Emma's War

Emma's War

DEBORAH SCROGGINS

PANTHEON BOOKS   NEW YORK

All rights reserved under International and Pan-American Copyright
Conventions. Published in the United States by Pantheon Books,
a division of Random House, Inc., New York.

Pantheon Books and colophon are registered trademarks of Random House, Inc.

Portions of this book originally appeared in slightly different form in *Granta* magazine.

Library of Congress Cataloging-in-Publication Data
Scroggins, Deborah.
Emma's war / Deborah Scroggins.
p. cm.
ISBN 0-375-40397-3
1. Sudan—History—Civil War, 1983–
2. Scroggins, Deborah—Journeys—Sudan. I. Title.

DT157.672.S37 2002
962.404—dc21   2002022033

www.pantheonbooks.com

Book design by Robert C. Olsson

Printed in the United States of America

First Edition

2 4 6 8 9 7 5 3 1

For Colin

Woe to the land shadowing with wings, which is beyond the rivers of Ethiopia:

That sendeth ambassadors by the sea, even in vessels of bulrushes upon the waters, saying Go, ye swift messengers, to a nation scattered and peeled, to a people terrible from their beginning hitherto; a nation meted out and trodden down, whose land the rivers have spoiled!

All ye inhabitants of the world, and dwellers on the earth, see ye, when he lifteth up an ensign on the mountains; and when he bloweth a trumpet, hear ye.

For so the LORD said until me, I will take my rest, and I will consider in my dwellingplace like a clear heat upon herbs, and like a cloud of dew in the heat of harvest.

For afore the harvest, when the bud is perfect, and the sour grape is ripening in the flower, he shall both cut off the sprigs with pruning hooks, and take away and cut down the branches.

They shall be left together unto the fowls of the mountains, and to the beasts of the earth: and the fowls shall summer upon them, and all the beasts of the earth shall winter upon them.

In that time shall the present be brought unto the LORD of hosts of a people scattered and peeled, and from their beginning hitherto; a nation meted out and trodden under foot, whose land the rivers have spoiled, to the place of the name of the LORD of hosts, the mount Zion.

—Isaiah 18

Author's Note

"Emma's War" was the name some members of the rebel Sudan People's Liberation Army (SPLA) briefly gave to the warfare that broke out in 1991 between the followers of John Garang, the SPLA leader, and those of his lieutenants, Riek Machar, Lam Akol, and Gordon Kong. Machar had married Emma McCune, a British aid worker, only two months before he and his fellow rebel commanders mounted a coup against Garang. Though McCune had little to do with either the plot against Garang or the violence that followed it, the SPLA leader initially blamed Machar's foreign wife for the schism within the movement. The factional fighting within the SPLA that grew out of the quarrel between Machar and Garang lasted many years after Emma McCune's death. It had political and philosophical as well as ethnic underpinnings, and it killed tens of thousands of people in southern Sudan. It is one of various subconflicts that have made Sudan's civil war the longest-running in Africa. Today the southern Sudanese no longer speak of "Emma's War." Instead they refer to the mutiny and the interethnic fighting it set off as "the split" or "the division" or sometimes "the war of the educated." I have chosen to look at the early period of this Sudanese conflict through the lens of McCune's life, with the intention of illuminating for Western readers the larger civil war and especially the suffering of the more than two million southern Sudanese whose lives it has taken. Calling this book *Emma's War* is, I hope, not to do a disservice either to them or to her.

I have adopted the Sudanese practice of calling many people, including political leaders, by their first names. In Sudan as elsewhere, there are exceptions to every rule. John Garang, for example, is commonly referred to by his last name.

Since 1988 I have interviewed hundreds of Sudanese and others about the events described in this book. Among those who have informed many different chapters are Lam Akol, William Anderson, Abdullahi An'Naim, Douglas Archard, Carol Berger, Millard Burr, Robert Collins, Aldo Ajou Deng, Francis M. Deng, Sally Dudmesh, Elizabeth Hodgkin, Sharon Hutchinson, Wendy James, Douglas Johnson, Andrea Kwong Ruijang, Ezekial Kutjok, Bernadette Kumar, William Lowrey, Angelina Teny, Riek Machar, Bona Malwal, Emma Marrian, Johnny McCune, Richard Mulla, Rory Nugent, Peter Adwok Nyaba, Detlef Palm, Jemera Rone, John Ryle, Alastair Scott-Villiers, Patta Scott-Villiers, Hania Sholkamy, François Visnot, and Alex de Waal. Many others to whom I am also indebted prefer not to be named.

Much of the dialogue in this book comes from those interviews. Sometimes my informants or I were able to refer back to contemporary notes and letters, or had a strong recollection of what was said. I have rendered this dialogue in quotation marks. Less conventionally, I have rendered a few dialogues without quotation marks. My point in these cases is to give the gist of a conversation as remembered years later, by me or by others, without pretending to be exact.

I have not cited material drawn from personal interviews or my own memory. However, quotations and other information taken from books, articles, and other published materials are listed in the endnotes and bibliography.

Emma's War

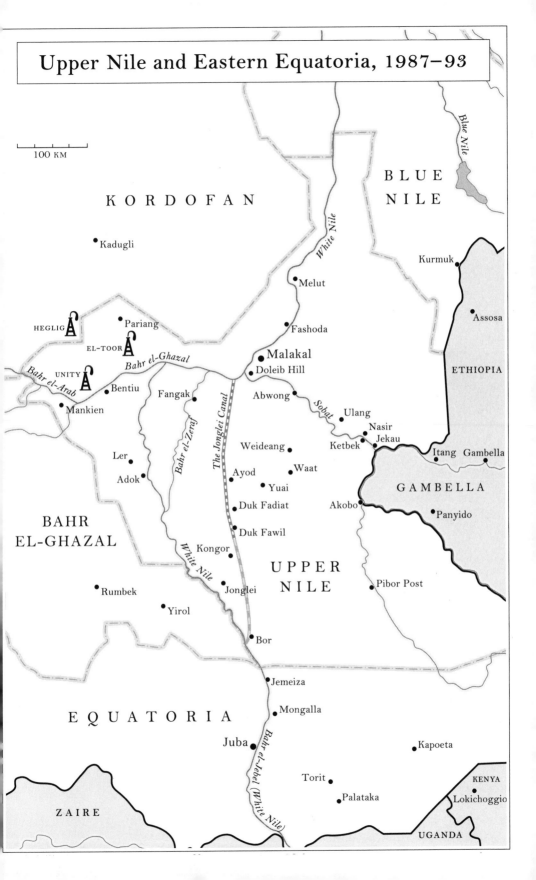

Upper Nile and Eastern Equatoria, 1987–93

100 KM

KORDOFAN

BLUE NILE

Kadugli

Kurmuk

Melut

White Nile

Assosa

HEGLIG

Pariang

EL-TOOR

Fashoda

Bahr el-Ghazal

Malakal

UNITY

Doleib Hill

Bentiu

ETHIOPIA

Bahr el-Arab

Fangak

Abwong

Mankien

Sobat

Ulang

Nasir

Jekau

Weideang

Ketbek

Itang   Gambella

Ler

Ayod

Waat

GAMBELLA

Adok

Yuai

Bahr el-Zeraf

Duk Fadiat

The Jonglei Canal

Akobo

Panyido

BAHR
EL-GHAZAL

Duk Fawil

Kongor

White Nile

UPPER
NILE

Rumbek

Jonglei

Pibor Post

Yirol

Bor

Jemeiza

Mongalla

EQUATORIA

Juba

Kapoeta

Bahr el-Jebel (White Nile)

Torit

KENYA

ZAIRE

Palataka

Lokichoggio

UGANDA

Blue Nile

Prologue

Even now, in the deep sweet busyness of a summer evening on Myrtle Street, I think of them. I'll be giving my daughters a bath, there will be chatter and commotion and slippery little-girl bodies, and then suddenly I will hear the strange hum of the famine camp at Safaha, the sound of thousands of people coughing and gasping for breath, and I'll remember how I lay awake listening to it. I will see my husband reading his book, and I will remember the contorted faces of the starving men who crossed the river and came to tell me something in a language I couldn't understand. I will look out the window at the sun setting over the Atlanta skyline, and instead I will see Africa's great violet ball of a sun sinking down over the river at Nasir. As the moon floats into view behind the branches of the big oak tree outside my house, I remember how it lit up the encampment outside the feeding center at Safaha, turning the plain into a field of silver skeletons.

I think of them, and I remember Emma. I met her more than a decade ago in Nasir, a place that has been shrouded in ambiguity and irony from its beginning. An Arab slave-hunter hired by an Englishman to end slavery founded the town. A hundred miles east of the White Nile and eighty miles west of Ethiopia, it lies on the eastern edge of the seasonal swamp that makes up the better part of southern Sudan. Early in the twentieth century, the British established a command post there over the local people, a tribe of exceptionally tall and fearless cattle-keepers called the Nuer. By the time I reached it, Sudan's civil war had destroyed most of the old town. The United Nations was delivering food at a crude airstrip made from the rubble of destroyed buildings. The rebel Sudan

People's Liberation Army (SPLA) had located its provincial headquarters in a mud compound a few miles up the Sobat River from the ruins.

This was in December 1990, well before Emma McCune scandalized the region's aid workers and diplomats by marrying the local warlord and going to live with him and his gunmen in that weapon-studded compound. But even then there was something unsettling about her. I was in Nasir working for the Atlanta newspaper. A photographer and I had been there for about ten days, reporting on the war between the Islamic government in the north and the Christian and pagan rebels in the south. I had been interviewing teenage soldiers and starving children. Since the war began in 1983, perhaps a million people had died, a quarter of them during the famine of 1988, which I had covered closely. Still there was an eerie beauty to this part of Sudan. The years of fighting had sealed it off from development, turning the blue-green wetlands between the White Nile and the Blue Nile into a vast wilderness refuge, whose silence was interrupted only by bombings, gunfire, and the haunting songs of the local people.

The photographer, whose name was Frank Niemeir, and I had been waiting for several days for a UN plane to fly us back to Kenya. The plane had been delayed for the usual obscure reasons. Perhaps the government had banned flights to rebel-held areas; perhaps the UN was punishing the rebels for threatening to shoot down UN planes. No one knew. Or if they knew, they weren't telling. Each day we walked up and down the banks of the Sobat, watching lyre-horned cattle roam through the ruins of what had once been a marketplace. We had seen a blue heron roosting on the wreck of an ancient steamer and marabou storks floating down the river on lily pads. In the evenings we had returned to the UN house, a derelict concrete structure of two rooms attached to a moldering compound that had housed the American Presbyterian mission in Nasir. The missionaries had been expelled from Sudan nearly thirty years earlier, in 1964, but their houses were still the best Nasir had to offer. At night we played cards by the light of a kerosene lantern until we fell asleep on metal cots swathed in mists of purple mosquito netting we had brought from Nairobi.

At last an SPLA officer with bloodshot eyes and a T-shirt that bore the legend "Martin's Restaurant, St. Paul, Minn.," came to tell us that the UN had radioed and a plane would be arriving shortly. We gathered up our backpacks and carried them through the ruined town to the edge of the airstrip, where we sat on top of them. The morning sun seemed to be looking down on us like a giant white eye. A couple of rebel soldiers stood around in flip-flops, listening for the plane. The first thing over the horizon wasn't a plane but a man. He came out from behind the rusted hulk of a bus that lay on its side near the airstrip. He was a middle-aged Nuer with loose skin and the six parallel marks of manhood across his forehead. He wore a bunch of pink flowers in each ear, brass armbands, and a pair of navy blue cotton underpants. His hair was dressed in corn-rows, and he was singing and dancing his way toward us. Our rebel escorts stirred uneasily.

"Who's this?" I asked.

"He is no one," one of the rebels answered shortly. The soldier's face was a mass of scars in the intricate dot patterns with which the southern Sudanese decorate their bodies; slung over his right shoulder was an AK-47.

The man with the flowers was only a few feet away now, gesticulating wildly, hopping up and down and pointing at us, singing at the top of his lungs.

"What's he saying?" I asked.

"He thinks he is a prophet," the first soldier said. "He says he has had enough now. You have been coming and going, but you don't bring anything."

"He is a madman," the other soldier declared.

Frank took the man's picture. I had been keeping a sort of diary of our trip in a small pink notebook I'd picked up in Nairobi. I took it out and wrote on the cheap brown paper:

> *Madman*
> *flowers in his ears*
> *feather in hair*
> *shells on right arm*
> *piece of notebook tied to left*
> *like a mime*
> *ring in nose*

Those are the last words in that Nasir notebook, for just then we heard a high-pitched whine. For a moment I wondered what it was, still transfixed by the prophet. Then we saw the shadow of the plane's wings. It was coming down in the tight corkscrew the pilots always performed in case someone started shooting at them. It landed, the engine sputtered into stillness, the rebels ran to open the door, and out jumped Emma. Frank and I stared. She was almost six feet tall, pale, dark-haired, and slender as a model. She was wearing a red miniskirt. An SPLA officer climbed out behind her; she and the officer were laughing about something. Emma threw her head back. She had large white healthy teeth. It was hard to believe she was flying in on an emergency relief mission. She looked as if she ought to be stepping out of a limousine to go to a party.

In a way, I was not surprised. I had heard about Emma. Young, glamorous, and idealistic, she had sent a ripple of excitement through the social circles of the aid business when she went to work for a Canadian aid group called Street Kids International. In Nairobi, headquarters for East Africa's burgeoning humanitarian industry, she had gained a reputation for wildness: adventures in the bush, all-night revels in the city. She was an Englishwoman with entrée to the city's most exclusive expatriate circles, yet she was said to feel most at home with Africans. Some admired her nerve; others considered her dangerously naïve. I'd caught sight of her myself a few weeks earlier at the mess tent in Lokichoggio, or Loki, as we called it, the staging ground inside Kenya for the UN relief operations into southern Sudan. She had been drinking beer with a table full of African men, and she was talking with great animation. I couldn't hear what she was saying, but I could tell that the men did not want her to stop.

Now in Nasir I thought I understood the current of disapproval that followed the stories about Emma. That gorgeous splash of a miniskirt seemed almost indecent in a place filled with sick, hungry people catching their breath between bouts of vicious killing and mass starvation. To look happy seemed tactless—a flaunting of one's good fortune. It occurred to me that the modest T-shirts and khaki shorts or blue jeans that were a kind of unofficial uniform for most of us expats were in some way an attempt to make ourselves sexless, at least in our own minds. We imagined that it announced "We are not here to have a good time." It was like a surgeon's scrub suit or perhaps a modern version of sackcloth and ashes: an unspoken signal that we thought we were wiser and more virtuous than the Sudanese and were in a kind of mourning for them. Not that the Sudanese were fooled. In truth the average aid worker or journalist lived for the buzz, the intensity of life in the war zone, the heightened sensations brought on by the nearness of death and the determination to do good. We wanted to be here, we were being paid good money to be here, and the Sudanese knew it.

On second thought, Emma's miniskirt seemed to me a refreshing departure from the usual pieties. It suggested that she was more honest than the rest of us, that she wasn't afraid to admit she was here because she wanted to be here. She and I exchanged pleasantries, nothing more, and when I turned around to pick up my backpack, the man with the pink flowers in his ears had disappeared. I never saw him again, and I didn't see Emma again for a long time. Frank didn't take her picture, and I didn't write about her in my notebook. But as the plane took off, I began to think about her for another reason that had nothing to do with clothes. I knew that she had been working closely with the SPLA's "education coordinator," a man called Lul Kuar Duek, to reopen Nasir's schools. I myself had spent days in Nasir interviewing Lul about his plans for the schools. He had claimed to be a great friend of Emma's. He was the kind of man the Nuer used to call a black *Turuk*, a name they took from Ottoman Turks who first introduced the Nuer to modernity when they invaded a century and a half earlier and that now extended to anyone who could read and write and wore clothes. Like most Nuer, Lul was dark as a panther, tall and thin with a narrow head and a loping walk. He was a former schoolmaster and an elder in the local Presbyterian church. He was also a bore and a bully. In the afternoons, he would drink Ethiopian gin out of a bottle and lecture me in his straw shack about the martyred American president John F. Kennedy and why southern Sudan was so backward and anything else that came into his mind. "The stage we are at now is the stage of the European in the stone age. We are in the age of stones," he would say, pointing his finger at me. "And you! You be careful. You should know you are talking to someone who knows everything."

Lul's baby son slept in a hammock next to his father's automatic rifle during these conversations, and Lul would frequently offer to give him up for the cause of liberating Sudan from the domination of the Islamic government in the north. "Even this boy, he shall fight! Even if he should die! Even if it should take a hundred years..." He recited the SPLA's slogans with noisy fervor, insisting that the south would never settle for secession but would fight until the whole country had a new, secular government, though he was to be equally enthusiastic less than a year later when his fellow Nuer commander led a mutiny against SPLA leader

John Garang on the grounds that the south ought to give up trying to change the north and start fighting for southern independence.

Like everyone else in Nasir, Lul was obsessed with a prophecy from the Book of Isaiah that he and the others believed foretold the future of southern Sudan. Whenever he had gotten about halfway through one of his gin bottles, he would wipe his hands on his red polyester trousers, take out the Bible from the crate beside his bed, and start banging his hand on it. "It is all here—it is written!" he would announce. Frank and I would exchange weary glances. "Isaiah eighteen. God will punish Sudan. People will go to the border with Ethiopia. 'The beasts of the earth and the fowls shall summer upon them and all the beasts of the earth shall winter upon them.' I have seen all this come to pass. But it says that in the end, we shall have a new Sudan."

Lul was talking about the years in which hundreds of people had starved to death or been killed in the fighting around the town before the SPLA captured it from the government in 1989. Even then I wondered how Emma could stand it, handing out pencils to Nasir's surviving children, while Lul raved on about fighting for another hundred years to make a new Sudan out of that blinding emptiness. I always made sure that Frank was with me before I went to visit Lul in his grass hut. But according to Lul, he and Emma got along famously. In fact, Lul was more interested in telling me about Emma than about the schools he was supposed to be running. "You know, Em-Maa"—he pronounced her name with a satisfied smack—"is just like one of us. She walks everywhere without getting tired. She is bringing us so many things we need, like papers and chalks and schoolbooks. You people should know, our commander likes Em-Maa very much. Very much! And she likes him! She has been here, looking for him." Underneath the praise, there was something leering in his voice.

It was hard to imagine why my newspaper would want to know about an SPLA commander's feelings toward a low-level British aid worker, and so I paid very little attention to Lul's lewd suggestions. But when I learned, six months later, that in fact Emma McCune had married Lul's commander, Riek Machar, the one who had "liked Em-Maa very much," I remembered the mingling of lust and envy and contempt in Lul's voice, and I felt obscurely frightened. Naturally I knew of "Dr. Riek," as the southern Sudanese called him. He was another black *Turuk,* but with a Ph.D. from Bradford Polytechnic in England that made him the best-educated Nuer within the ranks of the SPLA. Westerners found him unusually smooth and affable, but we also knew that he was part of a violent and secretive guerrilla movement that was capable of the most ruthless cruelty. The news of Emma's marriage provoked a surprising jumble of emotions in me. At twenty-seven she was just two years younger than I. I knew her only slightly, but the world of the *khawaja*—the Sudanese Arabic term for white people—is a small one, and she and I shared many friends and acquaintances among the aid workers, journalists, and diplomats in Sudan. The same interesting British couple who had helped Emma get her job with Street Kids International, Alastair and Patta Scott-Villiers, had given me the tip two years earlier that led to my first big story in Sudan. A few days after I returned to Nairobi from Nasir in 1990, the Scott-Villierses had invited me to join Emma and a bunch of other people who were spending Christmas at Mombasa on the Kenyan coast (an invitation I had to decline, as I spent the holidays working in Khartoum that year). I had been writing about Sudan, off and on, for three years: it was the deepest and furthest part of my experience. Now here was Emma going deeper and further than I had ever dreamed of going, crossing over from the *khawaja* world into a liberation army led by men like Lul and the scarred gunmen at the airport, men responsible for some of the horrors she had been trying to alleviate as an aid worker. What, I wondered, had driven her to take such an extreme step? Later, after it was all over, I got the idea that her story might shed some light on the entire humanitarian experiment in Africa. Or at least on the experiences of people like me, people who went there dreaming they might help and came back numb with disillusionment, yet forever marked.

Part One

My first impressions of Sudan were rather blurred and uncertain;
I was so much more interested in myself than I was in my surroundings.

—Edward Fothergill, *Five Years in the Sudan,* 1911

Chapter One

ID MAKES ITSELF out to be a practical enterprise, but in Africa at least it's romantics who do most of the work—incongruously, because Africa outside of books and movies is hard and unromantic. In Africa the metaphor is always the belly. "He is eating from that," Africans will say, and what they mean is that is how he gets his living. African politics, says the French scholar Jean-François Bayart, is "the politics of the belly." The power of the proverbial African big man depends on his ability to feed his followers; his girth advertises the wealth he has to share. In Africa the first obligation of kinship is to share food; and yet, as the Nuer say, "eating is warring." They tell this story: Once upon a time Stomach lived by itself in the bush, eating small insects roasted in brush fire, for Man was created apart from Stomach. Then one day Man was walking in the bush and came across Stomach. Man put Stomach in its present place that it might feed there. When it lived by itself, Stomach was satisfied with small morsels of food, but now that Stomach is part of man, it craves more no matter how much it eats. That is why Stomach is the enemy of Man.

In Europe and North America, we have to look in the mirror to see Stomach. "Get in touch with your hunger," American diet counselors urge their clients. Hunger is an option. Like so much else in the West, it has become a question of vanity. That is why some in the West ask: Is it Stomach or Mirror that is the enemy of Man? And Africa—Africa is a mirror in which the West sees its big belly. The story of Western aid to Sudan is the story of the intersection of the politics of the belly and the politics of the mirror.

It's a story that began in the nineteenth century much as it seems to be ending in the twenty-first, with a handful of humanitarians driven by urges often half hidden even from themselves. The post-Enlightenment triumph of reason and science gave impetus to the Western conviction that it is our duty to show the planet's less fortunate how to live. But even in the heyday of colonialism, when Western idealists had a lot more firepower at their disposal, Africa's most memorable empire-builders tended to be those romantics and eccentrics whose openness to the irrational—to the emotions, to mysticism, to ecstasy—made them misfits in their own societies. And the colonials were riding the crest of a wave of Victorian enthusiasm to remake Africa in our own image. If the rhetoric of today's aid workers is equally grand, they in fact are engaged in a far less ambitious enterprise. With little money and no force backing them up, they are a kind of imperial rearguard, foot soldiers covering the retreat of a West worn down by the continent's stubborn and opaque vitality. They may be animated by many of the old impulses, idealistic and otherwise, but they have less confidence in their ability to see them through. It takes more than an ideal, even an unselfish belief in an ideal, to keep today's aid workers in place. Emma had some ideals, but it was romance that lured her to Africa.

Chapter Two

S HE WAS BORN in India, where her parents, Maggie and Julian McCune, had met and married in 1962, and the direction of her life, like theirs, was pounded and shaped by the ebbing tide of the British Empire. Maggie, a trim and crisp former secretary, still calls herself an ex-colonial, though the sun was already setting on colonialism when she was born in 1942 in Assam. She published a memoir in 1999 called *Til the Sun Grows Cold* about her relationship with Emma. The child of a loveless marriage between a British tea planter and an Australian showgirl who met on board a wartime ship, Maggie spent a lonely colonial childhood as a paying guest at various English homes and boarding schools. Emma's father, Julian—or "Bunny," as Maggie called him— was an Anglo-Irish engineer who had knocked around Britain's colonies for at least a decade before he and Maggie settled down in Assam.

Theirs was an unfortunate match from the start. Maggie, shy and wounded, was only twenty-one when she was introduced to Julian on a visit to her father in India. She married him, she admits in her book, mainly to escape England and the hard-drinking mother whose theatrics she despised. With depths of neediness her husband never seems to have fathomed, she wanted nothing more than to bring up lots of children in the safe and conventional family she felt she had been denied as a child. Julian, fourteen years older, was a charming sportsman who thrived on admiration. He also liked his whiskey. He seems to have been unprepared to bear any responsibilities beyond excelling at *shirkar,* the hunting and fishing beloved of British colonial administrators in India. Perhaps their marriage might have survived if they had been able to stay in India, where Julian, simply by virtue of being an Englishman who had attended some well-known public schools, was able to provide the luxurious lifestyle they had both come to expect.

In Maggie's words, life was "heavenly" for the British hired in those days by London tea companies to run the Assam tea estates. The British lived in comfortable bungalows, the adults attended by Indian servants and the children watched by Indian nursemaids. The men began work at six o'clock in the morning, but after two hours they broke for breakfast. At noon it was time for lunch, and after lunch everybody took two "golden and silent" hours of siesta. After siesta, Maggie writes, "there was a little more work to do, leaving time for tennis, a round of golf or a chukka or two of polo before the sun sank. Then the sun-downer drinks parties began, followed by dinner and dancing" at the club. But by the time Emma was born in 1964 and her sister Erica in 1965, it had become plain that the postwar world was going to have a lot less room for people like the McCunes.

For India, as for so many other colonies, the end of the Raj in 1948 was only the beginning of the slow and subtle process of loosening Britain's control over the country. In the first few years under the new Indian government, the British tea companies operated pretty much as they had under British administration. But by the late 1960s, they were under pressure from the government to replace British employees with Indians. Julian lost his job supervising the maintenance of the equipment used to grade and prepare tea leaves. Maggie's father was pensioned off and decided to return to England. In her book, Maggie says that she and Julian enjoyed mixing with people of all races in Assam, but the only Indians she mentions socializing with were the petty royals for whom the dissolution of empire was almost as much of a disaster as it was for the British. Julian talked about emigrating to Rhodesia or South Africa, where many of their British friends from India had already gone, but Maggie worried about moving to another refuge that might prove temporary. She wanted to spare her children the uncomfortable colonial sense she had always had of never quite fitting in England. She wanted "Home" to really feel like home for them. In 1966 the McCunes decided to move to Yorkshire, where Julian had gone to school and had family. Emma was two.

There was an old manor house on the windswept edge of the Vale of York that Bunny McCune had never forgotten in all his years of wandering. Julian's parents were dead, but his mother had come from Leeds, and as a boy he had attended the Aysgarth School in North Yorkshire before going on to Winchester College. Cowling Hall, a long, thin brick-and-plaster Queen Anne mansion not far from Aysgarth on top of a hill overlooking a spectacular view of the Yorkshire Dales, had first captivated his imagination when he was a schoolboy. The house was shaped like an L, and the oldest part had been built from the ruins of a despoiled abbey. It was empty when the McCunes arrived. Local people said it was haunted. A child had died in the house, and a man had suffered a nervous breakdown. It was an imposing, if dilapidated, piece of architecture, but in the winter a bone-chilling wind whistled right through it. The house was so cold that Maggie tells in her book of warming butter for toast by the coal fire in the drawing room. But with six bedrooms, it was more than big enough for what would become a family of six—Jennie was born in 1967 and Johnny in 1970—and Julian had to have it. He had already invested his inheritance in a franchise he planned to set up in North Yorkshire for a firm marketing closed-circuit-television monitoring systems. Charmed by Julian's manners, the titled owners of Cowling Hall agreed to rent it to the McCunes for the nominal sum of six pounds a week.

A number of Aysgarth old boys still lived into the area, and these former classmates helped the McCunes settle into North Yorkshire's county set. Wensleydale is the heart of James Herriot country, a misty green landscape of ancient stone villages and black-and-white cows that occupies a large place in the sentimental imagination of England. Bunny hunted and fished in the area's magnificent forests and streams; Maggie organized cricket teas and was elected to the local cancer research committee. There were ponies for the children: Maggie saw a moral purpose in such outdoor pursuits. "Ponies are such good discipline," she told me once. "When you come back from riding, you can't just think about yourself. You have to brush down the horse." And there were the all-important public schools. After attending the local primary, Emma became a weekly boarder at Polam Hall in Darlington. Emma is positively radiant in photographs from these years, her cheeks freckled and ruddy as she poses in front of Cowling Hall or astride her pony, Misty.

Julian and Maggie were a popular couple. If Julian had one talent—and by all accounts, it was an unusual talent in a place as rigid and class-bound as North Yorkshire in the 1960s—it was for striking up friendships with people of wildly different backgrounds. "Julian was a thorough gentleman," Peter Gilbertson, an old schoolmate from Aysgarth, reminisced many years later. "He could go into any worker's cottage or any stately home with his boots on and his spaniels at his heels, and he'd be fine. He'd put two bottles on the table and say, 'Right! We're having a party.'" Among their close friends, the McCunes counted Bedale's local squire and his wife, the doctor, and the vicar. Maggie, who had been raised Catholic, converted to the Church of England. Julian, whose political views Gilbertson describes as "conservative—*very* conservative," became the treasurer of the local Conservative Association. The genteel McCune facade was impeccable, and Emma's father seems to have felt that this really ought to have been enough. Like so many upper-middle-class public schoolboys of the period, he had been educated to serve the empire. He really had no other skills. After nearly twenty years abroad, he was at first baffled, then angry, to learn that in the Britain to which he had returned, his social graces and his old school tie would not by themselves translate into a sizable income. As Maggie later wrote, his indifference to work, easy to overlook in India, was harder to ignore in Britain. When his security franchise failed to prosper, he went to work for a cousin selling farm equipment to large landowners. After a year or so, the cousin fired him. Julian never discussed business matters with Maggie, and he did not tell her when he lost his job. Nor did he look for a position he considered beneath him. Instead, he pretended he was going off to work each day. After saying good-bye to her and the children, he would drive to a nearby river, park his car, and sit in it reading newspapers. Maggie never guessed that he was unemployed until his cousin finally phoned her to say he had fired Julian more than a year earlier for being "bone-idle, a scrounger, and a liar."

When Maggie confronted him, Julian acted as if he were above worrying about money, the opinions of others, or even the law. He was arrested for drunken driving. He took up with a woman who lived in the local village. He was taken to court in Leeds for debt. He continued to come home with expensive presents that Maggie had no idea how he bought. Then he was charged with using his position as a treasurer of the local Conservative Association to steal Tory funds. When a judge asked Maggie why her husband had not appeared with her in court the day the two of them were summoned for failing to pay the rent at Cowling Hall, she had to tell him that Julian was too busy fishing for salmon on the river Tweed. In 1975 local bailiffs evicted the McCune family from Cowling Hall. Maggie and the children went to live in a cottage on the grounds of the Aysgarth School; Julian retreated to a crofter's hut high in the Dales, where he found occasional work as a farm laborer. Emma was ten when the family broke up. "Her childhood ended there," her mother writes.

The very night Maggie discovered that her husband was having an affair with another woman, she happened to be reading one of Emma's favorite childhood stories, Hans Christian Andersen's "Thumbelina." The tale of a tiny girl rescued by a swallow from having to marry a mole, then flown to the warm lands of the south, where she became a princess, must have recalled to the McCunes the magical days in Assam, before they were exiled back "Home." As their troubles mounted in England, perhaps it was only natural that the family should recall their years in India as a time and place in which they had been free to be the aristocrats that Julian, at least, felt himself to be. After a few drinks, Julian was wont to regale the local pubs about how, in India, he had been able to take the law into his own hands and do as he pleased. He loved to tell the story of how he had gotten himself out of jail after accidentally hitting a sacred cow with his car in Calcutta. He never could get used to how the roguish behavior that his fellow expatriates had found so entertaining in India met with disapproval in England. When he invited the Yorkshire policemen who had caught him driving drunk to join him for a brandy before their court appearance, an English judge was not amused.

It was not Julian's assumption of superiority that bothered his Yorkshire friends. Imperialism had not gone out of fashion in that part of the world. People did not mind if Julian complained about missing his Indian servants at the same time as he boasted about having "given service to the colonies." They didn't care if he saw it as his right to live like a lord. After all, some of his old school friends were lords. No, it was not Julian's pretensions that set him apart from the society in which he found himself. It was his inability to maintain them. "I just think he was born too late," Gilbertson said sadly. "He should have been born forty years earlier and with a hell of a lot of money." In the end, much of it did come down to money. To Maggie's intense anger and humiliation, Julian pleaded for leniency at his embezzlement trial on the grounds that he stole to finance his wife's extravagance. The two were divorced in January 1976. A few weeks later Julian killed himself.

Emma, who was eleven, was visiting the city of York the day it happened. Her father had never stopped seeing her. Indeed, he was the more playful of the McCune parents, forever taking the children out for a ride or a shooting expedition while Maggie fretted over how to buy groceries. That weekend he had invited Emma to go to the horse races with him, but she decided to go to York with her sister instead. She later told friends how much she regretted not going with him that day. She said she always wondered if she might have saved his life. With Julian's death, the days of pony school and ballet lessons were truly over. Maggie and the children entered a period of their lives as grim and cheerless as the bleakest Yorkshire winter. Maggie, who had not worked outside the house during her marriage, embarked on a heroic struggle to support all four children. For a while, she had to pump gas at the local service station to make ends meet. At last she found a job as a secretary to a headmaster at a state primary school in nearby Catherick Garrison. In her book, she chronicles the family's series of moves from borrowed cottages to a gray cement council house before she and the children finally landed their own small semidetached house in the village of Little Crakehall.

As the eldest child, Emma went from being the petted darling of Cowling Hall to becoming her mother's second-in-charge. Maggie leaned on her to help with the housework and look after the other children. Emma had to learn to shop and cook and sew. She also had to console her mother, who was so depressed and angry and fearful that she came home from work each evening longing to crawl into bed. "After my father died, Emma was like my mother's husband," her brother Johnny remembers. One of Emma's friends from Kenya said that Emma told her she dreaded coming down to the kitchen in the mornings as a teenager to see the list of chores her mother would leave for her. The family worried constantly about money. None of the houses they lived in had central heating, not even the Little Crakehall cottage that Maggie bought and lovingly restored. The electricity was on a coin meter, and occasionally it went off because they did not have enough coins. It was so much like one of those fairy tales in which a princess is brought low that Emma might have lain in the freezing room she now shared with her sisters, dreaming of Thumbelina and a swallow who might spirit her away to someplace warm where her rightful identity would be restored.

Despite their reduced circumstances, the McCunes remained part of the Yorkshire gentry. Maggie's closest friends continued to invite her and the children to fancy dress balls at their Georgian estates. They and Maggie's sister even helped with fees so that Emma could stay in public school, first at a Richmond convent, then at Godalming College in Kent. Maggie writes in her book that she hoped everything would come out all right if her children could just stay in the same schools and keep the same friends. "I think education is the most important gift you can give your children, don't you?" she told me. Emma was a hard worker, and she was good at organizing people and getting them to do what she wanted, but her strengths were not academic. Several of Emma's friends from Yorkshire have grown up to be well-known writers, editors, and artists; among this rich and clever group, Emma was considered a slow student. "Dippy," "not very well read," "not very articulate" are some of the less charitable phrases they privately used to describe her intellect. Emma knew what they thought and resented it. Intensely competitive, she was frustrated and disappointed when her test scores were not as high as those of some of her friends.

She came off better outside school. Her set liked to show off, riding to hounds, holding extravagant parties, and challenging each other as to who was the most adventurous. They all intended to live dangerously; reckless behavior was part of what they regarded as their aristocratic sensibility. (Typical of the epic tone was a young man who rented the entire town cinema so that he and his friends could watch the 1948 movie *Scott of the Antarctic* over and over again. He went on to become a UN ambassador and to write several books about Arctic exploration.) This was an arena in which Emma shined. Even as a teenager, she loved hearing people gasp at her latest exploit. At an age when most people want only to fit in, she strove for glamour. Unlike her straitlaced mother, who favored straight skirts and wore her hair neatly pulled back, Emma loved dramatic costumes with big hats and lots of jewelry. Once when she couldn't afford to buy a gown for a grand party, she made one for herself out of black plastic garbage bin liners. After passing through a gawky stage, she blossomed into a long-legged beauty, with pale freckled skin and a slow, seductive manner of speech. A classmate at the Convent of the Assumption school in Richmond remembers the entrance Emma made at a party when she was about sixteen. "Emma arrived wearing a striking black-and-white dress she'd made, and long evening gloves. The dress was long and straight. Everyone else was wearing conventional ball dresses, and no one could take their eyes off Emma. Our duckling had become a swan."

Still, Emma knew that in clubby North Yorkshire, she would always be her father's daughter. Behind the admiring glances lay pity. The condescension stung. North Yorkshire is a place with long memories. The sound one most often hears in its pubs and mansions and brick Georgian hotels is the deep ticking of grandfather clocks. Emma's school friends all remember hearing the gossip about Maggie and Julian. More than twenty years later I had no trouble finding neighbors who recalled every detail of Julian's disgrace. "Their father's downfall was quite a scandal," said one of Emma's friends. "It must have been very painful for them to have stayed there." None of the McCunes stayed in Yorkshire any longer than they had to. Maggie herself moved to London as soon as her youngest child went off to boarding school.

When I first met Maggie in 1997, I asked how she thought her husband's suicide had affected Emma. She paused. We were having lunch at a restaurant near St. Paul's Cathedral, where Maggie then worked as a secretary to the registrar. I was interviewing her for a magazine article about Emma. Maggie comes across in person as rather shy and reticent; several times in her book, she mentions moving though her life as if it were "a strange dream." That day she was particularly reserved. She had already warned me that she did not want to talk about Julian. "I think it made her less materialistic," she said finally of his death, and she made it clear that the subject was closed. Some of Emma's friends think Julian's suicide might have helped create a split in Emma's psyche between the sensuality and freedom she linked with her father and abroad, and the discipline and frugality she associated with her mother and England. Though as an adult Emma seldom talked about her father, she knew that in Yorkshire she would always be the girl whose father started out as an empire-builder and died living like a tramp in a crofter's cottage. "She had a lot to hide, and she hid it well," said one childhood friend. "She knew everyone would always know, but no one would ever say anything." Whatever the reason, by the time Emma was offered a place to study art and art history at Oxford Polytechnic in 1982, Africa already beckoned to her.

Chapter Three

FOR THOSE who care to look, Africa is all over Oxford. It's in the glass boxes at the Pitt-Rivers Museum, the iron-ribbed museum of a museum that the Victorians built to display the shrunken heads and feathered curiosities of the peoples they were about to introduce to Progress. It's in the odor of borax at Queen Elizabeth House, an institution where some of Britain's last colonial training courses were held before it was reinvented as a center for development studies. It's in the quiet stucco Quaker meetinghouse in St. Giles where some of the earliest antislavery meetings were held. It's at the ugly cinder-block headquarters of Oxfam, the antifamine group founded by Oxford pacifists during the Allied blockade of occupied Greece that has become Britain's wealthiest international charity. Oxford has updated the ethic of service to the colonies that it preached a century ago when Rudyard Kipling wrote of "the white man's burden." Nonetheless, dozens of its university graduates still set off for Africa each year with what might be described as a modern version of that urge, an ambition to "develop" Africa that arouses much the same pleasurable hopes and feelings as did earlier pledges to serve Kipling's "lesser breeds without the law."

Emma first found Africa at Oxford among her fellow students at the polytechnic. A redbrick institution in the suburb of Headington, Oxford Polytechnic then had a reputation as a haven for well-bred students who couldn't get into more prestigious universities, let alone Oxford University itself. She was seventeen and in her first year when she met Sally Dudmesh, a sweet-faced blond anthropology student standing beside a university notice board. Sally holds a British passport, but she was raised in Africa and considers herself a white African. She now designs jewelry in Kenya, though when I first spoke to her in 1997, she was spending the summer in England, as she does every year. She said she and Emma felt an instant attraction, particularly when Emma learned of Sally's connection to Africa. "I felt like I was meeting my own sister," Sally remembered. "At that time she was very arty. She always dressed exotically. She had this sort of very wonderful calmness. She just glided into a room." Emma wore a long purple velvet coat. She was pale, with a husky whisper of a voice and a smile full of sparkle and mischief. "She made fun of disasters with people. She had wicked sense of humor, a really fun, bad-girl side." The two girls struck up a fast friendship.

Sally lived with Willy Knocker, a white Kenyan from a well-known colonial family who was studying at London's School of Oriental and African Studies. Through Sally and Willy, Emma was drawn into a circle of friends who shared a fascination with Africa. They liked to dress in African clothes and talk about African politics while smoking pot and listening to African music. They wanted lives with an edge. Although many of them came from colonial or diplomatic backgrounds, they all abhorred the British Empire and blamed colonialism for most of Africa's problems. They felt their romance with Africa somehow set them apart from the restraint and tedium of middle-class English life. "It was just sort of a wildness—a spirit of adventure," said Sally, trying to explain the allure Africa had for her and Emma. "There's an incredible freedom and scope to Africa that you don't find in England. In England everything is so controlled. In Africa there's an intrigue and a fascination and a sense that you can really expand. In England you have the feeling that you're always having to play a certain role. You could always see that we would not end up living in England. We were not ordinary English girls."

Sally and Willy's house was a meeting point for other young people on their way to Africa. Emma met Alastair and Patta Scott-Villiers at a party there in the early 1980s. Patta—her given name was Henrietta, but she'd been called Patta since childhood—was studying international development with Willy in London. She and Alastair planned to move to Sudan as soon as she finished her master's degree. Alastair and Patta were a couple of years older than Sally and Emma. Alastair was compact, sandy-haired, and snub-nosed. His father had been with the Foreign Office, and he had spent part of his youth in Canada. Alastair seemed to have picked up some freewheeling North America ways in Canada. He was brash and friendly, an endlessly inquisitive chain-smoker. Patta was more reserved and watchful. She came from an aristocratic family but never mentioned her connections. She had soft brown hair and a magnolia complexion. She seldom wore makeup and liked to dress in blue jeans and T-shirts. Like many of Emma's friends, she seemed to feel more relaxed outside England. In 1983 she and Alastair moved to Sudan. Patta went to work for the international charity CARE. Alastair, who had been dealing antiques in London, went along hoping to find some kind of work once they got there.

It was exactly the sort of adventure that appealed to Emma and Sally. Already Emma was restless living in Britain. She had visited Europe several times on holiday. In 1985 she took off the better part of a year to fly in a Robin Aiglon single-engine plane to Australia with a young man named Bill Hall. Hall was the son of a distinguished Oxford professor. He had already finished university and gone to work for his family's engineering business when Emma and a friend rented a house from his parents in the nearby village of Littlemore. A solidly built, meticulously careful man in his twenties, he was an accomplished pilot. He had always wanted to fly his single-engine plane to Australia, where he had family. He invited Emma to come along with him. In those days without satellite navigation, it was much more risky than it is now to fly all the way across Europe, Asia, and the South Pacific in such a small plane. Emma knew nothing about flying, but she threw herself into the organizational details of the trip. She made the arrangements for their stops along the way, traveling to London to apply for visas at the embassies of half a dozen countries. For instance, Emma convinced the Saudi embassy to grant them a visa, even though as an unrelated, unmarried couple, she and Hall should not have been allowed to enter Saudi Arabia.

Emma talked her lecturers into letting her use the aerial photographs she planned to take as coursework for her art degree. *The Oxford Times* covered the pair's departure. "We will fly through extremely varied landscape, including jungle, desert and ocean," Emma proudly told the reporter from the paper. She persuaded newspapers in Australia and India to write articles about their thirty-thousand-mile flight. One of them took a marvelous picture of her and Hall in the cockpit. Hall is looking up from a map, while Emma simply looks ravishing in pearls and a colorful print dress.

The trip took her to India for the first time since her family had left in 1966. Hall remembers that it brought back memories of her father and his wild colonial exploits. When Emma and Hall stayed at the Tollygunge

Club in Calcutta, the manager told them a story about how Julian had been on a plane flying to Calcutta when the plane got lost. "Seems Emma's father was a bit drunk, and he went up to the cockpit, pushed the pilot away, and flew the plane back to Calcutta," Hall remembers the man telling them. Emma celebrated her twenty-first birthday in the foothills of the Himalayas, not far from where her father and grandfather had been stationed during the Raj. The trip settled in her mind the notion that she must have a life outside the bounds of everyday English experience. And it taught her useful things about maps and radios.

Hall and Emma were only friends, but Emma's mother half hoped the trip might spark a deeper relationship. Hall was kindly and dependable. He was the sort of man who could afford to indulge Emma's appetite for adventure and yet provide her with the security that Maggie herself had always longed for. But Emma didn't want to make her forays into other cultures from the safe confines of the West. When they left England, Hall gave Emma a wad of cash to keep in case of emergency. Emma promptly spent all the money in Luxor on clothes. Hall liked to stay in expensive "international" hotels such as the Hilton or the Meridian, where you could count on air-conditioning and clean sheets. Emma preferred to scour the back streets for humble guesthouses frequented by local people. Fortunately she had inherited her father's gift for appreciating vastly different characters. She and Hall remained fond of each other long after the trip was over. But what she really longed for was a much stronger experience. Even the exciting but essentially Western lives that her friends like Sally and Willy envisioned for themselves in Africa were not what she had in mind.

She had always been attracted to African men, though she can hardly have laid eyes on many Africans in Yorkshire. Her attraction was frankly erotic. She found black men more beautiful than white men, even joking with her girlfriends that the penises of white men reminded her of "great slugs." She loved the warmth of African laughter and the rhythms of African music. She often said that, with all their troubles, Africans enjoyed life more than Westerners. After she came back from her airplane journey in 1985, she started waitressing at a trendy Indonesian restaurant on the way to the Oxford railway station. The restaurant was a hangout for some of the university's more swinging lecturers, particularly those who specialized in Asia and Africa. One night Emma overheard Barbara Harrell-Bond, the American director of the university's new Refugee Studies Programme, at Queen Elizabeth House, talking with some others about how they needed student volunteers. Among those speaking most animatedly at the table was a tall, thin African man with long fingers. This was Ahmed Karadawi, the Sudanese co-founder of the Refugee Studies Programme and a penetrating critic of Western relief efforts. When Emma brought Karadawi his food, he rewarded her a smile so broad, it seemed almost too big for his face. Grinning back at him, Emma interrupted Harrell-Bond to volunteer for the program.

African refugees and famine were in the air that summer, not only in Britain but in Europe and America, too. Ethiopia and Sudan were in the grip of the great 1984–85 famine. In October 1984 Emma and the rest of Britain had watched the film that the television correspondent Michael Buerk brought back for the BBC nightly news from the Korem famine camp in northern Ethiopia. As the Irish pop singer Bob Geldof later wrote in his autobiography, *Is That It?*, Buerk's film showed pictures of people "so shrunken by starvation that they looked like beings from another planet." As the images appeared on the screen, Buerk spoke in tones of somber outrage. "Dawn, and as the sun breaks through the piercing chill of a night on the plain outside Korem, it lights up a biblical famine, now, in the twentieth century. This place, say relief workers, is the closest place to hell on earth." Geldof had come home that evening anxious and depressed about the failure of his latest album. Like thousands of television viewers, he found that the broadcast from Ethiopia "put my worries in a ghastly new perspective."

Geldof described the reaction Buerk's misty images of starving Ethiopians huddled under ragged blankets aroused in him. "Right from the first few seconds it was clear that this was a tragedy which the world had somehow contrived not to notice until it reached a scale which constituted an international tragedy. What could I do? I could send some money. Of course I could send some money. But that did not seem enough. Did not the sheer scale of the thing call for something more? Buerk had used the word 'biblical.' A famine of biblical proportions. There was something terrible about the idea that 2,000 years after Christ in a world of modern technology something like this could be allowed to happen as if the ability of mankind to influence and control the environment had not altered one jot. A horror like this could not happen today without our consent. We had allowed this to happen, and now we knew that it was happening, to allow it to continue would be tantamount to murder. I would send some money, I would send more money. But that was not enough. To expiate yourself truly of any complicity in this evil you had to give something of yourself. I was stood against the wall. I had to withdraw my consent."

Geldof helped galvanize Britain, then the Western world, with his moral outrage over the Ethiopian famine. Like millions of young people, Emma bought the Band Aid record "Do They Know It's Christmas?" that Geldof produced for the charity he founded to help feed the famine victims. Her brother remembers her sitting in front of the television in the summer of 1985, mesmerized by Geldof's Live Aid concert. Emma herself had always been good at fund-raising. She didn't mind asking people for money; in a backhanded way, she almost enjoyed it. As a child she had enthusiastically joined in various charitable campaigns sponsored by the *Blue Peter* children's television program. She liked the feeling of working together with others, and she liked the way championing a worthy cause forced adults to take her seriously. Geldof touched the conscience of people all over the world—Band Aid and Live Aid ultimately raised more than $100 million, and some 1.5 billion viewers in 152 countries watched the Live Aid concert—but in Britain he struck an especially deep chord. His appeals to help faraway and less fortunate people awakened so many memories of Britain's crusading past that to this day British journalists call Geldof, now a multimillionaire businessman, "Saint Bob." His heartfelt pleas on behalf of the Ethiopians awakened in Emma, as in many others her age, a sense of possibilities, a feeling that idealism still had a place in the world even in the waning last years of the cold war, when the aged prophets of capitalism, Margaret Thatcher and Ronald Reagan, seemed to have no larger vision for the future than of getting and spending.

Chapter Four

NOW IN HER last year at the poly, Emma took up with Ahmed Karadawi, the elegant African intellectual with the brilliant smile whom she'd first met at the restaurant. Married and eighteen years older than Emma, Karadawi came from Kordofan, a dry and sandy province in northwestern Sudan. He cast a sardonic eye on the self-congratulatory Western hoopla over Band Aid and Live Aid. He was touched by the sincere enthusiasm of the young people who thronged his lectures at Oxford, but he argued that, too often, the Western aid agencies they went to work for were more interested in pandering to the prejudices of their donors than in actually helping needy Africans. Karadawi was witty and urbane; he could make you weep with laughter at the ridiculous mistakes the self-important *khawajas* made in Sudan, and he could be just as withering on the subject of the Sudanese government's indifference to human suffering. In any event, he always said, no aid program could fix the civil wars that had caused the hunger in Ethiopia and Sudan. Only the people who lived there could do that. Emma knew nothing about Sudan and its politics. But she was about to learn from a master.

Bilad al-Sudan. How languorously those Arabic words glided off of Karadawi's tongue, like a magic spell in an Arabian wonder tale. But Karadawi did not romanticize his unhappy country. He was the first to tell Emma about the Arab proverb that says, "When God made Sudan, He laughed." (Some Sudanese say God laughed with pleasure, but far more suspect the diety was laughing at his gigantic creation.) Karadawi knew that Sudan had been the frontier between southern black Africa and the northern cultures of the Near East two millennia before the Arabs named it "The Land of the Blacks." He told her about how ancient Egyptians and Israelites knew the land south of Egypt first as the land of Cush and later as Nubia and as Punt. The Greeks and Romans called it Ethiopia or "The Land of the Burnt-Faced Ones." Not until the Muslim conquest of the Middle Ages was it named "the Sudan," or just "Sudan," as it was commonly called today. From Karadawi, Emma heard about *The Aethiopika*, the third-century Greek novel about an Ethiopian princess who was mysteriously born with white skin and was raised as a Greek, who had to travel to the ancient Sudanese city-state of Meroë to find true love and her rightful throne. From him Emma learned how the Nile River snakes out from the Sudd, the world's biggest swamp, all the way through the deserts of Sudan and Egypt to the Mediterranean.

In ancient times, the Sudd marked the limits of the world known to geographers. The Egyptians, Greeks, Romans, and Arabs sent expeditions to discover whence came the river that gave birth to Egypt, but the swamp defeated every attempt to find out. The people of the Sudan included hundreds of ethnic groups, each with its own language and customs. The northern two-thirds of the country was mostly dry, while the southern third was wet and tempting, with good grazing, fat cattle, and rivers teeming with fish. With the exception of the Nuba Mountains, the northern people were mostly Arabic-speaking and Islamic. Meanwhile the Nuba and the southerners remained "noble spiritual believers," as Karadawi liked to call them, clinging to their African languages and religions. The struggle between the lighter-skinned desert peoples, drawn by the south's water, slaves, gold, and ivory, and the darker-skinned peoples of the swamp, who violently resisted intruders, had marked Sudanese history for thousands of years. Sudan's contemporary civil war was in some ways a continuation of this antediluvian clash, Karadawi said.

Like most people in Britain, Emma had learned about the existence of huge refugee camps along Sudan's eastern border with Ethiopia only during the famine of 1984–85. But Karadawi explained that there had been Ethiopian refugees in Sudan long before the famine. Ethiopia's civil wars (like Sudan's) had deep roots, and so did the tensions between the two countries. Christian Ethiopia had been at odds with Muslim Sudan since the Middle Ages, and supporting each other's enemies had always been a feature of the contest. In 1961 the UN gave Ethiopia sovereignty over Eritrea, a partly Muslim former Italian colony that lies between

Ethiopia and Sudan. When the Eritreans rebelled against Ethiopia, they set up bases in eastern Sudan with the help of the Sudanese government and its Arab allies. As refugees who had crossed an international border, the Eritreans and their families came under the protection of the United Nations High Commissioner for Refugees (UNHCR), which fed them. Meanwhile, Ethiopia gave sanctuary to Sudan's rebellious southern pagans and Christians. Ethiopia's patron, Israel, also gave the southern Sudanese rebels military assistance, as a way of weakening the Arab coalition.

Karadawi had been a child when the Sudan gained its independence from Britain and civil war broke out in the south. The war was still dragging on in 1970, when he went to work for UNHCR in the Eritrean camps along the eastern border right after earning his degree from the University of Khartoum. The southern rebels called themselves Anyanya, or "poison," and they often behaved as poisonously to each other as to the northern army. In many ways, the tactics of the northern army resembled those of the nineteenth-century slave-traders. The army operated from inside garrison towns that had been founded on the sites of the old thorn-fence enclosures called *zaribas,* from which Arab slave-hunters had once armed their local allies and encouraged them to take captives. Now, as then, Arab army officers now handed out weapons to allied southern peoples, urging them to attack their local enemies and loot them of their cattle, women, and children. The southerners were easily manipulated, and it seemed as if the fighting might go on forever. Then a series of events suddenly changed the climate. Jafaar Nimeiri, a military officer, took over the Sudanese government in a 1969 coup and began searching for a way out of the war. Then Israel concentrated its flow of arms on a single southern rebel commander, the Equatorian Joseph Lagu, enabling him to gain control of what had been a hopelessly fractured movement.

From his position in the camps, Karadawi watched how Nimeiri used the Eritrean refugees as one card in the political game that finally led to a 1972 peace agreement between northern and southern Sudan. When Nimeiri wanted to pressure Ethiopia, the southern rebels' patron, he simply made it easier for the Eritreans to get weapons and supplies, including food, from friendly Arab countries. When he wanted to mollify Ethiopia, he squeezed the camps. In 1971 the aged Ethiopian emperor Haile Selassie agreed to act as a mediator in Nimeiri's talks with Lagu and the Anyanya. Largely united under Lagu, the southern rebels leaders were able to seize the opportunity for peace. In 1972 they and the government signed the Addis Ababa agreement that gave the south partial autonomy and ended seventeen years of civil war.

The Addis Ababa agreement ushered in a decade that Karadawi remembered as one of tremendous hope and promise. Sudan was going to be "the breadbasket of the Middle East." Nimeiri agreed to support the Camp David accords between Egypt and Israel. The United States rewarded him by making Sudan the next-biggest recipient of American foreign aid after Egypt and Israel. Sudan's Muslim neighbors across the Red Sea were awash in oil money. Nimeiri's government was able to borrow more than $12 billion from the International Monetary Fund and the World Bank and the Arab countries of the Gulf to finance its development schemes. *Biggest* was the watchword of the day. With a population of only about 26 million, Sudan had a land mass the size of Western Europe. It was the biggest country in Africa, and it was going to have the biggest of everything. International businessmen spent Gulf money to construct the world's biggest sugar factory south of Khartoum at Kenana. An Anglo-French consortium brought the world's biggest digger to Sudan and spent $75 million to construct the Jonglei Canal, a massive scheme that was going to use water from the Sudd to irrigate northern Sudan and Egypt. There were many dreams, but by the end of the decade the dreams, as well as the money, had vanished into the hands of Nimeiri's cronies and the Western expatriates who administered so many of the foreign projects. Meanwhile the Sudanese public was saddled with a debt twice the size of the country's gross national product.

The old siren song of treasure in the south spelled the beginning of the end. Following the 1973 oil crisis in the West, George Bush, U.S. president Richard Nixon's ambassador to the UN, visited Khartoum at the invitation of Nimeiri's foreign minister. Nimeiri had started out as a socialist, and the United States had kept its distance from him during his first few years in power. Now Bush, a former oilman from Texas, advised the Sudanese government that satellite remote-sensing intelligence available to the U.S. government showed that oil might be found in the southeastern part of the country, especially the triangle of land located in the Sudd region between Bentiu, Nasir, and Malakal. Bush named some American companies he said might be willing to undertake such a venture. In 1974 the American oil company Chevron was granted a license to look for oil in parts of the south and southwest. Chevron also signed a secret agreement to explore the Kafi-Kengi region in northern

Bahr el-Ghazal, where uranium deposits that could be refined for use in nuclear weapons had been found near the border with Darfur.

The Middle East was just beginning to churn with what the followers of political Islam call "the Islamic awakening." Disappointed with the failures of independence, young Muslims were turning to Islam in search of a more natural and authentic system of governance than the secular nationalism imported from the West. Political Islam found especially fertile ground in northern Sudan, where the biggest political parties already were associated with religious brotherhoods. After Nimeiri's communist allies attempted to overthrow him, the president drew closer to these Islamic parties. They had opposed his peace agreement with the south on the grounds that it gave what the agreement called the south's "noble spiritual beliefs" and Christianity equal place with Islam in Sudan's constitution. They also thought the agreement gave the south too much autonomy. They had mounted three armed uprisings against Nimeiri, in 1970, 1975, and 1976, the last two with the backing of Libya. The president did not have the strength to resist them forever. In 1977 he invited their leaders to come back from exile.

The Islamic politicians pressed Nimeiri to make Sudanese law—until now a colonial hybrid of customary, Islamic, and Western law—conform with classical *sharia,* or Islamic law. In their view, the purpose of a Muslim government was to enforce *sharia.* But southerners bitterly resisted any proposals to make *sharia* the source of all the country's legislation. Islamic law provides for harsh punishments such as amputation, stoning, and flogging. More important, under *sharia* law, unbelievers may not rule over believers, so that the imposition of *sharia* law would effectively close off the highest political offices to non-Muslims. Christians and Jews, as "Peoples of the Book," have fewer civil rights under *sharia* than Muslims; followers of Africa's traditional religions have virtually none at all. Nevertheless Nimeiri continued his drift to the right. Naming Hassan al-Turabi, the leader of the Muslim brotherhood, as his attorney general, he embarked on a program of making Sudan's laws more Islamic. He set aside his safari suit and began appearing at Friday prayers in the mosque in the skullcap and *jallabiya* of a Muslim scholar.

Then in 1978 Chevron struck oil just north of the town of Bentiu, in a mixed Nuer-Dinka area a little south of the north-south border. The oil well was located on a spot known as Pan Thou, or "thorn tree," in the Nuer language. In a move suspicious southerners saw as a clue to Arab plans to seize the southern oil, Chevron and the government insisted on changing the Dinka name of the spot to Heglig, the Arabic name for the same tree. Extracting Heglig's oil was to prove thornier than the company ever realized. Chevron had confined most of its dealings to the central government. But under the terms of the Addis Ababa agreement, the southern regional government was to receive the revenues from any minerals or other deposits found on southern land. Rather than see that happen, Nimeiri and his Islamist attorney general in 1980 tried to change the boundaries between north and south so that the land under which the oil and uranium lay would belong to a new northern province that the government named Unity. The south erupted in riots, and the president backed down. But the tension and mutual distrust kept mounting.

In the Bentiu area near the oil fields, angry Nuer men formed themselves into a militia they called Anyanya II; small clashes broke out in various parts of the south. In 1983 a battalion of southern soldiers stationed in the town of Bor mutinied over a pay dispute with their commanders. Colonel John Garang, a taciturn Dinka army officer with a Ph.D. from Iowa State University, was sent to mediate. Instead, Garang fled with the men of the 105th Battalion across the border into Ethiopia. From there he urged the Sudanese to rise up against Nimeiri's government as part of his newly formed Sudan People's Liberation Army (SPLA). This time, Garang said, the south and its allies would fight not for independence but for a secular, socialist Sudan. A few months later Nimeiri imposed an unusually harsh version of *sharia* law on all of Sudan. The civil war was on again.

Ethiopia welcomed Garang and his mutineers, just as it had embraced the southern Sudanese rebels of the 1960s. Ethiopia's wars and famines were a mirror image of those in Sudan; the same whirring cycle of disaster had rekindled that country's civil war. For a short while after the signing of the Addis Ababa agreement, the Ethiopian government had gained the upper hand in its battles with the Eritrean rebels. Then famine struck northern Ethiopia in 1973. A widely publicized BBC broadcast accused Emperor Haile Selassie of having ignored the famine. The United States and Europe withdrew the aid that had propped up his regime. A Marxist military regime seized power, and Sudan resumed its support for Eritrea. With Sudanese support, a slew of new Eritrean and Tigrean groups opposed to Ethiopia's government sprang up in the refugee camps on the border.

Like most Africans, Emma's friend Karadawi took it as obvious that to feed and house people on one side of a conflict was to help that side. He considered the UN agencies' pretensions to neutrality a laughable bit of Western hypocrisy. In Sudan he had been one of the first to suggest that the government recognize the humanitarian wings of the rebel armies fighting in Eritrea and neighboring Tigre province, allowing them to raise funds and import materials just like every other foreign relief organization. In Oxford Karadawi had gained a certain fame for his willingness to criticize all sides involved with aiding Sudan. When he and Emma met in 1985, President Nimeiri was refusing to ask for international assistance even though thousands of people in western Sudan were starving. A BBC journalist asked Karadawi where the fault lay, and he did not hesitate. "With the government," he replied. At the same time, he was engaged in writing a doctoral dissertation arguing that the West had turned refugee aid into a self-perpetuating industry that often did more harm than good in Sudan. His colleague Barbara Harrell-Bond ultimately incorporated many of his insights in her book, *Imposing Aid.* Alex de Waal, a fellow student at Oxford with Karadawi, is today Britain's best-known critic of humanitarian aid. De Waal credits Karadawi with inspiring him. He dedicated his 1997 book *Famine Crimes: Politics and the Disaster Relief Industry in Africa* to Karadawi.

Karadawi could go on for hours brilliantly analyzing the Islamic concept of *barakat,* or "blessings"—the wealth and power that naturally flow to the pious—always with cigarette in hand. In 1985 a group of army officers overthrew Nimeiri but refused to dismantle the *sharia* law he had enacted. It was going to be much harder to get rid of Islamic law than it had been to get rid of Nimeiri, Karadawi predicted. Islam, he said, was a genie that would not go back into the lamp. He explained that Islamist politicians would accuse any Muslim who tried to revoke Islamic law of being an apostate, a crime punishable by death under *sharia.* Meanwhile the abolition of Islamic law remained the key demand of the southern rebels. The officers who had seized power wanted to hold elections, but Garang and his SPLA refused to participate unless a constitutional conference was held to decide the place of religion and "nationalities" in Sudan. The officers, mostly conservative Muslims, refused. When a vote was held in 1986, the Islamic parties were the winners. Karadawi told Emma that this probably spelled the end of any peace talks for a while. "*Malesh,*" he would exclaim, using the half-amused, half-bitter Arabic expression that means something like "What a pity!" but can also mean "So sorry" and "Too bad."

Karadawi introduced Emma to many of the young Africans studying

at Oxford University. Heirs to the university's tradition of training colonial elites, the Africans tended to come from the most privileged families
in their own countries. Some were hereditary chiefs. Most had held or
were on their way to holding top positions in their governments or military—perhaps with the next coup. In their papers and in their seminars,
they spoke of economic development and the need for democracy and
institution building. But in private they talked of power as a family affair,
a game of intrigue and honor and greed into which they had been born
and in which they might well die.

Emma had never shown any interest in ideology, though as an art
student she had disavowed her father's Conservatism. The left-leaning
political opinions she voiced could have come straight out of the pages of
The Guardian. She felt a little insecure in the highly intellectual environment of the refugee program. But Karadawi assured her that as an artist
she had at least as much to offer refugees as the so-called experts who
were always blathering on about "early warning systems" or "coordina-
tion planning." "Most of the refugees in Sudan can't read. You can use
your pictures to teach them," he told her, one friend remembers. In any
event, it was not a political program that attracted her to the world of
Karadawi and his friends. It was more like the high drama of it all, the
almost Shakespearean sense that behind the sham parties and borrowed
ideologies, character is all. A few people, some of them her friends, might
decide the fate of whole countries. She could speak as glibly as anyone
else about the need for refugee participation and grassroots involvement,
but her friends believe that inside, she thrilled to the stories of kings and
queens, prophets and warriors, heroes and villains.

Karadawi never discussed his relationship with Emma, but everyone
at the refugee program knew they were having an affair. When Emma
staged an exhibition at Oxford's Poster Gallery of the aerial photographs
she had taken on her trip with Bill Hall, Karadawi invited all his friends
to come. The relationship distressed Karadawi's wife, Selma, but she kept
her feelings to herself. Sudan, like most of Africa, is polygamous. While
northern Sudanese men expect strict fidelity from their wives, few
Sudanese women are in a position to demand the same from their hus-
bands. "Let us just say Ahmed's wife was very tolerant," a Sudanese colleague of Karadawi's laughed indulgently when asked about Selma's
response to the affair. And Karadawi was not the only Sudanese man to
fall for Emma. Hamid el-Tayeb Zaroug, another northern Sudanese
refugee official, met her while on sabbatical at Oxford. Zaroug was a

Sudanese government administrator of the Ethiopian refugee camps that Emma had heard much about from Karadawi. He continued writing to her after he returned to Sudan.

Emma finished her degree in early 1986. For a short time, she went to work for the art department of the London magazine *Harper's & Queen*. The job didn't work out. The magazine's fashion mavens expected the young girls they hired to model the smart clothing featured in its pages. Emma insisted on wearing her trademark Indian caftans and big wooden bangles. When Tayeb Zaroug invited her to make a field trip to the refugee camps at Showak, she decided to take him up on his offer. She had saved some money from waiting on tables. At the end of 1986, she wrote Zaroug that she had booked a flight to Khartoum. She planned to make a display of her photos for refugee children. Alex de Waal remembers her coming over to the Oxford apartment he shared with his Eritrean girlfriend, excitedly asking for help translating captions for her photos into the Tigrinya language.

Zaroug wrote back immediately. "I read [your] letter three times to make sure I went over every word," he said. "Your face with that beautiful smile is always in front of me.... You don't believe how much I do want to see you my sweet untamed cat who trained me so much in UK on how to accept pain from whom you love. All I need from England is that I do want Emma and please tell her to come soon."

Chapter Five

*S*UDAN HAS A MAGIC that takes hold of you for better or worse," Emma told her interviewer in *The Warlord's Wife,* a 1993 ITV television documentary about her. "I've known other people who've fallen under its spell. It's not a beautiful country. It's the people who are so charming." The most famous Briton to fall under the spell of the Sudan was General Charles George Gordon. In Gordon's story lie all the seeds of the Western century in Sudan; but for his raptures and visions, the Western project in Sudan might not have had its peculiarly high-minded, moralizing tilt. Without the blindness that ultimately doomed him, his successors might have left more to show for their work. Until Emma met Karadawi, Gordon was only a name she vaguely recollected from school. But in Sudan, Gordon's story would follow her everywhere she went.

It started with the antislavery movement. In the nineteenth century, five hundred years into the Atlantic slave trade between Africa and the Americas, the Christian West experienced an extraordinary change of heart. In a remarkably short period of time, much of the West came to regard the bondage of human beings not just as a vice but as a sin, a deadly sin that had to be extirpated from the earth. Quakers and other nonconformists who started the first antislavery campaigns in the eighteenth century managed to persuade first the better part of Britain, then Europe and the pope, and finally the United States that African slavery, an immense and ancient institution that had brought huge wealth to Europe and its colonies, was not only wrong but evil—a crime, in fact.

This, the grandfather of all Western human rights movements, took on such religious fervor that in 1807, only twenty years after it began, Britain, the richest and strongest slave power of all, outlawed the trade to its subjects. Thirty-one years later, Britain freed the last slaves in its dominions.

In Egypt at the time, the spread of Western technology and capitalism was having the opposite effect on the even older slave trade between Africa and the Near East. Egypt's Muhammad Ali, the Ottoman sultan's *khedive* or viceroy, was one of the first non-Christian rulers to employ European advisers and technology to reform his army. His innovations swiftly made him the strongest ruler in the Middle East, but he needed a steady supply of recruits. Egypt had depended since antiquity on slaves from Sudan to man its armies. (The prophet Isaiah evidently met some Nilotes in the seventh century B.C., prompting him to issue his legendary prophecy of doom about their country's future.) In 1820 Muhammad Ali decided to invade Sudan to seize slaves and create an army loyal only to himself. "You are aware that the end of all our effort and expense is to procure negroes," he wrote in 1825 to the commander of his forces in Sudan. "Please show zeal in carrying out this matter." The Egyptians—or "the Turks," as the Sudanese called the invaders, since Muhammad Ali was technically a representative of the Ottoman Empire in Constantinople—established a garrison at the confluence of the Blue and White Niles named Khartoum. In 1840 the Egyptians managed to penetrate the Sudd for the first time in recorded history. Over the next decades, a rabble of Egyptian, Turkish, northern Sudanese, European, and Greek traders found their way to Khartoum, intent on hunting slaves with new European-made firearms.

Slavery had always been the business of Sudan. Ancient Egyptian records from the third millennium B.C. tell of thousands of slaves and cattle captured in the African lands to the south. Cush and Meroë were only the most famous of dozens of Sudanese kingdoms that prospered over the centuries from their role as middlemen in the slave trade between Egypt and sub-Saharan Africa. The Sudan's many ethnic groups historically raided each other for captives, especially women and children. The captives were sometimes adopted into local lineages and sometimes sold or exchanged or given away in the form of tribute. There were also more complicated transactions involving rights in people. For example, a lineage might give one of its members to another as compensation for a death or for the theft of cattle. In Sudan, as in other African societies with few material possessions, people and livestock historically have been the most important forms of capital.

The Arabs who spread out across the deserts of northern Africa in the Middle Ages gave this ancient trade a new tone. They brought horses and specialized cavalry operations that gave them an advantage over the local people. They had connections with Middle Eastern markets. And they had a rationale for what they were doing. In classical Islamic thinking, the pagan black peoples to their south belong to *Dar al Harb*, "the House of War," against whom *Dar al Islam*, "the House of Islam," is obliged to make jihad. Muslim jurists argued that while it was immoral to enslave other Muslims, slavery was the divinely ordained punishment for unbelief. "It is known that in accordance with the *sharia*, the reason why it is allowed to own [others] is [their] unbelief," wrote the celebrated Timbuktu jurist Ahmad Baba in the seventeenth century. "Thus whoever purchases an unbeliever is permitted to own him, but not in the contrary case." Like Christians in the American South who insisted that slavery was a civilizing institution for barbarous Africans, many Muslims considered slavery a blessing for pagan blacks because it exposed them to Islamic civilization. The Quran exhorted Muslims to treat slaves kindly, and religious tradition held that freeing slaves who converted to Islam would weigh in the favor of slave-owners on Judgment Day.

With the arrival of the Turco-Egyptians and their firearms in the nineteenth century, Muslim tribes such as the cattle-herding Baggara moved south in search of pagans to raid. They traded the slaves they captured for goods with small-scale traveling merchants called *jallaba*. The *jallaba* transported the slaves to Khartoum, Egypt, and other markets. For the northern Sudanese, the primary effect of the Turco-Egyptian invasion was the ruinous taxation that the new rulers exacted. For the Nilotic and other peoples who lived in the meandering wetlands of the south, the coming of the *Turuk* was a catastrophe that they call "the time when the world was spoiled." Until the coming of firearms, the Dinka, the Nuer, the Anuak, the Shilluk, and the many other peoples of the south had lived in their boggy homeland for more than five thousand years on a mixture of cattle-herding, fishing, and grain cultivation. Of the cattle-herders, only the Shilluk, who lived closest to the Arabized tribes of the north, were organized under a king, or *reth*. The Dinka and the Nuer mostly lived in stateless societies based on the bonds of kinship. Their lineages were loosely grouped into clans, which were even more loosely grouped into tribes. Lineages and clans, and more rarely tribes, united and divided on the basis of shifting patterns of alliances and feuds. Left alone, the Nilotes had flourished under this headless form of social organization. Now it left them horribly vulnerable to the manipulation of better-equipped and organized outsiders.

Accompanied by bands of armed men, European and Arab traders from Khartoum set up fortified stations they called *zaribas* along the rivers of the south. From within the *zaribas,* the traders concocted alliances with stronger groups, offering to lend the southerners weapons and men to attack the grass and mud villages of their enemies. In return, the traders received half the booty. At first they used the captured people and cattle mainly to barter for ivory, but eventually the slave trade proved more lucrative than the ivory trade. The *zariba* trade opened up new avenues for the *jallaba* from northern Sudan, many of whom set up their own companies and *zariba* networks. The Turco-Egyptian officials sometimes competed with the traders to capture slaves for the Egyptian army. Other times they worked together with them to line their pockets in a predatory and increasingly profitable commerce that soon made Khartoum's slave market one of the biggest in the world.

But the Western technology and capital that had been Muhammad Ali's strength was his successors' weakness. Egypt's dependence on Western money left it exposed to Western meddling, just as antislavery agitation was growing in Europe. If the abolition of the Atlantic slave trade ended the rather crudely capitalist form of empire that had given birth to Europe's American colonies, it soon gave life to another and far more seductive form: empire as a moral mission, with antislavery as its flagship. The victorious evangelicals who had led the campaign against British colonial slavery now lobbied to put the power of the Royal Navy behind a crusade to end African slavery everywhere. Between 1820 and 1870, the Royal Navy stopped and seized nearly 1,600 ships and freed 150,000 African slaves destined for the Americas. Britain also used its navy to bully most coastal African states into signing a series of treaties banning the Atlantic slave trade. In this climate it wasn't long before the Sudan and the Islamic slave trade gained the attention of Britain's antislavery activists.

European travelers had been writing about the cruelty of the Sudan slave trade since the 1830s. In 1839 an Austrian businessman, Ignaz Pallme, made a harrowing report to an antislavery society about an Egyptian government slave-raiding expedition into the Nuba Mountains in Kordofan.

Pallme's account was so shocking that it inspired a Catholic missionary from the island of Malta to set up Sudan's first modern Christian mission in Khartoum in 1848, with the explicit aim of fighting slavery. In the 1860s the British missionary explorer David Livingstone caused even more Western outrage with his revelations about the violence and cruelty of the East African slave trade. Abolitionists had maintained for years that Europe's capitalist free-labor system was not just morally right but essential to material and technological progress. Livingstone argued passionately and with great effect that Africa's backwardness owed a great deal to the local custom of slavery. He claimed that until African leaders had alternate means for acquiring European guns, cloth, and trinkets, they would go on selling their fellow men to obtain them. He declared that the only way to save Africa was to open it up to "the three C's": Commerce, Christianity, and Civilization. His readers were quick to interpret the three C's as a call to empire.

Early on, Muhammad Ali's grandson Khedive Ismail scented the danger that the self-proclaimed humanitarians represented to his empire. Ismail had grand ambitions to modernize all of Egypt on the Western model. He opened Cairo's first opera, and he built the Suez Canal. To do this, he used British and French money. On his ascension, he closed the public slave market in Khartoum and banned the introduction of slaves into Egypt from the south. But reports from missionaries in Khartoum and other European observers made it clear that the ban was in name only and that the slave trade continued as virulently as ever. If Ismail shared the abolitionists' moral indignation—and some historians think he did—the majority of Egyptians and Sudanese emphatically did not. Abolition was a Christian crusade; as a popular cause, it never really caught on in the Islamic world. As the historian Ehud R. Toledano has written, "Ottoman slavery and the slave trade were never seriously debated, either on the political or on the intellectual plane. It was as if one party barged in, fully armed with moral, economic, social and political arguments, imbued with a strong sense of justice, while the other timidly turned its back, refusing to engage in a dialogue, claiming that there was basically no common ground, no common language, no frame of reference through which a true discussion could take place." Slavery's legitimacy, Toledano writes, "derived from Islamic sanction and the unshakable conviction that Islamic law was predicated on deep human concern (*insaniyet*) and could not possibly condone any practice that was not humane, caring, and cognizant of the suffering of the weak and poor members of society."

Sudanese slave-owners saw Egypt's measures to outlaw as yet another hated concession to infidels bent on undermining Islam. Practically every one of Ismail's officials in northern Sudan was involved in the trade. Ismail himself had granted some of the big slave-trading firms in Khartoum their concessions to operate in the Upper Nile region. What steps the khedive had taken against slavery concerned only the selling of slaves. Owning them remained perfectly legal in Egypt and Sudan. Most northern Sudanese families owned at least one domestic servant. Ismail himself owned hundreds of people, as did most of his relatives and ministers. For Ismail, intent not just on keeping in the good graces of the European powers but on getting them to bankroll his even more grandiose plans to extend Egypt's reach beyond Sudan into modern-day Ethiopia and Uganda, the tirades of Livingstone and the other anti-slavers could have been an inconvenience—had he not hit upon an idea of his own. If the abolition of the slave trade had become a legitimate moral justification in Western eyes for all sorts of takeovers and conquests, why not make it the justification for his own?

One of the guests at the splendiferous 1869 celebrations of the opening of the Suez Canal was the British explorer Sir Samuel Baker. "Baker of the Nile," as he was called, had won fame a few years earlier when he and his wife, Lady Baker, attempted to traverse the Nile and discover its source. (They did not manage to clear up the entire mystery, but they did reach the other side of the Sudd.) Baker had written disapprovingly of how the slave trade disrupted and brutalized life on the route he traveled in the Upper Nile region along the Sobat River. The prince and princess of Wales read his book and were properly horrified; they were also titillated by the (truthful) rumors that Baker himself had bought his Hungarian wife at a Turkish slave auction. They invited the Bakers to travel with their party to the festivities at Suez. "It is almost needless to add that, upon arrival in Egypt, the Prince of Wales, who represented at heart the principles of Great Britain, took the warmest interest in the suppression of the slave trade," Baker later wrote.

Khedive Ismail felt the heat. At a fancy dress ball, he took Baker aside and made him a proposal. In return for a salary of ten thousand pounds and the title of pasha, he asked Baker to go back to Upper Nile in charge of a military force that would officially annex Upper Nile to Egypt and suppress the slave-raiding Baker had condemned. (Since Egypt up to then had never established formal claim to southern Sudan, its officials in Khartoum had always been able to maintain they had no authority over what went on in the hinterland.) Baker accepted with alacrity. Within a year's time, he and Lady Baker were once more headed up the Nile, this time in fifty-nine boats with sixteen hundred people under his command. For the next two years, the Bakers and their men struggled up the choked passages of the Nile, battling the slave-traders and their local allies and raising the Ottoman flag over rivers filled with splashing and grunting hippopotamuses. Baker named the province he staked out for Egypt "Equatoria."

In terms of actually ridding Upper Nile of slavery, Baker's expedition was ineffectual at best. He had brought along stores to feed his European party for four years, but he expected his Sudanese and Egyptian soldiers to live off the land. Some accused him of making matters worse by allowing his men to raid southern villages for grain. The notion that one man in command of a small flotilla could single-handedly extinguish a trade that had been millennia in the making absurdly underestimated its tenacity. In fact, as the khedive must have known, the plan was so unrealistic as to reassure any Sudanese slavers who had feared he actually intended to put them out of business. But in terms of appeasing British antislavery sentiment, it worked like a charm. Hiring an Englishman and giving him the Herculean task of stopping Sudan's slave trade assuaged Britain's vanity as well as its moral indignation. With the empire reaching its zenith under Queen Victoria, the British public had no trouble believing that a lone Englishman or two could take on any number of barbarian gorgons. The picture of British officers, seemingly armed with little more than moral superiority, curing entire peoples of their savage customs was a staple of the British penny press. When Baker's contract ended, Ismail cast about for a replacement. He found an Englishman who had already won national celebrity in one of these imperial set pieces. His name was Colonel Charles George Gordon, and his appointment set in motion all that was to come.

As a young British officer, Gordon had been a bit of a misfit, a loner who disliked the army's rules and regulations and who was given to extravagant religious musings. People who met him commented on his unusually pale blue eyes and his fine, almost feminine features. Then, at the age of thirty-one, he revealed the knack for bending foreigners to his will that was to make him the stuff of British schoolboy fantasies.

Posted to China in 1860, he was unexpectedly given charge of a Chinese army defending the Manchu dynasty against the Taiping rebels, a confused quasi-Christian group espousing agricultural reform. Gordon reorganized and trained his "Ever Victorious Army," and under his command it retook the cities the Taipings had captured until the rebellion was at an end.

The British press covered each step of this campaign, naturally giving their man all the credit. "Major Gordon Captures Soochow on December 5" was the headline in *The Times* of London on January 22, 1864. In this age of heroics, what the reading public liked best of all were stories in which the British showed through some personal act of bravery how superior they were to all other peoples. The newspapers were full of tales about how "Chinese Gordon" walked up and down the battlefield, smoking a cigar and holding a walking stick, indifferent to the bullets whizzing around him. When one of his men fled, he was said to have chased the man down, spun him around, and forced him to shoot using Gordon's own shoulder as a gun rest. When the civil war ended, Gordon wanted to stay on in China. He wrote to his sister that it was better to be a British officer abroad than at home. "In England we are nondescripts, but in China we hold a good position." But he had promised his mother he would come home, and after refusing all sorts of honors and offers of money, he left China at the end of 1864.

Back in England he was bored, especially when the War Office gave him the wearying task of constructing some new forts along the Thames at Gravesend. His eccentric piety irritated his more orthodox countrymen. He was endlessly patient and generous with Gravesend's young street urchins, for whom he set up a school paid for out of his own pocket. But he scorned what he called the "hollow emptiness" of his own class. He spurned invitations to dinners and soirees in London, preferring to stay at home with his Bible. In 1872 the prime minister of Egypt asked him to recommend someone to replace Sir Samuel Baker as pasha of the newly minted Egyptian province of Equatoria. Gordon had had a hankering to visit Africa since childhood. He recommended himself.

When Khedive Ismail offered him the job, Gordon took his orders to eradicate slavery as a Christian call. To show Ismail that he did not worship "gold and silver idols," he refused the generous salary that Baker had gratefully pocketed, instead asking for a stipend of only two thousand pounds. "I am like Moses who despised the riches of Egypt," he wrote his sister proudly. At first he seems to have thought he would be able to overwhelm Sudan's slave-traders by sheer force of character. "About the slavery question," he wrote confidently not long after arriving in 1874, "I shall have no trouble at all." The first time he ever got on a camel, he rode so hard that he reached his destination 250 miles away three days before the fastest caravan could have done. He rode into a slave-trader's camp ahead of his men, hoping to awe the trader with his courage.

What effect his theatrics had on the Sudanese is not clear. Gordon spoke only a bit of pidgin Arabic and never seems to have tried to learn more. He could not read or write Arabic at all. As the historian Douglas Johnson has written, "He was largely ignorant of the customs of the Sudanese and had to rely on 'reading the faces' of his Egyptian subordinates and Sudanese subjects to judge their characters." In Equatoria he relied on a handpicked staff that included Americans, Italians, Frenchmen, Englishmen, Germans, and Austrians. When these Western colleagues one by one died or were sent home with malaria, Gordon became even more isolated, shutting himself up to commune with his Bible. The Book of Isaiah was his special favorite.

Proceeding to the junction of the White Nile and the Sobat, he soon discovered that slavery was far more entrenched than he had realized. In the first month after Gordon established a garrison that could intercept boats, he caught a caravan of three hundred slaves. In the months to come, he liberated hundreds more from riverboats, often finding the slaves hidden under piles of wood or ivory. At first his determined efforts seemed to bear fruit. Gordon closed down a *zariba* on the Bahr el-Zeraf. After imprisoning its leading slaver, a northern Sudanese named Nasir Ali, for two weeks, Gordon ordered him to open a new station aimed at interdicting slaves in a spot called Nor Deng on the Sobat River. "He is not worse than the others," Gordon wrote by way of explanation. Nasir Ali did as he was told, naming after himself the *zariba* from which the town of Nasir took its name. But the more Gordon learned about slavery in Sudan, the more he began to wonder whether he was doing any good.

The slaves Gordon released from the riverboats were often reluctant to leave his garrison. They seemed as fearful of being killed by the neighboring Shilluk people as of being kept and sold as slaves to the Arabs. Some years earlier the Anti-Slavery Society in London, the oldest and biggest of the Western abolitionist groups, had pressed the khedive to create a river police to intercept slave-trading boats. But the river police simply inducted most of the slaves they caught into the Egyptian army, leading the Sudanese merchants to regard their seizures as a barely veiled form of taxation. The slave-hunters who melted away from the rivers when Gordon and his men started patrolling did not disappear. Instead they created new overland routes for the trade, marching their captives across deserts without food or water. The traffic was no longer visible to the European consuls and missionaries in Khartoum, but the slaves were suffering more grievously than ever. Gordon, who before coming out to Sudan had been a rather uncritical admirer of the Anti-Slavery Society, began to have doubts. "Up to the present, the slave is worse off through your efforts," he wrote the Anti-Slavery Society. "I am sure a poor child walking through the burning plains would say, 'Oh I do wish those gentlemen had left us alone to come down by boat.' "

Slaves did all the work in Sudan that domestics and laborers did in Britain. Gordon himself estimated that two-thirds of the population of Sudan were slaves and that abolition would cost the country two-thirds of its revenue. Sudan's Arabized tribes had a higher standard of living than its African peoples, and most blacks, Gordon came to believe, "would give their all to be enslaved in a good Cairo house." (This view was widespread among slave-holders; whether the slaves themselves agreed is less certain.) Though Muslims would not marry their daughters to non-Muslims, Islamic law gave masters the right to use their slaves sexually, and the children of such unions were born free. Some of Sudan's most celebrated sultans and slave-raiders were born of slave mothers. Even the African peoples who suffered the most from the slave trade were used to it. They knew nothing of money and wage labor; slavery was the only form of employment outside the family and clan they knew. To obtain servants, Gordon himself had to break down and pay four pounds of *durra*, the local grain, for two Shilluk boys aged nine and twelve.

Gordon knew that his Egyptian or Sudanese *mudirs*, or subgovernors, saw nothing wrong with slavery at all. "Has the khedive or the Pashas ever moved a little finger against the slave-trade except under coercion from without?" Gordon wrote. "Is it not true that the moment this coercion ceases the slave-trade recommences? It is engrained in the bones of the people." Time and again he had to discipline his officers for seizing for themselves the slaves he was trying to liberate and even selling the men under their command into slavery. Gordon and his men looked at the same wretched boatload of African slaves and saw very different things. Gordon saw robbery and murder; the Egyptians and Sudanese, he felt, saw a way of life they accepted as inevitable and perhaps the chance to make a bit of money. "When the trees hear my voice and obey me, then will the tribes liberate their slaves!" he wrote. And those were the slaves Gordon could recognize as slaves, for as he soon learned, his subordinates often took advantage of his ignorance to carry on the trade right under his nose. Claiming that the Africans in their care were their own wives and children, they used his caravans to transport slaves from the south and west to Khartoum. "The Khedive writes me quite harshly to stop this slave-trade, and you see his *mudirs* help it on," he angrily wrote his sister in 1874.

He was bitterly frustrated, not only with the khedive and his failure to put down the trade, but also with the abolitionists in London, who seemed to assume that it was so easy to put Sudan to rights. When the khedive complained that he was spending too much money, he resigned, then relented in 1877 when Ismail offered to make him governor-general over the entire country. The title theoretically gave him absolute authority over the whole of Sudan, a million square miles extending from the Libyan Desert to the equatorial rain forest. But it could not change the petty, venal reality of the Egyptian occupation, and soon Gordon was in despair again. No matter what he did, he could not escape the fact that exploitation was Egypt's reason for being in Sudan. His officials took bribes and connived with the slave-traders because they saw nothing wrong in it and because they were paid little else anyway. (The two thousand pounds to which Gordon had been so proud to reduce his salary was still many times more than any Egyptian or Sudanese official made.)

As governor-general, Gordon forbade his officials to use the hippohide whip to collect taxes. The Sudanese regarded the new policy as weakness and stopped paying taxes. He replaced the Egyptian officials he considered most corrupt with Europeans and Americans. Carl Christian Giegler, the German who had been in charge of constructing a telegraph system, was made deputy governor-general. Rudolf Slatin, a twenty-one-year-old Austrian officer, was named governor of southern Darfur, a region the size of England. Dr. Mohammed Emin, an enigmatic Austrian doctor, became governor of Equatoria. If the new pashas knew as little as Gordon himself about what was going on around them, they were at least conversant with his Western vision of good government. But no amount of fantasizing could conceal the fact that Sudan still had no transportation, no reliable postal service, no police, and virtually no administration—just the governor-general and his handful of pashas dashing about on camelback offering on-the-spot justice and harassing the slave caravans that kept chugging across the desert.

The British correspondents who wrote about Chinese Gordon in Sudan saw none of this. For them, as for their readers, the Sudan was not so much a real place as a magic mirror that reflected back a heroic picture of themselves and their culture. In this sentimental mirror, Gordon was "the world's greatest living expert on the Sudan." Through his hypnotic hold over the "native mind," the reporters wrote, he had brought "peace and orderly government" to an area the size of Western Europe. Gordon himself was not immune to such illusions. As governor-general, he could still write of his grandiose plans to stamp out Sudan's slave trade. "Consider the effect of harsh measures among an essentially Musselman population, carried out brusquely by a Nazarene—measures which touch the pocket of everyone. Who that had not the Almighty with him would dare do it? I will do it." But he was pessimistic about the prospects for ending slavery itself. The Anti-Slavery Society published an article criticizing him for buying slaves to use as soldiers. Gordon roared that they failed to see the weakness of his position. "People think you have only to say the word and slavery will cease...I need troops—how am I to get them but thus? If I do not buy these slaves, unless I liberate them thus, they will remain slaves, while when they are soldiers, they are free from that reproach...I need the purchased slaves to put down the slave-dealers." The same year Gordon was writing to his sister, "When you get the ink out of the ink-stained blotting paper, then slave-holding will cease in these lands."

He launched a violent campaign against the slave-dealers and their leader, Suleiman, the son of Zubayr Pasha, a notorious slaver and the former governor of Bahr el-Ghazal province. His Italian lieutenant defeated Suleiman and had him executed. Riding hard through Kordofan and Darfur, sleeping out on a Sudanese rope bed, Gordon captured hundreds of slave-dealers and thousands of slaves. But he knew that many more caravans had gotten away. At Shakka in southern Darfur, his camels had to pick their way through the skulls of dead slaves. In a fury, Gordon ordered the locals to pile hundreds of skulls up as a memento to the crimes of the slave-dealers; they obeyed his orders with impassive hostility. He stripped and flogged the slave-dealers he caught, then let them go. "I cannot shoot them all!" he cried out to his diary.

What to do with the slaves he had liberated was an even more devilish problem. Released in the middle of Darfur, they would only be captured again or perish of hunger and thirst. "Poor creatures! I am sorry I cannot take them back to their own countries, but it is impossible to do so." He tried distributing them among his own men as "wives" and servants. Fights broke out among them about how to divide up the slaves. When he tried to inject some realism into his correspondence with Britain, he succeeded only in alienating his humanitarian fans. "An escaped slave is like an escaped sheep, the property of those who find him or her," he wrote the Anti-Slavery Society angrily, after its activists sermonized that returning runaway slaves to their owners "entails complicity with slave-owning." "One must consider what is best for the individual, not what may seem best to the judgment of Europe. It is the slave who suffers, not Europe." But Europe did suffer when its good intentions were thwarted, and Gordon was at heart a European who cared more than he liked to admit about the judgment of Europe.

The Bloomsbury writer Lytton Strachey later wrote in a celebrated essay about Gordon, "Ambition was, in reality, the essential motive in his life—ambition, neither for wealth or titles, but for fame and influence, for the swaying of multitudes, and for that kind of enlarged and intensi-fied existence 'where breath breathes most—even in the mouths of men.'" Perhaps. Or perhaps he was simply sick at heart. "I declare that if I could stop this traffic I would willingly be shot this night; and yet strive as I can I can scarcely see any hope for it," he wrote on his way back from Darfur. After four years as governor-general, he came to the conclusion that "I could not govern the country to satisfy myself." He wrote to his sister that he was "longing with great desire for death." At the end of 1879, he resigned again, and this time a new khedive accepted his resignation.

In Britain and Europe, the conviction was gaining ground that the only way to extinguish African slavery was to bring the continent under direct European control. Like Khedive Ismail, Belgium's King Leopold saw in the public zeal for antislavery an opportunity to carve out a pri-vate African empire for himself. When Gordon returned to England in 1880, King Leopold invited him to Brussels to try to enlist him in the ven-ture. What Leopold really wanted from Congo was ivory (and later rub-ber), and he would get it at a vast human cost to the people he claimed to want to help. But his humanitarian rhetoric duped Gordon, as it did most of Europe. Gordon wrote to a friend that the Belgian king "wished merely to help a wretched people, suppress slavery, and promote Chris-tianity—all under an international flag." In 1884, after a year or so of biblical researches in Palestine, he was on the verge of resigning his commission with the War Office to accept Leopold's offer. Then all of a sudden Britain, which had occupied Egypt in 1882 to put down a nationalist rebellion, learned that Egypt's southern empire had risen up against "its government" under the leadership of a mysterious Muslim holy man who called himself "the Mahdi" or "the Expected One." They asked Gordon to go back.

In the four years since Gordon had left Sudan, Mohammed Ahmed, a smiling Arab boat builder's son, had rallied almost the whole of northern Sudan behind him in rebellion against "the Turks." Mohammed Ahmed told his followers that the Prophet Muhammad had appeared to him three times in dreams to say that he was the man who, according to some Muslim traditions, was expected to rise up and vanquish Islam's foes. He had the marks of a prophet: a mole on his left cheek and a gap between his front teeth. People listened. For years no Sudanese had dared to engage the Turco-Egyptians with their fearsome Remington rifles and cannons. But when "the Turks" tried to cut down the Mahdi at his home on Aba Island, his enraged followers rushed at the soldiers and killed them with their lances and spears. This defeat of the seemingly invincible Egyptian army convinced many pious Muslims that God was on the Mahdi's side. In 1881 the Mahdi wrote to Gordon's replacement in Sudan as well to all his *mudirs*, warning that "whosoever doubts my mission does not believe in God or his prophets, and whosoever is at enmity with me is an unbeliever, and whosoever fights against me will be forsaken and unconsoled in both worlds."

The Mahdi promised those who flocked to hear his preaching that if they would give up the godless ways of "the Turks"—the clothes, the alcohol—he would throw out the foreigners and liberate Egypt, Mecca, and Constantinople. One of his first converts was Abdullahi al-Tashi, from the cattle-herding and slave-trading Baggara tribes of southern Kordofan and Darfur province. The *jallaba* among the Mahdi's own tribe, the Danagla, and the neighboring Jaalin joined his Ansar movement by the thousands. Dressed in patched white smocks symbolizing their virtuous poverty, the Ansar defeated Egyptian forces sent to quell them in 1881 and 1882. In 1883 the Mahdi's army captured the town of El Obeid in Kordofan, marching the European nuns and priests from the Catholic mission in the nearby Nuba Mountains to the Mahdi's camp for imprisonment.

To European observers, the Mahdi's rule seemed cruel and primitive, but he was wildly popular in the Sudan. Gordon and the other British officials who blamed Egyptian misrule for the rebellion underestimated the religious appeal of the Mahdi's pledge to throw out the unbelievers. Life was and is so hard in Sudan that sometimes it seems as if the Sudanese prefer to think about death and the supernatural—as if the language of dreams and visions is the country's only common tongue. The Mahdi preached of heavenly delights awaiting those who took part in his jihad. He also maintained a rough discipline among his troops. When his men captured towns, they were required to place their plunder in a communal treasury. Beautiful women were the only indulgence the Mahdi allowed himself and his men; there were terrible punishments in his camp for drinking or smoking. In this as in all else, he claimed to follow the model of the prophet Muhammad.

There were signs and portents in the Mahdi's favor. In 1882 the appearance of a comet had foretold that the town of El Obeid would fall to the Mahdi. Eleven months later the Egyptian government sent ten thousand men under the command of a British officer, Colonel William Hicks, to recapture the town. The Ansar annihilated Hicks and his men and seized their guns, machine guns, and rifles. "Nothing could have exceeded the savage grandeur of the Mahdi's triumphal entry into El Obeid after the battle," wrote Rudolf Slatin, the young Austrian whom Gordon had appointed governor of southern Darfur. "As he passed along, the people threw themselves at him and literally worshipped him." Slatin was abandoned by his men and forced to surrender to the Mahdi and to convert to Islam. Gordon's other Austrian appointee, Dr. Emin or Emin Bey, hung on in Equatoria but was increasingly isolated. The Mahdi was ready to march upon Khartoum.

The uprising in Sudan presented Britain's Liberal government with a conundrum familiar to modern Western governments. The London government wanted not so much to do anything about this African catastrophe as to be seen to do something about it. Prime Minister William Gladstone freely admitted that he cared nothing for Egypt's southern possessions. Gladstone had a sneaking sympathy for the Mahdi as a nationalist. "Yes, those people are struggling to be free and they are rightly struggling to be free!" he told the House of Commons when urged to action. But within his own Liberal Party, antislavery sentiment was strong, and there was a worry that the Mahdi was a front for Sudan's slave-traders. Forced to take a stand, the government came out in favor of evacuating all the Egyptian garrisons south of Wadi Halfa. But that was more easily said than done. Thousands of Egyptians as well as a few hundred Europeans were scattered throughout the country in distant, isolated stations. How were they to reach Egypt without falling into the hands of the Mahdi, as Hicks and the European missionaries already had done. The British establishment was agreed that it was not worth spending British lives or treasure to save the Sudan. At the same time, Britain did not want to injure its sense of propriety by allowing people, most especially white Europeans under its de facto protection, to fall into harm.

In the midst of this debate, the influential London paper *The Pall Mall Gazette* came up with its own solution. Why not send Gordon, the hero, to extricate the Egyptian garrisons? "We cannot send a regiment to Khartoum, but we can send a man who on more than one occasion has proved himself more valuable in similar circumstances than an entire army." Here was a painless, cost-free way out of the quagmire and one that the British public, fed for years on a diet of stories about Gordon's near-magical abilities, enthusiastically endorsed. Even Queen Victoria took up the call. Gordon behaved as if he believed as much as anyone in his own legend. Though he had opined that it was necessary to defend Khartoum at all costs, he accepted the charge to evacuate the besieged city. On January 18, 1884, he set off for Sudan so quickly that, as Strachey later wrote, it almost seemed as if he had wanted to be back there all along. From Cairo he traveled south by train to the end of the line at Asyut. There he boarded a sailboat. As he left Egypt, Gordon assured a huddle of well-wishers that he knew what he was doing. "I feel quite happy, for I say, If God is with me, who can or will be hurtful to me?" Arriving in Khartoum on camelback exactly one month from the day he left London, he told the crowd assembled for his opening address that he had been unhappy away from them. "I come without soldiers, but with God on my side to redress the evils of the Sudan. I will not fight with any weapons but justice," he said.

The crowd cheered, and the young correspondent for *The Times* traveling along with Gordon was rapturous. "In that distant city on the Nile where a few days before all was misery, despondency and confusion, the coming of one noble-hearted Englishman, resolute, righteous and fearless, has changed despair into hope and turned mourning into joy," he wrote. But without weapons Gordon could in fact do very little. To Slatin, imprisoned in the Mahdi's camp, he seemed disastrously delusional. "The mere fact that Gordon had come without a force at his back proved to these people that he depended on his personal influence to carry out his task; but, to those who understood the situation, it was abundantly clear that personal influence was at this stage a drop in the ocean.... Had Gordon not been informed of the Mahdi's proclamations, sent to all tribes after the fall of El Obeid? Was he not aware that these proclamations enjoined all the people to unite in a religious war against Government authority, and that those who disobeyed the summons and were found guilty of giving assistance to the hated Turk, were guilty of betraying the faith and as such would not only lose their money and property, but their wives and children would become slaves of the Mahdi and his followers?... How could Gordon's personal influence avail him for an instant against the personal interests of every man, woman and child in the now abandoned Sudan?"

In Gordon's mind, it was a point of honor that he not leave without handing over power to some sort of government, however hastily contrived. To do otherwise would be to admit that all the "progress" of the last few decades was lost. Gordon knew there was no such thing as an antislavery party in Sudan. Everyone with any power was involved in the trade; the differences among them on the issue were a matter of degree. But when he attempted to cobble together a Sudanese coalition that might conceivably stand against the Mahdi, first by announcing that his government would not interfere with slave-owners and then by proposing that Egypt set up the notorious Sudanese slaver Zubayr Pasha as his successor, he infuriated antislavery opinion in Britain. "What is the use of his prestige if he has to do this?" sputtered one influential London daily. Gordon claimed that Zubayr, the former governor of Bahr el-Ghazal, would at least try to curtail the slave trade (in exchange for a hefty Egyptian subsidy), whereas the Mahdi openly called for its revival. But the Anti-Slavery Society denounced his plan, calling it "a degradation to England and a scandal to Europe." Better to abandon the slaves to the Mahdi than for Britain to sully its honor by consorting with known slavers. The cabinet was ready to veto Gordon's proposals, but in a barrage of telegrams, the general persisted in arguing the point. At last the Mahdi stepped in and ended the debate. On March 10 his forces swooped down on the telegraph line south of Khartoum and cut the copper wire that had been laboriously laid under the Egyptian regime. The line to the outside world went dead.

Gordon and the few Europeans left in the city could have escaped. The Mahdi sent word offering Gordon safe passage if he would simply go without a fight. But he refused to abandon the Egyptian and Sudanese troops who had remained loyal to him to face the Mahdi alone. Instead he tried to act as a sort of human shield to force the British into evacuating his men. He sent messages to Cairo warning that "*I will not leave the Sudan until everyone who wants to go down is given the chance to do so,* unless a government is established that relieves me of the charge; therefore if any emissary or letter comes up here ordering me to come down, I WILL NOT OBEY IT BUT WILL STAY HERE AND FALL WITH THE TOWN AND RUN ALL RISKS." Slowly and reluctantly, the British government began preparations to send a relief expedition. As the siege intensified, Gordon sat in his shuttered palace along the Nile, chain-smoking, writing in his journal, and reading his Bible. Food ran low. His tribal allies betrayed him. He sent boats down the Nile warning that the city could not hold out much longer. The Mahdi captured them and killed their British commander along with all his crew. In the end, there was nothing left but the sheer spectacle of Gordon's quixotic belief that he ought to be able to save the place. "I am ready to die for these poor people," he wrote, and yet it is not clear whether the Sudanese for whom he thought he wanted to give his life had the foggiest notion of what he was doing there. In a last angry scribble to the British government, he wrote, "You send me no information though you have lots of money. C.G.G." He died in the fighting around the palace on January 26, 1885, the day the Mahdi's forces finally overran Khartoum.

Hearing sounds of rejoicing, Gordon's former protégé Rudolf Slatin crawled out of his tent in the Mahdi's camp on the afternoon of the twenty-fifth. Three of the Mahdi's slave soldiers were marching toward him at the head of a noisy crowd. One carried a bloody bundle in his hand. As the slaves approached Slatin, they stopped for a moment, smirking. Then the one holding the bundle unwrapped the bloody thing. It was Gordon's head.

" 'Is not this the head of your uncle, the unbeliever?' he said. 'What of it,' Slatin managed to reply. 'A brave soldier who fell at his post. Happy is he to have fallen.' "

The expedition sent to rescue Gordon arrived two days later and was repulsed easily by the Mahdi's troops. "TOO LATE!" the headlines screamed when the news reached London. The British could have blamed Gordon for the disaster. After all, he had misread the situation. But to do so would have been to admit that the Sudan of the mirror was not the real Sudan at all. Better to blame the British government for failing to relieve Gordon sooner than to admit that Sudan's wars and famines were more than a stage set for heroes and saviors from the West. Queen Victoria was beside herself with rage and humiliation. "Mr. Gladstone and the government *have*—the Queen *feels it dreadfully*—Gordon's innocent, noble heroic blood on their consciences," she wrote to her private secretary. The leader of the relief expedition was first ordered to "smash up the Mahdi." But when the prime minister informed Parliament that it would cost approximately 11.5 million pounds to overthrow the Mahdi, cooler heads prevailed. All British and Egyptian troops were withdrawn from Sudan. The country, north and south, was left to the Mahdi and, when he died of typhus six months later, to his successor, the Khalifa Abdullahi.

For thirteen years, Europeans and Americans devoured a series of memoirs from prisoners like Slatin who had escaped from captivity to describe the Sudan's descent into tribal warfare, famine, and slavery. It was said that up to five million Sudanese died under the Mahdiya, as the Mahdist regime was known. It was not to save them that a Conservative government finally made up its mind to reconquer Sudan in 1896. The government wanted to foil French designs on the Sudd and to secure the precious waters of the Nile for Egypt. But British officers who carried out General Sir Herbert Kitchener's plan to advance up the Nile meant to avenge Gordon. With the British army's new Maxim guns and magazine rifles, they could be sure of achieving both objectives at far less cost than they would have in 1884.

"Remember Gordon!" they cried at the 1898 Battle of Omdurman as their Egyptian troops mowed down the Sudanese warriors who came at them on foot, camel, and horseback in patched white gowns, banners fluttering behind them. Perhaps ten thousand Sudanese armed with spears died in the battle outside the mud-walled warren of alleys and mosques, across the Nile from the ruins of Khartoum, where the Mahdi had made his capital. The British celebrated their victory on the grounds of Gordon's palace. Journalists warned British and American readers that Britain could not expect any material gain from the addition to the empire. It was the honor of England that had been saved. "The vindication of our self-respect was the great treasure we won at Khartum and it was worth the price we paid for it," concluded G. W. Steevens in *With Kitchener to Khartum*. "The poor Sudan! The wretched, dry Sudan! Count up all the gains you will, yet what a hideous irony it remains, this fight of half a generation for such emptiness…the Sudan is a God-accursed wilderness, an empty limbo of torment for ever and ever."

And yet—what better to remake than an empty limbo of torment? Perhaps because Sudan really had nothing Britain's 19th capitalists wanted for themselves, the field was left open to those tempted by its hallucinations and visions, to those for whom the mirror was enough. For Rudyard Kipling, Omdurman was England's finest hour. Three months after the battle, he wrote what became imperialism's defining poem, "The White Man's Burden," urging Americans to join Britain and

> *Take up the White Man's burden*
> *The savage wars of peace—*
> *Fill full the mouth of Famine*
> *And bid the sickness cease.*

Chapter Six

I N LONDON THE BRITISH still place loving notes and flowers at the base of the brooding statue of the martyr of Khartoum that stands along the Embankment. If you don't hear much about the "white man's burden" any more, savage wars of peace and Britain and America's duty to fill full the mouth of famine remain staple news fare. In Khartoum the great clash between Gordon and the Mahdi is remembered differently. The Mahdi's Oxford-educated great-grandson, Sadiq el-Mahdi, is the head of the Ansar sect as well as Sudan's largest political party. After President Nimeiri was overthrown in 1986, Sadiq, as the Sudanese call him, was elected prime minister. In 1987, the year Emma made her first visit to Sudan, Sadiq declared the anniversary of his great-grandfather's victory over the British hero a national holiday. On January 26 crowds thronged Omdurman's outdoor theaters to watch children reenact the killing of Gordon. When the Ansar ran their spears through the Englishman—dressed in one skit in a red minidress over a pair of black bell-bottoms—the sky overhead burst into fireworks. Emma arrived in time for the celebrations, but she appears to have paid them no mind. To her mother, she wrote rapturously of the Sudanese men in their loose white turbans and long flowing gowns and of the hot breeze that in Khartoum smelled of exotic spices. Right away she wanted to stay.

In his letter, Emma's admirer Tayeb Zaroug promised that he would prepare "*All Showak* to wait for you." Evidently he kept his word. A friend of Zaroug's picked Emma up at the Khartoum airport and drove her to the refugee administration center 150 miles to the east in Showak. From there, Emma wrote her mother that the Sudanese treated her "like a queen." She was given her own room with a garden in an old British guesthouse. Every morning she opened the large wooden shutters on her windows to the cloudless desert sky. At the end of the day, Tayeb and the other refugee administrators would change out of their gray safari-style uniforms and into long white *jallabiyas,* and she would join them for a communal meal under an acacia tree in the garden of the administration compound. She never asked for a fork and knife but used the flat, pancakelike Sudanese bread called *kisra* to scoop up spicy Sudanese stews just as the men did. After dinner she and Zaroug might sit outside, drinking the bootleg alcohol called *aragi* and looking at the stars. Most of the men had left their families at home when they moved to Showak, and in any event it is customary for men and women in Sudan to eat separately. But Emma didn't mind being the only woman. She liked it. As a guest of the government, she was not allowed to cook, wash, iron, make her bed, or go anywhere unaccompanied. Far away from judging English eyes, she felt free, free to lie in bed as long as she liked, free to show up late for appointments, free to stuff herself with food if she liked. "It is a very conducive lifestyle," she wrote her mother.

Showak had grown up around the railroad line the British built in the 1920s to transport cotton to Port Sudan from the fertile Gezira land south of Khartoum. It was a scrubby little town of flat-roofed Arab buildings with a few acacia trees. In colonial times, the British had run some cotton farms near Showak. (The Anglo-Egyptian administration financed itself by running large agricultural schemes for profit.) Now the refugees from Ethiopia were the town's main industry. UNHCR had its headquarters there, as did most of the private Western charities working in eastern Sudan. The gleaming white Land Cruisers favored by the aid agencies nearly, but not quite, outnumbered the donkeys on the town's sandy unpaved streets. In the government compound where Emma stayed, several dozen pins in a map on the wall showed the location of camps in the desert between the old railroad line and the border with Ethiopia. The camps had names like Um Rakuba (Mother of Shelter) and Hakuma (Government) and Tawawa and Central One and Central Two.

In the 1970s, the Eritrean People's Liberation Front (EPLF) had been joined by other ethnic liberation groups seeking to overthrow Ethiopia's by then communist government. The Tigrayan People's Liberation Front (TPLF), the Ethiopian People's Revolutionary Party (EPRP), and the Oromo Liberation Front (OLF) each claimed to be battling to create an Ethiopian state. In addition to the bewildering acronyms of their names, they professed an opaque mixture of Marxist, Maoist, and even Albanian ideology. The only thing that really united all the fighters was the desire to oust the Amhara people, who had dominated Ethiopia first under the emperor and then under Colonel Mengistu Haile Mariam.

Behind the thorn fences that surrounded every camp, the refugees were divided according to religion as well as ethnicity and political affiliation. Many of them had fled to Sudan during the Ethiopian famine of 1984–85. Others had come a decade earlier to escape the famine that struck Ethiopia's northern provinces of Tigre and Wollo in 1973. Still others had been in this part of Sudan since the 1960s. The Eritrean camps, which were the oldest, had the best facilities. Over the years, some Eritreans had been able to build flat-roofed mud houses with painted metal doors like those of the Sudanese who lived in the region. It was possible to find an acacia tree or two in the Eritrean camps. More commonly the refugees found shelter from the sun in the round thatched *tukuls* they made out of mud and sticks and plastic sheeting donated by the aid agencies. The *tukuls* were set off with little fences made of thorn. They could be surprisingly cozy inside, with Ethiopian needlework hung on the walls and teakettles bubbling on the charcoal stoves that the refugees made out of tin cans. Beyond the camps were the graves of the dead, an endless expanse of mounds that rippled out into the desert, seemingly all the way to Ethiopia. The Tigrayans and Tigrinya-speaking Eritreans, who were Christian, put crosses on their graves. The Muslim Eritreans covered theirs with thorn bushes. The sand swallowed up both with equal indifference.

The camps teemed with political intrigues; what the West saw as purely humanitarian acts were never viewed as such in Showak. Anything the aid agencies gave to one camp was assumed to be intended to benefit whatever ethnic or political group was in charge there. Emma soon learned that each liberation group had its foreign backers, even its foreign groupies. There were always rumors of secret deals and deliveries; somebody was always paying somebody else off. One day Saudi Arabia was supposed to be sending the EPLF a truckload of new AK-47s hidden beneath sacks of grain and milk powder. Another time she heard about a U.S. embassy official who had been seen meeting with the members of the Ethiopian People's Democratic Alliance. Then a group of stubble-chinned Frenchmen who said they were journalists but whom the Sudanese suspected were spooks were seen hanging around town for a few days, waiting to cross the border with the TPLF on one of the rebels' secret runs into Ethiopia.

The human consequences of this skullduggery were plain for Emma to see. Every third or fourth *tukul* contained its legless or armless young man; at any tea shop, she could find a table of war veterans smoking and arguing furiously in Tigrinya or Arabic. After big battles inside Ethiopia, the wounded would come flowing back from the event into Sudan by cover of darkness, like a kind of human sonic boom. The next morning she saw them lying in their bloody bandages on the stretchers their comrades had used to carry them down from the mountains. The camps were full of disease—malaria and tuberculosis above all—as well as suffocating idleness. The Ethiopians were forbidden to work in Sudan. Many Ethiopians worked illegally anyway in towns like Kassala and Gedaref and Khartoum, but they were subject to periodic roundups called *kasha* in which they might be returned to the camps, if not imprisoned. The local Sudanese envied them their free food and medical care, but the camps were hardly havens of safety. Occasionally one would hear the sound of gunfire. Rival factions would assassinate each other's members. Murderous rivalries broke out among hungry, bored people crowded into small spaces.

But to *khawajas* of a certain temperament, Showak's appeal was all the more alluring for being less than obvious. (And in this self-enclosed world, Emma was quickly assigned a place: From the moment she set foot outside the administration compound, dancing children followed her wherever she went, pointing and shouting, "*Khawaja! Khawaja! Khawaja!*" Her nationality and her pro-African sympathies meant little to the refugees, just as their nationality—Ethiopian—and their political sympathies—democratic, Marxist, royalist—meant little next to their more fundamental ethnic and religious loyalties. To them, she was a white woman, plain and simple.) From a Western point of view, the refugees were so pitiful, so poor, so utterly bereft that it seemed as if almost anything one did for them would help. The rush, the thrill, the excitement of living on the edge in itself gave the aid workers an excuse for all sorts of wildness that never would have been tolerated in their own countries. What was tedious for the refugees could be exciting for expatriates. Here as in the rest of Africa, *khawajas* were forever turning to one another to say, with pleased surprise, "Did you know my brother is a stockbroker?"—and then smiling in mutual satisfaction for having escaped such a fate. And in

Emma's case, there was the haunting sense of kinship she felt with the Sudanese—the sensation that, in Sudan, she had come home.

But a haze of suspicion hung over Westerners in Showak. In the nearby Tawawa camp not for from Showak, Emma met some of the Ethiopian Jews left behind a few years earlier when Israel managed to spirit away some sixteen thousand *falashas,* as the Ethiopians called them. It had been against the stated policy of Sudan to assist the Jewish state in any way, but with American help, the Israelis spread around enough cash that they were able to land a plane more than once outside Showak and load the Ethiopian Jews onto it. Ahmed Karadawi had often pointed to the Ethiopian Jews as another case of Western hypocrisy, noting that U.S. and Jewish charities raised $300 million to finance Operation Moses, the most dramatic of the Israeli airlifts, and care for its 8,000 beneficiaries— ten times the amount raised in the United States at the height of the famine to care for 600,000 refugees remaining in Sudan. When news of the *falasha* affair broke, the Sudanese media portrayed it as an outrageous violation of Sudanese sovereignty by a conspiracy of Zionists, CIA agents, and humanitarian agencies. The outcry helped lead to Nimeiri's downfall. In the trials and investigations that followed, several refugee administrators lost their jobs. Those who remained tended to view the *khawaja* commotion over the famine in Ethiopia as a smoke- screen for the West to pursue its own interests, such as aiding Israel and making the Soviet Union look bad.

Emma's Sudanese friends assumed she would have no trouble finding a job with one of the Western aid agencies. Zaroug and the others were forever complaining about the arrogant young foreigners who ran so many of the refugee programs. Just as the Victorians in the nineteenth century trusted Gordon and Baker more than the Egyptians to carry out their antislavery agenda in Sudan, so twentieth-century North Ameri- cans and Europeans trusted their own nationals more than Africans to carry out their schemes for African improvement. Frustrated by what they perceived as the inefficiency and corruption of African govern- ments, they channeled an increasing amount of their aid through private, nongovernmental organizations such as World Vision and Oxfam. The overseas aid workers often were hired not for their knowledge of Africa but for their familiarity with Western ideas about what should be done for Africa. In the 1980s, that meant concepts such as women's rights and "grassroots development."

In the eyes of the Sudanese, the Western aid agencies' preference for hiring *khawaja* over Sudanese managers looked at best like a case of tribal favoritism, at worst like a neocolonial plot. To them, these university-educated Europeans and Americans seemed painfully incompetent. Few spoke any of the languages of Sudan or Ethiopia. They seldom knew anything about the way the refugees had lived back at home. They were hardly capable of penetrating the internecine politics of the camps. They outraged local mores with their clothes and their music.

Volunteers hired in their home countries to work for organizations like Britain's Voluntary Service Overseas (VSO) for about $100 a month lived closest to the people. Their stipend was still almost four times the average annual Sudanese income of $360. After gaining some experience, however, expatriates who liked the life could graduate to better-paying jobs with an established charity such as Oxfam or Concern or CARE. At the top of the aid caste system were the high-ranking UN officials and Western diplomats in charge of dispensing the government money that kept the whole system operating. They did not visit the camps often, being busy in Khartoum with logistics and paperwork, but they sailed back and forth in air-conditioned vehicles between their offices and walled villas with cooks and gardeners. The United Nations and its specialized agencies such as UNHCR and the United Nations Children's Fund (UNICEF) regarded Sudan as a hardship post. In addition to an annual salary of $50,000 to $100,000, such expatriate officials in the country received a per diem of $100 a day. To obtain one of these jobs, certification from a Western university in development studies or refugee affairs was usually the ticket. The aid workers in Showak welcomed Emma to their Friday-night rooftop parties. But with a degree in art history and no aid experience, she didn't have the credentials for them to hire her.

After a month in the east, she gave up looking for work in Showak and went to Khartoum. In the capital, she found a short-term position funded by the VSO, teaching English and art to children at an Italian convent school. Initially she hoped to extend her contract. But the sprawling Sudanese capital was not Showak. According to her mother and her friends, something happened to cool her initial infatuation with Sudan. The air started smelling to her of diesel fumes rather than exotic spices. She began to see the cruelty that lived alongside the Sudanese charm.

She learned about the northern Sudanese custom of "circumcising" girls. When a Muslim girl reaches the age of four, a midwife cuts off her clitoris and all the surrounding flesh. The midwife then stitches the remaining tissue together, except for a small opening maintained by inserting a small stick into the vagina. The operation is intended to preserve virginity, but it gives women excruciating health problems, not to mention a loss of sexual pleasure. When the British ruled Sudan, they sought to discourage female circumcision through public education. More recently, the United Nations has named it a human rights violation. Almost every Muslim Sudanese girl has the operation anyway. Emma's male Sudanese friends claimed to detest the practice, but she learned that their sisters, wives, and daughters were all circumcised. Yes, it was unfortunate, they admitted, but superstitious women refused to give up the custom. Sudanese women were more frank when she asked them why they mutilated their daughters: No Sudanese man would marry an uncircumcised girl. No, no, no, they laughed, a bride must be *tahur,* pure, clean, not dirty and smelly with a clitoris hanging down between her legs like an infidel. Besides, everybody knew that Sudanese men liked a tight vagina—tight and dry. The women demonstrated for Emma with their hands the way their men liked it. Emma may have laughed, but privately she was horrified.

She visited the squatter camps outside the city where hundreds of thousands of southerners fleeing the civil war had gathered. She saw now why the Sudanese officials at Showak often said that many Sudanese wished they were lucky enough to be Ethiopian refugees. Conditions were much worse in the squatter camps than anything she had seen in the east.

On her VSO salary, she could barely afford to live in a cheap Sudanese guesthouse. She wrote her mother that she no longer slept inside her stifling room, but lay outside swatting at flies and mosquitoes on a rope bed in the courtyard. The way the Sudanese ignored the flies and let them land on their eyes and mouths had begun to disgust her. She complained that the men at the guesthouse treated her like a female servant. Possibly she was sexually harassed or worse. In traditional Sudanese culture, a woman traveling alone without the protection of a husband or male relation is considered sexually available. Emma adored flirting and playing sexual games, but she reserved the right to say no. She wanted to stay in Sudan, but not like this. Some three months after arriving, she asked her mother to book her a ticket back to London.

ON THE AIRPLANE, Emma met Khalid Hussein al-Kid, another learned, married Sudanese exile who wanted to take her to bed. Khalid was a former army officer and Communist Party member, a poet and a hilarious raconteur. In Sudan the Communists were the only northern party that did not call for Sudan to become an Islamic state. Khalid told Emma about how he had tried to lead a 1966 coup against Sudan's then-parliamentary government. The Sudanese government had outlawed the Communist Party and arrested its officials after a visiting Syrian Communist had ridiculed Islam in a speech. Khalid and his friends struck back by trying to take over the Khartoum radio station and thus overthrow the government. His punch line was always that he had been so drunk, he hadn't known what was happening anyway. After he was exiled, he earned a degree in literature from Reading University in England. He was teaching literature when Emma met him.

Emma told Khalid that she planned to return to Showak as soon as she could. But that proved more difficult than she had anticipated. In London the VSO turned her down for a permanent teaching position in eastern Sudan. Then she heard that Sally and Willy's old friend Alastair Scott-Villiers had found a job as Band Aid's representative in Sudan and was temporarily working out of London. She approached Alastair with a proposal to send her back to start a magazine or a library in Showak. Emma's friends at the Sudanese refugee commission had told her that the town needed a library. There were no books of any kind in Showak and especially none about refugees and development. Nor did the town have any language tapes that refugees and administrators could use to learn each other's languages. They had also spoken of the need for a refugee magazine. Emma wrote her friends at the refugee commission to see if she could seek funding on their behalf. They endorsed her plan.

If Emma was anything, she was a self-starter. She rushed around London collecting information on the cost of producing a magazine. She wrote away to British magazines volunteering to work as a production assistant so she could learn something about the publishing business. But her proposal discomfited Alastair. Every since he had lucked in to the Band Aid job two years earlier, he'd been inundated with appeals for money from friends with one plan or another for Sudan. Now here was Emma, a very young, very inexperienced Englishwoman coming forth with a proposal on behalf of a Sudanese government agency. If the Sudanese government wanted a library in Showak, why not ask for it themselves? To make matters worse, Emma kept playing up their old acquaintance, hanging around the Band Aid office in London and looking beguiling. "But I've just got to get back there," she moaned, seeming not to understand that it was against the unspoken rules of aid to admit that all one really wanted was to get away from home. Alastair turned her proposal over to an Ethiopian colleague, an Amhara refugee expert named Belay Woldegabriel.

Belay decided not to give Emma the money. He said that if Band Aid wanted to fund a project run by the Sudanese refugee commission, it should fund the commission directly, rather than through an expatriate with no particular expertise in library work or publishing. Belay observed that in the supercharged atmosphere of the camps, starting a magazine that was "above politics," as Emma promised, was impossible. As Alastair later recalled, the camps "already had newspapers. The EPLF had a newspaper, the OLF had a newspaper, and all the parties mounted this sort of propaganda campaign to bring the refugees around to their point of view. So to come marching into the middle of it with a new publication that was supposed to be for everybody and to try to stop rivalries was very dangerous."

Alastair and Belay were right. Sudanese and Ethiopians were always suspicious of *khawajas* who were so eager to leave the comforts of the West to come live with Africa's poor. Apparently a letter Emma wrote about her plan to start a magazine in Showak sparked rumors that she was a spy, rumors that dogged her for the rest of her life. Just what the letter said remains unclear, but it was something about the political personalities in the camps. Her friend Khalid al-Kid, who read it, defended Emma, saying she'd been defamed by refugees who thought that every foreigner who took an interest in Ethiopian politics was an intelligence agent.

Belay had another reason to scotch Emma's scheme to get back to Showak. The two of them had become lovers. When Emma realized that she would not be going back to Sudan anytime soon, she moved into Belay's council apartment in east London. Tall and quiet, Belay impressed Emma's friends with his intelligence and calm air of authority. So far as his British colleagues knew, he remained scrupulously above politics, yet the Ethiopian factions in the camps all seemed to hold him in high esteem. Even Emma's family liked him, but the relationship was turbulent. Emma seems to have been suffering from the alienation that so often afflicts people who return home from wars and places of deep suffering, though Showak was tame compared to what she was later to experience in southern Sudan. She kept telling her English friends about the awful things she'd seen and heard, as if she wanted to shock them out of their complacency. She spoiled a dinner party at her mother's house with a graphic description of female circumcision. She and Belay showed up hours late at her aunt and uncle's house, then acted as if they were small-minded for being irritated with her. The reaction she got was defensive; her friends assured her that they had traveled, too, and didn't need to be lectured about the existence of poverty and injustice in the world. And behind that, at least for some of them, was the unspoken implication that Emma was not quite serious, that perhaps she was using Sudan and its refugees as means for self-dramatization, and that she would be better off to put the whole experience behind her and start getting on with her own life.

Emma retreated into the demimonde of East London's African exiles, a world of thin-walled apartments and studios smelling of fenugreek and coriander, of tired women in bedroom slippers serving sweet tea to men arguing politics while television blared in the background and little children in ill-fitting school uniforms struggled with their homework on the coffee table. The exiles shared Emma's fascination with the Horn of Africa, but in a different way, they were just as skeptical as her old friends of her newfound political ardor. These were their countries, after all. Emma was indignant, even outraged, about the misery she'd seen in the Ethiopian refugee camps, whereas for the exiles the misery and the camps were established facts of life. For a while they would let her go on, but eventually they, too, got fed up with her emotional tirades and wanted to talk about something else. "She was a lovely-looking girl, but too bossy," said one.

In the summer of 1987, she discovered that she was pregnant with Belay's child, and she seems to have wanted to have the baby, but she miscarried. She became depressed, ill, lost weight. She stayed out all night, snorting cocaine and dancing in half-illegal African nightclubs to homemade cassettes of music from Zaire. She and Belay argued. When Khalid came to visit her in September, she told him she had been drinking too much and smoking lots of hash. Khalid packed Emma off to the household of the Hodgkins, a highly intellectual British family whose ties to Africa and the Sudan spanned several generations. Crab Mill, the Hodgkins' golden stone house in the Cotswolds village of Ilmington, had been a refuge for all manner of eccentrics for many years. Dorothy Crowfoot Hodgkin, the brilliant, gentle seventy-seven-year-old matriarch of the family, was Britain's only female Nobel laureate. Her daughter, Elizabeth, or Liz, as her friends called her, was working on a doctorate in African history. The Hodgkins helped Emma recover her romance with the Sudan.

Before winning the Nobel Prize for chemistry in 1964 for her work on X-ray crystallography at Oxford University, Dorothy had spent part of her youth in the Sudan. From 1916 to 1926, her father had served as Sudan's director of education under the Anglo-Egyptian Condominium. Her mother wrote and published *The Flowering Plants of Northern and Central Sudan*. Dorothy's late husband, Thomas Hodgkin, a left-wing writer and lecturer, had been one of the first Western intellectuals to write sympathetically about African nationalism. In 1948 Thomas Hodgkin had traveled around British Africa advising the colonial authorities on how to set up adult education systems that would prepare Africans for independence. Like Khalid, Thomas had belonged to the Communist Party. He got to know many of the heroes of African independence, including Ghana's Kwame Nkrumah. Liz Hodgkin taught for several years on the staff of the University of Khartoum. The Hodgkins' generous internationalism extended to their easygoing personal life. At Crab Mill, the door was always open; Dorothy invited any guests who showed up to help themselves from a pot on the stove.

Dorothy and Liz knew Khalid's wife well. At first they were disconcerted when he showed up at Crab Mill with a young English girlfriend in tow. But the Hodgkins were not the kind of people to pass judgment on the sexual morality of others. And the weekend they met Emma turned out to be one of those magical autumn interludes in the Cotswolds when the leaves turn all shades of gold and crimson. Emma and Dorothy talked for hours. They had more in common than anyone could have guessed. Dorothy's recollections of being sent away from her parents' Khartoum villa, with its banana trees and its lush rose garden, to the chilly gloom of England were like the stories Emma had heard about her mother's youth. In the four years of World War I, Dorothy and her sisters had seen their mother only once and their father not at all. By the end of the weekend, the Hodgkins agreed that Emma was a "wonderfully interesting person." When Khalid suggested that Emma stay with them at Crab Mill for a while, it did not seem as outlandish as it might have a few days earlier.

Dorothy had been afflicted for several years with a particularly painful kind of arthritis that made it difficult for her to walk, much less to do the kind of entertaining that she enjoyed so much. She was beginning to cut back on the trips she made for various international scientific and peace groups, especially those campaigning for East-West disarmament. Britain's Conservative prime minister, Margaret Thatcher, had been Dorothy's student at Oxford. Thatcher admired her former professor so much that she kept her portrait on the wall at 10 Downing Street. When Emma came to stay in 1987, Dorothy was trying to use her connections with Thatcher and with Soviet scientists to convince the prime minister that the new Soviet premier, Mikhail Gorbachev, really represented something different from his predecessors. All of this required domestic and secretarial assistance. Liz was frantically trying to finish her doctoral thesis and did not have much time to help. When Emma volunteered help with the housework and gardening, the two women accepted gratefully.

At forty-six, Liz was more than twenty years older than Emma. The politically committed, rigorously international milieu of the Hodgkins could not have differed more from the provincial, class-bound world of the Yorkshire gentry in which Emma was raised. Nevertheless, Liz and Emma became great friends; to this day, Liz remembers her with enormous warmth and tenderness. Liz understood Emma's desire to throw herself into a cause. After spending her twenties teaching in Zambia and Sudan, Liz had gone to North Vietnam in 1973 to teach English and edit English publications. She became disillusioned about the prospects for socialism in Vietnam, but she retained the longing that she had inherited from her parents and grandparents to make the world a better place. Emma's generosity of spirit touched her. "She had this ability to get close to people and to accept people even if they were very difficult to accept," Liz told me in an interview. "She was capable of great love, and she inspired great love."

The two months Emma spent at Crab Mill were a period of rest and reflection. Liz and Dorothy did not ask too many questions, but they gathered that Emma was in some way estranged from her own family. They tried to make her feel at home with them. Liz recalls that Emma became like another "daughter in the house," cooking up huge stews with carrots and peas and lots of cumin for the Hodgkins' many visitors. In a letter to Belay, Emma wrote that spending the winter in Ilmington brought back happy memories of her early childhood in Cowling Hall. "I like good snow. There is a purity and silence about it. When we were children, winter heralded new adventures, sledging, skating, building snowmen and igloos. Sometimes a blizzard would block the roads, school was closed and a free day appeared." Under the gentle influence of Liz and Dorothy, Emma agreed to try taking a more conventional route back to Africa. She applied and was accepted to begin work on a master's degree in African studies at London's School of Oriental and African Studies.

Liz had finished her Ph.D. Emma helped with the last frenzied printing and photocopying of her dissertation, and the two women moved to
London at the end of 1987. Khalid helped Emma find a part-time position
administering student grants for Sudan's cultural center in Knights-
bridge. Emma encouraged Liz to apply for a job as a researcher for the
human rights group Amnesty International. They celebrated together
when Liz got the job. Once Khalid satisfied himself that Emma was settled, he decided to stop seeing her. Their romance had been sweet, but as
he and Emma later told Liz, he was not prepared to leave his wife, and he
felt that Emma deserved better than to be a mistress. For a while Emma
moved back in with her Ethiopian boyfriend, but eventually they split up
for good. Belay was too secretive, Emma told Liz. "I just don't understand
Ethiopians the way I do the Sudanese," she said. "I just don't know what
they're thinking."

A decade later I went to England to try to track down Ahmed
Karadawi and Khalid al-Kid. I wanted to ask them whether Emma had
really understood the Sudanese as well as she thought she did. But they
were both dead: Karadawi of lung cancer in 1995 and al-Kid of injuries he
suffered the same year after he was hit by a car on his way to a Sudanese
political meeting in London.

Finally I reached Emma's supervisor at the London School of Oriental and African Studies. Michael Twaddle remembered her well. "She
was one of the better students we've had," he said. "A very original person." He never asked her why she wanted to go back to Sudan so badly.
"No, we take it as a given that we're all hooked, as it were," he said. Nor
was he surprised later, when he heard that she had married a guerrilla
and got mixed up in the civil war there. "A number of our students do
marry dangerous people," he said. "People who get involved in Africa
often do get involved in terrible things."

Part Two

If God punished man for his sins, not one creature would be left alive.

—The Quran, 16:56

Chapter Seven

THIS IS A NILOTIC MYTH. Once there was a rope from heaven to earth. Anyone who became old climbed up by the rope to heaven to be made young again, then climbed back down to earth. One day a hyena and a durra bird climbed up the rope. Knowing the nature of these two guests, God gave instructions that they were to be closely watched and not allowed to return to earth, where they would surely make trouble. Nevertheless, they escaped one night and climbed down the rope. When they were near the earth, the hyena cut the rope. The connection between heaven and earth was thereby severed, and forever after those who grew old had to die, for what had happened could not be made not to have happened.

What has happened cannot be made not to have happened, and often in Sudan I have felt that what has happened cannot be made to stop happening. The British-Sudanese writer Jamal al-Mahjoub once said that to understand the Sudan, you need a layered map like one of those cellophane diagrams of the human body that used to be in encyclopedias. As you peeled away the top piece of cellophane labeled "Sudan," you would find a succession of maps lying underneath. A map of languages, for example, and under that a map of ethnic groups, and under that a map of ancient kingdoms, until, as Mahjoub wrote, "it becomes clear the country is not really a country at all, but many. A composite of layers, like a genetic fingerprint of memories that were once fluid, but have since crystallized out from the crucible of possibility, encouraged by the catalyst of the European colonial adventure." I have often thought that you need a similar kind of layered map to understand Sudan's civil war. A surface map of political conflict, for example—the northern government versus the southern rebels; and under that a layer of religious conflict—Muslim versus Christian and pagan; and under that a map of all the sectarian divisions within those categories; and under that a layer of ethnic divisions—Arab and Arabized versus Nilotic and Equatorian—all of them containing a multitude of clan and tribal subdivisions; and under that a layer of linguistic conflicts; and under that a layer of economic divisions—the more developed north with fewer natural resources versus the poorer south with its rich mineral and fossil fuel deposits; and under that a layer of colonial divisions; and under that a layer of racial divisions related to slavery. And so on and so on until it would become clear that the war, like the country, was not one but many: a violent ecosystem capable of generating endless new things to fight about without ever shedding any of the old ones.

Not that I had any idea of all this when I first arrived in Sudan in 1988, clutching a plastic shopping bag full of newspaper articles about the war in Sudan, the war in Ethiopia, and the war in northern Somalia—the whole mess that was the Horn of Africa. It was February, the month the Nuer call "Fire." "Welcome to the seventh circle of hell," a morose and sweaty Iranian at the UN press office told me by way of greeting. I was twenty-seven years old. It was my first foreign assignment for *The Atlanta Journal-Constitution*. The newspaper had embarked on a long-term project looking at famine in the Horn of Africa. I was in the country to write about the mass starvation that the U.S. State Department claimed was about to cause tens of thousands of people in nearby Soviet-backed Ethiopia to seek refuge in Sudan.

I knew that Sudan itself had suffered a few years earlier from the same famine that struck Ethiopia in 1984–85. My Khartoum hotel, the Acropole, had been the nerve center of the relief effort. So many aid workers had stayed there in 1985 that journalists dubbed it the "Emergency Palace." On the wall of the hotel office was a letter from Bob Geldof teasing the three Greek brothers who owned the Acropole about their "empire." But I did not think much was happening in the Sudan now. Sudan in early 1988 had fallen out of the news. Two years earlier, in 1986, the United Nations had warned that another famine was developing in the south. The Mahdi's great-grandson, the democratically elected prime minister Sadiq al-Mahdi, responded by expelling the UN secretary-general's special representative to Sudan and closing much of the south to foreigners. Meanwhile the southern rebels threatened to shoot down any airplanes, including those carrying relief, that flew into the south. Since then the international press seemed to have forgotten Sudan's wars and famines.

So *The Sudan Times* came as a surprise to me. Written in English by southern Sudanese and printed on cheap brown paper, it came each morning at the Acropole along with fruit, eggs, and cereal. Its lurid black headlines reported such apocalyptic goings-on that I used to cast a covert eye around the dining hall to see how my fellow guests were taking their morning news.

TWO MILLION IN DANGER OF STARVATION IN BAHR EL-GHAZAL

ARMY ACCUSED OF TORTURING CIVILIANS IN KURMUK AND GISSEN

FOUR RELIEF AGENCIES EXPELLED FROM THE SOUTH

125,000 IN DANGER OF STARVATION AS MALAKAL RUNS OUT OF FOOD

No one ever looked alarmed. Two ancient Sudanese waiters in turbans and long blue robes padded across the black-and-white parquet floor, silently pouring coffee. The ceiling fans creaked, and the dozen or so guests murmured to one another. They were mostly European and American relief workers, although later I met a few more exotic characters, like the ancient Pole who once stepped out of his room into the atrium and fell down face forward, stark naked and reeking of illegal vodka, or the squat coal-black Ugandan with the bloodshot eyes who told me over spaghetti and meatballs that he was in Khartoum shopping for surface-to-air missiles. Shocking reports of torture and starvation, polite requests to please pass the butter: Breakfast at the Acropole gave me my first inkling of the weirdly seductive contrast between Sudan's hot and sleepy silence and the murderous events rippling underneath it.

I wanted to go straight to the Ethiopian border, but journalists needed permission from the government to travel outside the capital. Each morning after breakfast, I presented myself at the Ministry of Foreign Affairs, a shabby reinforced-concrete building with outdoor walkways that looked like a spectacularly dilapidated American motel. I usually made it over to the Ministry of Information at least once a day, too. Sadiq al-Mahdi's government was threatening to expel all the Ethiopian refugees from Sudan if UNHCR did not pay the Sudanese government more to administer their camps. Before they would approve my trip to the east, the Sudanese insisted that I listen to a long series of background interviews about the alleged stinginess of UNCHR.

They were a handsome breed, these Sudanese officials sipping their hot, spice-scented tea behind battered metal desks while their gorgeous secretaries sat outside examining the henna designs on their hands and winding and rewinding long white Sudanese veils called *taubs*. Most of them were northerners, coppery Muslims with high cheekbones and long, elegant fingers who spoke a mellifluous Arabic. Few bore the tribal marks or scarification so common in the south and the west. I spent so much time waiting around in their offices and I became so tired of hearing about their currency-exchange disputes with UNHCR that I started asking them about the stories in *The Sudan Times*. I noticed they had a way of brushing off questions about the war in the south with a flick of their scarves. "*Malesh*," they would say. "It is a very sad and complicated problem. It goes on."

But then the Sudanese seemed to take everything with the same slightly melancholy, slightly self-mocking good humor. I could see why they were famous for their charm. They punctuated every statement of action with the caveat "*Inshallah*," or "God willing"; when the electricity flickered off, as it did at least once every day, they ignored it. Telephones almost never worked. I rattled around in a taxi, leaving notes for officials, making appointments to make appointments, but mostly I wasted my time. Government offices opened at eight A.M., but not long after that everyone took a break for morning prayers. Then around ten o'clock they went off for a breakfast of *ful*, or bean stew. At one P.M. it was time for lunch and siesta. In theory employees returned after four P.M. for another three hours of work. In practice I usually found myself back at the Acropole in the early afternoon, the official day over.

The hotel was located in the center of the old British town that had been laid out in spacious avenues by Lord Kitchener after the Anglo-Egyptian conquest of Sudan in 1898. Sometimes I took a walk after lunch past the old British railway and the great brown mosque, with the men standing out front in tattered *jallabiyas* and skullcaps, selling melons and tooth-cleaning sticks. At the train station, a line of empty cattle cars stood on the track, their open doors gaping stupidly at the Sudanese women tripping through the midday heat like so many birds-of-paradise in their sandals and diaphanous rainbow-colored veils. Washing hung out the windows of the sandstone British hospital across the street, and cats yowled from the roof. The main building of the Acropole had originally been part of a commercial arcade. Across the street, a hotel annex was located in an office building built around the time Sudan gained its independence. An abandoned shopping plaza at the end of the same street was littered with empty plastic bags. Clearly someone had once anticipated lots of Western visitors with hard currency in this part of town. But whoever it was had long gone.

The dirty windows of the little tourist shops in the arcade were piled high with unsold ivory carvings. When a dust storm blew up, the sandy streets seemed to swirl up into the sky, and the buildings merged into one another like the shapes in a brown dream. The whole colonial city seemed half abandoned, faded and crumbling and going back to sand, like the ancient pyramids in the deserts farther north that I had read about. Government offices, the foreign embassies, and foreign clubs were still located on the south bank of the Blue Nile along with Gordon's reconstructed palace. But the crowds, the construction, and the life of the Sudanese metropolis had moved across the river to Omdurman, the mud-walled stronghold of the Mahdi, and to Khartoum North, the new suburb where the aid agencies and wealthy Sudanese were building houses behind walls edged with jagged glass. Khartoum proper was quiet, so quiet that in the afternoon you could stand in the shimmering heat and hear nothing but the rustling of litter in the streets.

I would go back to the Acropole and sit under the fans in the atrium reading back issues of *The Sudan Times,* smoking cigarettes, and drinking the tangy red hibiscus tea the Sudanese call *karkaday.* After a while, one of the relief workers might come over and start talking in a hushed voice, and in this way I began to learn a bit more about the war in the south. The SPLA leader John Garang was a Dinka, and the Dinka, the single largest people in the south, formed the mainstay of the rebellion. The Khartoum elite supplied southern and western tribes hostile to the Dinka with machine guns and encouraged them to form militias to raid the Dinka for cattle and, some whispered, even for women and children. The reward for the militias was the booty they captured and, in the case of Muslims, the promise of paradise. There was an Arabic saying that summed up the strategy of the northern elite: "Use a slave to catch a slave." The south and its borderlands were divided among many tribes, many militias. Baggara, Toposa, Murle, Fertit, Didinga, Ruf'aa, Nuer, Latuka, Acholi— it was hard to keep them straight. The region was also home to smaller, weaker peoples who had no weapons at all, peoples like the Uduk, the Berti, the Bongo, and the Moru. They were everyone's victims. For the Sudan People's Liberation Army did its share of raiding, too, in the areas it controlled, and those areas were growing.

There were more modern things to fight about: oil, water, and uranium, as well as education and the elusive development often promised and never delivered. The war had started about many grievances, and the longer it went on, the more it collected. It was an ugly business of robbery and revenge, and the army presided over it, disavowing the deeds of the militias in public and working with them in private. Some officers were making a fortune, colluding with merchants in the closed garrison towns of the south to jack up the price of grain and to smuggle out ebony, ivory, rare animals, and anything else of value.

Southern refugees were pouring into the capital by the hundreds every day. No one knew exactly how many there were altogether, but the UN guessed it to be around 700,000. The Nilotes, who made up most of the refugees, were visibly different: eggplant black, taller than most northerners—quite a few Nilotic men as well as some women stand well over six feet five inches tall—and with shorter and crinklier hair, extraordinarily high cheekbones, and facial scars. The Nilotic men wore on their foreheads the distinctive Shilluk raised dots or the parallel marks of the Nuer and some Dinka. Their lower incisors were removed; many decorated other parts of their bodies with cicatrices. They walked with the loping gait of rural people accustomed to traveling by foot. I was told that in the south they might have worn little besides beads and perhaps a pair of shorts, but here in the Arab capital they dressed in ragged Western castoffs. Their sullen demeanor set them apart as much as their clothing. The Arabic-language newspapers called them "traitors" and accused them of bringing disease, alcohol, and prostitution to the city. Since the southerners had not crossed an international boundary, they had no legal right to protection from international agencies such as the UNHCR. Regarding them as a potential fifth column for the SPLA, the government discouraged private relief groups from working in their camps, although some groups did anyway. Once I learned how to recognize the southerners, I saw them everywhere: dusty little boys selling cigarettes outside the Acropole, broad-shouldered women washing clothes in buckets outside Arab houses, statuesque Dinka doormen at the Hilton Hotel.

The government and the SPLA were engaged in a dance of negotiation at the time over Sadiq al-Mahdi's campaign promise to repeal *sharia* law. At the same time, the Arabic-language newspapers were full of gossip about al-Mahdi's desire to form a coalition government with his brother-in-law Hassan al-Turabi's hard-line party, the National Islamic Front (NIF). Al-Mahdi's flirtation with the NIF, whose entire program centered on creating an Islamic state, cast doubt on the sincerity of his promises to rescind *sharia*. But the first southern refugees I ever asked about the war said little about Islam or Christianity. Instead they told me they had been driven off their land because the northerners wanted the oil underneath it. An American named Bob who worked for Save the Children had invited me to come with him on a visit to one of the southern squatter camps outside Khartoum. Right after breakfast we climbed into his Land Cruiser and drove over the bridge across the White Nile to a big camp on the other side of Omdurman called Hillat Shook. From the bridge, I could see Omdurman's minarets and the shining gold dome of the Mahdi's tomb. We passed residential neighborhoods surrounded by high walls studded with broken glass, industrial areas, a camel market, desert strewn with trash. On the outskirts of the city, the road petered out, and we bumped onto a dirty expanse of sand. Finally we reached a vast garbage dump over which hung a whitish, chemical-smelling fog of smoke. In the midst of the garbage, people milled around hundreds of low, round igloolike huts made from scraps of cardboard and plastic sheeting and burlap. This was Hillat Shook.

Bob and I got out and started picking our way through broken glass and twisted metal toward the huts. Some tall, bony men came out, waving their arms and shouting at us. Bob said they were speaking Dinka. "I hope they aren't drunk," he said under his breath. The men pulled us by the arms toward one of the huts. They did smell of *merissa,* the local beer, and I wondered about that, because alcohol was illegal in Sudan under Islamic law. But they seemed sober enough. Outside the hut a woman appeared to be cooking something over a burning tire. Despite the awful smell and industrial debris, the scene was recognizably African. To my citified mind, it looked as if an avant-garde artist had been given the task of creating an African village out of toxic waste materials. I crouched down and crawled inside the hut behind one of the men. It stank of shit and sweat and burning rubber. A naked old man lay on the dirt floor. His eyes were open but covered with a thick whitish film. A woman squatting next to him in a faded floral cotton dress spoke imploringly to me, wringing her wrinkled hands. I couldn't understand a word she said.

Outside I could hear Bob talking to a man who knew some English. Bob seemed to be explaining that we were not doctors.

A gurgling sound came from the old man's throat. His foot jerked, then lay still.

The woman, who had been looking at me expectantly, began to wail. People crowded into the hut. They jabbered angrily. I backed out, making apologetic signs.

I've told them you are a journalist, Bob said when I emerged. This man is ready to talk to you.

I took out my notebook with relief. Taking notes I knew how to do. A gaunt old fellow dressed in what appeared to be a dirty white nightshirt came forward. He carried a large stick. The men who had dragged me and Bob over to the hut set down some wooden crates for the three of us to sit on. Surrounded by a noisy and ever-growing crowd of Dinka, the old man began to tell us his story. Another man attempted to translate. The old man spoke with passion and vigor, often thumping the ground with his stick for emphasis. The listening crowd shouted added details at key points in his story. All the while the woman inside the hut kept up her monotonous wailing. The smoke from the tire burned my nostrils and made my head ache. All I could make out through the translation was that the man and the others who lived in this section of Hillat Shook came from a village called Pariang in Upper Nile province, near the Heglig oil field. They were Dinka. They had owned many cows. Then two times, the year before and the year before that, the Baggara Arabs had come to Pariang with guns. The Baggara rode on horses and donkeys. The government had given them the guns. The Dinka had no guns. The Baggara shot some people and captured others, particularly children. The people who survived the second raid on Pariang came here. The children of Pariang had never been found.

A man in the crowd shouted "Chevron," and angry babble erupted. Wiping the sweat off of my face, I asked the translator what the man had said.

"They say the *jallaba* are stealing their land for Chevron. Chevron has found oil on their land, and the *jallaba* want it."

I looked at Bob.

He nodded. Pariang was near Bentiu. Chevron, which held the oil concession in that part of Sudan, had first discovered oil in commercial quantities in Bentiu in 1978. But the company had suspended its operations after southern rebels killed four of its workers in 1984. A lot of southerners claimed the government was arming the Arab militias to attack southern villages in that area and clearing the land so Chevron could resume work. But there was no way to confirm such reports, since the oil fields were located in the war zone and the government seldom gave foreign journalists permission to visit them.

I asked about conditions in the camp.

Everyone began to shout. They had no medicine, not enough food. They pointed to their bellies and turned their palms up in supplication. Children were dying of diarrhea. Children got hungry and ate the garbage. A man pulled me up from the crate, past a blur of cardboard shanties. There! he exclaimed, pointing at some children who were poking through a field of garbage with sticks. The rest of the crowd caught up with us. Someone else pointed to a lone Arab riding through the camp on a donkey loaded with a tank of water. They had no water except what they could buy from *jallaba* like him. People were dying from malaria, diarrhea, measles, tuberculosis, meningitis.

Bowls of *merissa* appeared. The voices became slurred, angrier. A man pushed his way forward, yelling and jabbing his finger at me and Bob.

"He wants to know why people are hearing this in Britannia and Europa and are not helping us. You have lots of money, but you do not help us."

I had no answer.

THE NEXT MORNING I went to the big brown Chevron office building in the center of town. I wanted to ask about the attacks the camp dwellers said had driven them out of Pariang. But the Sudanese watchman said the office was closed. I went to see a Canadian journalist I'd met at the Acropole. Carol Berger knew as much as anyone about Chevron's dealings in Sudan. She'd spent three years there as a stringer for the BBC before being deported for breaking the news of the rebel attack on the oil company's Rub Kona base camp. (She returned a year later after Nimeiri was overthrown.) She was tall and slim, with short brown hair, blue eyes, and a slight limp. She loved the insanity of Sudan, and she had seen a lot of it, having covered the last famine as well as the waning days of Nimeiri's regime. She laughed when I told her how shocked I was by Hillat Shook. What would I think, she asked, if I knew that in addition to everything else, Hillat Shook was actually the site of a hazardous waste dump? When Carol arrived in Khartoum in 1981, the Chevron building had been a hive of activity. In those days, the oil company expected to annually produce oil worth $275 million by 1986. But after Nuer rebels killed four

Chevron workers, the oil company shut down its operations. At Chevron's request, Carol said, Nimeiri began supplying the Baggara tribes of southern Kordofan in early 1984 with automatic weapons to secure the oil fields. But this only intensified the fighting between the local Nuer and Dinka people and the Baggara. Finally Chevron told the Sudanese president that "some kind of political settlement in Upper Nile" would have to be a precondition for oil exploration to resume.

Nimeiri had pinned all his hopes on the oil. He entered into a secret deal with Saudi arms dealer Adnan Khashoggi. In return for equipping and training a southern militia that could keep the SPLA out of Bentiu, Khashoggi was to get half the proceeds of any oil revenues that would accrue to the Sudan government. Khashoggi was to draw his militia from the Nuer people who made up most of the population in the Bentiu area and were traditional rivals of the Dinka. But the Khashoggi deal failed when the Nuer kidnapped the team Nimeiri sent to negotiate with them. (Carol was particularly amused by this twist.) Nimeiri then tried to open negotiations with the SPLA, relaying an offer to make John Garang, the SPLA leader, vice president of Sudan and economic administrator of the south, and to give six of his colleagues cabinet posts. But Garang turned down the offer, and a few months later Nimeiri was overthrown by his generals while on a visit to Washington. (The United States, aware of Nimeiri's increasing unpopularity and fed up with his corruption, did nothing to stop the coup.)

When Sadiq took power after the 1986 elections, he stepped up arms deliveries to the Baggara militias known as the *murahaleen.* The Baggara had been the backbone of the Mahdi's rebellion, and they retained their loyalty to his great-grandson. They traditionally pastured their cattle and horses along the Bahr el-Arab and Bahr el-Ghazal rivers, which ran through the oil fields. In 1984 and 1985 the Baggara Arabs cleared the land around Bentiu of its inhabitants. The Nuer who lived closer to Bentiu were told to move south of the river. The Dinka were driven off toward the north, the people I met from Pariang probably among them. The following year the SPLA led an assault on the oil fields that gave control of the area to the rebels. As Carol and I sat talking in Khartoum, the *murahaleen* were fighting all along the Bahr el-Arab to take control of the pastureland and the oil beneath it.

Sadiq's government was even more desperate than Nimeiri's to get the oil flowing. In the early 1980s, foreign aid had paid for almost three-fourths of Sudan's annual budget. But with the cold war waning, the United States and other rich countries were losing interest in the Horn of Africa. U.S. aid to Sudan had shrunk from $350 million in 1985 to about $72 million, and the embassy expected it to fall further. After all the excesses of the 1970s, Sudan owed more money to the International Monetary Fund than any other country in the world. Carol was frustrated with the Western diplomats who believed Sadiq's high-flown protestations about his plans to develop Sudan. They thought he was like them because he'd gone to Oxford, she said. To her, he seemed more like the feudal leader of a Muslim clan that spent much of its time bickering over how to divide up the country's wealth.

Sadiq's cousin, Mubarak al-Mahdi, had argued violently not long before with some Chevron executives. Mubarak was Sadiq's closest confidant. He was also close to Colonel Moammar Qaddafi, the president of Libya and a patron of Sadiq's who had given him the backing to stage several armed rebellions against Nimeiri. Reportedly Mubarak had been entrusted with the funds Qaddafi gave Sadiq to win the 1986 elections. After his victory, Sadiq had given his cousin a vital new task: to get Chevron to resume drilling. But the Americans refused, citing the danger the rebels presented to their personnel. Oil prices were at a low of $16 per barrel. As the U.S. ambassador to Sudan, Norman Anderson, later wrote, Mubarak accused the Americans of using Sudan's civil war as an excuse to wait for the price of oil to go up. Mubarak warned the Americans that if Chevron didn't want to drill in the south, the Sudanese would find another company that did. The French company Total, for example, already owned large concessions in the far south, near the towns of Bor, Kapoeta, and Pibor. Total might be willing to drill where Chevron was not. Chevron held its ground. The company had invested more than $1 billion in Sudan, but as Anderson wrote, it did not want to "make itself again a target" or "incur large new expenses in uncertain political and economic conditions without reasonable prospects of a return on investment." The al-Mahdis fumed, but the oil remained underground.

I KNEW OF ONLY one person who had visited the Sudan for pleasure. She was a friend from London who'd gone to visit Patta Scott-Villiers, an old schoolmate who also happened to be a friend of Emma McCune. When I called my friend to say I was going to Khartoum, she suggested I look up Patta and her husband, Alastair, who was Band Aid's representative there.

By coincidence I had spent my first night in Sudan in a room at the Acropole that Band Aid kept as an office. The walls were decorated with posters of Bob Geldof and Princess Diana. The floor was stacked with yellowing telegrams addressed to the Scott-Villierses about famines past. Clearly, they had seen all of this before. I left a message for Alastair and Patta, and a few days later they invited me to dinner. When Alastair came to pick me up at the Acropole, I was in high spirits. I had just received my permit to travel to the Ethiopian refugee camps.

What do I remember about that night? An apartment a little less empty than most—wooden furniture mostly has to be imported in Sudan, and foreigners who don't plan to stay long seldom bother to buy more than a few chairs and a bed—the smell of curry, a couple of British aid workers sprawled out on a couch smoking a joint, the Police playing on the cassette deck, and Patta's kind smile as she came out of the small kitchen wiping her hands on a dish towel. How Alastair and the others laughed indulgently when I told them I had come to check out the U.S. reports of starvation in Ethiopia. How Alastair later took me aside to say that the famine I was looking for wasn't in Ethiopia but more than two thousand miles in the other direction, in the far western province of Darfur, on the Bahr al-Arab River in the land of the Baggara Arabs—and that this was a famine the United States wasn't talking about.

Safaha. It was a whisper, a word on a report, a squiggly half inch of italic writing on a map over Alastair's desk, and yet I swear felt a chill when I first saw the name. Alastair and I had been discussing an article in *The Sudan Times* that said thousands of people were starving in the town of Wau. The last foreign aid worker, a Dutch doctor, had been evacuated from the town a month earlier. I was saying that I believed the stories, but unless I could see and describe the starving people myself, nothing I wrote would have any impact. Or something like that. Alastair gave me an appraising look. Now that I understand what he knew then about the slaughter going on in Wau, I can only imagine what he was thinking. But he didn't say anything. Instead he took me into another room. You might want to read this, he said, handing me a folder. It's an Oxfam report from southern Darfur that was handed out at an aid meeting this week.

I read quickly. *A large influx of destitute southerners has been moving into south Darfur since December. Their arrival is connected with the collapse of security in and around Wau . . . Confidential: Two thirds of the children in the feeding center have MUAC ratios of 60 percent and less . . .* MUAC means "muscle-upper arm circumference." I knew from my reading that MUAC ratios of 60 percent was aidspeak for saying that two-thirds of the children had lost almost half their body weight.

How do you say that again—Safaha? I asked.

Yes, said Alastair, and he turned on the light so that I could see the map of Sudan on the wall. There it is, he said, pointing to a tiny strip of letters in the empty lower left of the map next to the crooked line of a river. *Safaha.* It's on the Bahr el-Arab River, he said, the boundary between north and south. Bahr el-Arab means "The River of the Arabs," but Dinka call the river the Kiir. The Dinka and the Arabs both used to water their cattle at Safaha, but for the last year or so there have been reports of fighting there. His finger moved up the map to a town called Ed Da'ein. About a year ago there was a massacre of Dinka here, he said. Thousands were killed. A bloodbath really. A couple of lecturers at the University of Khartoum wrote quite a good report about it. They said that some of the surviving Dinka were sold into slavery. You could probably get a copy from one of them.

Alastair put the Oxfam report back in its folder and reached to turn off the light.

Safaha lies above the northern boundary, he said. Technically, it's outside the war zone. Oxfam and the Belgian branch of Médecins Sans Frontières (MSF) are working there. Maybe you could get permission to visit one of them.

We went back to the living room.

Just remember, you didn't get it from me, he added.

Patta called everyone to dinner.

Chapter Eight

IT WAS AN UNUSUAL and expensive thing for the Atlanta newspaper to send a reporter to Africa. I had been hired only a few month earlier and I feared that if I failed to come up with a story, I would spend the rest of my career checking suburban police blotters. After four days in the Ethiopian refugee camps at the border, I had seen some of the unhappiest people on earth. But not one of them appeared to be starving. I made up my mind to go back to Khartoum and pursue Alastair's tip. A Quaker couple staying with me at the government guesthouse made me feel distinctly callous. Chris and Clare Rolfe were British and in their mid-thirties. He had light brown hair and a beard; she had a shy smile that crept up the corners of her mouth. Their pale, open faces radiated honesty and compassion. In their cheap cotton clothes, the Rolfes looked like English hippies, but they were lit inside by the same religious beliefs that had propelled the early Quaker abolitionists. They were in Showak with their two young children, three-year-old Tommy and one-year-old Louise. They both spoke softly, as if even their voices had been trained in nonviolence, and they ate their vegetarian meals alone with their children in the guesthouse. They were waiting for permission from the Sudanese government to start a community self-help project in the camps.

Before coming to Sudan, the Rolfes had spent three and a half years in Somalia working on a Quaker project making small-business loans to Somali refugees from the Ogaden region of Ethiopia. Clare told me in her gentle way that she'd wanted to have Tommy in Somalia, but the London office had talked them into going back to England for the birth.

While they were gone, fighting had broken out in the Ogaden. Somalia's president Mohammed Siad Barre had been arming the Ogaden refugees to fight his Somali enemies. His enemies retaliated by torching the refugee camps. The Quakers had to shut down their lending program. The small businesses the Rolfes had nurtured were abandoned. I thought that if I had been in the Rolfes' position, I would have been embittered. But they were not discouraged. If they ever got the necessary papers from the government, they were planning to start over among the Ethiopian refugees in Sudan.

Chris chuckled to himself as he described his patient attempts to negotiate the bureaucratic maze of the Sudanese refugee commission. The Rolfes' serenity fascinated me. It also made me uneasy. I couldn't help but wonder why they weren't more frustrated at the waste of all those years, all that money in Somalia. How could Clare have wanted to have her baby in a refugee camp rather than in England? I wondered what the Somalis and Ethiopians made of them. While the Rolfes waited at the refugee commission all day, a round-faced Ethiopian nanny looked after their children. I often heard Tommy snuffling and whining in the room next to mine. His eyes bulged oddly. He seemed to be ill. One morning as I was leaving for the camps, I saw him pressed against the chicken wire surrounding a little dirt yard by the side of the house, sobbing. He looked up at me when he heard the door open. His face was angry and pink. It dripped with perspiration. He swatted helplessly at the flies swarming around his eyes. The nanny stood behind him, impassively rocking his baby sister. I felt obscurely guilty. The boy so clearly did not belong.

Later that day I asked a Sudanese refugee administrator who had been taking me around the camps what he thought about the Rolfes bringing their children to Showak. After all, even the Sudanese bureaucrats left their families at home when they came to this ugly place.

Who knows why you *khawajas* do anything? he laughed. Believe me, everyone else in Sudan would rather be in London!

I TOOK A BUS back to Khartoum and got a copy of the human rights report Alastair had told me about from one of the authors, Dr. Ushari Ahmad Mahmud. A University of Khartoum linguist, Dr. Mahmud belied the stereotype that all Arab northerners were indifferent to the suffering of the southern Sudanese. When I found him at his university office, he described with quiet precision the massacre that had taken place a year earlier in the town of Ed Da'ein. He and Suleyman Ali Baldo, the coauthor of the report, estimated that a thousand Dinka had been killed at Ed Da'ein, while another three thousand Dinka children had been taken into slavery. Mahmud and Baldo had visited the town to collect the information for their report. After it was published, Sudan's Arabic newspapers had called them traitors and liars. Both men were interrogated, and Mahmud was imprisoned. He had only just returned to his post at the university.

The British had founded the University of Khartoum as Gordon College. Now many young women on campus had taken to wearing the Islamist uniform of a scarf and a long dress. I took Ushari's report back to the Acropole to read. Ed Da'ein, the report said, was a railway town of about sixty thousand people, most of them belonging to the Rizeigat, a Baggara tribe of Muslim cattle-herders who considered themselves Arabs. Rizeigat territory bordered the land of the Dinka. In the nineteenth century, the Rizeigat had been great slavers. In recent years, Sadiq al-Mahdi's defense minister had been giving them and another Baggara tribe, the Misseriya in neighboring Kordofan province, automatic weapons and hand grenades. The government claimed the Baggara needed to use arms in self-defense against the SPLA. Dr. Mahmud said they were using them to burn houses and fields and steal cattle throughout the Dinka lands of northern Bahr el-Ghazal and Upper Nile provinces.

In January 1987 an SPLA company ambushed a Rizeigat militia along the Bahr el-Arab at Safaha. In more peaceful times, Safaha had been a center for trade between the Dinka and the Rizeigat. Now southerners claimed the Rizeigat militia gathered at Safaha had been raiding Aweil District across the border in Bahr el-Ghazal. The SPLA killed 150 Rizeigat and captured four thousand cattle in its attack on Safaha. For months thousands of Dinka refugees had been streaming north past Safaha to Ed Da'ein. On March 27 the Rizeigat retaliated for the SPLA attack by firing on the Dinka refugees and burning down a Dinka church at Ed Da'ein. The Dinka gathered for safety at the Ed Da'ein railway station, where a train was supposed to leave for the town of Nyala the next day. After the Dinka clambered on board the train, the enraged Rizeigat set fire to the wagons. Hundreds burned or were suffocated to death in the cars nearest the station. The Dinka in other cars managed to start the train with the help of some railway workers. As the train moved, the Arab mob ran through the town killing and mutilating any Dinka they found. The police joined in the attacks. The perpetrators were never arrested, and the government clearly wanted to keep the matter quiet. For months it denied that any massacre had occurred. Then in June the Sudanese minister of interior announced that only 183 people had been killed at Ed Da'ein. The University of Khartoum investigators put the number at more than a thousand.

Mahmud and Baldo said that the Rizeigat militia made a practice of selling Dinka women and children to Arab families in South Darfur for use as servants, farm workers, and sex slaves. "The kidnapping of Dinka children, young girls, and women, their subsequent enslavement, their use in the Rizeigat economy and other spheres of life and their exchange for money—all these are facts," their report said. "Moreover the existence of slavery in the area has generated some beliefs among the Rizeigat that the Dinka is subhuman. All psychological barriers to terminating his existence have been broken down—that was what made the massacre at Da'ein possible—without fear of reprisal from the government whose representatives were present."

The report said the Rizeigat took the captured slaves to Safaha.

I WROTE A COUPLE of stories about the Ethiopian refugees at Showak—with Carol's help, as I had never seen a Telex machine before—and I sent them to Atlanta. A little while later, the machine lit up and a reply clattered back: THIS FINE, BUT WHERE FAMINE???

COMING, COMING, I typed slowly.

Why wasn't it enough to write about how hundreds of thousands of Eritreans and Tigrayans and Oromos were stuck out in the sands of Sudan, waiting for the whirlwind of war and famine that had ripped them out of their homes to cease? That meningitis had recently broken out in the Tawawa camp and that Tigrayan children were dying without vaccines? That great set battles involving tanks and artillery were taking place in mountains between the Eritrean People's Liberation Front and the Ethiopian army and that one day an Amhara deserter wounded by shrapnel and for some reason carried down into Sudan by the Eritreans died on a stretcher in front of me, his black velvet eyes suddenly going gray and glassy like the eyes of a rocking horse I'd had as a child?

I knew the answer. At that historical moment, one year away from the fall of the Berlin Wall, famine was still a kind of totem to the West.

Refugee camps, terrible poverty, sickness, epidemics, AIDS—all this we accepted as unfortunate third-world realities. But mass starvation was different. Bob Geldof had shown that famine could still outrage Americans and Europeans. They bought newspapers to read about it. There was simply too much food in the world. It was embarrassing to think that thousands of Africans might be dying of hunger while we gorged ourselves, especially since fattening up the skeletons we saw on television appeared to be a purely technical matter, requiring nothing more than the money to buy grain and the knowhow to move it. Africa's other tragedies might be borne, but against famine a line must be drawn.

I suspected that American readers would be equally disturbed to learn about a revival of slavery. As Primo Levi wrote that same year of the Nazi camps, to whose survivors the starving Ethiopians had carried such a disturbing resemblance: "How much of the concentration camp world is dead and will not return, like slavery and the dueling code? How much is back or is coming back? What can each of us do, so that in this world pregnant with threats, at least this threat can be nullified?"

IN DARFUR, I MIGHT FIND SLAVERY, I wrote.

The machine was silent. Then it lit up again.

GOOD. BUT HURRY, it said.

AT THE U.S. EMBASSY, no one seemed to know anything about Safaha. But officials of the two aid agencies that Alastair had told me were working there, MSF-Belgium and Oxfam, went quiet when I asked about it. If you can get permission from the government to go to Safaha, we will be glad to show you what we are doing, Oxfam's freckled, red-haired country director said finally. But for now I can't talk about it. It's an army garrison subject to military secrecy.

Carol had broadcast the report for the BBC on the Ed Da'ein massacre that prompted Dr. Mahmud and Suleyman Ali Baldo to undertake their investigation. I asked her for advice on how to get to Safaha. She warned me not to ask the Ministry of Information outright for a permit. Don't even say the word "Safaha," she said. The minute they find out you're interested in Safaha, you can forget about going anywhere. I did as she suggested and instead asked for permission to visit Nyala. Two hundred and fifty miles north of Safaha, Nyala was the nearest town with air service. The United States had mounted a huge relief effort in Nyala during the last famine. Fertile grasslands had once surrounded the town, but now they were turning to desert. The Sudanese government blamed drought. I told the Ministry of Information that I wanted to see what Oxfam and MSF were doing to help the nomadic Arab camel people who lived there.

The Oxfam report had said the Dinka influx into southern Darfur was connected to events in Wau, the capital of Bahr el-Ghazal, the huge province south of Darfur that had been fertile slave-raiding territory in the nineteenth century. Wau had been under seige by the SPLA for more than a year. The army and the rebels had blocked overland relief shipments to Wau. Pilots had refused to fly into the south ever since a plane chartered by the aid agencies had been shot down over the town of Malakal a year earlier. There were many rumors in Khartoum about what was going on in Wau. In January the acting governor of Bahr el-Ghazal, a southerner, had sent a message to the prime minister. "Right now, citizens are starving to death in villages," he wrote. "Wau town has run out of essential food items like grain." He urged that food shipments be sent "to avert a very devastating human tragedy." No grain had been sent. Some whispered that the army commander at Wau, a man called Abu Garun, was a psychopath; others said he was simply following orders from Khartoum. He was said to have personally master-minded atrocities against civilians, including crucifixions. Fighting was reported between the Dinka police and wildlife services in the town and a government-armed militia drawn from the Fertit, a black African tribe. Carol had obtained Wau police reports showing that the Fertit were killing an average of ten Dinka a day. Next to many of the victims' names, the notation "cult" appeared, meaning that the body had been ritually dismembered and disemboweled. The Fertit were also said to be kidnapping Dinka women and children and selling them to the Baggara as slaves. On Christmas Eve, a Sudanese army unit had carried out a particularly gruesome massacre. Hundreds of Dinka were said to have been machine-gunned and thrown into the river that flowed through the town.

In October 1987 the army expelled World Vision, an American relief agency, and three other agencies from Wau. Dick and Carol Steuart, the couple who had worked for World Vision in Wau, came from Clarkston, Georgia. The Steuarts had been accused of telling the BBC about a massacre of 160 to 200 Dinka refugees at Wau. American diplomats told me the army had taken away their radio transmitter and threatened them in other ways. They said there was almost no food left in Wau. I wanted to find the Steuarts, but they had already left the country. A month before my arrival in February 1988, a UNICEF pilot had flown into Wau on a special mission to extract the last remaining foreigner in Wau, a doctor for MSF-Holland. Another Dutch medical worker, a woman, had escaped Wau earlier by hitching a ride with an army convoy going to buy beer and cigarettes in Zaire. The Dutchwoman was now in Khartoum. She was said to be shattered from her experiences, maybe even having a breakdown. I went to the tin-roofed MSF house in Khartoum to see if she would talk to me.

I found her rocking in a chair on the shady veranda of the old bungalow, a pale, wan-looking woman with circles under her eyes and whitish faded hair. Beside her a barefoot Dinka boy wearing a neatly mended shirt and short trousers squatted on a wooden crate. The Dutchwoman's chin began to tremble slightly when I asked about the stories of murder and starvation that had been trickling out of Wau. The agencies had been expelled for "security violations." What exactly had happened?

The aid worker rocked slightly in her chair. She didn't look at me.

I told her I understood that after what had happened to World Vision, the aid workers from Wau were afraid to talk about what they had seen. But wasn't it time to consider whether relief workers could do more good by speaking out than by staying on and trying to alleviate the damage caused by the perpetrators? Our conversation would be totally off the record—

The Dutchwoman interrupted me.

You are right, it is too late to sit in Wau with no food, watching—ach, she said. Her voice quavered for a moment.

I have decided to do something, she said. She took the boy's slim black hand into her pale one. This is Marial.* His parents are dead. I knew them. . . . Those things you have heard about the situation in Wau, I am not going to talk to you about them. Just now I am waiting for the government to give this boy an exit visa. I am going to take him to Amsterdam. I am going to leave this, this, this—she searched for the word—this *cursed* country, and I am going to take him with me to Europe.

She stood up.

*I have changed the boy's name.

It is one thing—the one clear thing I can do. Everything else is muddled. Even if I told you, what difference would it make? I'm sorry I cannot help you. It's not because of Médecins Sans Frontières. It's this boy. I can't take a chance with his exit visa. Anyway, after you have been in this country for some time, you will see that it is not so simple to find the truth.

She smiled, a forced grimace that made her look more tired than ever, turned, and went inside. The boy followed her, silent as a shadow. The screen door slapped behind him. All I could hear was the buzzing of flies.

Another week passed. I got my permit to go to Nyala. I rushed to tell Carol. She was on her way to Sadiq al-Mahdi's beautiful old Omdurman villa that afternoon to collect a couple of quotes for a story on the Sudanese economy. She invited me to tag along. I thought it rather odd and hilarious to just pop in on the prime minister, but Carol insisted that it was standard Sudanese practice. After all, it's not as if the telephones worked and we could call and make an appointment! she said, laughing. That clinched the argument. We grabbed one of Khartoum's tiny old yellow taxis and jerked across the bridge to Ombdurman in it, passing the Madhist fortifications built to withstand the British. When we reached the al-Mahdi villa, the car door wouldn't open, and Carol had to climb out the window to open it from the outside. It wasn't a very dignified entrance, but the guard let us in anyway. He led us up a long staircase and told us to wait in the hall. On the landing, I saw a fine oil painting of a turbaned man charging across the desert on horseback, sword drawn. I guessed it must be a portrait of the Mahdi. It gave me a little shiver. For the first time, I wondered what it must have been like to be raised as the scion of a Muslim messiah. Was it really so surprising, I wondered, that creating an Islamic government seemed more important to Sadiq than ending the war or reviving the economy? The guard came back and said, "The prime minister is playing tennis with the World Bank," and that made us giggle, too.

After a long wait, the door to the hall burst open, and Sadiq strode in, dressed in tennis whites and still sweaty from his game. He was a very elegant-looking man, with hooded black eyes, a long nose, and a graying goatee. I'm terribly sorry, but I can't give you more than a minute, he told Carol apologetically. She asked her questions about the economy quickly, while he wiped his face with a towel. His English was exquisite. After her interview, Carol introduced me.

Deborah's going to Darfur tomorrow, she said.

I want to go to Safaha, I added suddenly, watching his face. It seemed inconceivable that this donnish tennis player would forbid my trip. I wanted to see his reaction to the name *Safaha*.

How interesting, he said, with polite indifference. I couldn't tell if he had ever heard of the place before. He stroked his goatee.

You must come and tell me all about it when you get back, he said.

Chapter Nine

OXFAM HAD A SUDANESE administrator in Nyala. His name was Adam. He wore a white *jallabiya* and skullcap with a ballpoint pen tucked behind his ear. He stood up behind a desk covered with papers and clasped my hand in two of his. "*Al-hamdillallah*—my excuse has arrived!" he said, laughing and pulling up a plastic chair for me. "Anything to get away from this paperwork."

I was relieved. Pierre, the Belgian administrator for MSF in Nyala, had not been so welcoming. In fact, he asked me to leave the MSF house when I told him I wanted to visit Safaha. Running his hands through his curly blond hair, Pierre said the Sudanese army had forbidden MSF's Belgian doctors to take photographs at Safaha. The army might expel them if it suspected them of helping a Western journalist get there. But Adam did not seem as nervous as his European counterpart. Flinging himself into a chair opposite me, he assured me that Oxfam would be glad to take me to Safaha. All I needed was permission from the police. As a matter of fact, a staffer would be driving there in a few days. I could catch a ride with him. Oxfam was running a feeding program there. The police estimated that thirty thousand Dinka had passed through Safaha since February. Hundreds more were arriving each day. Yes, they were in a pitiful condition. Oxfam did not have enough food for all of them. Many had died. It was tragic.

Why were they coming to Safaha? I asked.

Adam shrugged sadly. There was the war between John Garang and the government in the south. And the drought.

I asked about the reports that Dinka children were being sold into slavery.

"Slavery is very strong word," Adam replied. His expression was pained. "A harsh word. There is a war in the country. Some of these tribes like the Dinka and the Rizeigat have some traditional customs that are hard for foreigners to understand. They have something they call 'pawning.' In a time of famine, a family will pawn their child to a richer family. The richer family will pay for the child. The child will work around the house, he will be fed. When times improve, the parents can buy the child back.... This seems strange to you, but when people are hungry, they will do anything to save themselves and their families."

He walked me out to the waiting room. A dark-skinned muscular man wearing blue jeans and sunglasses was sitting there, his long arms and legs akimbo in a plastic lawn chair. He was a Dinka, by the looks of the scars across his forehead.

Ah, here is Gaudensio, Adam said, eyeing the Dinka. He is the one who will take you to Safaha.

Inshallah, I said.

Yes, *inshallah,* Adam agreed.

AT THE POLICE STATION, a tiny whitewashed cube of a building, a uniformed officer with a large Afro took my application for a permit to Safaha without comment. Come back in a few days, he said.

Adam had told me I could find people who had passed through Safaha at a camp called Abu Jiira. But the taxi driver instead took me to a freight train that stood still on the tracks in the desert. "Dinka, Dinka," he insisted, nodding vigorously and pointing at the cattle cars. "We find them here." We got out and started walking through the sand toward the silent train. As we drew closer, southerners came climbing out of the train to greet us. One of them, a woman wearing a loose cotton dress, spoke a bit of English she said she'd learned at a mission school. Her name was Mary Awatch. She said the Dinka on the rusting train had escaped the Ed Da'ein massacre the year before. She herself lived in the third railway car from the front. She had watched from the open window of the same car as a man shot and killed two of her children who had been trying to climb on board the train during the massacre. Another child, a girl, had disappeared in the confusion of the attack, and she never saw her again.

The fifty or so Dinka on the train kept to themselves, she said. They were afraid of the Arabs who lived in the nearby villages. The Arabs gave them work carrying water and serving meals, but the Dinka knew they weren't liked. They got some clothes and a little food from the Catholic mission in town, but they were hungry, very hungry. They hoped to make enough money somehow to get to Khartoum. Mrs. Awatch showed me a thick scar she said she had suffered when a man knifed her in Ed Da'ein. "It is better on the train than in Da'ein," she said. "They will kill Dinka in Da'ein."

I thought about Ed Da'ein. Alone out of all the atrocities committed in Sudan in 1987, the massacre at Ed Da'ein had been documented. Mahmud and Baldo said they had written their report "to show the need for immediate assistance for the survivors of the massacre" and "to call on public opinion, both local and international, to exert pressure and to agitate for the dismantling of the institution of slavery in the Sudan." The massacre was debated in the Sudanese parliament and reported in the international press as well as in the Sudanese papers. The U.S. State Department had mentioned it in its annual human rights report. Anyone who had anything to do with the Sudan knew all about it. All these words, and yet here was the result—a motionless train sitting in the desert.

The taxi driver and I continued across the sand to a cluster of conical thatched huts we could see in the distance. The Dinka on the train had said the Arabs of this village sometimes employed them. The Arabs were camel-herders who had come to Nyala from Kordofan province after they lost their animals during the big 1984–85 famine. At this time of the day, the women had the village to themselves. They fluttered about in blue and crimson veils. A buxom woman named Bakhita Adam seemed to be their leader. I wanted to ask her about the Dinka, but I thought I'd better ease into the subject, so I asked her to describe a typical day for me.

The woman giggled at the question. The taxi driver translated her answer. "She wakes up, she clears the house, she feeds the chicken. She washes clothes. She makes food, she buys food. She visits her neighbors. She makes dinner." She had a Dinka servant who pounded millet for her family. It took the girl about five hours of pounding to prepare enough millet to feed the family each day. She was a big help, but Mrs. Adam said she didn't like her—didn't like any Dinka, in fact. She wanted the provincial government to move the train people somewhere else.

Why? I asked.

She had stopped laughing. Her coffee-colored face twisted into an ugly scowl. "Because they are ugly and black," she said.

EATING GOAT STEW at a long table in the Nyala souk, I met a Sudanese journalist who worked for one of the Khartoum newspapers published by the National Islamic Front. I had read about the NIF. Headed by Sadiq's brother-in-law and Nimeiri former attorney general, Hassan al-Turabi, it was the most hard-line of the Islamic parties. Turabi and most of the other NIF members belonged to the Muslim Brotherhood, the oldest of all the modern movements seeking to return the Islamic world to Islamic law. Founded in Egypt in 1928, the Brotherhood called on Egyptians to eject Britain from their country and replace Egypt's Napoleonic legal code with *sharia*. From there it spread to Sudan, Kuwait, Palestine, Lebanon, and elsewhere. As one country after another freed itself from colonialism, the Brotherhood continued to agitate for a return to *sharia*. "Islam is a state and a religion" was one of its slogans. "No constitution but the Quran" was another. I asked the journalist why the Muslim Brothers were so determined to make *sharia* the only source of law in Sudan.

He was happy to tell me. Islam, he said in between bites, was a complete system, covering every aspect of life. This is what Sudanese Muslims forgot when they let the British talk them into making religion a private matter, outside the purview of the state. The Islam is *sharia,* or the "straight path," he went on, and the Sudanese would not be fully Muslim until they lived in a state committed to enforcing it. There was a oneness, a unity, to Islam that made it impossible for Muslims to pick and choose among its rules and regulations; the faith had to be swallowed whole or it was no good. That's why no Muslim could oppose *sharia.* If he did, he was an apostate. Young people like him were turning to the NIF because it was the only party prepared to stand up for Islam against the West and its unbelievers. Sadiq al-Mahdi and other corrupt politicians like him claimed to be Muslim, but in fact they were in the pay of the West. Only the NIF was determined to create a Sudanese state with the holy Quran as its constitution. "Democracy, socialism, nationalism—all these imported systems have failed," he concluded, waving his arms for emphasis. "It is time for us to return to our own tradition—Islam."

But what about the southerners and other Sudanese who aren't Muslim and don't want to become Muslim? I asked. What place is there for them in an Islamic state?

Actually Islam is the only unifying force we have in Sudan, he said slowly. "Without Islam we are just a bunch of tribes."

I persisted. What was so wrong with being "a bunch of tribes"?

The journalist gave me a hard stare. I'm not surprised to hear you say that, he said. That's just what the British said when they were here. They closed off the south to the north and invited Christian missionaries to go there and teach the southerners to hate Islam. They wouldn't allow the southerners to wear Arab clothes or speak the Arabic language. They turned the south into a "human zoo."

He seemed to be working himself up. The so-called aid workers stirring up trouble in the south today are part of the same old Christian-Zionist conspiracy against Islam, he said. The NIF had no illusions about what they were up to. "You crusaders think you will be able to stop the march of Islam into Africa, but you are mistaken," he sneered. "You will see. The Islamic revolution is going to begin in Sudan and from here it will go all over the world."

I didn't know then that "crusader" was a common Islamist epithet for Westerners, and as an agnostic sort of Christian, I was too astonished to be called one to focus on his predictions of revolution. "But no one is suggesting that Sudan become a Christian country," I sputtered. "What the southerners are saying is that a secular state could provide guarantees for all religions—"

The journalist interrupted. "A secular state *is* a Christian idea—a Christian plot to prevent Muslims from fully realizing Islam," he asserted. "It was the missionaries who gave the southerners these ideas, who taught them these things in their schools.

"Yes," he went on, "John Garang is a 'child of the missionaries.' It is you people who are to blame for these wars!"

NATURALLY THE AMERICAN priest at the low, whitewashed Roman Catholic mission in Nyala disagreed. The priest pointed out that in Darfur, the Rizeigat were using their arms to attack the Muslim Fur people as well as the pagan and Christian Dinka. Religion is a useful mask for greed, but in the Sudan it was no defense against a stronger tribe who wanted your land, your animals, or your women, he said. The northerners would be attacking the southerners even if the southerners had converted to Islam. The south's problem was not Christianity. It was weakness. Most southerners were not really Christian anyway. They just called themselves Christian because they knew the northerners were even more prejudiced against pagans than they were against "Peoples of the Book." The southerners also thought *khawajas* would be more willing to back them against the north if they claimed to be Christian. They needed all the allies they could get. You didn't have to be Christian, he said, to know that in Sudan no one was without sin.

He went on: "You can't just blame the Baggara." The politicians and the merchants in Khartoum were manipulating them, too. The agribusiness schemes funded by the World Bank and the Arabs in the 1970s had cut into their grazing lands. One of them right outside of Nyala was called the Western Savannah Development Corporation. In the name of development, the corporation had relocated the Baggara to areas dependent on motor-driven water pumps. Now foreign aid was dropping, and the government had no hard currency to buy fuel for the pumps. The nomads were left with no water for their cattle. The Baggara had lost more than a million cattle in the 1984–85 famine. The Umma Party was giving them arms and telling them to replenish their herds at the expense of the Dinka. Was it really so surprising that they took up the offer? "The sad thing is, when the SPLA retaliates," the priest concluded, "it will be the Rizeigat and the Misseriya who suffer, not Khartoum."

The priest lent me one of his Dinka students to translate at the Abu Jiira camp. The people in the camp crawled out from the same sort of igloo-shaped *tukuls* made from plastic sheeting that I had seen at Hillat Shook, but they seemed even skinnier and more despondent than the people outside Khartoum. Some of them shuddered visibly when I mentioned Safaha. "They have all passed through Safaha to get here," the Dinka student replied when I asked why they seemed frightened. "It is very dangerous there. The Rizeigat are there. If you have money, you can leave. If you do not have money, you cannot leave."

"Have any of them sold their children?" I asked.

The catechumen said sternly, "No person in this life sells his baby. They have rented their babies to rich people—rented them—see?"

"What rich people?" I had yet to see one.

"Baggara. Between Safaha and Ed Da'ein, they have found rich people from the Baggara. This is how to find money for their food and to live and to be sure that their babies will live."

Evidently the Baggara farmers and nomads who were the objects of international charity were comparatively wealthy in the local scheme of things.

A short, weathered woman spoke up in the high-pitched *tick-tock* sounds of the Dinka language. "Her name is Amaow Akok. She had one son, name of Akol. She rented him for fifty pounds at Safaha. She doesn't know the name of the Baggara who gave her the money."

The woman rubbed her belly and held out her upturned palm in supplication.

"She is hungry," the catechumen said.

I remembered the Iranian press officer who had told me Khartoum was the seventh circle of hell. I was beginning to think there must be more than seven circles for those damned to live in the Sudan.

I WENT TO THE POLICE station every day. I was now staying outside Nyala at the Western Savannah Development Corporation that the priest had told me about. It was a mostly empty expatriate village of brick houses with neat driveways that seemed to have been beamed down into the desert from suburban England. A British engineer living there had invited me to stay. The police told me I need permission from army security to go to Safaha. An army security officer told me flat out that I could not go. But after about ten days of sitting around drinking tea with the police, I wore down one of the them, and he gave me some sort of stamp. I took it straight to Oxfam. Gaudensio and his driver picked me up the next morning while it was still dark. We drove southeast into the desert, following the old British railroad tracks.

Just after sunrise we heard the sound of singing. A tall man with a short cloak tied over his shoulder, carrying a staff, was walking toward us, chanting a song. He looked like a character out of the Bible, and as he got closer, I saw that he had all sorts of little amulets and charms hanging off of him. We stopped for breakfast and gave the walker a drink of water. He set off into the desert again, still singing. I felt as if I had stepped back centuries in time.

We jolted past miles and miles of brown thorn scrub. Except for the railroad tracks, we saw not a hint of human endeavor. We saw no animals except a baboon and a few gazelles. Where are all the animals? I finally asked Gaudensio. He had been snoring beside me when a large bump woke him. He lifted his dark glasses. "All of the animals have run away to Central Africa," he said slowly before he dozed off again. Finally we started to see some acacia trees, and soon after that we began passing ragged little groups of tall, skinny people sitting or lying under the trees.

I could tell they were Dinka from the scars on the men's foreheads and the way the women were bareheaded and sometimes bare-chested.

Gaudensio woke up and pointed at them from the window. "These people are coming from Safaha," he said. I wondered about him. He was a Dinka himself, one of the tiny educated minority. He had told me he came from around Wau. He was a former mission boy, educated by the Verona fathers. Working for Oxfam, he had a rare opportunity to help his family and his people. Instead he had shown up at Western Savannah reeking of illegal *aragi*. At breakfast he pulled out a canteen and started drinking again. He had to know he was playing in to every Muslim stereotype about unbelievers. Was he doing it to express his rage and frustration over the plight of the Dinka, or did he just not care?

Near Ed Da'ein we had engine trouble. We decided to spend the night in the town. I noticed that Gaudensio stayed in the car and let the Arab driver do the talking at Ed Da'ein. I stayed in the car, too, and studied the Rizeigat from the window. They were magnificently handsome, tall, big-boned men with high cheekbones, chocolate-brown skin, and slightly tilted, almost Tartar eyes. In the nineteenth century, they had captured Gordon's governor, Rudolf Slatin, and held him prisoner not far from here. Somewhere among them today were the murderers who one year before had shot, knifed, and burned to death the relations of the Dinka on the train outside Nyala. I wondered what their spotless white cotton robes and swirling turbans must have looked like that day. Gaudensio fingered his canteen unhappily. Ed Da'ein seemed to make him anxious.

After the driver came back, we drove slowly through the town. The mud bricks of the buildings in the town center gave way to fenced compounds of straw, and then, just out of sight of the town's conical thatched roofs, we saw a group of about five hundred Dinka sitting under a grove of trees. As the truck drew closer, some of them came running toward us. They were dressed in torn scraps of Western and Arab clothing. When I stepped out of the truck, a gaunt old man with a long walking stick cried out and rushed toward me, weeping and talking rapidly in Dinka.

"What's he saying?" I demanded, feeling acutely uncomfortable.

Gaudensio wore a sardonic expression. "He is their chief. He says now that he sees your white face, he knows help has come."

I felt ashamed, as if I had misled the old chief by my very presence. He thought I was the advance party—for what? An aid agency? A colonial force? But I knew there was nothing behind me, nothing at all. I could see people lying in the sand. It seemed they were too weak to stand. I got out my notebook and started asking questions. They were Dinka from Aweil. They had gone to Safaha looking for food, but there was none. They had paid to be trucked out of Safaha. The trucks had dropped them here three days earlier, and they had no money to go any farther. The authorities had forbidden them to enter the town after citizens complained that the Dinka were urinating near their houses. They had no food or water or shelter. Two of their party had died the day before.

I had never before seen so many sick, frightened people.

The chief said something that caused everyone to murmur in mournful assent. I looked at Gaudensio.

"He said, 'We left because we were dying in the south. Now it seems that we will die here anyway.' "

I asked the chief if any of his group had rented their children to the Rizeigat. Before the chief could answer, five or ten people crowded around and shouted "me" and "I rented my child." The chief fluttered his hands in great agitation. He said that it would take time to collect the names of all the children who had been rented. If we could come back tomorrow, he would give us a complete list. He was still crying. I felt like crying myself. By being here, I was giving him false hope. He seemed to think that if he supplied us with a list, we would be able to recover the children. I asked if I could walk around. I took out my camera and strolled over to the trees where the bulk of the chief's people were camped. The chief and his men followed at a distance.

The sun was starting to go down. The figures leaning against the silver-barked trees were bathed in lavender light. The people seemed to have nothing more than a few quilts they had strung up in the trees for shade, and some calabashes and plastic jerry cans. They were all bony. Some were plainly close to death. A little way apart from the rest, I saw an older man and a skeletal young boy sitting under a tree of their own. The boy was sitting in the man's lap, staring out into the desert with blank eyes. His collarbone stood out like a harness; the skin across his protruding rib cage was wrinkled like an old man's. The man was gently rubbing the boy's huge, knoblike knees and bony shins with water from an old cutoff plastic jerry can beside him. With infinite patience, he dipped his hand into the water, then carried it to the boy's legs, then dipped his hand in the water again, speaking to him softly in Dinka. I stood, transfixed with pity and horror. Gaudensio stepped up beside me, whispering in my ear like Dinka Virgil: "The boy is dying. The father is trying to cool his pain, to make it easier for him to go." I reached into my backpack and found my wallet. I had about seven hundred Sudanese pounds on me in cash. It was worth about seventy dollars.

Gaudensio turned away. "Better not give them all your money. You will see worse at Safaha," he said.

I took a picture of the father bathing his dying son. Then I gave the old chief five hundred pounds and hurried back to the pickup truck.

THE NEXT DAY we set off again. The land was getting greener, with more trees and tall grass. We began to see herds of cattle with long horns twisted in the lyre shape that I'd read that the Dinka trained their cows' horns in. The Dinka culture and religion centered on their cows. But these Dinka cattle now belonged to the Rizeigat. We stopped at a village of rectangular grass houses called Nabagia. Some pretty Rizeigat girls with long braided hair had been fetching water from a village pump— the gift of the Western Savannah Development Project, no doubt—and they flocked around me in their yellow and pink veils, touching my hair and smiling with their big, white teeth. While I was taking the girls' photos, a couple of tribesmen carrying automatic weapons came over to the driver, speaking urgently to him in Arabic. When he agreed to whatever they had said, they clapped him on the back and jumped into the back of the Oxfam truck. They were laughing and talking excitedly among themselves. They greeted me with a speech of thanks. Evidently they thought I was the boss who had agreed to give them a ride. I heard the word *abid* several times. I knew that *abid* meant "slave," but that it was also used as a general derogatory term for southerners. Gaudensio stood behind me, glowering at the new passengers.

What are they saying? I asked him.

They are going to the police at Safaha to complain that a slave they bought there has run away, he said between clenched teeth. The boy was a Dinka. They are saying they beat him the night before, but not hard.

We got back into the truck and rode on without speaking. It was March 28, 1988.

Chapter Ten

SUDDENLY THE DRIVER made a sharp turn, and we banged down a hill to a grassy clearing. Gaudensio turned to me, grinning like a demented tour guide. "Safaha," he cried, and with a wave of his big hand, he gestured toward a field spread out below us.

I had already heard and thought so much about it, and yet it was not at all what I had been expecting. It was like a landscape painted by Hieronymous Bosch, a succession of almost inhuman figures and odd cameos set in an almost bucolic landscape: a naked child lying underneath a cloudless sky in a puddle of urine, flies crusted around his eyes and his nose...Dinka women on their knees, furiously weaving straw...the bones of an old man's buttocks protruding through his torn gown as he dragged himself along a grassy path with a walking stick...a Rizeigat merchant with a turban like whipped cream, walking through a crowd and snapping a long whip as birds chattered in the background.

The Land Rover came to a halt in front of a grass shack with a sign bearing the Oxfam logo. Gaudensio and the driver jumped out. I followed slowly. I felt as if I had stepped into a strange dream. The Rizeigat men in the back had tumbled out and were smiling and thanking everyone in elaborate Arabic. I could hear moaning in the distance. From out of the Oxfam hut came two African men in their twenties wearing Western clothes. They were shorter and stockier than Gaudensio, with flatter, broader features and large Afros. Gaudensio said they came from Central Africa. Everyone shook hands all around. It seemed that they had been waiting for us. I looked at my watch. It was not quite noon.

Get back in, Gaudensio said. It is time for the distribution.

He held the door open for me. The two other men climbed onto the back of the Land Rover. We drove a few hundred yards through the camp, right up to the muddy bank of the brown and green Bahr el-Arab River. Across the river crowds of wasted human beings, some dressed in rags, some naked, stood waiting their turn to cross the water. On their shoulders, they carried their naked children, whose skin hung from their abdomens in grotesque folds of loose flesh. Other bony forms lay sprawled in the mud. Some people were already wading the waist-deep river. After they crawled up the bank, they formed a line in front of two uniformed policemen seated at a folding table under a little canopy. Gaudensio explained that this was where the police registered each arrival.

I got out of the truck. The shriveled people swarmed around me, wailing in Dinka. I walked over to a group of new arrivals who had collapsed on the ground behind the registration site, moaning monotonously. There were about twenty of them. They were women with withered breasts and young boys, their faces buried in their hands. Gaudensio followed reluctantly. Ask them what happened, I demanded.

They crowded around me, still wet from the river, moaning and crying. The boys thrust out their arms and lifted their rags to show me bruises and burns. I could not tell the welts from the scars all over their bodies. What were they saying? I tried to hear Gaudensio's translation over the tumult. The boys said they came from Marial Bai, a village near Aweil. Their cattle had been stolen, their village burned, and they had no food. All the villages around theirs were deserted. They had been walking for three days. Last night the Rizeigat militia had attacked them in the forest on the other side of the river. The boys said militiamen had whipped and burned them. They also had taken seven children and one woman away with them.

I was writing down the names of the children when Gaudensio motioned for me to put my notebook away.

"The police are looking at us," he said. "Safaha is a Rizeigat camp. The men who took their children are probably here now."

Behind him I saw masses of people who had crossed the river that morning now crouched on their bony haunches, waiting for food under the pitiless white eye of the sun. One of the Central Africans walked through the crowd smoking a cigar-sized joint as he separated naked children from their families and lined them up in a special queue. Many of the children had lost so much weight that their heads looked huge and unnatural. The driver and the other Central African opened one of the giant burlap sacks we had brought in the Land Rover from Nyala. It was filled with woolen sweaters. The children with the strength to stand waited obediently while the Oxfam men worked their way down the queue. It was a struggle, but they wrestled a hot, itchy, ill-fitting sweater over the head of each child. I imagined cold English days, with old ladies sitting next to a gas flame, knitting sweaters and mittens to take to the little Oxfam shop on the high street. What would they think if they could see their handiwork now?

Why do they have to wear sweaters? I asked Gaudensio.

"Because they have none," he said, as if that were an answer. He was unloading more bags and boxes from the truck. The sweaters seemed like madness in this heat, but perhaps clothes were some kind of defense against the Muslim contempt for nakedness. Later I learned that many of the sweaters ended up on the heads of Dinka men, who tied the sleeves in knots. They made interesting hats.

Suddenly a great clamor broke out a few yards away from the Land Rover. Hundreds of starving Dinka were rushing toward the driver, who was opening bags, cans, and boxes of food and soap. A policemen came over, waving a long whip and yelling at the people in Arabic to form a line.

"Give one of these to each woman," Gaudensio told me, dumping a box of soap in front of me. The women were already pressing forward with calabashes and old plastic jerry cans. The odor of wet, unwashed bodies assailed me. The relief workers were supposed to give each recently arrived woman a shallow, foot-wide basketful of sorghum, a cup of cooking oil, and a bar of soap. With more than five hundred people crossing the river each day, it was all the Oxfam workers could do to deal with the new arrivals. The Dinka chiefs in the camp were supposed to hand out a subsistence ration that they got in bulk from Oxfam to the twenty thousand or so people already at Safaha. But there were so many new arrivals, all crowding forward, all pleading to be fed, that in the confusion some of the camp dwellers who had been there for days joined the mob and demanded food—or so I was given to understand from the outraged reaction of the Oxfam workers, who called the entire operation to a halt until those who were asking for more got out of the way. During the frenzy, an old Dinka woman fell down in convulsions. Her head and feet banged on the ground, and foam dribbled from her mouth. No one paid the slightest attention. When the distribution resumed, she was nearly trampled to death.

Gaudensio was walking up and down the line, writing down the name of each person who was to receive food, but so many of the people had the same names that his list seemed pointless. Over where the children were still waiting for sweaters, a shaggy-haired young white man wearing thick black glasses had joined the Oxfam workers. The white man was weighing children on a set of scales he had hung from a tree. He wrote down the weight of each one, stopping often to wipe the sweat off his glasses. Gaudensio said the man was one of MSF's Belgian doctors. He was looking for children to take to the special feeding center that MSF ran on the hill next to the army camp. Children had to weigh half as much as normal for their age to qualify for the feeding center.

All the food and the sweaters had been handed out. I got in the back of the Land Rover. My head was pounding. It was terribly hot. We began driving slowly back through the camp. The air was hazy from the smoke of cooking fires. On either side of us, thousands of people were sitting and lying on grass mats on the flat open plain beside the river. It looked like a gigantic picnic of skeletons. Farther off I saw white-robed militiamen carrying automatic rifles marching some bare-breasted Dinka girls toward a sort of alley of grass shelters where a lot of Rizeigat men seemed to be milling about. The truck swerved to avoid hitting a shriveled little boy lying in the dirt beside a woman. I thought of the trembling Dutchwoman in Khartoum. *I'm going to do one clear thing,* she had said. "Stop," I said suddenly, and then I said it again louder. I felt foolish, because in truth I had hardly ever shouted a command at anyone in my whole life, but I said it again. "Stop!"

The truck stopped. I climbed out and walked back to where the little boy was lying. He was barely breathing, barely able to blink his enormous eyes against the flies swarming around them. A pair of spindly legs poked out from his bloated belly. The scrawny woman beside him struggled to sit up, then fell back, wheezing. Gaudensio caught up with me. Why isn't this child at the feeding center? I demanded. Gaudensio shrugged and spoke to the woman in Dinka. She said nothing, but another woman watching from a nearby mat spoke up.

At length Gaudensio answered: "The child's mother is very ill. Maybe she has pneumonia. She has no relatives to take the boy to the feeding center."

We can take them, I said. We can take both of them to the feeding center. Gaudensio shrugged again. He shouted to the driver, who slowly backed the Land Rover to where we were. A crowd gathered around. Some men picked up the mother and laid her in the truck bed. When I sat down in the back beside her, they put the boy in my arms. He felt like a hot papery bundle of little bones. His eyes were closed, but I could see a vein throbbing underneath the skin stretched across his skull. Every time the truck jolted, I was afraid he might break. We drove up the hill and parked in front of another long rectangular grass hut. An MSF Land Cruiser was parked in front. Surrounding the hut on three sides was a large U-shaped lean-to made of woven grass and filled with women and children. This was the feeding center.

I got out of the truck, still carrying the boy. The doctor I had seen earlier at the food distribution emerged from the hut wiping his mouth.

Sorry, he said, taking the child from me. He had a high-pitched Flemish accent. We were just eating our lunch, he said. I'm Eric Hendricke.

I told him my name and that I was a journalist.

Dr. Hendricke lifted the boy into another pair of scales hung from a tree. There was another journalist here, he said. British. He was arrested yesterday. The police were taking him to jail in Nyala today.

I mulled this over as Hendricke recorded the boy's weight. It was 4.2 kilograms. The mother was sitting up now in the back of the truck and able to speak. Hendricke questioned her while Gaudensio translated. She said the boy was three years old and his name was Atot. Three years old, and he weighed ten pounds. Was it possible?

The second doctor with glasses I had seen weighing children by the river came out of the hut bearing an aluminum cup filled with hot milk. He introduced himself as Koen Henkaert and took Atot's mother and the boy inside the feeding center. I followed. He squatted next to Atot's mother, pantomiming how she ought to give it to the boy to drink. The Dinka women in the center chimed in, nudging the mother and motioning for her to give the boy the milk. But she was too ill and sank down in the dirt. Finally one of the other women took the cup and began feeding the boy with it. To my surprise, he opened his eyes and drank, slowly at first and then in gulps.

I asked Henkaert if he thought Atot would live. He shrugged and stood up. Who knew? It was good that he was drinking. But very few children survived if the mother was not strong enough to feed them. That's why the rule at the feeding center was that each child had to be accompanied by an adult. The children at the center needed to be fed every three hours. Henkaert and Hendricke could hardly feed all 264 themselves. Even if they could, they didn't have enough food for more, and it was better to save it for the children who were likely to survive. And those were the ones who had someone to care for them.

Hendricke interrupted to ask if I wanted some lunch.

It seemed somehow shameful to eat among the starving. But I was hungry, so I followed him into the MSF hut. There was no furniture, only blankets and clothes strewn on the dirt floor, a couple of backpacks, and a kerosene burner with some brownish stew cooking on it. Hendricke flopped down on a blanket and scooped stew onto a couple of tin plates. He handed me one and started eating. I ate a spoonful. It was very chewy and full of gristle. What is it? I asked.

Gazelle, Henkaert answered, laughing at my expression. We bought it in the market.

I was surprised to learn that there was a market in a famine camp like this. Who had anything for sale?

The doctors laughed again, bitterly. Oh, but everything was for sale in Safaha—*durra,* the meat of goats, cloth, even human beings. For those who have money to buy, Safaha is a shopping paradise, Henkaert muttered.

Hendricke interrupted. Actually they had never been to the market. The army did not allow them to leave the feeding center except to go down to the river to weigh children at the noon distribution. They had to send their Sudanese staff to buy food. But they had heard about it.

They were both haggard and unshaven. No wonder, I thought, feeding over two hundred children every three hours. The three of us sat chewing for a minute. Then I asked if I could stay with them in the MSF hut. I volunteered to help. They agreed, so long as I stayed out of trouble. For God's sake, don't try to buy a slave, groaned Henkaert. That's how the other journalist got caught.

What other journalist? I asked.

He was British, that's all they knew. How he got to Safaha, what he was doing there, they couldn't say. One day he appeared at the feeding center, snapping photos. When they saw that, they shooed him off the place. Next thing they heard, he had been arrested.

Henkaert made instant coffee with canned milk. I offered him and Hendricke some of my American cigarettes; they took them gratefully.

We lay on the blankets, inhaling luxuriously. The cigarettes tasted better than the gazelle. It felt very good to be full. In fact, it seemed to me that I had never really noticed how satisfying it was to be full.

In the afternoon, Gaudensio and I went to register with the police. Their station was a card table under a thorn tree. As the policemen sat in their folding chairs looking at my passport, a truck full of soldiers rolled up. The soldiers appeared to be guarding a beardless white man with a crew cut and bright blue eyes. I guessed the prisoner to be in his early twenties. He didn't seem frightened. He waved to me and asked in English for a cigarette. He was the British journalist the doctors had told me about.

I walked over to the truck and handed him some Marlboros. He told me that he was an investigator for the Anti-Slavery Society in London as well as a journalist. He said he'd had a dreadful time getting to Safaha. The police wouldn't give him a permit. He finally paid a merchant to take him. The merchant helped him make the connections in the market to buy a slave. Another merchant from Ed Da'ein, a big fat fellow, was going to handle the whole thing. He was going to buy a seven-year-old boy for forty pounds. The Ed Da'ein merchant was going to get a four-pound commission out of that. It was all arranged, but then the Rizeigat militia got wind of it, and now the police told him they were taking him to jail in Nyala on charges of trying to buy slaves.

The bastards have taken all my notebooks and my film, he said. He drew a cigarette out of my pack and lit it. Do you mind if I take a few? I've given all of mine to these blokes.

I told him he could have the whole pack.

Quickly he tucked it inside his shirt.

I was still trying to take in what he had said. You're working for the Anti-Slavery Society? As in the abolitionist group that Gordon was always writing to? I asked. With his pluck and audacity, he seemed almost like an apparition from Gordon's day. I had seen the jail in Nyala. It had a single window covered with iron bars. I didn't think I would be so cheerful if I were headed there. But what about this pawning business? I asked him. The people I'd interviewed at Abu Jiira had said they were only renting their children to the Baggara.

Yes, that's why it's so maddening that I got caught, because I made it very clear that I was going to be taking the boy abroad, and the merchant was still quite happy to sell him to me. I told him I needed the boy to clean my house in England!

He laughed out loud, apparently at the ludicrousness of the idea that he needed a slave to clean his house. Then he lowered his voice. "Safaha is a funnel," he said softly. "South of here the Rizeigat are burning villages, stealing, murdering. This is where the militia divides up the loot— the cattle and the slaves. All those villages you passed on the way from Ed Da'ein are filled with slaves."

The driver of the army truck started the engine. The soldier who had been talking to the policemen shouted an order in Arabic.

Time to go, the antislavery investigator said. He was already climbing onto the back of the army truck with the soldiers.

Where is the market? I called out.

He gestured with his thumb in the direction of the alley in which I had seen the soldiers marching the Dinka girls earlier in the day.

I SCRIBBLED DOWN the antislavery investigator's words in the safety of the doctors' hut. The police hadn't said anything, but they'd kept my passport. I had to be careful not to be seen taking notes. I didn't mind. I thought every moment would remain engraved forever in my mind. And yet after all these years, what comes back most powerfully is the sense of being hurtled from one incomprehensible situation to the next, the sensation of being in a dream from which it is impossible to wake. At the feeding center that night, Henkaert showed me how to boil the water and mix it with powder to make the hot milk and how to give the children the UN remedy for the dehydration brought on by diarrhea. When the formula was made, we poured it into metal buckets. Every few hours we took buckets and a kerosene lantern and walked along the rows of women and children huddled under the lean-to, ladling out milk into calabashes and cups. I remember the women whispering to me from the shadows, holding up their cups, "Sister, sister, please." They looked even more skeletal in the moonlight, like living corpses. And of course some of the shapes did not whisper. In the morning, these shapes were found to be dead bodies.

After a feeding, the doctors and I would fling ourselves onto the blankets back in the hut. Hendricke would produce a bottle of *aragi*. He had worked for MSF in Ethiopia, and he had seen the camp at Korem, of which the BBC correspondent Michael Buerk had intoned, "*This place, say workers here, is the closest thing to hell on earth.*" "This place is worse than anything I saw in Ethiopia," Hendricke whispered. "Higher death rates—"

How many have died? I interrupted.

Henkaert sat up, irritated. "How could we know?" he said. "We've told you, we're not allowed to leave the feeding center."

"Here in the feeding center, the death rate is higher than we recorded in Ethiopia," Hendricke went on. "We can only imagine how many have died out there in the camp. Nobody knows, not even the police. There are so many people coming and going, not even the police know who is here." (Later an American historian who tried to estimate just how many people died in southern Sudan in 1988 concluded that one in ten people at Safaha that spring died.)

Hendricke and Henkaert knew how to perform brain surgery, but here in Safaha they were reduced to feeding children out of buckets. Anyone could have done it, but no one else was doing it. MSF had tried to hire Sudanese workers in Nyala, but they couldn't find anyone who would go to Safaha. Evidently the army expected the SPLA to attack Safaha at any time. The doctors speculated that the army commander might have invited the aid groups to Safaha to avert such an attack, but they really had no idea why they had been allowed to come. If the SPLA attacked, the Rizeigat were likely to slaughter the Dinka refugees farther north in retaliation. Oxfam had signed a contract with the army to truck all refugees to safer locations outside Nyala, but the agency had not been able to purchase the vehicles and the fuel they needed. The Arab merchants who controlled such things were making more money here than they could get from Oxfam for their trucks. In a few weeks, the rains would come and the savannah would melt into a sea of mud. If Oxfam didn't get some trucks soon, the refugees would have to leave on foot, at the mercy of the Rizeigat militia. The sticklike children whom the doctors had been feeding would surely die on such a march.

That was why many parents refused to accompany their children to the feeding center, the doctors explained. The parents could not afford the time it would take. Instead of sitting around at the feeding center, the parent could be working—weaving a mat, for example—and saving a few more piastres toward the eventual purchase of a ticket out of here on one of the Rizeigat lorries.

"We want to feed the children first because they are the weakest and the most innocent," said Hendricke. "But this goes against the African way, which is to feed the adults, the strongest, first, since they are the most likely to live. Theirs is an ethos of scarcity, ours is an ethos of luxury. And yet here especially one clings to the idea of preserving innocence, since the strongest are inevitably the worst—how can they not be, in such conditions?"

It was dark. I took out my sleeping bag and shook it. A scorpion fell out. Henkaert killed the creature and held it up to the light. It was poisonous, he said, and for some reason it struck me and Hendricke as very funny. If it had stung you, we would have no antidote. We laughed and laughed. For a while, our laughter drowned out the sound of the thousands of people coughing and retching outside the hut, a heaving cacophony so loud and deep it seemed to be coming from inside the earth.

"Opportunistic infections," Hendricke said, when he saw that I had stopped laughing and was listening to the mournful racket. "Pneumonia, bronchitis, diarrhea—this is what kills most of them after they are weakened by hunger."

From the bowels of the camp came deep-throated bellows and drunken roars.

Fucking—the militia are fucking the Dinka girls, Hendricke groaned. Henkaert pulled a blanket over his head. I wondered who could think of sex in a place like this? But of course the place throbbed with sex—from the Rizeigat swaggering through the rows of bare-breasted Dinka women to the tension between me and these Belgian doctors. Perhaps it was the naked sense of having food when others didn't. Or maybe it was the terrible fear. It's a funny thing about these camps, Hendricke said. The less food there is, the more bodies you find in the morning—the more fucking goes on. All three of us lay in the hut listening to the shouts and grunts coming from the direction of the market. Finally Henkaert stood up and broke the mood. It's time for another feeding, he said.

THE NEXT MORNING Henkaert said, "If you want to know how many people have died, why don't you look at the graves in the camp? They cover them with brambles." As I walked around the camp that day, I counted many dozens of bramble-covered mounds. Gaudensio arranged for me to interview four Dinka elders in the Oxfam hut. The elders carried long walking sticks, and they wore the Oxfam sweaters on their heads. "The *jallaba* want our land and our cows—that is why they are killing us," they said. The elders said many people had already starved to death or been killed in their villages before they set off on the trek to Safaha. As they struggled toward the camp, they said, wild animals had killed and eaten the children and old people too weak to keep walking. That morning at the feeding center I had seen a boy of about nine whom Hendricke said had survived a hyena attack. The hyena had ripped off the right half of his face, including his nose and his eye. He was walking around the feeding center, naked except for a scarf wrapped around his head to cover his wound.

At first glance, the camp had looked like chaos. But after a day or so there, I realized there was an order to it, an order all the more rigid for being panic-stricken. From the first hard light of morning until the sun went down, every refugee who could sit up was working. The strongest women kept walking out to cut the tall yellow thatching grass surrounding the encampment, carrying it back in great bundles on their heads. Other women sat in the dirt or under flimsy grass shelters weaving the grass into long rectangular mats. They sold the mats to the Rizeigat merchants, who could resell them in the north. The northerners used the mats to make their rectangular huts. It took one woman one day to weave a mat. She was paid one Sudanese pound, about ten cents, for it. After a woman had made and sold fifty mats, she could give the merchant who bought them the fifty Sudanese pounds he had paid her. Then the merchant would let her ride out of Safaha. Her children could ride with her for free—if she didn't have too many. All day long the merchants collected mats, stacking them one by one on the trucks. Late in the afternoon they began to pack the trucks with people, too. Fifty or sixty refugees rode out at a time on top of a stack of mats they had woven.

For those who weren't strong enough to cut grass or weave mats, there was one other way out: to sell their children. Nubile girls commanded the highest prices. Small children came next. The doctors said the price of a healthy boy of eight or nine, who could care for goats or cows, had been as high as three hundred pounds back in February. Now the price had sunk to fifty pounds, exactly the price of a ticket to Ed Da'ein. The police recorded the transactions in a big book on their card table under the tree, allegedly so that the parents could ransom the children back at double the original price. The illiterate Dinka parents signaled their assent by making a thumbprint in the book. I wondered how they would ever find their children again, since they couldn't read and write and would soon be leaving Safaha. Gaudensio snorted when I asked him what good the police record would do. "The police just want to make sure they get their cut from the Rizeigat," he said.

I had stayed away from the shanties where the British antislavery investigator had told me the actual deal making took place. As the appointed time arrived for the souk trucks to leave, I noticed a number of gaunt Dinka parents leading children in that direction. One of the women sidled up to me. Earlier I had smiled at her daughter, a naked toddler who looked healthier than most of the children in this grim place. She plucked at my sleeve, saying something in a pleading voice.

"She wants to know if you would like to buy this girl," Gaudensio said.

Some soldiers were standing not far away in a trench. I was afraid they might charge me with trying to buy a slave if I asked the girl's price, but I wanted to know more about how this system worked. "Ask her what such a young child could do," I told him.

Gaudensio spoke to the woman in Dinka. The mother got down in the dirt and put her hands around my ankles, wailing something in Dinka. What was she saying? The soldiers were definitely watching us now. My heart was pounding with fear and shame. I fumbled in my backpack for some money to give her. "*La, la, la,*" I kept saying. "No, no."

"She says the child will get bigger," Gaudensio said. His expression was inscrutable behind his dark glasses.

"Tell her we can't buy the girl!"

I gave her a hundred pounds. She let go when I thrust the bills into her hand, crying out her thanks, her face smeared with dirt and tears. I hurried into the Land Rover before the other parents could reach me. As I sat in the truck, I tried to think of something I could do. I had only about a hundred Sudanese pounds left, but I had traveler's checks in U.S. dollars. Would the Rizeigat merchants take traveler's checks? I wondered wildly. I could buy a ride out for at least a few hundred people. But that would only get them to Ed Da'ein—hardly a safe harbor. And the merchants would raise the price for the thousands left behind. No, it wouldn't do any good. The Dinka pressed their faces against the glass of the window, but at least I couldn't hear their cries. Now I understood why Gaudensio always drove the truck rather than walking the short distance from the hut to the food distribution.

.   .   .

ON THE THIRD NIGHT, Atot's mother died. All that night I fed Atot myself. Each time he seemed to drink a little more from my cup. I will stay here and keep giving him milk until he is well, I thought. But before the sun was up, the doctors and I heard the roar and rumble of an army truck. It came to a stop in front of the hut. We heard footsteps, saw a light. "I have come for the woman," a soft male voice said.

It was the camp commander, Major Hussein Hamid. He was going to Nyala. He said I had to go with him.

I stammered something about getting my things. I was thinking about Atot. If I asked to take him with me, I would almost certainly be accused of trying to steal a child. Besides, his sister was somewhere in the camp. I could not take him away from his family. I remembered the words of the Dutchwoman in Khartoum, *I'm going to do one clear thing.* Was it possible to see one clear thing in this country? I wondered.

You will keep feeding Atot, won't you? I asked Henkaert.

"Of course," he said. His face was gray with exhaustion.

I climbed into the cab of the army truck beside Major Hussein Hamid.

IT WAS A FOURTEEN-HOUR drive back to Nyala. Somewhere along the way, a pain started stabbing behind my eyes, then in my intestines. I slumped down in my seat. I felt as if a volcano were erupting in my gut. "Please stop," I croaked. When the truck rumbled to a halt, I sprang out of the cab. For a moment I looked back. A dozen or so Sudanese soldiers armed with AK-47s stood up in the back, regarding me curiously. The faces of the major and his driver swam through the cab window. They looked worried. My teeth were chattering. How strange to be standing under the blazing sun freezing to death. There wasn't a stalk to hide behind. I pulled down my jeans, squatted, and let my bowels explode in the dirt.

Somehow I got back into the truck. There was a silence. Then the major asked me a question.

Is everyone in America rich?

No, not everyone, I answered, struggling to squint against the sunlight jabbing at me through the window. Some Americans are rich and some are poor.

Does everyone have a toilet inside their house? he wanted to know.

Yes, I said. Almost everyone.

Then why do you say they are not rich? he said. He laughed and laughed, slapping his knee. It took me a few minutes to get the joke, but then I laughed, too. It did seem absurdly luxurious, a world in which everyone had a flush toilet. There was only one place like it in Nyala: the Western Savannah Development Corporation. I had criticized Western Savannah when I was staying there, but now I swore to myself that if only I could get back there, I'd never say anything bad about it again.

The major told me the police at Safaha wanted him to take me to jail. The stamp in my passport wasn't the right kind. The police had radioed Nyala and been told that I knew I wasn't supposed to go there. But when we were almost to Nyala, the major seemed to change his mind. He asked me where I wanted to go.

The Western Savannah Development Corporation, I whispered.

Of course, said the major. His teeth glinted white against his face. The *khawaja* compound.

He gave directions to the driver. Once again the miraculous English suburb materialized in the desert. I pointed out the engineer's house. His servant, Abdul, ran out, gaping at the army truck. Major Hussein ordered him to take my backpack inside. As we said our good-byes, the major made me promise to come visit him in town when I felt better, to meet his wife and children. Tears of gratitude came to my eyes. I felt I owed him my life. *Al-hamdillallah*, I mumbled. *Inshallah.*

The major's truck drove off. I backed into the house, staggered into the bathroom, lay down on the cool white tiles next to the engineer's toilet, and passed out. The fever lasted four days. A Belgian doctor who came and gave me an injection said it was typhoid. At the end of the week, I managed to get out of bed. I got on a flight to Khartoum, then another flight to Kenya. Soon I was in Nairobi, in a hotel room, trying to think what to write. My head still ached. I scribbled out a few words on the hotel stationery: "There are places so sad the mind goes queasy trying to understand." It was a start.

THE ARTICLES I wrote about Safaha were some of the first to appear in the West about what became known in Sudan as the famine of 1988. Not many people outside Sudan remember that famine now. It never really pierced public consciousness in the West. Partly that was because for a long time the United States and its allies did not care to make an issue out of a famine in a fragile but friendly African democracy. But as the months passed, aid workers and reporters like Carol Berger, and Jane Perlez of *The New York Times,* sent back dozens of reports showing that tens of thousands of southerners seeking refuge in the north were starving in places like Abyei, El Meiram, El Muglad, and Babanousa. When it was over, the UN estimated that 250,000 southern Sudanese had died. A later report called "Quantifying Genocide" by J. Millard Burr for the U.S. Committee for Refugees put the number closer to 500,000. Like so much else in Sudan, the truth about how many died in the famine will never be known.

Chapter Eleven

EMMA WAS ONE of the few Westerners who did take notice of the famine. In 1988 she was a graduate student at London's School of Oriental and African Studies and thus was in the heart of what her friend Alex de Waal, the aid critic, calls "the Humanitarian International" of Western aid workers, human rights advocates, diplomats, journalists, and missionaries who make foreign disasters their business. By now she had come to know a few southern Sudanese through her job at the Sudan Cultural Center. She had seen how contemptuously some of the Arabic-speaking diplomats at the center treated the southerners, sometimes calling them *abid,* or "slave," behind their backs. Her friends Sally and Willy were now living in Nairobi. Through them she heard that Alastair had gotten involved in a covert effort to transport food from Kenya into parts of southern Sudan long closed to foreigners. She heard from southerners she met about the "Trail of Bones," so called because of the skeletons that littered the hundreds of miles of paths that the starving southerners took to the refugee camps in Ethiopia. The famine brought out the campaigner in Emma.

She began agitating for the British government to take a stand against Prime Minister Sadiq al-Mahdi's support for the government-allied militias such as the Rizeigat that were raiding the south. Liz Hodgkin was working at Amnesty International, where she was privy to the reports of southerners being detained and tortured in the squatter camps around Khartoum. She and Emma joined a fledgling group called the Sudan Committee for Peace and Reconciliation. Some of the British members of the committee had gone out to Sudan as volunteer teachers in the

1970s and 1980s. Like Emma, they had been caught by the country's spell. They made an uncertain living working for Africa-related groups and newsletters. They took long journeys by subway to attend meetings on how to draw public attention to starvation in southern Sudan. They wrote letters to members of Parliament and newspapers, trying to drum up support for peace.

Michael Wolfers, a close friend of the Hodgkins, was on the committee. Wolfers is one of those people whose tombstone ought to read, I'D RATHER BE IN AFRICA. A former Africa correspondent for *The Times* of London, he had also put in some time working for Mozambique's socialist government. "Africa is my life," he often says in all seriousness. Emma was a novice compared to old Sudan hands like Wolfers, and yet she had a charisma that made them welcome her. "I don't remember her as a political analyst," Wolfers said. "I can't remember her having any particularly strong opinions. My strongest memory of her is how beautiful she was."

Gillian Lusk, the editor of *Africa Confidential,* was another member. Gill was a friend of Carol Berger's who had spent years in Sudan, first as a teacher and later as a journalist. She now lived alone in Greenwich, a few blocks from the church, as she often told visitors from Sudan, where General Gordon had been christened. Gill was impressed by Emma's sincerity and commitment to Sudan: "She seemed like a person who was deeply offended by oppression." Emma's infatuation with Sudan reminded Gill of her younger self. Gill's office wasn't far from the Sudan Cultural Center. She and Emma sometimes got together to have drinks and to write letters to Sadiq al-Mahdi and John Garang, to the leaders of Sudan's political parties, and to the country's small human rights groups. They produced a pamphlet about the prospects for peace in Sudan. Gill remembers that Emma was always willing to take up a collection or do some typing. "She was not a bullshitter. If she said she was going to do something, she did it." The Sudanese diplomats at the cultural center, of course, bitterly resented what they considered meddling Western groups such as the Peace and Reconciliation Committee. Gill and Liz Hodgkin say that Emma eventually started to feel so uncomfortable working there that she quit her job.

Some members of the peace group believed that the United States and Europe had the leverage to push the Sudanese government into making peace with the south, if only they would use it. After all, Western donors were still paying for roughly half of the Sudanese government's recurrent expenditures. With the Soviet Union disintegrating, the government seemingly had nowhere else to turn for support than the West. But President Ronald Reagan's administration remained silent about the starvation in Sudan throughout most of 1988. The election of George Bush at the end of that year seemed to signal a change in policy. Bush had surprising connections with Sudan. In the 1970s, he had helped U.S. oil companies make contact with Nimeiri's government. As vice president, he had visited Sudan to examine the U.S. relief effort during the famine of 1985. Already in the fall of 1988, Julia Taft, the head of the U.S. Office for Foreign Disaster Assistance, had shocked Secretary of State George Shultz into taking a harder line against the al-Mahdi government by showing him footage taken by the NBC television network of skeletal southern Sudanese children. The Sudanese government had been resisting the aid agencies' efforts to deliver food to the south. Less than a week after Bush was inaugurated, Washington announced that it would begin delivering food to civilians in the south whether the government liked it or not.

The response from Sudan was immediate. Forced to choose between a UN relief operation that would remain at least partly under government control and direct U.S. aid to the rebel areas, Sadiq's government entered negotiations with the United Nations Children's Fund (UNICEF) to start a relief program that, for the first time in UN history, would deliver food and supplies to both sides of a civil war. (Paralyzed by the cold war, the United Nations seldom got involved in civil wars until the late 1980s. Its agencies took the position that any recognition of rebel groups was a violation of a member state's sovereignty.) The relief effort was to be called Operation Lifeline Sudan (OLS). Though it came too late to save many lives, Operation Lifeline represented a huge victory for the "Humanitarian International" who had turned Sudan's famine into a cause.

The antifamine coalition knew that Sudan needed more than relief to end starvation. In 1988 one of Sudan's traditional Islamic parties, the Democratic Union Party (DUP), had signed a peace agreement with the SPLA. In the agreement, the parties agreed to freeze Islamic law until the country could hold a constitutional conference on the role of the religion in a unified Sudan. Hassan al-Turabi's NIF took a strong position against the agreement, arguing that the Muslim north could not compromise on the issue of *sharia*. Sadiq had tried to sabotage the agreement, placating the NIF and dithering on talks with the SPLA. Then, a month after President Bush took his new hard line with the government, the Sudanese army delivered the prime minister an ultimatum: Either make progress toward peace and begin disbanding the militias within one week, or there will be a coup. Sadiq capitulated. His Umma Party formed a coalition government with the DUP. Despite NIF protests, the Sudanese parliament voted to freeze Islamic law. Emma and her friends were overjoyed. Peace seemed to be at hand.

She had been saving money for months to visit Sally and Willy. Willy was working as an aid consultant in Kenya, while Sally was designing jewelry. In March 1989 Emma flew to Nairobi. With its cool, wet highlands, Kenya had always been the polar opposite of austere desert Sudan. The British had forbidden foreigners to buy land in Sudan during the colonial period. In Kenya they gave away thousands of acres to white settlers. The White Highlands near Nairobi became especially popular with aristocrats and wayward millionaires drawn to its blue-green scenery and spectacular wildlife. At the turn of the century, these fugitives from Europe sought to establish a sort of feudal lifestyle in Kenya. Their "Happy Valley" outside Nairobi became as famous for its dissipated pleasures as for its superb villas. The Danish author Karen Blixen added to the mystique when she published her ode to the white aristocratic ideal, *Out of Africa,* in 1937. Kenya had been independent since 1963, but Nairobi was still the white capital of East Africa when Emma arrived in 1989. In a region plagued by war, Kenya was at peace. It had telephones that worked, tarmac roads, and a thriving tourism industry. The Western press corps used Nairobi as its base, as did the swelling disaster relief industry.

Sally was thrilled to have her best friend in Nairobi. She took Emma everywhere and introduced her to everyone. With its low, tin-roofed bungalows and its gaudy Asian mosque, Nairobi's center retained a colonial flavor, but cheap cinder-block high-rises were overtaking the older buildings. Beyond the city center, most of the city's residents lived in wooden shantytowns spread across the hillsides like fungus. White Kenyans seldom ventured there. Instead their world centered on Nairobi's shopping district and its fragrant white suburbs such as Langata and Karen, named for the author of *Out of Africa.* Emma and Sally would dress up and meet for drinks at the colonial-era Norfolk Hotel, then go dancing at the Florida 2000 disco around the corner. Or they would head for dinner under the flame trees in Langata, where Willy and Sally lived.

Willy and Sally introduced Emma to a circle of naturalists, aid workers, artists, and journalists who included some of white Africa's most dashing young people. Willy's parents still lived in Kenya, in a rambling old house near Mombassa. Willy was an outdoorsman who had been on trek with Masai warriors; he knew the habits of the eland and how to roast a goat over an open fire. His and Sally's friends included the artist David Marrian and his wife, Lady Emma Marrian; the Italian writer and documentary filmmaker Francesca Marciano; the (in Sally's words, "drop-dead handsome") artist Tonio Trzebinksi, whose mother, Erroll Trzebinski, had published a book about the notorious 1941 "White Mischief" murder of Lord Erroll that did much to spread the legend of Happy Valley; and the younger Douglas-Hamiltons, whose father, Iain Douglas-Hamilton, had spearheaded the movement to save the Kenyan elephant and whose Italian mother, Oria, had been raised in an art deco palazzo beside Lake Naivasha.

If the expatriates of the 1980s did not entertain in quite the baronial style of their Happy Valley predecessors, they still lived with a kind of magnificence that would have been quite impossible in London, Paris, or Washington. But for the scent of their charcoal fires, Nairobi's slums could seem as remote from the villas of Langata or Karen as from Europe or North America. The interminable African waits—for permissions, for visas, for repairs, for equipment—allowed for a leisurely pace of socializing almost forgotten in the West. At Nairobi house parties, Emma and her hosts played badminton on thick carpets of kikuyu grass or went for a dip in backyard swimming pools overhung with bougainvillea, amused by the antics of monkeys and warthogs. Servants delivered them cool drinks on patios overlooking the Ngong Hills. At dinner, they would take turns sniffing cocaine in the bathroom and gossip about who was sleeping with whom. On weekends they competed to organize the most adventurous safaris. Mombassa and its beaches were only a train ride away, and many expats kept a boat or a summer house there.

Some of them had been born in Kenya. Others had come seeking excitement and escape. It was a point of pride for them to take risks, to scorn the Western cult of safety. They stalked big game. They relished sports like hang gliding and parachute jumping. They would party all night, then take someone's small airplane to the top of a mountain to watch elephants swimming in a lake. They were always looking for the ultimate wave, the most extreme sensation, and it was part of their avowed code never to settle for mediocrity in anything. Trzebinksi, a painter who was conducting a passionate affair with Sally, liked to repeat a line of the artist Francis Bacon's, which became the group's motto: "It is all so meaningless that we might as well be extraordinary."

It was an intoxicating lifestyle, and when Maggie McCune came out to visit a few years later, she immediately and enthusiastically recognized it as "colonial." But the younger generation of whites had largely given up the colonial dream of actually investing and creating wealth in Kenya. They had seen what had happened to white farms and businesses after independence. Instead they catered directly to Western fantasies of Africa. Some led safaris for rich tourists. Others took pictures, wrote books, or made films celebrating the people and animals of the continent. Some went to work for the aid business. Others got involved with wildlife preservation. Or, if they were journalists, they wrote about articles about Western people doing all these things.

The dwindling band of Westerners was nonetheless the object of tremendous African resentment. "Security" was a constant preoccupation. The whites made more money "helping" Africa than all but a very few Africans. They used it to rent secluded villas surrounded with razor wire, iron gates, electric fences, and armed guards, but that didn't ease their fears. For all they knew, their Kenyan cooks and gardeners and guards were in league with the police and the gangs rumored to be robbing white compounds. Their bedroom doors were covered with metal screens so that intruders could not kill them with panga knives in their beds. Yet everyone knew of someone who had been murdered by thieves. The knowledge that the price of being so extraordinary might be death added to the rush of it all.

Alastair and Patta had moved from Khartoum to Nairobi. They were invited to all the same parties, but they were too busy with Operation Lifeline Sudan to socialize as much as some of the group. In March 1989 Sadiq finally gave the United Nations permission to fly food into SPLA-held areas. He also signed an agreement to freeze Islamic law. Getting the reclusive SPLA leader John Garang to agree to let the UN distribute food to the starving people in his territory had been almost as hard as getting Sadiq to agree to it. On the face of it, Garang had everything to gain from this recognition by the UN. But, like Sadiq, he had to consider every move in the context of a regional chessboard.

Garang's protector, Ethiopia's Colonel Mengistu, opposed Operation

Lifeline. Mengistu was fighting for his life. His own patron, the Soviet Union, was crumbling before his eyes. In northern Ethiopia, Tigrayan rebels aligned with the separatist Eritreans had seized the entire northern province of Tigre. Mengistu was bombing relief convoys going into Tigre from Sudan. He feared that Operation Lifeline would set a precedent that would open the door for the UN to assist other rebels opposing governments that were unpopular in the West, such as his own. At one point, Mengistu told Garang that he would have to choose between military support from Ethiopia and relief from the United Nations.

But after a string of military victories, Garang was riding high. He knew that the Ethiopian dictator needed the SPLA almost as much as the SPLA needed him. In southern Ethiopia, the Sudanese rebels almost functioned as Mengistu's personal army of occupation, keeping an eye on potentially rebellious Ethiopian peoples such as the Oromo. Meanwhile in Sudan, the SPLA had started winning not just countryside but garrison towns such as Kapoeta, Torit, Bor, and Nasir. Ignoring Mengistu's warnings, Garang sent his "foreign minister," a former engineering professor named Lam Akol, to conduct the final negotiations with the UN leading up to Operation Lifeline. On April 1, 1989, almost a year after I left Safaha on Major Hussein's truck, the first UN plane flew out of Loki into rebel-held southern Sudan. A few weeks later Garang announced a unilateral cease-fire with the Sudan government.

Emma was a visitor to the lushly landscaped UN campus outside Nairobi during those exciting first days of Operation Lifeline. She met Vincent O'Reilly, the humorous, black-haired Irishman who was to be in charge of OLS operations in the south. (Operation Lifeline pledged to send equal amounts of relief to northern and southern Sudan.) She heard from Alastair and Patta about the semisecret mission they had made for MSF-Holland to investigate conditions at the height of the famine in Ler, a Nuer village behind SPLA lines. "There was a look of desolation and shock on people's faces—as if years of war and suffering had left them numb with the horror of it," Patta later wrote.

These early encounters with the SPLA—or the SPLM (Sudan People's Liberation Movement), as the rebels liked to be called—seemed to some Western aid workers like entering the cave of nocturnal creatures unaccustomed to light. In their camps inside Ethiopia, the rebels had been able to do pretty much what they liked with the aid they received. Although UNHCR tried to keep tabs on whom it was feeding, its officials were not allowed in the camps after dark. Relief commodities officially destined for the approximately 200,000 Sudanese camp dwellers at Itang also fed the military training centers and headquarters that the SPLA maintained in the nearby camps of Bonga and Bilpam. Peter Adwok Nyaba, a former rebel officer who has written a book about his years with the SPLA, says that high-ranking officers seized most of the food and other supplies. They then made the civilian refugees work for the rebel movement as porters and servants in return for it.

Like the Eritrean and Tigrayan rebels in Sudan, the SPLA had its own supposedly civilian relief organization, the Sudan Relief and Rehabilitation Association (SRRA). The group was notoriously thieving and incompetent. Even before Operation Lifeline began, Band Aid, Oxfam, and Save the Children had tried to teach the SRRA about Western methods of accounting and ideas about restricting relief to noncombatants. The experiment was a disaster, but it showed aid officials how far Garang and his cronies would go to protect their absolute control over any money that came the rebels' way. When Band Aid and the others gave the SRRA about $60,000 to maintain its tiny office and telephones in Nairobi, the money disappeared into an Addis Ababa bank account. The SRRA director was an Equatorian lawyer named Richard Mulla. The aid groups badgered Mulla to confront John Garang and his top henchmen with evidence of malfeasance. Mulla was reluctant. The SPLA was at that moment in the midst of a brutal conquest of Equatoria, and relations between Mulla's people and the Dinka were bad. But eventually he made the complaint the foreigners asked him to make.

It was a few weeks before Mulla and the agencies heard from Addis. Then orders came that Dr. Justin Yaac, a balding, pear-shaped Dinka gynecologist close to Garang, would be coming from Ethiopia to replace Mulla. Mulla held an angry meeting with Dr. Justin at a hotel favored by the SPLA. After it was over and as Mulla was leaving, a truck came out of nowhere and forced his car off the road. The Equatorian suffered serious head injuries in the accident. He told Western aid workers who came to see him that he suspected the SPLA had set up the accident. But when the aid officials complained to the Kenyan police, the police arrested Mulla for making false accusations. The Westerners managed to get him out of the Kenyan jail. By that time, he was ready to resign. Under Western pressure, Garang sent Lam Akol to Nairobi to smooth things over. Mulla was made the rebels' spokesman in London, while Dr. Justin went back to Ethiopia.

Such intrigues did not put off Emma; indeed, they fascinated her. She begged Alastair and Patta to help her find a job with Operation Lifeline. She returned to London after a few weeks but immediately began making plans to return to Kenya for good. She told her teachers at the School of Oriental and African Studies that she wanted to do field work there for a master's thesis on refugees. One of Emma's projects for the Sudan Committee for Peace and Reconciliation had been to raise money to start a newsletter dedicated to collecting information about Sudan. On June 10 SPLA representatives met with the Sudanese government in Addis Ababa to discuss peace. The war looked so near to an end that some in the peace group wanted to cancel plans for *Sudan Update*, as it was to be called. Emma talked them into going ahead.

The first edition came out in June 1989; *Sudan Update* has been in continuous publication ever since. The peace that seemed so tantalizingly close was snatched away. On June 30, 1989, one day before the Sudanese National Assembly was due to suspend Islamic law and four days before Sadiq was due to meet face-to-face with Garang, a group of midlevel army officers overthrew Sudan's parliamentary government in a bloodless coup. The coup leaders proclaimed a "Revolution of National Salvation." They were soon revealed to be protégés of Hassan al-Turabi and the National Islamic Front. Sudan's experiment with democracy was over. The war that Turabi had always considered a holy jihad was on again.

Emma returned to Nairobi at the end of August. She was twenty-five. She never again lived in England.

Chapter Twelve

THE JOB THAT the Scott-Villierses found for Emma was the brainchild of a Canadian lawyer whom Alastair and Patta knew from Khartoum. Peter Dalglish was a Stanford University graduate who had given up a promising legal career after visiting an Ethiopian famine camp in 1984. (After seeing the camp, he told me, he decided "the world could do without one more corporate lawyer." But when he informed the partners at his Halifax law firm that he was leaving for Africa, one of them suggested he see a psychiatrist.) Dalglish had gone to work for UNICEF in Sudan. In 1986 he got to know some of the street children who begged outside the Acropole Hotel in Khartoum. Many of them came from the south. Some of them had seen their own parents killed. They lived in boxes and ate out of garbage dumpsters. The police considered them vermin and criminals. Dalglish later wrote that people spit at them and called them "monkeys" and "slaves." The violence and poverty of their lives outraged the young lawyer. To help them, he started his own charity, Street Kids International (SKI). Alastair was then representing Band Aid in Khartoum. George Patagoulatos at the Acropole introduced him to Dalglish. Alastair recommended that Band Aid fund SKI's first proposal, a technical training school for street children. A month later Bob Geldof approved a $50,000 grant for Dalglish to start the school.

After Dalglish left Khartoum, he convinced an American pilot he knew in 1988 to fly him into Ler, the same Nuer town Alastair and Patta had visited a few months earlier for MSF-Holland. Dalglish spent six days living with six Nuer children on an abandoned barge alongside a family of hippos in the White Nile. On the second day, about eight hundred naked boys appeared, walking in long and silent columns along the river's edge. "Behind is death," one of the boys told Dalglish. The boys said Baggara militiamen had torched their villages in Bahr el-Ghazal. They had walked hundreds of miles to reach Ler and had more than one hundred to go before reaching their destination, the refugee camps across the Ethiopian border. Along the way, some boys had been blown apart by land mines or eaten by crocodiles. Some had simply given up hope and refused to walk any farther. "Watching that day as the exhausted boys stumbled into the river, made pathetic attempts to pull younger brothers and best friends out of the formidable current, then slipped below the surface, I experienced a miserable epiphany," Dalglish wrote years later. "Bearing witness to the atrocities visited upon 11-year-old children by the government of Sudan and the rebels was now my responsibility."

Schools had been closed in the south for up to six years. The boys told Dalglish they were going to the refugee camps to get an education. But Dalglish knew the SPLA was more likely to induct them into the rebel army. His time in Khartoum had convinced him there was no future for southern children in the Arab north. He decided that SKI should try to help such children go to school at home in the south. In Nairobi, Dalglish worked together with Patta to develop a proposal for SKI to rehabilitate and equip southern primary schools under the aegis of Operation Lifeline. The aim was political as well as practical: Dalglish hoped the schools would become islands of stability that would protect children from the forces conspiring to suck them into the war. When UNICEF agreed to fund the program, Patta suggested that Dalglish hire Emma for the job.

Emma accepted eagerly. "Without education, these children have no future," she often said. In September she wrote her tutor to say she would be postponing work on her master's degree for at least a year. Dalglish said she ended up making about a thousand dollars a month. UNICEF gave her a Toyota Land Cruiser, an aging mimeograph machine, and a typewriter and told her to open a SKI office about fifty miles north of the border in the rebel-held town of Kapoeta. She made her first trip into the south in November 1989. From the thick plastic windows of the UN plane, she could see herds of giraffes and gazelles running across open grassland. She was elated and more than a little frightened. Later she wrote that she felt as if she were "on the cusp of the earth."

The SPLA had captured Kapoeta some eighteen months before Emma's arrival. The rebels had put up a sign in English and Arabic on the road entering the town that read "Welcome to Kapoeta Liberated Town." Another SPLA sign said "United We Stand, Divided We Fall." But the local Toposa people did not consider the SPLA's presence in Kapoeta a liberation, and they were anything but united in support for the rebels. The Toposa and their land of thorn scrub had been one of the last parts of the south to come under British administration. Like the Dinka and the Nuer, the Toposa were slim-hipped, long-legged cattle-herders who used cow dung to dress their hair in extraordinary shapes. The army had given the Toposa machine guns to fight the SPLA; oiled and greased young Toposa men wearing nothing but a brass earring and an AK-47 strapped across the chest had been known to attack relief trucks as well as rebel convoys coming up from Kenya. Just as often the Toposa used the guns to rustle cattle across the border in Kenya. When I was in Kenya in 1988, I had tried and failed to go to Kapoeta with one of the few relief groups then operating across the border. But the Kenyans closed the border with Sudan after the Toposa raided Lokichoggio, killing 110 people. "The Toposa have been disturbing people," a young SPLA man told me laconically when I asked about the attack. "That is their tradition—disturbing people."

For the Toposa and other people who lived around it, Kapoeta was the same *zariba*-like garrison town under the SPLA as it had been under the Sudanese army and, before that, the British. Dinka-led SPLA battalions left Kapoeta to steal grain and cattle from Toposa villages and call it tax-ation, as northern Sudanese and British troops had done before them. The SPLA also was secretly mining gold on Toposa land outside Kapo-eta. Relations were no better between the rebels and the fierce Murle people, who lived northeast of the Toposa, or between the Acholi and Didinga peoples, who straddled the border with Uganda to the south-west. The town itself was nothing more than the shells of a few colonial buildings and an abandoned Arab market. A Dutch journalist who was one of the first foreigners to visit Kapoeta after the town fell to the SPLA showed me pictures of a Dinka doctor operating with an old-fashioned straight razor on patients in the former hospital building. The doctor had begged the journalist to bring him on his next visit a handsaw so that he could perform more advanced amputations. Barefoot SPLA soldiers guarded the rubble of the town behind rocket launchers and machine-gun emplacements.

Emma moved into a bullet-scarred concrete house with a corrugated iron roof that the UN had claimed for *khawajas* working in Kapoeta. It was the dry season. The temperature hovered around 120 degrees. A former Burmese government official named Mynt Maung was the UN's resident program officer in Kapoeta. One former colleague said that Maung followed Emma around Kapoeta "like a puppy." Southern Sudan had no currency, but in Kapoeta a small market was beginning to develop where the aid workers could buy food in exchange for salt and soap. Outside the town, the earth was studded with land mines. In 1987 a Thames Television crew coming back from an interview with John Garang had run over a mine on the road from Kapoeta. The crew's director was thrown from the vehicle and died in the arms of a colleague.

The sense of isolation was unearthly. But to Emma it was the starting point for the discovery of another world. Emma's job was to deliver paper, pencils, textbooks, and chalk to help start schools throughout the province of Equatoria. From Kapoeta she sallied forth across the Nilotic plain, bumping over long-disused and overgrown dirt tracks to deliver her supplies. (The south was divided into three provinces: Equatoria, Bahr el-Ghazal, and Upper Nile. There was still too much fighting in Bahr el-Ghazal to consider opening schools there, and Operation Lifeline had not yet received permission from the SPLA to open schools in Upper Nile.) Her Land Cruiser was one of the only working vehicles in all of southern Sudan—an area as big as France and England combined—and it did not always work. The very first week she spent in Sudan, she and Maung got into a car accident driving back to Kapoeta from the Imatong Mountains. Maung was driving. The car overturned, but luckily Emma was unhurt and Maung received only a scratch.

The southerners' demand for education, as Emma learned, was second only to their demand for medicine. The helplessness they felt in the face of the mysterious powers of "paper" played a big role in their sense of being at a loss compared with the north. The north had an old, if not especially deep, tradition of literacy, owing to its contact with Islam and the Mediterranean world. Most northern boys learned at least the Arabic script as part of their religious training. But reading and writing were unknown to the south before the nineteenth century. The Shilluk people had laughed at the early missionaries for their habit of "dirtying little bits of paper." Not until after independence did most southerners begin to see the value of literacy. At that time, only a few thousand of several million southerners had learned to read and write in mission schools. Of these "children of the missionaries," very few had gone further than primary school. The tiny educated elite had not been chosen by their people, but on their shoulders rested the whole burden of bringing southern Sudan into the modern world.

Once the British left, the northern government moved against these "children of the missionaries," regarding the educated as hostile to Islam. The mission schools became government schools. Arabic replaced English as the language of instruction. The educated men of the south whom the Nuer and the Dinka called "the children of the red foreigners" rose up against the north in part because of these measures. But the wars into which they led their people did more damage to southern education than the most diabolical northern government could have done. A century and a half after the world of paper intruded into the papyrus swamps of Sudan, fewer than one in twenty southerners could read, and now the lack was seen as a horrible handicap. Schools, as a UN official later wrote, had assumed an "incantatory, almost ritualistic importance" in the eyes of the people. "In Bor district, children don't ask for food, they ask for pencils," Emma told a reporter.

Emma soon learned that the Land Cruiser would not take her far in a land without roads. If she wanted to find the people, she would have to go into the villages on foot. Towns were alien to the Nilotic peoples, who moved from season to season with their beloved long-horned cattle. From November to March or April, they lived in the grasslands close to the rivers. From April to October, when the rains came and the rivers flooded, turning the grassy plains to marsh, they moved to permanent villages of conical thatched houses on higher ground. The women and older people cultivated *durra,* groundnuts, pumpkins, maize, and okra, while young men tended the cattle in cattle-camps near the edge of the floodplain.

Poetry and song are the main art form of the Nilotes. They especially love to sing about their cows. Nothing about these beasts is too small for the Dinka and the Nuer to celebrate. As Terese Svoboda, an American writer who collected Nuer poems in the 1970s, has written, the color of their cows, their personalities, the quality of their milk, even the size of their testicles can be the subject of songs. Nilotic cattle-herders not only depend on their cows for milk and meat; they also believe that men and cows share a "oneness," and they use cattle sacrifice to atone for human sin and to seal marriages. Such prized possessions are the source of arguments. As the Nuer say, "More people have been killed for the sake of the cow than anything else." A man got his first ox at the time of his initiation. The only true way to enter Nilotic society was to pay cattle to marry a Nilotic woman, thereby becoming attached to a lineage. A father had no rights to a child born to a woman whose family he had not paid cows.

Emma's willingness to get out and walk from village to village won her respect from the southern Sudanese. Most *khawajas* were afraid to be parted from their machines—their cars and their airplanes. As a Dinka woman later recalled, people began to "twitter" about Emma: "This lady is different—that is the way people are talking." When she arrived in a village or cattle-camp with her backpack full of school supplies, old people would spit on her head in greeting. Children whose bodies were smeared in ash to keep off mosquitoes would prance about, trying out their English on her: "Good morning! Good evening! I love you!" Young men, their faces creased with intricate scar designs and their hair dyed orange from cattle urine, would spear river fish for her to eat. Stately mothers would clap their hands for their children to bring her bowls of warm cow's milk to drink. They called Emma "the Tall Woman from Small Britain." She was such a novelty that they drew pictures of her in her miniskirt on the walls of their wattle-and-daub *tukuls*.

Emma learned that many villages had already sent their young boys to join the rebels in Ethiopia. The boys' parents hoped they might gain the education in refugee camps that they could not get in the south—the education they saw as a passport to a *khawaja* lifestyle. The peoples of the south had traditions of sending young boys away from home to learn how to be warriors; the idea that the SPLA was also training their boys to use weapons was not as shocking to them as it was to Westerners. Nor was young children going away to school a new idea. During the colonial period, southern boys who went past primary school often had to travel for hundreds of miles to attend boarding schools. But nearly everyone would have preferred to have their boys go to school at home.

Even if southerners accepted the notion that boys past the age of initiation should be ready to fight for their people, they disliked the SPLA policy of putting soldiers of mixed ethnic backgrounds into battalions and stationing them in parts of the country where they had no relatives. The local people resented the "foreigners" from other tribes whom the SPLA sent to rule over them; they wanted "the sons of the area" to protect them. (The SPLA says it wanted to create a southern army that would rise above tribal and ethnic differences. The former SPLA officer Peter Adwok Nyaba says the rebel leaders also intended to prevent their troops from developing bonds with the local people that would allow them to challenge their authority.) And they knew that child soldiers often went hungry under commanders with whom they had no ties of blood. Nyaba later reported that in 1988 some three thousand young boys from the Nuba Mountains training with the rebels at Gambella camp in Ethiopia died of starvation and related diseases after the officer responsible for them sold their food. Hundreds of young recruits also died of neglect at the Dimma refugee camp, according to Nyaba.

The villagers wanted Operation Lifeline to restart schools in the south so they wouldn't have to send their boys to Ethiopia. Emma and UNICEF hoped that establishing schools in local communities would also have the effect of allowing more girls to attend. Few families were willing to send their daughters away to Ethiopia. They knew that unprotected girls were likely to be seized and made into "wives"—without compensation for the family's loss of income. Girls, who brought cattle into the family when they married, were too precious to lose. Their mothers needed them to help collect water, prepare food, weave baskets, and care for smaller children. But parents usually let them attend lessons in their own villages that did not interfere with their domestic duties.

Dalglish had feared Operation Lifeline would have to import teachers from Kenya, but Emma found out there were plenty of literate southern Sudanese willing to teach in return for a monthly allotment of soap and salt. Emma worked together with UNICEF's program coordinator, a German, to create a start-up kit that contained everything a community needed to open a school. One of the biggest obstacles to southern literacy was the lack of books printed in the southern languages. Someone in Nairobi discovered that the Christian missionaries who had been expelled a generation earlier still had the original printing plates they had created for a children's reader in the Dinka language called *Marial and the Cow*. Emma had the books reprinted and gave them to her teachers. She dug up other old books in the Nuer, Bari, and Latuka tongues. She gathered the wooden ammunition crates she found lying around and paid carpenters to turn them into desks and chairs for her schools. She read everything she could get her hands on in Nairobi about village education in rural Africa and ordered more books from England.

With the SRRA, Emma organized teacher-training courses and brought teachers from all over Equatoria to attend them. She supplied the courses with mattresses, kerosene lamps, cooking pots, books, and writing materials. The teachers learned how to use new textbooks and to

write lesson plans. They attended lectures about health and immuniza-
tion given by UN health workers. Each teacher was expected to go back
to his community to recruit and train teachers. Within a year, Operation
Lifeline and the SRRA had about twenty-two thousand pupils attending school in Equatoria. Most of the boys and girls had never done so
before.

The schools were rough. Most consisted of no more than a teacher
and some children sitting under a tree. When I visited one in Nasir in
1990, I winced through an English lesson. The teacher pointed to his ears
and shouted, "Repeat after me! 'These are my eyes.'" Dalglish was
pleased with the reports Emma faxed to Toronto listing the supplies she
had given out. Later he told me that she "knew exactly how many pencils
had been distributed at each school." But a distinguished British educator
with long experience of southern Sudan who visited the schools wrote an
angry report criticizing the program for measuring its success by superfi-
cialities. Barry Sesnan complained that Emma's teachers spent too much
time accounting for pencils and not enough time teaching. "There were
no figures about how much education was going on," Sesnan wrote. "No
figures were given for how many days were actually taught; how many
pupils were in the class; how much was actually learned in the given
period; how efficient the learning was. Yet, of course, that is what education is about!" Critics accused the rebels of inflating the number of children attending schools and the amount of learning going on in them, and
Emma of too credulously accepting their claims.

But ordinary southerners were overjoyed by her work. A woman
named Elizabeth left her village thirty-five miles away to come and work
for the UN in Nasir so her six-year-old son could attend the school
Emma had set up there. After pounding grain, cleaning fish, and boiling
water all day for visitors from the UN, Elizabeth would stay up late at
night, trying to teach herself to read from one of her son's books by the
light of a kerosene lantern. In Kapoeta, the children at Emma's school sat
on rocks in an abandoned building. Lual Agoth, a skinny boy who
thought he was thirteen years old, was typical. Agoth had walked more
than two hundred miles from a village near Aweil in Bahr el-Ghazal to
reach the school. (Aweil district was the place from which the starving
people I had seen in Safaha were escaping.) Before Agoth left his village
to join a group of boys walking south, he told his mother, "I cannot die
here, my mother. I'm going to look for food and an education."

It took Emma no time at all to figure out the political implications of her new role. She and the UN were helping the rebels provide their constituents with a greatly desired service. The contentious history of education in southern Sudan meant that even her choice of primers aroused controversy, for Khartoum believed it fostered the division between north and south to teach children to learn to read in their own language or in English rather than in Arabic. Emma was too new to ask the larger question: whether it made sense to be encouraging the southerners to put so much faith in a Western-style academic system that was designed to prepare people for an economy and a bureaucracy that the south had no means of supporting. "I don't see any future for southern Sudan without an educated population," she opined earnestly to a reporter in 1991. "Otherwise it is always going to be this hand-to-mouth existence." The schools program deepened her intoxication with Sudan. "It was just a wild place with a lot of opportunity for her," said Sally Dudmesh. "She had this incredibly powerful job. She was like the minister of education! I think she just found out that she could have this power. She could go places in Sudan."

She had power, and amid a war in which a cow, a pair of old boots, or a sackful of grain was considered a prize worth fighting over, that made her and her schools a target. The SPLA kept a wary eye on her. To make sure she did not see anything the rebels did not want her to see, three armed guards accompanied her on her trips outside Kapoeta. It was all right for her to deliver the supplies and the salaries to pay the teachers, so long as the schools and the boys remained firmly under SPLA control. Emma got along well with her counterpart at the SRRA, an angular young Dinka man named Ajith Akuei Awan with a quick smile, but her outspokenness soon attracted attention. "Emma was special from the start. She was willing to die for the people of Sudan; she didn't hesitate to go into areas which were very dangerous. She was braver than all the other aid workers. Also, she never feared to talk about South Sudanese politics. She was completely honest about her opinions," said David Oduho, a southern Sudanese consultant to Operation Lifeline.

The commander of southern Equatoria, a dour and suspicious Dinka named Kuol Manyang Juk, took an especially dim view of Emma's free ways and opinions. Kuol Manyang made many people shiver. Kuol was said to be the inspiration for the chant that the SPLA supposedly taught all recruits upon graduation from military training, which began with the line "Even your mother, give her a bullet!" Legend had it that Kuol Manyang had done just that. A Twic Dinka related to John Garang and a graduate of the University of Khartoum, Kuol was a man of many secrets. Reporters called him "the Butcher of Equatoria." His prisoners included Episcopal bishop Paride Taban, whom he accused of "feeding the enemy" because the bishop had distributed relief food in the town of Torit when it was under government occupation. He once told a correspondent pressing to know how many people had been killed in one of his assaults that he was "not very interested in casualties. War is war." Emma had her first run-in with Kuol over her habit of driving after curfew. In her girlish way, she tried to charm the tall Dinka commander by telling him what she was doing to build schools in his area. Kuol was not moved. He told her bluntly that if she persisted in defying him, she would be thrown out of Sudan—or worse.

A few months later their quarrel erupted into a full-fledged feud. Emma noticed that sometimes bright young boys who had caught her attention on a visit were no longer there when she came back. When she asked the boys' parents why, the parents seemed frightened and wouldn't say where the boys had gone. In March 1990 Emma and several other relief workers happened to stumble upon the sun-bleached ruins of a 1930s Italian Catholic mission called Palataka, which lay in a field of elephant grass about thirty miles southeast of Kapoeta. To their surprised dismay, they found some four thousand ten- and eleven-year-old boys living in the abandoned mission buildings. The boys said the rebels had turned the mission into a school. Emma knew Palataka wasn't on the list of schools she had been given to supply. The boys were dirty and sickly; they were scratching at lice and chiggers. They wore rags. The old brick buildings they called their dormitories were infested with rats. The aid workers saw that they had been making cooking fires on the floors and sleeping on homemade rope beds. The blankets they shared were torn and filthy. They were tending a herd of several thousand cattle, but they said they had to beg for food from neighboring villages. They sang a song that Emma felt reflected their misery:

> *Oh my mother,*
> *I want to leave you now.*
> *I am going to school, yeh,*
> *Don't sing for me again.*

The boys came from all over Sudan. They grew quiet when the aid workers asked whether they were receiving military training. While Emma and the others stood talking to the boys, some armed men appeared and told them to leave.

Palataka was only a few miles south of Kuol Manyang's camp at Torit. Emma drove there to ask the commander about the boys. If Palataka was really a school, why hadn't she been told about it? Why had the boys been sent such a long way from home? It went against the whole principle of the primary schooling plan, which was to let children attend school in their own communities. Kuol was sitting outside his *tukul* sharing a meal of *kisra* and goat stew with his guards when she arrived. When he heard what Emma wanted, he stopped chewing and gave her an icy stare. The boys were none of her business, he said. They were orphans under SPLA care. If she wished to give them some pencils and paper, she could leave the supplies with the commander, and he would have them delivered. Otherwise she and the other aid workers should stay away from Palataka. If she didn't, Kuol could not be responsible for the consequences.

Ignoring Emma, Kuol and his guards resumed their meal.

Emma went away angry and flustered. When she asked Ajith about the boys, he wouldn't look her in the eye. He seemed to hang his head. He said Kuol Manyang himself was in charge of Palataka, and there was nothing he or Emma could do about it. Emma and the other aid workers concluded that Palataka was a secret SPLA recruitment and training camp for child soldiers. Over the next few months, they learned that there were others like it in Equatoria. Operation Lifeline officials in Nairobi took up the issue with John Garang's office in Addis Ababa. At first the SPLA did not reply to their inquiries. Then the rebels informed the UN that Palataka was sponsored by an organization founded by Garang himself, called the Friends of African Children Educational Foundation, or FACE. In the "New Sudan," the rebels said, FACE was going to run many schools like Palataka. The students at FACE schools would pay for the cost of their schooling and learn self-reliance by tending cattle and growing crops for the rebel administration. If Operation Lifeline wanted to make a donation of books and supplies to FACE, that would be fine. In fact, Garang himself recommended it. Otherwise the *khawajas* should leave Palataka and other SPLA schools like it alone.

While Emma's superiors wrangled with Garang over the FACE "schools," she continued to ask the Sudanese villagers she met about

Palataka. She learned that many of the children at Palataka were not orphans, as Kuol had claimed. In fact, some of the boys missing from her own schools in Equatoria had been taken from their parents and force-marched to Palataka. Kuol Manyang had seized many of the cows the boys were herding at Palataka as fines in court cases. Top SPLA commanders were now using the cattle to marry local women. Emma fumed that Palataka was worse than a military camp: it was a forced-labor camp in which children slaved for the wealth of Kuol and his cronies. She became emotional when she talked about the FACE schools, and her voice took on a hushed quality. "Whatever they're producing goes to the movement," she would whisper dramatically. The boy soldiers became her personal cause.

Khartoum was now even more resistant than the rebels to Operation Lifeline. Hassan al-Turabi and the NIF had been opposed from the start to the agreement that Sadiq signed with the UN creating the cross-border relief operation. The Islamic government argued that the operation ceded too much sovereignty to the rebels. The government claimed to be willing to offer the south independence in exchange for a free hand to implement Islamic law in the Muslim north. But Garang insisted that the rebels did not want to separate from the north. Instead he maintained they wanted a secular constitution for the whole of Sudan with guarantees for ethnic and religious minorities—a position that was intolerable to the Muslim fundamentalist government, which argued that in an Islamic society government had no other purpose than to impose divine law. Starting in December 1989, the government threatened to shoot down any flight that left Lokichoggio without its approval. In a pattern that continues to this day, the Sudanese air force began bombing relief centers where large numbers of southerners gathered in search of food. A month after Emma arrived in Equatoria, government warplanes bombed the towns of Torit and Bor, killing dozens of people.

Emma saw her first Antonov, the Sudanese government's bomber of choice, over the Nuer town of Ler. There were so few mechanical noises in Sudan that you could always hear the Antonov well before it lumbered into view and so few buildings that you could usually guess its target. The Sudanese educator she was with that day insisted that Khartoum would not dare bomb a *khawaja*. Emma hid under a tree anyway. Not long after that, Emma and some other aid workers were caught in another government bombing raid at Bor. Crouched in a muddy dugout, they listened to the explosions around them. When they crawled out, the expatriates saw bleeding bodies. Five people had been killed. The bombs had blown off other people's arms and legs. The wounded were screaming. The SPLA medical team had disappeared. One of the aid workers, an American who had served in Vietnam, climbed into a UN vehicle and drove around in circles, frenzied with rage. Emma stayed calm. She seemed almost exhilarated. She went to Bernadette Kumar, the young Indian surgeon who was the lone UN representative in Bor, and offered to help with the wounded. She radioed for a UN plane to come and pick them up. She helped bury the dead. The bombing of Bor taught her something she hadn't known about herself: She was good at war.

She also made a friend at Bor who was to become her closest female confidante in southern Sudan. On the face of it, Emma and Bernadette Kumar did not have much in common. The surgeon was tiny, with short black hair and black eyes; next to Emma, she looked even smaller. She came from a distinguished Indian family, had been an excellent student, and spoke several languages fluently. Though she shared Emma's love of adventure, she had an orderly mind, and she respected rules. But once again Emma's gift for friendship trumped all differences in personality and culture. A decade later, when I reached Bernadette by phone in Beijing, where she was married to a Norwegian diplomat and working for UNICEF, she remembered Emma with the warmest affection. "Whenever Emma was around, it was always good fun," Bernadette said. "We kind of bonded, the way women do, especially in a place like that where you're really on your own."

Like Emma, Bernadette was said to be very brave. Despite repeated bombings, she refused to evacuate Bor. She lived alone with a cat in an old British house with a corrugated iron roof, where she operated around the clock on the wounded. The Sudanese marveled that such a small person could find the strength to keep dragging their long bodies onto her makeshift operating table to clean out shrapnel, cut off limbs, or close the eyes of the dying. "It was a very emotional time in my life," Bernadette told me. "I still haven't gotten over it. It was all-involving and engulfing and painful being so close to death every day, and yet I never really appreciated life as much as I did there."

Emma would whiz up to Bor in her Land Cruiser regularly, heedless of bombs. After a long day of operating, the exhausted doctor would come home to find Emma waiting for her, cigarettes and a bottle of *aragi* in hand. The two women would share a meal of canned spaghetti; they would talk and talk about the situation in southern Sudan. In no time,

Emma's imitations of their colleagues or the SPLA officers they knew would have Bernadette weak with laughter. "Emma, you are *crazy*," the doctor would say, but she felt that Emma's visits helped keep her sane. To Bernadette, her zany English friend seemed like the impetuous personification of the life force. *Khawajas* were supposed to stay indoors after sunset, lest they be mistaken for spies, but Emma did as she pleased. She would drive after dark, joking and laughing about land mines and what she had told the rebels at the last roadblock along the way. "Emma was very strong-minded," Bernadette said. "She was stubborn. She didn't care about structure, about rules."

Emma made no secret of her attraction to the tall Nilotic men. She and her SRRA counterpart Ajith were rumored to be having an affair. She told Bernadette about flings she'd had with other rebel officers. She had a vision of overcoming racism through romantic love. She wanted to break the seal of her whiteness—to "make herself that bridge between black and white," in Bernadette's words—to join in some sort of mystical union with Sudan. She felt that the other aid workers who constantly criticized the Sudanese were influenced by racism, whether they knew it or not. She was acutely conscious of the way the aid workers appeared to the Sudanese, how they could be so infuriatingly self-righteous, so ignorantly superior, and it made her squirm. "She hated the snobbery of the Europeans—she really wanted to go against that," recalled Bernadette. "She would sleep with a man just to prove a point." She told her surgeon friend that she identified with the struggle of the southern Sudanese. She said she felt her destiny was here, with these people.

Bernadette would say, "Emma, really, I can't understand this."

Emma would reply simply, "In my heart, I'm Sudanese."

Her carefree attitude toward sex shocked and delighted Bernadette, who, like Emma, had attended convent school. Emma could always make Bernadette giggle with one of her rude jokes and her favorite line: "You know what they say—convent girls are always the worst." But the doctor worried about the medical risk Emma was taking with her sexual adventures. Southern Sudan was so isolated that AIDS hadn't had much chance to spread inside the country, but many of the rebel officers had lived in Ethiopia and Kenya, where the disease was rampant. "I said, 'Emma, the only thing I'm going to say to you is, from a medical point of view, you've got to be safe, and if you need condoms, I can happily supply them.'" Emma just laughed. She called Bernadette a puritan. If she was in one of her fanciful moods, she might muse about her fondness for more than one lover. "You know, I love them all in my own way," she would say.

Bor, where Bernadette was based, was a steamy, mildewing former garrison town in the swamps at the end of the White Nile. During the rainy season, the river disappeared altogether into a crocodile-infested mess of reeds and water lilies. As the scene of the 1983 mutiny that led to the formation of the SPLA, Bor was one of the government's favorite bombing targets. It was also a good place to get a sense of how different the civil war looked when viewed from the bottom up. All the big issues of ideology and religion vanished into a relentlessly local fugue. The Bor mutiny, for example. The SPLA leadership presented the 1983 mutiny as the beginning of its fight for a unified, secular, democratic Sudan. But in Bor, people remembered it as squabble that initially broke out when two southern army majors fell out with their Arab commanding officer over an illegal plan to ship elephant tusks, leopard skins, and locally mined gold to Khartoum for sale. The Sudanese government often disparaged the SPLA's pretensions to represent the south, calling it a "Dinka" movement, but in Bor, Emma could see that even Dinka-ness, so to speak, was a very relative term. The Jieng, as the Dinka called themselves, were divided into more than sixty sections and many hundreds of lineages. Their dialects were so different that it was often difficult for a Dinka from Bahr el-Ghazal to understand one from Bor. With few roads and no modern means of communication, they knew little about each other. To ordinary southerners, even the section was an abstraction: Their deepest loyalties belonged to their lineage and their *wut*, the cattle-camp.

The southerners often were more engrossed in their own feuds than in the larger issues of the civil war. During Emma's time in Kapoeta, the Dinka were divided over how to treat a Bor man named Paul Kon Ajith. Paul claimed to be a Christian prophet. He walked around the south naked except for a waist belt and a cross, ringing a bell and beating on a drum, telling people that the Christian God had commanded him in a dream to gather all the wooden posts and sacred symbols of the Dinka religion and burn them at a place outside Bor that he called Zion. He said this sacrifice at Zion would be the present "brought unto the Lord" that the biblical prophet Isaiah had foretold twenty-seven centuries earlier. If southern Sudanese heeded his words, peace and prosperity would return. But if they failed to listen, he warned, God would punish them. The Bor commander Kuol Manyang laughed at the prophet. But

Christians and non-Christians in the district began fighting over whether the Dinka ought to burn their holy spears and drums as he ordered.

Emma made light of her own feud with Kuol. "He's just mad at me because I won't sleep with him," she scoffed to Bernadette. Bernadette was as dismayed as Emma by the condition of the boys at Palataka, but she worried that her friend did not understand how dangerous it could be to cross a commander like Kuol in a place like southern Sudan. She feared that Emma's romantic fantasies prevented her from seeing how brutal and ruthless the rebels were. "She lived in an artificial bubble," she said. Bernadette knew that, despite all the SPLA rhetoric about democracy and the "New Sudan," men like Kuol Manyang were the real face of the rebel movement.

The SPLA conquest of Equatoria had made Kuol the absolute ruler of the province. The reality was that only Kuol's kinsman, John Garang himself, had the power to question his decisions, and that was because only Garang, who maintained strict control over the outsiders supplying the movement's finances, had the power to cut off weapons and supplies to him. (Likewise, only Mengistu and Garang's other foreign patrons had the power to question Garang, because he was "eating from them," and only they had the power to cut off his guns and ammunition.) Bernadette had come to Sudan in early 1989 to replace another doctor whom the rebels had accused of stealing a sacred leopard skin. The man had been held prisoner for three months in a pit dug in the earth before the French medical charity who sent him to Sudan could persuade the SPLA to release him. Bernadette tried to tell Emma to let her superiors at Operation Lifeline handle the situation at Palataka. But Emma wouldn't listen. "She didn't exercise the caution that was required," Bernadette said. "Hers was really at times a reckless nature."

THE DANGER and the sense of menace in southern Sudan could be oppressive, but—unlike the southern Sudanese—the Operation Lifeline workers had an escape hatch. When bombs started falling or when Sudan simply became too much for them, the *khawajas* could radio for a UN airplane to pluck them out of the south and back to their base camp at Lokichoggio. Loki in 1989 was not yet the "5-star dude ranch, complete with a swimming pool and restaurant," that foreign reporters would mock a decade later. Visitors at Loki slept in army tents, on camp beds. They took showers outside in sun-warmed water and ate in a communal

*Emma McCune at home in Nasir, after her 1991 marriage to rebel commander
Riek Machar. "She wanted to make herself that bridge between black and white,"
said her friend Bernadette Kumar.* (Photo by Peter Moszynski)

Left: Cowling Hall, a Queen Anne mansion built on the ruins of despoiled abbey, became home for the McCune family after they returned from India in 1966.
(Photo by Deborah Scroggins)

Above: After Emma's parents were divorced and her father committed suicide in 1976, the family was forced to move to this block of public housing.
(Photo by Deborah Scroggins)

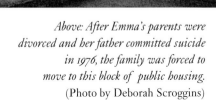

Left: As a student at Oxford Polytechnic, Emma took the better part of a year off to fly around the world in a single-engine airplane with her friend Bill Hall.
(Photo by Clive Hyde)

Above: A southern squatters' camp outside Khartoum.
(Photo by Deborah Scroggins)

Right: A Dinka man bathing his dying son outside Ed Da'ien in south Darfur. (Photo by Deborah Scroggins)

Emma first traveled to Sudan in 1987 to help Ethiopian children in refugee camps on the Sudanese border. She soon learned that southern Sudanese fleeing Sudan's civil war to squat in camps outside northern cities lived in even worse conditions than the Ethiopian refugees. The year after her visit, more than 250,000 southern Sudanese died in the famine of 1988, leading the United Nations to create Operation Lifeline Sudan so that relief could reach Sudanese in the rebel-held south as well as the north.

Left: Emma's job for Street Kids International was to help open schools inside the southern war zone for Sudanese children like these Nuer boys. (Photo by Peter Moszynski)

The leader of the National Islamic Front (NIF), Hassan al-Turabi, backed the radical Islamist regime that took power in Sudan in a 1989 military coup. (Photo by Scott Peterson/Liaison)

John Garang, the chairman of the Sudan People's Liberation Army (SPLA), antagonized fellow rebels with his overbearing ways and his insistence that they keep fighting until the whole of Sudan was unified under a secular government. (Photo by Scott Peterson/Getty Images)

Tiny Rowland, the British chairman of Lonrho Corporation and one of the SPLA's financial backers, tried to persuade Garang to make peace with Turabi's regime, but Garang refused. "Garang is a very difficult chap," Rowland said. (Photo by Eamonn McCabe/ The Observer)

Emma met Riek Machar, the SPLA zonal commander in the Upper Nile province, in January 1989, just as Riek was growing disenchanted with Garang's stance. Emma and Riek were married two months before he and other rebel commanders mounted a 1991 coup against Garang. (Photo by Deborah Scroggins)

ove blooms among the bullets in Sudan

Tom Haley　　　　　　　　　　　　　　　　　　　　　　　　　　Richard Ellis

d: Sudan's SPLA guerrillas are waging war against the government – and each other

Deadly waters: Emma McCune with her dog Come On and a refugee. She says she is the first to run for cover when the bombs fall

he white woman' says
es to guerrilla leader

by Richard Ellis
Nasir, southern Sudan

swampy outback
Sudan, reached by
flight from Nai-
-minute boat ride
stuary of the Nile,
note, bush head-
an African guer-
fighting a war of
e.

he compound of
basic: the lavatory
a the ground and
om the straw roof.
siders the size of
ls, snakes, scor-
rats. Crocodiles
iver, and recently
mauled eight

id such primitive
s, there is some-
a copy of Vogue,
side table, featur-
have tweeds"; a
dal Sassoon con-
ampoo. The rebel
amander, Italian
holster, steps for-
oduce his second
all brunette from

year-old Emma
ne to be in such a
story that might
from the pages of
n. A former con-
e had a thirst for
After studying art
hnic, she worked
centre in Oxford.
ecame touched by
of the southern
largely Christian
dominated by the
o and fiercely Is-
erners.
rs ago she was
outhern Sudan to
o schools, which
into touch with
guerrillas, the Su-
s Liberation Army
e met, and fell in
Rick Machar, one
r commanders, an
ter university lec-

Rick Machar: two wives

turer in mechanical engineering.
It was a difficult courtship,
because he was often away at
the front. Travelling was dangerous: one trip took McCune
10 days and meant cutting a
path through 18 miles of acacia forest.
Five months ago, she ac-
cepted Machar's proposal of
marriage. She had few qualms
about becoming his second
wife: his first, a southern

Sudanese woman, lives with
his three children in Bradford,
where he did his PhD. "I
know her, and like her a lot,"
said McCune.
She sometimes laughs at
what the reaction would be of
the nuns who taught her at
Richmond Convent of the
Assumption. "I should think
they would keel over if they
knew one of their former pupils had entered into a polyga-

mous marriage. But they do
say convent girls are always
the worst."
It was only after the simple
open-air wedding in June that
she plucked up the courage to
tell her mother in England
(her father died when she was
11). "She was slightly shocked
at first, but she has been
tremendously supportive."
Life at the commander's
two-roomed mud hut near the
devastated town of Nasir has
been tough. One night, Mc-
Cune awoke to find a rat
gnawing at her forehead. She
has been bitten by a scorpion,
and endured amoebic dysent-
ry. The only concession to
comfort is the light provided
by a solar panel. Yet that, too,
has its problems: it attracts
tens of thousands of mosquitoes, moths and crickets,
which bring in frogs and bats
to feast on them.
The biggest danger, though,
is the war. The government in
Khartoum recently used aircraft to bomb Nasir, killing 33
people. There is a bomb-shel-
ter a short sprint away from
their home. McCune con-
fesses she is the first into it at
any sight of the MiGs. "I'm
not very brave," she said.
But she has taken hardship
in her stride. The only things
she misses are the cinema and
theatre and, occasionally, a
juicy steak – the couple live
almost exclusively on river
fish.
She keeps in touch through
the BBC World Service, a
subscription to the Guardian
Weekly and the magazines
given to her by workers at a
nearby United Nations camp.
"I'm very happy," she said. "I
know exactly what I was letting myself in for. When you
are in love with someone you
can go through anything."
Machar, 39, in the unique

position of having a southern
Sudanese wife in Britain and a
British wife in southern Sudan, marvels at how McCune
has coped with the bush. "I
complain about it more than
her," he said.
She is devoted to her work
with the children of southern
Sudan, many of them refu-
gees. As a representative of
Street Kids International, a
Canadian-based organisation,
she has helped set up dozens
of schools.
Travelling from refugee
camps by boat, she is greeted
like a favourite aunt. "Ha-
waga," the children shout happily, announcing the arrival of
"the white woman" and her
constant companion, a
brown-and-white puppy
called "Come On". "It had
another, proper name," said
McCune. "But Rick's soldiers
always heard me shouting
'come on' to it, and thought

that was her name. Now it's
stuck."
McCune's position, though,
has recently been complicated
by a split in the SPLA: her
husband and two other commanders have broken with
John Garang, the rebel movement's autocratic leader, and
the two factions have been
fighting for supremacy.
Hopes of a reconciliation
were dashed 10 days ago when
hundreds of Garang's soldiers

commandeered a Red Cross
barge in Bor, and sailed up
river to attack Machar's
troops near his home village,
close to Adok.
The threat of a raid on
Machar's headquarters at
Nasir, either by Garang's
troops or by the government,
cannot be discounted. The
rainy season is nearing an end,
the traditional time for offens-
ives in a stalemate war that
has lasted, on and off, since

independence 38 years ago.
Machar explains his move-
ment's aims, marking out his
strategy for victory on a
photocopy of a Michelin map.
Inevitably, as a foreigner
married to the breakaway
commander, McCune has at-
tracted attention. Garang's
side has accused her of being a
British spy and of having influenced her husband to
launch his "creeping coup"
against the SPLA leader.
She dismisses this as ridiculous, but is passionate in her
opposition to the tactics of
Garang's SPLA, which have
included taking up to 50,000
boys as young as seven away
from their parents and
herding them into "schools"
for milary training.
"I have seen children being
turned into little warriors, almost being brainwashed into
joining the struggle, and it is
so wrong. They are already
suffering so much. I have to
speak out against it – it has to
be stopped," she said.
The last chapter of Mc-
Cune's story remains to be
written. If her husband eventually succeeds in his war, she
might become the first lady of
an independent southern Sudan. If he fails, a more grisly
fate might await her. "There
are some people out there who
would gladly put a bullet
through my head," she said.
"But I'm sure it won't come to
that."

The news of Emma's marriage to Riek was splashed across the pages of The Sunday
Times *on Nov. 17, 1991. Emma laughed at the thought of how the nuns who had taught her
in Yorkshire would react. "They would keel over if they knew one of their former pupils had
entered a polygamous marriage," Emma told the reporter. "But they do say convent girls are
always the worst."* (Photos by Tom Haley & Richard Ellis/ The Sunday Times)

Emma outside her tukul at Ketbek. Local women decorated the walls with paintings of geometric shapes, animals, and people. Emma persuaded Riek's soldiers to plant a garden next to the tukul from seeds she had saved and dried. "She was determined to get the soldiers to put down their Kalashnikovs and plant," recalled an aid worker. (Photo by Peter Moszynski)

Emma sitting on her bed at Ketbek. "I really admired her for living totally the Sudanese way," said Bernadette Kumar. (Photo by Peter Moszynski)

Emma and Riek at work. After Emma lost her job, she threw herself into Riek's cause. "I faithfully type out draft constitutions, programs, plans, and policies for my beloved husband," she wrote in June 1992. (Photo by Peter Moszynski)

Emma and Riek with their bodyguards. "There are some people out there who would gladly put a bullet through my head," she told The Sunday Times. *"But I'm sure it won't come to that."* (Photo by Peter Moszynski)

Crowds gathered to meet the plane that brought Emma's body to Riek's hometown of Ler for burial. "When we got there, thousands of people were waiting for us," her brother Johnny recalled. "Some of them had walked for days. Riek had to stand on a truck and use a megaphone before we could get out." (Photo by Peter Moszynski)

Emma's grave at Ler was all that was left of Riek's family compound after a Nuer militia allied with the government and opposed to Riek razed the town in 1998. (Photo by Peter Moszynski)

mess hall. From the Western point of view, they were still roughing it. But that was not how the Sudanese saw it. An SPLA commander who visited Loki that year later described it to the human rights group African Rights. "When I saw the UN compound in Loki, it was amazing," the commander said. "When people talk about Heaven...Heaven is where you enjoy life.... When you want to drink something cold, you go for it. When you want to drink something hot, you go for it. Some people are enjoying Heaven. There are people who are enjoying our war in southern Sudan, and I was sorry for that because people are dying in the hundreds." Southern Sudanese like this commander assumed that relief workers like Emma were in it for the money; they often remarked that such people must be failures in their own societies to want to come to Sudan.

From Loki, Emma flew to Nairobi. She spent part of every month in the Kenyan capital. She had to go there to fax Dalglish the reports she wrote on her solar-powered laptop about all the pencils and blackboards she was delivering to the schools. And she needed to replenish her supplies. Sometimes she stayed with Willy's sister, Roo. Willy and Sally had broken up more than a year earlier, though they remained close friends. He and Emma started dating. Emma adored Willy's family. The pair talked of marriage. At the end of 1989 Emma canceled plans to go home to Britain for Christmas to spend the holiday on the coast with the Knockers. Emma's mother had her fingers crossed about the match. She liked Willy and considered him a stabilizing influence on Emma. But it was not Willy's expatriate Africa that appealed to Emma's deepest nature; it was another Africa less hedged and bounded and safe. After Willy spent much of the Christmas holiday away on safari, leaving Emma alone with his family, the couple quarreled.

Peter Dalglish finally met Emma on one of his periodic visits to Nairobi from Toronto. He was standing outside the Fairview Hotel when she drove up in Willy's mud-splattered Land Rover. Languidly unwrapping her long legs, Emma informed Dalglish with an impish smile that the truck was named Brutus. Her panache and enthusiasm for the work took her new boss's breath away. "She was extremely beautiful, striking, ferociously independent," Dalglish remembers. Dalglish, unmarried and only a few years older than Emma, was smitten. "Who wouldn't be?" he said later, ruefully. "Everything about Emma had a story." Dalglish saw in her a kindred spirit who, like him, was prepared to spurn the materialism that he felt had paralyzed so much of their generation. "You know, a lot of people Emma's age are back in the City of London now, driving Range Rovers that cost forty thousand pounds," he said. "Emma had no interest in those things. She was very compassionate. She clearly had a real interest in children, in helping kids." She enthralled Dalglish with tales of her escapades. She invited him to go camping with her and Willy. They looked at flamingos and swam nude in a lake outside Nairobi.

Emma's work impressed Dalglish even more than her flair. With money from UNICEF and help from the rebels' relief group, Emma and Ajith had opened 110 schools in areas where there had been no formal education for seven years. They had persuaded dozens of teachers to come back to southern Sudan. She had been stung by scorpions and bitten by rats and braved ruthless rebel commanders, yet she had emerged with her spirits high. Dalglish had known a lot of relief workers, but he wrote that Emma was the most extraordinary one he ever met. Late in 1990 she took him on a tour of some bush schools. Their first stop was Kapoeta. There was a young orphan boy there named Kachinga who was deaf and mute. Emma thought Kachinga's hearing might be restored with proper medical care. She had brought a Walkman with her to test Kachinga's ears. She placed the headphones on the boy and gradually turned up the sound. Dalglish later said he would never forget the moment when Kachinga heard his first notes of music: The boy leaped into the air, weeping with happiness.

Dalglish was an amateur classicist, and on that trip, as he and Emma were jolting along a mined road in the back of a truck, they got into a conversation about the *Iliad*. Didn't this world of warriors remind Emma of the heroic age of Greece? Wasn't all this talk about honor and fate and feuds right out of the great epic? And what did Emma think about Achilles' preference for a short but spectacular life over a long, dull one?

Oh yes, Emma agreed. She'd much prefer the fate of Achilles to that of ordinary mortals.

By that time, she had already met Riek Machar.

Part Three

Smoke from poor guns smells like exhaust.
Girls hate those guns like they hate
the monitor lizard. The dance is ruined
even if everyone keeps the beat.
Girls hate those guns like they hate
the monitor lizard.

—Daniel Cuol Lul Wur, "Strutting with my rifle,"
in *Cleaned the Crocodile's Teeth: Nuer Song,* 1985

Chapter Thirteen

 FTER I CAME BACK from Sudan that first time, I felt as if I'd taken a potion or been initiated into some kind of mystery cult. Everything about Atlanta seemed bland and insignificant in comparison. Luckily, my editors allowed me to spend long stretches of 1988 writing about the famine and Washington's failure to acknowledge it. It wasn't just that I missed the drama. It was also the feeling that in Sudan, what I wrote could actually make a difference. While I was still in Kenya, *The Sudan Times* reprinted my articles about Safaha, and the BBC interviewed me about the situation there. A little later I heard that Oxfam had managed to move all twenty thousand people out of Safaha. The aid agency's press officer told me that after my articles appeared, the army had suddenly found the trucks Oxfam needed to move them. He said I had saved lives by exposing the plight of the Dinka there. I heard from others that Sadiq's government was very angry at me. I even received an anonymous death threat. It gave me a sense of power: I had never saved anyone from anything before. But very soon the Sudan revealed a death's-head face that wilted my heroic fantasies.

"Did you say Khartoum? Didn't I hear on the radio this morning that some hotel there got blown up?" I still remember the icy shock I felt when a doctor I was visiting gave me the news that the Acropole had been bombed. Thirteen years later, in the dreadful autumn of 2001, Americans are becoming accustomed to this ominous tickle of dread. *It's them again,* we think as we rush to our television sets to find out about the latest hijacking, the most recent anthrax infection, the last plane crash. Once you find out you have enemies, it's horribly easy to start seeing them everywhere. But I first felt that searing sensation thirteen years ago as I hurried out of the doctor's office back to the newspaper. There I read on the wires about how a man had hurled a backpack full of hand grenades into the dining room of the Acropole, killing seven people and injuring seventeen others, while several more gunmen shot up the Sudan Club down the street. The club was a British colonial relic complete with yellowing photographs of the young Queen Elizabeth II and a cracked shell of a swimming pool where Carol and I had often gone for a lemonade. Among the dead, I learned, were a British family: Chris and Clare Rolfe and their two young children, Tommy and Louise.

It was the Quaker couple from Showak. I'd seen them in the Acropole dining room the night before I left Khartoum for Nairobi. They told me they'd come back from the east to lobby bureaucrats in the capital for permission to start their community-lending program in the Ethiopian refugee camps. The news article said they'd secured their permit from the government and had been celebrating when the bomb went off. The blast had beheaded one of the children. With a sickening rush, I remembered little Tommy's angry pink face behind the fence that day in Showak and the irritation I'd felt when he kept crying. Why had the Rolfes ever taken their children to Sudan? I asked myself again. I felt like crying, but my eyes were dry: A strange side effect of that first trip to Sudan was that for a long time afterward I couldn't cry.

The killers, who were quickly arrested, had issued a statement saying they were Palestinians waging a terrorist campaign against Britain and the United States. They accused the guests at the Acropole of "using their humanitarian work as a cover for espionage." In another communiqué, they claimed to be working for "the Cells of the Arab Fedayeen" and ranted on for seven pages about political and economic conditions in Sudan, calling the Acropole and the Sudan Club "nests of foreign spies." The American embassy in Khartoum claimed that the terrorists were working for Abu Nidal and that Libya was behind the attack. Even if that was true, I wondered whether some Sudanese parties might have had a hand in it, too. Sadiq's Umma Party was known for its closeness to Libya and Qaddafi. Sudan's Islamist press made a habit of labeling Western aid workers spies and missionaries. The killers arrived in Sudan with valid Sudanese visas. The Libyan Arab Holding Company was right around the corner from the Acropole. I'd often walked past its office on my way to the Ministry of Information. According to the U.S. embassy, its Libyan director was a known terrorist. He was also an intimate friend of Sadiq's cousin Mubarak al-Mahdi, the one who had been entrusted with getting Chevron back to work in the oil fields. If someone had wanted to send a message to the troublesome *khawajas* trying to disrupt northern plans to clear the lands along the Bahr el-Arab of their rebellious inhabitants, the Acropole would have been a logical place to deliver it.

I couldn't stop thinking about the whispered conversations at the Acropole about the carnage in the south, the shuttered and fearful faces of aid workers like the Dutch nurse from Wau. Curiously enough, the Rolfes had never lost their frank and open expressions. That must have been because they were just about the only *khawajas* I'd met in Sudan who seemed to take absolutely no interest in the civil war.

IN MARCH 1989 I went to see the bomb damage to the Acropole. I found birds nesting in the shattered rafters of the atrium where the Rolfes and their children had been blown to bits. It seemed that the Sudanese landlord who owned the building did not care to fix it, and so it remained, an unacknowledged memorial to an undeclared war. The Patagoulatos family had reestablished the hotel across the street, but the brothers and their wives looked older, as if the explosion had drained them of their sap. One of the wives told me she went out of her way to avoid parking in front of or even looking at the wrecked building because of the memories it brought back of that day: the man who ran past the office with the fatal rucksack; the boom of the explosion; the bits of human flesh and blood splayed on the steps; the screams of her dying employees and customers.

I had come to Khartoum to cover the press conference announcing Sadiq al-Mahdi's agreement with UNICEF to start Operation Lifeline Sudan, but I found myself spending most of my time at the hotel, because the government put me under house arrest as soon as I arrived. At the Ministry of Information, a furious government spokesman accused me of traveling to Safaha the year before without permission, of orchestrating a conspiracy against Sudan from my base in Atlanta, of misquoting aid officials, et cetera, et cetera. He even claimed that the plastic grips on the purple nylon money pouch I wore around my neck contained a concealed listening device. When I laughed out loud in nervous astonishment, he fairly throbbed with rage. Finally he ordered me to go to my hotel and stay there.

A colleague from the paper had to come and negotiate my release, with the result that I was expelled from the country. The night before I left, I slipped out of the hotel to attend a party held by some aid workers from the Irish group Concern. It was one of those dusty Khartoum nights when the whole town seems to be smothered in a hot brown fog. The aid workers were dancing on the roof to a boom box. As I stood around talking, I saw someone I recognized standing off by himself, drinking whiskey and watching the dancers leap through the dust. It was Pierre, the young administrator with the tight blond curls from MSF-Belgium in Nyala who hadn't wanted to help me go to Safaha. He saw me and waved me over.

All these months he'd been in Darfur. His eyes were wild and bitter. He was also quite drunk. So you're back, he said, and he motioned vaguely, inexplicably toward the darkness beyond the roof. You're back, and what are you going to do now?

I said I wasn't doing anything, that the government was putting me on a plane to Nairobi in about six hours.

He didn't seem to hear me. It's still happening, he breathed. The same as when you were there. Safaha and all that.

I was puzzled. I said, But I thought you were able to move the people out of Safaha.

He made an impatient gesture. Yes—so they could die outside of Nyala, he said roughly. Then he straightened up for a moment. That wasn't fair, he corrected himself. Moving the people was good. It was something, anyway. But it hadn't changed the situation that had brought the Dinka to Safaha in the first place. And it hadn't changed things for them once they reached Nyala. They were still traitors and unbelievers in the eyes of the local people. The children they had sold at Safaha were still enslaved by the Rizeigat. And besides, the Dinka from Safaha had been only the first wave. After them hundreds of thousands of starving southerners had poured into towns all over western Sudan. Tens of thousands remained at the mercy of the militias in camps across southern Darfur and Kordofan. Aid workers traveling through the desert had seen the corpses of southerners. They watched the Arabs marching the Dinka off to toil on their farms. Those who dared to speak out were threatened with expulsion.

But what about Operation Lifeline Sudan? I asked. At the press conference announcing the agreement, Sadiq had spoken of opening "corridors of tranquillity" so that aid could flow to dispossessed southerners in the north as well as the south.

Pierre laughed. Don't you know by now that the words of the Sudanese are like birds? he said. They are so beautiful, but they fly away, up, up into the sky, and you cannot catch them....

He stopped and looked at me. The words change, but they do the same things, he said.

Forget about Operation Lifeline, I persisted. What about the peace agreement the moderate Islamic parties were on the verge of signing with the SPLA? Relief was a half measure at best, but peace would allow the Dinka to return to their homes.

Pierre snorted. What makes you think the north wants peace? he demanded angrily. The merchants, the generals, the militias are all making too much money off the war to end it. The slaves, the animal skins, the uranium—they've got a million rackets. And besides, there's the oil. Mark my words—the north will never give up the oil. The northern Sudanese think they're so high and mighty with their Arab blood, but they know the Arabs in the Middle East think they're no better than mongrels. People like Hassan al-Turabi can't wait to get their hands on some of that oil money the Saudis have been lording over them. Then they're going to show the world who the true Muslims are—the Muslims of the land of the Mahdi!

But surely if the United States and the European Community really cut off the money they've been giving Sadiq's government, the northerners will have to make peace—

Pierre's lip curled. The real money in Sudan comes from the Gulf—from the remittances of the Sudanese working there—and the NIF controls that. Sadiq's government will be blown away like a stack of cards, and there's not a thing in the world the West is going to do about it, he said scornfully. Do you think the United States—or Belgium—cares what happens to these people? All the donors want is for the Sudanese to play along, to let us hand out some grain, to keep our politicians looking good to the nice white people at home. I go to these meetings all the time here in Khartoum. I tell the donors, "The Sudanese say one thing and do another. It's like a game for them, a shell game. They say we have permission to go somewhere. Then we get there, and they won't let us work. Good cop, bad cop." I tell them thousands of people are dying. These guys from the embassies just look at me. They don't want to know.

He paused for a moment, then chuckled harshly to himself. Even if the donors did want to know, what could they do? he said. After all, we've already tried colonizing this place.

Then he dragged me off to dance, singing in a crazy doomed way to the Tears for Fears song that was such a hit with the aid workers, "Everybody Wants to Rule the World."

> *Welcome to your life.*
> *There's no turning back.*
> *Even while we sleep*
> *We will find you acting on your best behavior*
> *Indecision after vision*
> *Everybody wants to rule the world.*

A visiting American congressional delegation got me a new visa that brought me back to the Sudan a few weeks later. And pretty soon Sudan had a new government that proved Pierre right.

Washington had been expecting a military takeover for some time. It was the complaints of the Sudanese generals about the conduct of the war in the south that had forced Sadiq to enter negotiations with the SPLA. But the coup that toppled him on June 31, 1989, came not from the army's leadership but from its middle ranks. And it soon became clear that it was not Washington but the wily Hassan al-Turabi and his NIF who were behind it. At the head of the rebellious army officers was a quiet and self-effacing colonel named Omar al-Bashir. Bashir had been stationed at El Muglad, the former headquarters both of Chevron and of the Misseriya militia accused of raiding Nuer, Dinka, and Nuba villages near the oil fields. He and his fellow conspirators were known for their Islamist sympathies. Turabi's NIF quickly threw its support behind the officers' "National Salvation Revolution."

The West had underestimated Turabi. He had buck teeth and a high-pitched giggle, but he was smart and determined. And he was already well on his way to reaching his goal of crushing the south, taking its oil, forging links with other anti-Western Islamists around the world, and financing an Islamist revolution.

He was born in 1932, the son of an Islamic judge, and in 1955, while studying at the University of Khartoum he helped found the local branch of the Muslim Brotherhood. Later he won a scholarship to study law at the University of London, and went on to get his doctorate at the Sorbonne. By the mid-1960s, he was back in Sudan, deep in Islamist politics, and dedicated to improving the movement's finances and organization. In Saudi Arabia in the 1970s, he befriended Prince Mohammed al-Faisal, the royal family's biggest contributor to Islamist causes. He also got to know two other Muslim Brothers, the Palestinian academic Abdullah Azzam and the blind Egyptian preacher Sheikh Omar Abdel-Rahman. All three men wanted to create an "Islamist International" that might compete with international Communism, and with creeping Western humanitarianism—the aid workers and the journalists whom they saw as a front for "the Crusader-Zionist conspiracy."

Their first step was to create an independent Islamic banking system. In Sudan, President Nimeiri let Turabi set up the Faisal Islamic Bank with funding from the prince. The bank avoided interest, relying instead on shared profits. It attracted depositors among the Sudanese Muslims working in the Gulf, whose remittances were larger than the pay of Sudan's domestic work force. It also collected zakat, Islam's prescribed charity, from its customers. And it funneled this money into a network of Islamic organizations established by the Brotherhood and its friends. "It is not a major exaggeration to say that Sudan was bought and sold in these years," writes Alex de Waal. At the same time, the Brotherhood began a slow and patient infiltration of the Sudanese government, especially the judiciary and the military. "Having become the owners of Sudan," continues de Waal, "the Moslem Brothers concluded...that they were entitled to govern it."

Turabi's interests went far beyond Sudan. In the 1980s, he threw himself into the jihad against the Soviet occupation of Afghanistan. His old friend Abdullah Azzam had moved to the Pakistani border town of Peshawar to head up the Brotherhood's campaign to bring Muslims from all over the world to fight the Soviets. Turabi visited Peshawar at least six times to offer his support. He also renewed contact with Sheikh Omar Abdel-Rahman, who turned up in Peshawar in 1985 after serving three years in Egyptian prisons on charges of authorizing the assassination of President Anwar Sadat. After the Soviets withdrew from Afghanistan in 1989, Turabi exhorted Muslims not to give up the jihad, but to keep fighting for Islamic rule worldwide.

Turabi's party, the NIF, seized power in Sudan later that year. According to Yossef Bodansky, former director of the U.S. Congressional Task Force on Terrorism and Unconventional Warfare, in 1991 Turabi invited the international Muslim Brotherhood to use Sudan as "a springboard to other Arab and African countries" in return for substantial financial support for his regime. Khartoum stopped requiring visas from Muslims. Some of the Islamic world's most famous radicals were soon moving there, including Sheikh Omar Abdel-Rahman, Carlos the Jackal, Abu Nidal, and Osama bin Laden. Bin Laden, the son of a Saudi construction magnate, had served as a conduit for Saudi support of Azzam's Services Bureau. After Azzam was killed in 1989, bin Laden, who knew and admired Turabi, reorganized the Services Bureau and renamed it al-Qaeda or "the Base." At the invitation of the NIF, he began buying up land and businesses in Sudan.

Meanwhile, Sudan's new Islamic government suspended Operation Lifeline, imposed martial law, dissolved the trade unions, increased support for the Baggara militias, and arrested hundreds of dissenters. And it redoubled the pressure on Chevron to resume exploration of the oil fields near Bentiu in the south.

Chapter *Fourteen*

*H*ow Emma met Riek Machar Teny-Dhurghon was one of her favorite stories. I'm going to tell it here the way I heard it from her friends. I should start by saying that Riek is not handsome in the way of so many Nilotic men. He is tall, but among the towering Nuer he hardly stands out. He tends to fleshiness, and his black eyes are small. But, as Margaret Mitchell famously said of Scarlett O'Hara, people captivated by his charm seldom notice such flaws. He has the gap between his front teeth that some Sudanese regard as a sign of prophecy; Westerners often find his warm and ingratiating manner irresistible. Emma had heard about the SPLA commander long before she met him. "Dr. Riek," as the southern Sudanese call him out of pride and in deference to his Ph.D., was known to all as the most highly educated Nuer in the rebel leadership. Like John Garang, Hassan al-Turabi, and Sadiq al-Mahdi, he held a doctorate from overseas—in his case, from Bradford Polytechnic in Emma's own home county of Yorkshire. Like Emma's nemesis Kuol Manyang, Riek was a zonal commander, but unlike the grim and suspicious Kuol, he was said to positively like *khawajas*. In Ler, his hometown and the SPLA's administrative base in Upper Nile, he reportedly went out of his way to invite foreigners to come and discuss politics and philosophy with him in his fortified compound.

Alastair had told Emma about meeting Riek on his first trip to Ler in 1988, a secret mission for MSF-Holland to assess the severity of the famine behind rebel lines. Although Alastair saw plenty of suffering in Ler, he was struck by how forthright and cheerful the town's residents seemed compared to the cowed denizens of some other rebel areas they'd visited. When he and his colleagues were introduced to Riek, the commander invited them right away to start a relief operation in his area. Riek was not even dismayed when they suggested that the fastest way to get food to Ler might be on barges from the north. The members of the team were so impressed by the commander's relaxed confidence that they encouraged MSF-Holland to set up a hospital in Ler.

Emma wanted to expand her schools program into Riek's zone, but the SPLA leadership refused to give her permission to move beyond Equatoria. The rebel relief group had blocked Upper Nile teachers from attending her training courses in Torit and Bor. The SRRA had also prevented her from traveling freely in Upper Nile. Emma had heard that many Nuer parents were still sending their boys to the "children's camps" in Ethiopia at Itang and Panyido. She suspected that the rebels were trying to stop Operation Lifeline from opening village schools in Upper Nile because they might compete with their recruitment of child soldiers in the Ethiopian camp schools. When she heard that Riek Machar would be attending a relief conference at Nairobi's Pan Afric Hotel in January 1990, she decided to go there and try to meet him. She had some harsh things to tell him about the failures of education in southern Sudan. But everything she had heard about Riek Machar told her she was going to like him. Her premonition might even have been stronger than that. "She knew she was going to sleep with him before she went to meet him," says her friend Emma Marrian.

The Pan Afric, a shabby, stained, glass-and-concrete tower dating from the glory days of pan-African nationalism, stood just across the street from the Fairview, but it had a completely different ambience from the aid workers' hotel. As Emma made her way across the Pan Afric lobby, she passed the bar, with its clouds of cigarette smoke and weary-looking African prostitutes. She stopped here and there in the dimly lit halls to ask Sudanese she recognized whether they knew Riek Machar. At last she found someone who had gone to school with Riek and agreed to take her to the conference room where he was chairing a discussion on relief. She took a seat at the back and settled down to wait.

Riek Machar has a honeyed purr of a voice; Emma later would say it sounded to her like velvet. In his hand, he twirled the ebony and ivory cane of an African chief. He wore an olive-green uniform with bright red epaulets and a red beret. Emma could see the other southern Sudanese in the room straining to hear his responses. When the session finally ended and Riek's school friend introduced her, she was caught off guard. Riek held her hand for a long minute, looking straight into her eyes. A slow, gap-toothed smile spread across his face; his gaze seemed to swallow her up. Emma stammered that she had heard a lot about him. In his low, thrilling voice, he answered that he had heard about her, too.

Emma launched into the speech she'd prepared about the need for village schools, about how the boys in the Ethiopian refugee camps were being dragooned into the rebel army, how she needed his protection. Riek listened quietly, tapping his long fingers on the conference table. She later said she fell in love even before she finished her harangue. When she came to a halt, Riek stood up and snapped his fingers at his bodyguards. Let us talk alone, he said softly, and he dismissed everyone else until only the two of them were left in the room. Then he sat down again. Stretching his legs out in front of him, he leaned forward across the table, looking at Emma and stroking his short mustache with his fingers.

What you say is very interesting to me, he began. About a year ago John Garang sent a message that there were good schools in the refugee camps, if children wanted to go there. This seemed to me a noble idea. I started a campaign for the children in the liberated areas to go to school in the refugee camps. I vigorously pushed this in my command and also in the neighboring zones. There were no schools in the liberated areas. We had lost five years since the start of the SPLA, and we needed to make up for lost time. So we sent many children to Ethiopia.

Now you are saying Operation Lifeline wants to open schools in the liberated areas, he went on. This is a change. And you are saying the children in the refugee camps are not going to school. If this is true, it is wrong. Now that you have brought it to my attention, I will find out what is happening. Until then you may begin working with the SRRA to reopen schools in Nasir. Nasir is my new headquarters.

Reaching across the table for a piece of paper, Riek wrote out a permission slip. Then, with a hard thump, he stamped the paper with the official SPLA seal and signed it with his full name: RIEK MACHAR TENY-DHURGHON.

Here, he said, handing it to her.

Emma was bowled over. This tall man with the soft voice shared her dreams for the children of southern Sudan, she thought. With one signature, he had opened the whole of Upper Nile province to her. Thousands of children might go to school because of this. And he was honest enough to admit that the SPLA had been in charge of the campaign to send boys to Ethiopia, instead of pretending like the other rebels that southern parents had made the decision on their own to send their sons. He trusted her so much that he was going to investigate her reports that the boys were being trained for the rebel army! She could hardly believe her success. She said later that it was all she could do to breathe out a thank-you.

Riek watched her, a half smile playing across his face. So she was interested in his people, the Nuer, he said, leaning forward. Had she ever read the books of E. E. Evans-Pritchard?

Emma, of course, knew of Evans-Pritchard, the British anthropologist who had visited the Nuer in the 1930s and written a classic ethnographic trilogy about them. But she had to admit that she had not read a word of *The Nuer: A Description of the Modes of Livelihood and Political Institutions of a Nilotic People*, much less *Kinship and Marriage Among the Nuer* or *Nuer Religion*. Few Nuer lived in Equatoria, and she had more than enough reading to do about the Dinka, Toposa, Murle, and all the other peoples of her district. Nevertheless she was angry with herself for having come to the meeting without at least having looked at Evans-Pritchard. Willy and Alastair, she knew, had read his books. It made her sound like the sort of aid worker she despised—the kind who went around telling the Sudanese what to do without bothering to find out the first thing about their country.

I haven't, but I will, she promised.

Riek just smiled another slow gap-toothed grin and lifted his eyebrows.

You really should, he replied. It will tell you everything you need to know about my tribe.

Emma later told friends she could tell from the way he was looking at her that he was not going to hold her ignorance against her. Warming to the conversation, she asked him about himself and his family. If the surface of their conversation was still about SPLA regulations and Nuer customs, the undercurrent between them was running in another electric direction. They discovered the coincidence that he had done his graduate studies not far from where she grew up in Yorkshire. It struck them both as remarkable. If he'd stayed in England only a few years longer, Emma told him teasingly, she might have administered his grant for the Sudan Cultural Center.

It was getting late in the day. Riek's bodyguards were waiting outside. Emma gathered up her courage. She asked if Riek would go with her to the library the next day to borrow Evans-Pritchard's books. Laughing, he agreed. But they never did make it to the library. Next to this cultured and worldly freedom fighter, Emma must have wondered what dusty old Evans-Pritchard could have to tell her. Both of them later called their meeting at the Pan Afric "love at first sight"; Emma's mother writes that they slept together that night.

In Riek, Emma saw a way to unite all the threads pulling her to the Sudan.

Chapter Fifteen

I'VE NOTICED THAT when people talk about Riek Machar, even people who hate him, even those who wish him dead, an indulgent smile often flits across their faces, almost like a reflex. Riek is so amiable, so seemingly good-natured, that it is hard not to warm to him; only later does one sense the bottomless ego behind the little-boy pout. The Sudanese jokingly call him "the Bill Clinton of Sudan"; the comparison is not as far-fetched as it might sound, and not just because Riek, like Clinton the idolized son of a strong mother, is an inveterate flirt. Riek is a man who lives for admiration, a man who never wants to be alone, a man who hates to say no. He feels your pain even as he plots your end. He was, as he says, born "a political animal," in 1952, the twenty-sixth child of a headman of the village of Ler. In the Nuer language, the word *riek* can mean "the pole that holds up a house or a shrine." It can also mean "trouble."

When Riek was growing up, Ler was a shady village of beehive-shaped mud-thatch huts surrounded by a cornstalk stockade in the middle of the Sudd. The first sound that boys like Riek heard in the morning was a rooster's crow, and the last sound at night was the croaking of frogs. The villagers lived on a diet of sorghum porridge and cow's milk, sometimes flavored with cow's urine. They cooked their food and kept warm with dung fires. Men dressed their hair with cow dung; women wore nothing more than a short apron made of cattle hide. They moved with their cows from the village to higher ground according to the rhythms of the seasons. Then as now they had no electricity, no plumbing, and no telephone system. Then as now they were at war. But at least in those days they had their land.

Riek was one of a new breed of Nuer, a black *Turuk* raised to govern a people who traditionally had no government. The Nuer were like most southerners in that they lived in what Evans-Pritchard called a state of "ordered anarchy." Their leading men or "bulls of the herd" had authority because they were respected, but no Nuer man recognized another as his superior. The main deterrent against crime was the blood feud. The only way for a Nuer to guarantee respect for himself and his cattle was to show that he and his kin would respond violently to the slightest infraction of their rights. The most esteemed male virtue was bravery. "They strut about like lords of the earth, which, indeed, they consider themselves to be," Evans-Pritchard wrote. "Their respect for each other contrasts with their contempt for all other peoples."

The Nuer were known as ferocious warriors who took what they liked from other people, be it cattle, women, or children. They had conquered from the Dinka much of the swampland they inhabited. They were feared by their neighbors, especially smaller hunting and farming peoples such as the Uduk. It took the British until the 1920s to fully subdue the Nuer and then only after savage military campaigns. The Nuer were (and are) divided into tribes, segments, and sections and on down into lineages and families, each bound more and more tightly by the ties of blood and cattle to defend one another against aggression. Riek's tribe is known as the Dok Nuer. The Lou Nuer live to the east of Ler, around Waat, and the Jikany Nuer are clustered along the Pibor and Sobat rivers near Nasir and across the border in Ethiopia. In general, the Nuer resisted outsiders. But the Dok Nuer had a tradition of working with them.

The Nuer believe in an omnipotent God who sometimes communicates to humans through lesser beings they call "spirits of the air." Such spirits of the air take possession of individuals and speak the language of prophecy, which is also the language of poetry. Riek's grandfather was one of these chosen individuals. The spirit that seized him and his brother was known as Teny, and his family has called itself Teny-Dhurghon ever since. Prophecy is so close to madness that the Nuer sometimes wait to see if a person having visions is actually insane. Teny did not bring much luck to Riek's family. Riek's great-uncle was killed fighting the Egyptians in 1883. His grandfather's herd perished after another prophet cursed it. Teny then seized a cousin who, according to the historian Douglas Johnson, "had sex with women seeking cures from his divinity, until their enraged men folk seized him and cut off his penis." In the 1920s, Teny left Riek's section to possess an unrelated Dok man named Buom Diu.

The Dok at this time were hungry and their cattle were sick. Buom's spirit told them to stop fighting among themselves. Instead Teny said they should raid the Dinka living south of them for cattle. The British colonials had not yet extended their administration to Ler, but at a dance Buom prophesied their arrival: "Children, I will bring you a man whom you will deny, I will bring you a man to whom you will have to listen. He will beat you with a stick." A little later, just as he had predicted, the British district administrator for Nuerland, Captain V. H. Fergusson, paid a visit. The prophet invited Fergusson to be his partner in ruling the Dok Nuer. "The country is yours," he said. "Go where you like and do what you like, and you and I like brothers will govern these people." Having heard much about the warlike character of the Nuer, Fergusson naturally was pleased. He created an office for Buom: government chief.

The British gave government chiefs the power to hear court cases and collect cattle in fines. Riek's father became a subchief. In the 1930s Buom had allowed the Anglican Church Missionary Society to build a mission school and a hospital just outside Ler. After World War II the American Presbyterians already tending to the Nuer on the other side of the Sobat took over the mission at Ler. Few parents allowed their children to attend the mission school. Nilotic parents at that time saw school as a bad influence. Boys who went to school, they said, grew up to be "vultures who cared for no one but themselves." The family of Riek's mother, Nyadak, however, was an exception to this rule, and Riek has said he owes it entirely to her that he is not herding cattle today.

Nyadak was the third of Riek's father's five wives. Outwardly she was no different from the other village women. She and her children shared a compound with her husband's co-wives and their children. When she cooked food for her husband and his friends, she got down on her knees to bring it to them. If she became ill, she asked her husband to sacrifice a cow to make her well. But Nyadak had a cousin of whom she was inordinately proud. Her cousin had gone to school, becoming one of the first Nuer to attend the university in Khartoum. Now, in the late 1950s, he was a leader of the Anyanya rebellion. Nyadak saw that a mission education had given her cousin opportunities to which not even her husband, a chief, could aspire. Only school graduates could obtain government posts and the salaries that came with them, since, as the Nuer put it, only they knew "the ways of government" and could speak to the

Turuk in his own language—"the language of paper." Likewise, only school graduates capable of representing the south abroad could rise to the top of the rebel movement. Nyadak's eldest son was not interested in studying, but she made up her mind that her two younger boys should get an education.

Riek's father was himself more open than many Nuer to "the things of the *Turuk*." His family was the first in town to try out such inventions as a can opener and window screens. He acquiesced to Nyadak's determination to send her sons to school. Nyadak had Riek and his brother baptized Presbyterian—a common practice among parents of schoolboys, according to an American missionary who taught at Ler in the 1950s, "since there was no way of knowing where the secret of the white man's power lay"—and she helped engineer his older sister's marriage to one of the first Nuer to be ordained a Presbyterian pastor. When Riek passed the entrance examination to Atar Intermediate School and needed money for fees and clothing, Nyadak traveled alone to Khartoum to brew beer in a squatter's camp until she had earned enough to pay for everything he needed. Her sons rewarded her determination with academic success. After the war, Riek graduated from the University of Khartoum. Later he won scholarships to study in Britain, first at Strathclyde University and later at Bradford Polytechnic. His brother became a professor of veterinary medicine in Egypt. They were the only two of their father's thirty-one children to go to school.

Riek was only eleven when his mother and father sent him off on a great wood-burning steamer to Atar, a town about a hundred miles away in Shillukland. Studying at the "house of writing" set Riek apart from most Nuer boys in a thousand ways. In the school dormitory, he slept for the first time with blankets, under mosquito nets. While his older brothers and cousins were wandering with the family cattle between riverbanks and pastures, covered only in ash to protect them from mosquitoes, he had to learn to wear khaki shorts and a shirt and to sit still in a chair. The boys in the cattle-camps learned about the remote and mysterious nature of God, next to whom, the Nuer said, people were like "black ants." Riek learned that Jesus Christ was his friend. Other Nuer boys mastered the art of knowing what sins might bring down the wrath of God, and when and how to sacrifice cattle to make things right. Riek was taught that the rite of animal sacrifice was meaningless and that his people were backward. Other Nuer boys learned that it was taboo to eat fowl or their eggs. Riek was taught that it was tragic nonsense for birds to go uneaten in a land of hunger. Other boys learned about vengeance and the blood feud. Riek was taught that the Nuer, like all the peoples of the world, must henceforth live in nation-states, under governments, with laws written on paper. Other boys ate their meals from a gourd on the floor. Schoolboys like Riek had to learn to use enamel bowls, forks, and knives.

On holidays Riek's sister who was married to the Presbyterian minister was given the task of making sure he did not linger in the cattle-camp and fail to go back to school like most Nuer boys. Riek said his sister, herself illiterate, was keen for him to learn because "she saw what education could do and she thought to have a brother at the level of her husband would be good." As Riek's English improved and he tasted what he called "the thrill of reading and writing—to know what others have written, to get knowledge of others," his sister's job became easier. Riek began to take pride in his ability to "spear words on paper." At school he learned about Progress and that it was his duty as a member of the educated vanguard to bring it to the Nuer.

When it came time for the other Nuer boys of his age to prove their manhood by lying perfectly still while an older man carved the six parallel marks known as *gaar* across their foreheads, Riek failed to join them. It was a profoundly defiant act. Initiation turned a boy into a *wut* or a "bull of the herd"; it linked him to an age-set, the customary warrior force that led raids and defended villages, and gave him the right to have sex and sacrifice cattle. Not until the day of her son's initiation was a mother allowed to call herself by the honorific prefix *Man,* or "mother of," rather than *Nya,* or "daughter of." But Riek's missionary teachers discouraged the practice. They considered the operation barbaric and dangerous, and they thought tribal marking inhibited the development of national consciousness. The Nuer had a name for the breed of grown but uninitiated men produced in the mission schools. They called them "bull-boys," a term that suggested the unease with which the average Nuer regarded these men who were not quite men. There was something slippery about the bull-boys, something not quite trustworthy. They had not accepted their people's moral code. But Riek and his parents determined that in the new, spoiled world that outsiders had brought to the Sudd, it was the bull-boys and not the traditional bulls of the herd who would be running things.

Riek told me that it was his father who decided he would be better off unmarked. With his skill at reading and writing, his parents thought he would probably end up living in a town with people from many different tribes who might hold his Nuer marks against him, he said. Riek could have run away to a kinsman's house, demanding to be marked. That was what Nuer boys who wanted to be initiated traditionally did if their fathers said they were too young. But Riek did not run away. Under the influence of their teachers, many schoolboys like him had grown contemptuous of the *gaar*. Lul Kuar Deng, another bull-boy who worked under Riek in Nasir in the early 1990s, told me that scarification was "nonsense." (Lul also wanted clothing to be a top priority in the SPLA's "New Sudan." He said the people who did not want to wear clothes should be forced to wear them, because "nakedness is very bad.") Riek almost certainly agreed with these views. When he became the SPLA zonal commander of western Upper Nile, he went so far as to outlaw the *gaar* altogether.

During the civil war that raged all through Riek's childhood, the northern government hunted down and killed bull-boys and other educated southerners. The government argued that the missionaries had poisoned the minds of the south's educated young men against Islam and the north. But Riek's mother, and others like her, believed that the *jallaba*, as they called the Arab northerners, just wanted to keep the "black peoples" ignorant. At the time of independence, the whole of southern Sudan had only two secondary schools. During the civil war, one of these was relocated from the town of Rumbek to Omdurman because of the fighting. The indefatigable Nyadak sent Riek's younger brother, who was fourteen, across the border to Ethiopia to study under the protection of her cousin, the Anyanya leader. Meanwhile she sent Riek, who was sixteen, to Omdurman to attend Rumbek Secondary School. Riek's father died in 1971, but Riek stayed on in Omdurman. He graduated in 1972, the year the rebels and the government signed the Addis Ababa agreement ending seventeen years of fighting. The following year he was among the first one hundred southerners admitted to the University of Khartoum after the war.

Riek majored in mechanical engineering at the university, but he was always more interested in politics than in building things. For this first generation of university-educated southerners, the purpose of higher education was to gain the credentials for government office. In the south, where such meager commercial enterprises as existed had always been in the hands of Arab and Greek traders, politics and warfare were the traditional means of accumulating wealth and power. While other Nuer boys learned to use their spears to increase the clan's herd by raiding, school-boys like Riek sang songs about using their pens "as a spear for their peo-ple." One of Riek's earliest memories concerns a neighbor who came home to Ler from the civil war. He had lost an arm, and he made Riek feel the stub. Riek's mother had never made any secret of why she wanted him to go to school. She wanted him to become a big man, like her cousin. When Riek was suspended for leading his class in a chant for southern independence, she bought him his first pair of trousers as a reward. "Since my secondary school," Riek later told me, "I was a politi-cal activist. I made sure I attended all my lectures, but after the lectures I engaged in political activities."

Peace had not treated the rebel leader, who was Riek's relative, well. He managed to get a job in the civil service, but he was no good at it. After years in the bush, he had forgotten the law he'd studied at the uni-versity. He disliked taking orders from Arabs. He took to drink. When he was supposed to be at work, he could often be found in Omdurman's bars, railing against the *jallaba*. Riek spent part of his university years living in this cousin's household. He was saddened and ashamed by his relative's descent into alcoholism. The great man his mother had brought him up to emulate had become a laughingstock. Riek saw him as an example of the disappointments and shortcomings of the Addis Ababa agreement. He also made up his mind not to become a drinker.

The southerners at the university came from many different tribes and peoples. Some had been refugees during the civil war. Others had stayed in Sudan. All they really had in common was their exclusion from the Islamic parties and preoccupations that dominated the northern political scene. Riek and some other southern students formed a political party to represent the south that they called the African Nationalist Front. The front took the position that the Addis Ababa agreement had been a mistake for the southern rebels. The agreement, they said, had denied the people of the south an opportunity to vote on union with the north, much less on the composition of Sudan's government. "It was just an agreement between elites which they did not subject to the people," Riek told me later.

Riek was still at the university when he heard about a Dinka army officer who shared the southern students' disenchantment with the peace agreement. The officer was John Garang, the future leader of the SPLA. A decade older than Riek, Garang had spent the 1960s as a refugee in socialist Tanzania, where he attended high school with the future guerrilla leaders of Uganda and Rwanda, Yoweri Museveni and Paul Kagame. Later he attended Grinnell College, a liberal arts school in Iowa, on a scholarship. Immediately after graduation in 1971, Garang joined the Anyanya rebel movement. But before he had time to see much action, the Anyanya leader Joseph Lagu signed the Addis Ababa agreement. Garang was hugely disappointed. He had the temerity to send a message around to his fellow rebel officers, inviting them to disobey the cease-fire. The officers, some of them war veterans many years older than Garang, were astounded at the nerve of this "child of the red foreigners" who seemed to think his education gave him the right to order men twice his age about. Captain John Garang, they muttered, needed to be taken down a notch or two. They told him that he would have to put down his weapons with everyone else.

When peace came, Garang chose to join the Sudanese army. As Riek commented, "It was unusual, because the army was shunned" by educated southerners of the period who sought opportunities in the civilian bureaucracy. But Garang's career flourished. In recognition of his abilities, his northern superiors sent him in 1977 to the U.S. officer training school at Fort Benning in Georgia. Later he persuaded the army to let him stay on in the United States and earn a doctorate in agronomics from Iowa State University. But success did not change his opinion that the Addis Ababa agreement had failed to resolve any of the real differences between the north and south. "Dr. John," as southerners now called him, was the kind of man whom opposition only made more stubborn. From his position in the army, he lent a sympathetic ear to lower-ranking former southern rebels who complained about their treatment in the newly integrated army. In Khartoum, he got together with small groups of educated southerners who were outraged by Nimeiri's violations of the agreement. One evening a friend of Riek's who came from Garang's home district of Bor invited Riek to come along to one of these gatherings in a tea shop.

At the tea shop, a group of southern men sat around small tables, talking politics. Garang was thinner in those days than he is now, but he had the same pointed goatee and the same feline eyes. The debate over whether the south ought to go back to war usually hinged on whether the south would be better off independent from the north. Garang posed the issue a new way. The south needed to stop looking at the north as an indistinguishable mass of *jallaba,* he said. The majority of northerners were almost as disenfranchised as southerners by the Khartoum elite, except that their religious affiliation prevented them from recognizing it. The so-called southern problem was actually a Khartoum problem.

He pointed out that the question of whether Sudan was an African or an Arab country depended on how you looked at it. Sudan's 26 million people were two-thirds Muslim but only a little over one-third Arab. Muslim or not, most Sudanese were dark-skinned Africans. Yet the country's wealth was concentrated in the hands of the descendents of a handful of Arabs, mostly from the Nile Valley. Meanwhile, this Arab elite kept the black African majority divided and fighting among themselves. The solution to Sudan's problems, Garang said, was not independence for the south but a constitution and a government that would provide justice and civil rights for all Sudanese. And that would not happen until Muslim northerners began to see themselves as the Africans they really were.

Garang was an incisive and commanding speaker. In a country where most people were unable to see beyond ethnic and religious loyalties, he looked at things in terms of class and economics. His analysis impressed Riek. But his supercilious air irritated the young Nuer. One of the many divisions among southerners was between those who stayed at home during the civil war and those who went abroad. The southerners who had grown up in the refugee camps and been educated abroad sometimes looked down those who had remained in Sudan, seeing them as backward and insufficiently militant. Garang seemed to Riek a typical returnee, pompous and full of himself, but out of touch with the reality of Sudan. For example, he insisted on speaking English or Dinka to other southerners, when everyone else in the capital used Arabic as a lingua franca. "From those of us who got educated in the Sudan and those of us went to school abroad, particularly in East Africa, and those of us who went to school, who had our schooling in Sudan, there is a slight difference," Riek said later. "Sudanese society is open, very open. But Garang—" He shrugged. "He is not so open."

Garang, it seems, scarcely noticed the young Nuer student. Riek's happy-go-lucky manner was not in keeping with the aristocratic aloofness Dinka leaders like Garang cultivated. But Riek had not given up his mother's dream of becoming a big man. Behind his smiles, he was as ambitious as ever. He earned a first-class degree from the University of Khartoum in 1977, taking away many of the prizes that year for mechanical engineering. After graduation the university offered him a job as a teaching assistant. In 1979 Riek was awarded a chance at the most coveted credential of all: a foreign degree like Garang's. The boy who had seen the first "sky canoes" land at Ler was soon flying on one of them across the sea to Scotland to study management and production techniques at Strathclyde Polytechnic.

WITH HIS SHINY ROUND FACE and his legs too long for his trousers, the young Nuer who arrived at Strathclyde in the fall of 1979 hardly looked like the scion of a famous warrior people. Cold, rainy, stone-built Scotland was unlike anyplace he'd ever been, but Riek adjusted rapidly. His English was good enough for him to forgo Strathclyde's special language instruction and move straight into a dormitory with other students. With typical Nilotic bravado, he refused to be overawed by the wealth and technological power of the West. "I had read and heard so much about it that I was not surprised," he later insisted. "There was no culture shock." He fulfilled his course requirements dutifully, including a session as a trainee at a Scottish whiskey factory. But he never really immersed himself in British culture. Right from the start, it was exile politics that really occupied his mind.

Southern Sudan was restless and unhappy. After discovering oil in 1978, Chevron had built a large base just outside of Riek's hometown. The Americans who ran the place paid little attention to the local Nuer notables but went directly to Khartoum when they had a problem. Riek wrote his first political article for an exile publication lambasting Hassan al-Turabi, then Nimeiri's attorney general, for trying to change the provincial boundaries to remove the oil finds from the jurisdiction of the southern regional assembly. He had an inside source regarding Nimeiri's machinations over the oil fields. Thomas Kuma, one of his teachers from Atar Intermediate School, represented Bentiu, the town at the epicenter of the oil development, at the assembly. Kuma had been like a father to Riek ever since he arrived at Atar a scared, skinny boy of eleven. Their relationship had deepened when Kuma left teaching for politics after the civil war. Kuma set an example for Riek when he went to Britain in 1971 to study for a master's degree at Leeds University. Riek had grown up playing with Kuma's children. When Kuma returned from his studies abroad, Riek became reacquainted with one of his daughters, a girl named Angelina. Angelina was only thirteen, but Riek could see that one day she would make a perfect wife for him.

Thomas Kuma and his wife had made the unusual decision to send their daughters as well as their sons to school. While many Nuer girls wanted nothing to do with unmarked bull-boys like Riek, Angelina had been raised to settle for nothing less than an educated man. Like Riek, she belonged to the class of educated southern Sudanese who were in the process of adopting Western social mores. At boarding school in Kosti, she had learned about Christianity as well as "paper." Her English was at least as good as Riek's. Riek would never have to scold her for going outside dressed only in underpants, as happened to the first Nuer pastor in Ler, when he gave his untutored young wife her first set of *Turuk* clothes. Nor would he have to explain "the ways of government" to Angelina. Her father had taken his children to election rallies where Nuer charged about in battle formation, chanting war songs in honor of their candidate, as well as to the secret meetings where things were really decided. "We knew all about it, even the nasty bits," she remembered.

But Angelina was not only sophisticated and intelligent. She was also astonishingly beautiful. She had the build of a dancer and the look of a cat: long, slim legs, a straight back, high cheekbones, and uptilted eyes. Her mother came from a village near Dolieb Hill, the site of the first American mission in Sudan. She was linked on that side to the same prominent Christian Shilluk family as Lam Akol, the canny young engineering lecturer Riek had known at the University of Khartoum. Her father's kin included more than a few former mission boys now rising in the southern government. In marrying her, Riek would form a valuable political as well as personal alliance.

If Riek was less than adept at Nuer spear throwing and hunting, he excelled at the art of wooing. He courted Angelina in traditional fashion, paying her extravagant compliments and chanting poems in her honor. In the Nuer language, a woman is said to "agree" to the man she marries; "to agree" was the closest synonym the early missionaries could find to the English verb "to love." Angelina agreed to Riek when she was still in her teens, but her father insisted that she finish secondary school before she could marry him.

Her father set another condition to their marriage: Angelina was to be Riek's only wife. Riek was known to like the ladies. He already had one daughter with another woman. When Angelina protested that Riek had promised to be monogamous, her father cautioned her that she would need all the safeguards she could get to keep a Nuer husband from bringing home another wife. "Men will always take advantage of culture," he warned. Kuma insisted that Riek take his vows in the Catholic Church, considered the most strictly monogamous of all the Christian churches, in addition to paying the traditional Nuer bride-price for Angelina. "Not that it made any difference," Angelina laughed bitterly many years later.

The elders of the two families met many times to decide on the bride-price. After that it was up to Riek's father to find the necessary fifty cattle from among the family herd. For most Nuer, marriage was more like an ongoing process than an event. A young Nuer wife did not leave her own family to live with her husband until her first or even second child was born. But modern young people like Riek and Angelina had no time for such conventions. When Riek came home from Scotland in 1981 for his wedding, he had been offered a place to study for a Ph.D. at Bradford Polytechnic in Yorkshire. He talked Kuma into letting Angelina to go back to Britain with him.

Angelina was only eighteen. All her life she had heard about England. Now was her chance to see it. A diligent student, she hoped to study bio-chemistry at the polytechnic herself. In three or four years, she thought, she and Riek would return to the Sudan with their degrees. The couple left for England at the end of the summer. As they waved good-bye to their family and friends, Angelina never dreamed that it would be more than twenty years before she again laid eyes on the green, cattle-centered land that until then had been her whole world.

AND YET IT WAS already becoming clear even to those who supported the Addis Ababa agreement that the peace was dying. Nuer men from Riek and Angelina's home region of western Upper Nile had been returning to the bush to fight the government since 1975. While Riek was still at the University of Khartoum, he saw southerners fighting in the streets with northerners who they said treated them disrespectfully. In 1981 and 1982 the government expelled Nuer migrant laborers from Khartoum en masse. In late 1983 two well-known Nuer army officers, Colonel Samuel Gai Tut and Major William Abdullah Chuol, deserted the army to join up with other mutineers collecting in Ethiopia. The deserters called themselves Anyanya II and said they were calling for total inde-pendence for southern Sudan. Some of Riek's cousins joined them.

In Bradford, Riek wanted to support the Nuer rebels. He and a few dozen other southerners started meeting after classes in his and Ange-lina's cramped apartment. Calling themselves the Sudan Revolutionary Congress, they issued manifestos applauding the Anyanya II. If the

British students at Bradford noticed Riek and his Sudan Revolutionary Congress at all, it was probably with derision. To ordinary Westerners, African liberation groups with their acronyms, their sweeping abstractions, and their crudely printed leaflets can sound absurdly childish. But there were other foreigners on the lookout for men just like Riek—men who were willing to risk their lives to fight the Sudan government.

One of them was Libya's Colonel Moammar Qaddafi, who was then backing Sadiq al-Mahdi against Nimeiri. Riek has said that at the end of 1983, as he was finishing his doctorate, a private "contact" in Britain arranged for him and his Sudan Revolutionary Congress to visit the Libyan leader in Tripoli. He declined to name his contact, but in 1998 the British tycoon Tiny Rowland told me that he must have been the man who made Riek's trip happen. "My dear, I've been involved in the Sudan for forty years," the tall, silver-blond chairman of the Lonrho Corporation boomed from his mansion in Buckinghamshire when I happened to catch him by phone there one night. "I knew them all—I was everybody's friend."

ROWLAND WAS ANOTHER ex-colonial, born in 1917 in British India to a German father and an Anglo-Dutch mother. After World War II he emigrated to Rhodesia. There he became one of the first Westerners to see a business opportunity in the decolonization of Africa. Without the protection of colonial governments, most Western investors were afraid to invest in Africa. Yet few Africans had the capital or the skills to run the enterprises the colonials were leaving behind. Rowland's solution was to finance the bush rebels who were on their way to becoming the leaders of African's newly independent states. In exchange for Rowland's cash, friendship, and assorted personal services, African politicians gave his Lonrho Corporation contracts and concessions for land and minerals at bargain-basement prices. Even more important, they guaranteed Lonrho protection from the post-independence seizures and nationalizations that were so devastating to other white-owned firms. By the time he met Riek in the 1980s, Rowland had turned Lonrho from an unprofitable Rhodesian mining and ranching concern into a $4.7 billion London-based conglomerate whose tea plantations and gold mines and luxury hotels spanned Africa. Britain's prime minister, Edward Heath, called him the "unacceptable face of capitalism," but without a doubt he was

Africa's most influential businessman, and he attributed it all to his personal relations with the continent's often dictatorial leaders.

The Sudan occupied a special place in Rowland's heart. He often recounted to roars of laughter how he had rescued President Nimeiri from a 1971 coup attempt. Learning in London of the coup, Rowland had flown six still-loyal Sudanese officers from England to Libya, where Qaddafi allowed them to broadcast to the troops, saving Nimeiri's regime. (Qaddafi also helped by executing two of the conspirators against Nimeiri who found themselves in Libya at the time.) As a reward for his support, Nimeiri named Rowland sole purchasing agent for the Sudanese government in Britain. He also gave Rowland and Lonrho the contract to use Kuwaiti money to built the world's largest sugar plantation on the White Nile at Kenana. "Nimeiri told me, 'You could have any part of Sudan you want if you grow sugar for me there,' " Rowland would say. By the 1980s Lonrho's interest in Kenana had dwindled to less than 2 percent. Rowland and Qaddafi had fallen out with Nimeiri. But Rowland never lost interest in Sudan.

One of the ways that Rowland maintained his influence was to perform quiet favors for Western intelligence services. An early Lonrho director was a former member of MI5, and Rowland often boasted of his contacts with the agency. He also bragged about his close relationship with the U.S. State Department and the CIA. According to one biographer, a U.S. embassy official introduced Rowland to John Garang; another says the Mossad's David Kimche used the British businessman as his contact with the Sudanese rebel leader. For years Rowland made himself helpful to the Reagan administration and CIA director William Casey by building support for Jonas Savimbi's war against the Soviet-backed government in the oil-rich country of Angola. In 1985 Rowland put up the bridge financing so that Israel could sell Oak anti-aircraft missiles to Iran in the Iran-Contra arms-for-hostages scandal. Tiny Rowland could keep a secret. The flamboyant millionaire was never afraid to be seen shaking hands with even the most unsavory individuals, and that made him useful to governments and businessmen who, for reasons Rowland usually contemptuously dismissed as "establishment hypocrisy," preferred to remain in the shadows. Meanwhile he used his contacts with spies to further his business interests.

For African politicos in the 1980s, Lonrho's glass-and-chrome Metropole Hotel in London was the place to be. Rowland was said to have bugged every room and every telephone in the building. All the government ministers and all the liberation groups went there anyway. Ugandan guerrillas shared tables in the lobby bar with dark-suited African National Congress cadres enjoying a last beer before heading off for military training in Libya. (Among Rowland's patron Qaddafi's protégés from this period were the Liberian warlord and future president Charles Taylor and the Sierra Leonean rebel Soday Fankoh, between them responsible for some of the most gruesome atrocities of the 1980s and 1990s.) Uniformed waiters served tea to Renamo commandos from Mozambique, and the wives of Kenyan politicians compared the results of shopping expeditions. Bugged or not, Tiny picked up their bills at the Metropole, and that was more than most of them could resist. "You could meet everyone in Africa here," a Ugandan politician recalled nostalgically at the hotel a decade later. "It was like a bloody peace hall."

Rowland himself occasionally made an appearance, striding through the threadbare crowd in one of his impeccable Savile Row suits, smiling his enigmatic smile and stopping every so often to shake hands with a visitor who caught his eye. "My dear friend, how is Rebecca?" he would ask the awestruck recipient of his attentions in his clipped, upper-class accent, for he had the politician's gift for remembering the names not only of the people he met but also of their friends and families. "And little Lucy? What about Simon?" Cocking his head sympathetically, he would ask if there was anything else he could do for his dear friend from Angola. Or Zimbabwe. Or Sudan. Did he need an extra hotel room to use as an office? Help finding the right British boarding school for a child? Money to pay for a trip overseas? The name of a good immigration lawyer?

Rowland's ties to the rebels of southern Sudan and to Qaddafi were not widely known in the early 1980s, but he told me that Qaddafi had given him power of attorney at the time to act on his behalf. He never made any secret of his penchant for bankrolling politicians up and down the African continent. A former Zambian foreign minister once described Rowland as looking down at Africa from his Gulfstream jet and saying, with satisfaction, "There isn't a president down there I couldn't buy." Rowland did not remember Riek's particular student group. "My dear, I've supported so many national liberation movements. I've put 150 million pounds into national liberation movements," he told me. But he said he was likely to have done it, since he was arranging such matters for

Qaddafi at the time. "I was a founding member of the SPLM. All their uniforms were supplied by me—boots, everything. I still have a warehouse full of them.... I've put twenty or thirty million pounds of my own money into the SPLM."

Rowland was also a friend and sometime business partner of Adnan Khashoggi. After Chevron pulled its employees out of the Upper Nile oil fields in 1984, Nimeiri told Khashoggi he could have the concession if he could manage to equip and train a Nuer militia to defend the fields from the SPLA. When Khashoggi failed, Nimeiri turned to Rowland in desperation. Through Rowland, he relayed the message to John Garang that he could become vice president of Sudan if he would give up his rebellion. But Garang refused. "Garang is an extremely difficult chap," Rowland sighed many years later.

IN 1983 QADDAFI'S ALLY, Ethiopia's Colonel Mengistu Haile Mariam, also wanted to rekindle Sudan's civil war. But the Ethiopian dictator was lukewarm toward the newly formed Anyanya II. Its Nuer leaders wanted the south to secede from Sudan, and Mengistu was opposed to that. He had enough troubles with his own secessionists on his northern border with Sudan, in Eritrea. Besides, Anyanya II's vision of an independent southern Sudan might prove enticing to Ethiopia's own Nuer population in Gambella province. The colonial borders were the one Pandora's box that Africa had not opened since independence, and Mengistu wanted to keep it that way. Then, in 1983, Colonel John Garang and the 105th Battalion fled to Ethiopia after staging their mutiny at Bor. Garang was a Southern Sudanese leader whom Mengistu could support. He was a Dinka, and there were no Dinka in Ethiopia. Like Mengistu, he was a military officer with Marxist ideas. Best of all, he was not calling for independence. Instead he claimed he wanted to create a unified socialist Sudan along the lines of Mengistu's own regime in Ethiopia.

The two men formed a fast friendship. Mengistu agreed to channel all weapons and supplies destined for the Sudanese rebels through Garang, effectively anointing the Dinka colonel as their leader. When the Nuer leaders of Anyanya II refused to give up their goal of independence for the south and submit to Garang's leadership, Mengistu lent Garang his security forces to ambush Anyanya II, killing hundreds of Nuer at Gambella. The Anyanya II now had a bigger grievance against Garang than against the northern government. To get the arms to avenge themselves, they rejoined the government side.

The skirmishes between Garang and Anyanya II took place far from the gaze of the world press, which can scarcely differentiate one African country from another, let alone the intricacies of lineage and tribe that are the hidden reality behind the facade of nation-states and governments. But for Qaddafi and others who wanted to squeeze Nimeiri, what was rapidly turning into a Nuer-Dinka quarrel presented a problem. The bulk of the oil fields lay in Nuer territory. It was Anyanya II who had led the attack that shut down Chevron's operations. Now Nimeiri was negotiating with the Anyanya II leaders from the Bentiu area. If he could sign a separate agreement with them that would pacify Nuerland, Chevron might resume work, and Nimeiri might get the money he needed to stay in power. What Qaddafi needed was some Nuer from the oil fields who were willing to unite with Garang against the government. In Riek's Sudan Revolutionary Congress, the Libyan dictator found what he wanted.

From Tripoli, Qaddafi flew Riek and his fellow students to Addis Ababa to meet with Garang in September 1983. Many Nuer wanted nothing to do with what they regarded as a Dinka movement that was killing their kinsmen in Anyanya II. But Riek and his congress were attracted to Garang's modern vision. They wanted to rise above tribal loyalties, and their vaunted Western educations gave them some authority to do so. When they agreed to form the Sudan People's Liberation Movement under Garang's leadership, it was an important victory for him and his backers. It was also the beginning of Rowland's role as quartermaster to the SPLA, second only to Mengistu himself. Riek returned to Britain long enough to finish his dissertation and settle his affairs. A British insurance firm had offered him a job, but he turned it down without a second thought to return to Addis Ababa at the end of 1984.

Angelina had already postponed her university education after she became pregnant with Teny, the first of their two children born before Riek left for the war. Mimi had come along little over a year later. Now Angelina faced the prospect of staying on in Britain, alone with a toddler and a seven-month-old in an alien country. As the SPLA paid no salaries, she would have to go on the dole. She knew she and her children had it much easier in Bradford than their relatives in southern Sudan, but she could hardly pretend to be looking forward to Riek's departure. As Riek laughingly recalled, "Angelina wasn't—well, she wasn't for it. But she found out I was really thick!" Characteristically, Riek listened patiently to Angelina's worries, then did as he chose. "You won't get an argument from Riek," Angelina sighed many years later. "Perhaps that's why he gets away with so much." Angelina's family as well as Riek's agreed with him that it was his duty to join the rebellion. In their view, it was far more honorable for him to become a guerrilla than to go to work for an insurance firm. "She didn't really have a choice," Riek admitted. He had two tiny children, but he had never anticipated playing much of a role in their upbringing. "In our society, the stronger element is the mother," he said. "In our society, where a man might have five families, it is the mother who has responsibility for the children." Neither he nor Angelina expected the war to last more than a few years.

IF RIEK LABORED under any illusions about the violently authoritarian nature of the movement he had joined, they quickly were dispelled in the gloomy Ethiopian capital. The Ethiopian famine was at its height when he arrived in the winter of 1984. Bullet-riddled bodies were often found in the streets. No one dared ask where they came from. John Garang had gained a potbelly, and his oblong eyes were colder than ever. Garang was in favor because he modeled himself after his benefactor and steadfastly parroted Mengistu's Marxist jargon. The southern Sudanese who hung around the dingy SPLA office in Addis Ababa's "Super Market" shopping center likewise called each other "comrade" and wrote Marxist screeds denouncing Khartoum's "reactionary bourgeoisie." Privately they hoped that Garang knew better than to believe in such *Turuk* nonsense. They assumed that his rhetoric in favor of a united, democratic Sudan was just a tactic aimed at winning international support for the rebels and that, like most southerners, he knew better than to think the *jallaba* would ever share real power with the south. They saw the SPLA slogan "We Know What We Want" as a veiled acknowledgment of the movement's true aim: independence for the south. But since Garang never came out and admitted that his antisecessionist stand was really a subterfuge, they could not be sure what he really thought.

Addis was a snake pit, and yet somehow Riek managed to gain Garang's confidence. Not long after Riek arrived in late 1984, Garang made the affable young Nuer his office manager. The crucial factor may have been Riek's loyalty during the period in which Garang annihilated his Nuer rivals within Anyanya II. Riek had written to the Nuer leaders, earnestly urging them to reconcile with Garang. But while Riek was still in England, the SPLA commander Kerubino Kuyanin Bol ambushed and killed Samuel Gai Tut on his way to a peace meeting in Ethiopia. To show what became of those who failed to submit to Garang, Kerubino allegedly ordered his men to give the Nuer's body eighty lashes every day until it decomposed. Meanwhile the SPLA killed many Nuer who remained in rebel training camps as suspected traitors. In retaliation, the Nuer inside Sudan massacred thousands of Dinka youths who happened to be passing through Nuerland on their way to join the SPLA in Ethiopia.

Later that same year Benjamin Bol, a popular Dinka politician whom Riek had known in London, disappeared in Ethiopia, allegedly after a violent disagreement with Garang. In England Bol's wife asked that British anthropologist John Ryle try to find out what had happened to him. On behalf of the SPLA, Riek came to see Ryle at his hotel in Addis. He told Ryle that Bol had died of natural causes. Riek later told me that when he relayed Ryle's inquiries about Bol to Garang, "I was told the man had died of liver failure, which was rubbish." But if Riek knew it was rubbish at the time, he failed to tell Ryle.

In 1985 Garang finally sent Riek to the border for military training in the refugee camps at Gambella. After he was finished, the SPLA leader gave him command of a brigade of three thousand troops and told him to march with them more than a thousand miles to the Nuba Mountains in southern Kordofan. "I had to manage how to walk with them, how to feed them, all that," Riek remembered. For the first time, he said, his studies in management and strategic planning came in handy. While troops of other commanders starved to death, Riek managed to keep his alive.

The Nuba were one of the African groups in the north who felt exploited by the Arab government. In the years since oil was discovered on the part of their homeland bordering Nuer-Dinka territory, the Baggara had grown increasingly bold about attacking Nuba villages. The government had also seized large portions of their communal lands and given it to Arab landowners to run commercial farms on it. Riek and his men captured some Baggara *murahaleen,* then used them to negotiate a local peace. Later he agreed to let Baggara chiefs graze their animals on Nuer territory as long they paid tribute to his SPLA. In this way, he saved western Upper Nile from the worst of the Baggara raiding that led to the 1988 famine in Bahr el-Ghazal. In 1986 Riek's forces captured his hometown of Ler. He set up his administration there.

When the SPLA captured an area, it immediately proclaimed itself to be the government. The local rebel commander claimed the right to tax the local people, to fine them, and to settle their disputes. In theory, Riek and his fellow commanders were supposed to rule according to the SPLA military code. In practice, they could do whatever they wanted so long as they maintained control of their area for the SPLA. Garang favored educated men like Riek, but the people at home sometimes were not as impressed as the SPLA leader with the bull-boys and their degrees. As a man told the anthropologist Sharon Hutchinson, men who had not been cut "were not fully, 100 percent Nuer." In the nineteenth century, Ngundeng, the most famous of Nuerland's prophets, had warned the Nuer that one day "black *Turuk*" would come to rule over them. The Nuer had first identified the British government-appointed chiefs as black *Turuk*. Now they saw the SPLA and its bull-boys as the latest fulfillment of the prophecy.

The political philosophies Riek had learned at school meant nothing to the average Nuer, who was preoccupied with the workings of the supernatural. Even to Riek, concepts like "constitution" and "free market economics" began to seem more and more abstract. The SPLA's power grew out of the gun, a *Turuk* thing. "Whatever we want to create in town, that has no roots," Riek later said ruefully. "Maybe after generations it will have roots. But for we, the village children, from village schools, what we have acquired in towns, it's just a beginning."

Riek saw himself as a philosopher-king, bringing enlightenment to his people. Many southerners, especially the chiefs the SPLA was displacing, saw him and the rest of the rebels as a new group of oppressors, in their own way just as bent on destroying Nuer culture as the northerners were in theirs. "The SPLA was led by unmarked guys," a Nuer teacher from Waat told me. "They were forming a system which was unknown to the people. They had no respect for people. The Nuer were being forced to join them.... They would prefer to be the way they are." In Britain, Riek had always made light of his descent from a warrior-prophet. Back in Sudan he began to draw on this spiritual authority. He told Sharon Hutchinson that when he outlawed the *gaar* as well as the traditional extraction of children's lower incisors (thought to keep them from looking like hyenas), the prophets of western Upper Nile warned him that "our gods will reject this law." Riek retorted that he knew more than they did about the gods: "I told them that I am part of the gods since I am one of their descendants and this is my word!"

He used his religious authority to undermine the Nuer spiritual beliefs that dissuaded his soldiers from attacking fellow Nuer who disobeyed the SPLA. Before the coming of outsiders, the Nuer fought with spears and clubs. They believed that when a Nuer man killed another with his *wut*, or fighting spear, a mystical bond was forged between the slayer and the slain. As Hutchinson has written, the "embittered" blood of the slain was thought to enter the slayer at the moment of death. If he ate or drank before going through a ritual designed to release this "blood of vengeance," he was sure to die of a highly dangerous and contagious form of pollution known as *nueer*. Even after the slayer was cleansed of *nueer*, a "bone" was said to lie between his family and that of the slain, preventing them from eating or having sex with each other "forever." By paying blood-wealth and carrying out special ceremonies of atonement, the slayer's family might persuade the family of the victim to call off active vengeance. But the bone itself could not be removed. It existed as long as it was remembered. Evans-Pritchard called *nueer* "the most important of Nuer sin concepts."

The coming of guns had clouded these ethical rules. "Whereas the power of a spear issues directly from the bones and sinews of the person who hurls it, that of a gun is eerily internal to it," Hutchinson writes. "Not only were bullets (*dei mac*, literally, 'a gun's calves') more prone to unintentional release, but having been fired their trajectories—and hence fatal consequences—were often difficult if not impossible to trace accurately." Until Riek and the SPLA appeared, the Nuer of western Upper Nile had settled the issue by treating the victims of gunfire like those killed by lightning. Their kinsmen bought ghost wives for them and had children with the ghost wives, so that the dead men could live through their children. They offered cattle sacrifices in their honor, but they did not engage in feuds with their killers.

Riek decided he had to disabuse his men of these beliefs. Violent deaths associated with the civil war, he told the people, had no spiritual consequences. There was no need, he argued, for his men to undergo the bloodletting ritual designed to cleanse them of *nueer*, whether they killed with guns or with spears. Nor was there any need for them to provide the dead with ghost wives. Hutchinson, who talked with him about it, worried that Riek's radical notions were undermining some of the strongest moral ideas uniting the Nuer.

The Nuer style of decision making is very lengthy and cumbersome. If one man proposes a course of action, all the other men have a right to discuss it or make their own proposals. Each man must be allowed to talk for as long as he likes, and sometimes their speeches go on for hours. They talk about the cattle of their youth, the sayings of the prophets, what they had for dinner yesterday, and whatever else comes into their heads. If any man feels belittled or slighted in the tiniest way, the entire project falls to pieces and may actually erupt into fighting. Very few outsiders have the patience to sit through an entire Nuer meeting. But Riek was a master at orchestrating such events. He would listen with seeming attentiveness to the most interminable speeches, smile pleasantly at the worst blowhards, and slowly, slowly nudge the group in his direction until, at last, feeling their pride satisfied, they would go along with what he wanted in the first place. "He doesn't talk waving his finger," one Nuer man explained to me. "Riek is good and peaceful—he doesn't want to kill anyone."

At meeting after endless meeting, Riek told the Nuer that it made no sense for them to go on fighting each other. A bone lay between the Nuer of Anyanya II and Garang. But Riek also was Nuer, and he, not Garang, was in charge of the SPLA in western Upper Nile. In 1987 several key Nuer politicians switched to the SPLA side. In March 1988 the Anyanya II leader Major General Gordon Kong joined the SPLA, bringing with him two-thirds of Anyanya II's forces. The reconciliation was announced on SPLA radio with a song the prophet Ngungdeng was supposed to have sung:

Nuer and Dinka
Even if you hate yourselves
There will come a time when you will recognize me as your father.

As part of the agreement, the Nuer commanders Kong and Riek were made alternate—but not permanent—members of the SPLA's High Command. The reconciliation had an immediate effect on the proposed oil development. Acknowledging the impossibility of continuing its work in the face of unified Nuer opposition, Chevron began dismantling its rigs at the Unity field near Bentiu in 1988. In early 1989 the towns of Nasir, Waat, and Akobo fell to the rebels. With the exception of the towns of Bentiu and Malakal, the better part of eastern Upper Nile lay in SPLA hands. A large part of the credit for the victory was due to Riek. He was given sole command of northern and western Upper Nile and its more than a million inhabitants. His troops had killed thousands of people, but he had unified and organized the Nuer. His men began to talk about another prophecy they attributed to Ngungdeng. They said Ngungdeng had foretold that an "unmarked man would come from the west to lead you"; some versions had it that the unmarked man would be left-handed. Riek was unscarified and left-handed, and he came from western Upper Nile. People began to say that perhaps he was the Nuer savior Ngungdeng had predicted.

After four years in the bush, Riek was ready for a break. Angelina's distant cousin Lam Akol had replaced Dr. Justin Yaac in Nairobi as the SPLA's head of external relations for the rebels. In the fall of 1989, Lam offered to arrange for Riek to visit Angelina and the children in England for the first time since 1984. By the time her husband returned to Kenya later in 1989, Angelina was pregnant with their third child. A few weeks later, Riek met Emma at the Pan Afric Hotel.

Chapter Sixteen

*R*IEK HAD BEEN AWAY too long to let his marriage vows stop him from embarking on a romance with a bewitching young aid worker. Other, more secret considerations presented a bigger obstacle. Riek and several other SPLA commanders were getting restive with John Garang. The world was changing, and Garang didn't seem to be keeping up. The Soviet Union had collapsed. Communism was dissolving in Eastern Europe. The Soviet-backed regime of the SPLA's protector, Colonel Mengistu, was about to fall, too. Whole Ethiopian battalions were surrendering to the Eritrean and Tigrean rebels; in the southern part of the country, the Oromo Liberation Front was attacking the SPLA refugee camps. All three anti-Mengistu groups were backed by the Sudanese government. The southern Sudanese rebels were in danger of losing their Ethiopian safe havens as well as their major supplier.

Sudan's new fundamentalist government had made statements suggesting that its leaders might be willing to end the war by letting the south secede. That way, the Islamists said, the Muslim majority in the north would have a free hand to establish *sharia*. But Garang refused to test their offer. The old revolutionary didn't seem to have a plan to deal with the present situation. Instead he kept repeating the same tired slogans about fighting on to free the whole of Sudan for secular democracy. Garang's officers began to ask themselves if he really believed what he said about fighting for as long as it took to make the *jallaba* give up their dream of an Islamic state. All the old talk began to circulate again about how Garang was a pampered exile who didn't understand Sudan. Some went so far as to say that he preferred to keep the war going rather than submit to democracy himself in an independent south.

Lam Akol, the SPLA "foreign minister," first brought these rumblings to Riek's attention when Riek arrived in Addis Ababa on his way to London. Lam talked Riek and two other commanders into asking Garang to call a meeting of the SPLA's High Command. Lam was vague about exactly what they wanted to say to Garang. "We told him that the [Berlin] Wall had fallen," he told me later. "We just told him in general terms that we need to review policy, that we saw mistakes." Riek said they asked Garang to clarify what they were fighting for. "The SPLA did not have a conception of what the struggle was about. It was not clear if our main issue is *sharia* or oil or water or the formation of political parties or learning Arabic, or are we really saying we don't want Islam." In effect, the commanders asked Garang to spell out an endgame for the war.

Garang was not pleased. Lam and Riek agree that previously he would have had them both shot. But with Mengistu growing weaker by the day, the SPLA leader could no longer rely on Ethiopian security to do his bidding. Instead he started a whispering campaign among the SPLA against Riek and Lam. "He started saying things like 'They said all the prisoners must be released,' " Lam recalled. "And people were saying to us, 'That's irresponsible—you must be mad.' When in fact all we had asked was for investigation and trial of those being held." By the time he reached London, Riek was talking openly about his resentment of Garang's overbearing ways.

His old friend Tiny Rowland was also getting impatient with Garang. When I asked Rowland why he had soured on the rebel leader, he brushed off the suggestion that it had to do with money. "The business side of it isn't what interests me," he boomed across the international telephone line. "It's the people that interest me. I was going to bring Garang in. I told him, 'You've got to make peace. You're getting to be an old man.' " But Rowland knew very well that anyone who could obtain a political settlement in Upper Nile that would allow oil exploration to resume would be guaranteed a hefty reward. The Islamic government had said it would be willing to let the south separate in return for peace. According to Rowland's biographer, Tom Bower, Rowland made at least two attempts in 1989 to bring President Omar Bashir and Garang together to negotiate a settlement. But Garang maintained that Bashir and his allies couldn't be trusted. Rowland put Riek up in the Metropole's presidential suite, with room service and an international telephone line to use to his heart's content. When Riek returned to Nairobi, it was an open secret among the rebels that he and Garang had fallen out.

For one night he cast aside such intrigues to stay with Emma at the Pan Afric. The next day he was off to Zaire, where the SPLA and the government were holding peace talks under the auspices of the U.S. State Department. The talks broke down when the government refused to agree to hold a convention to write a national constitution based on "multipary democracy" and to withdraw from garrison towns in the areas the rebels occupied north of the Bahr el-Ghazal, Bahr el-Arab, and Sobat rivers—including the oil fields across the river from Bentiu at Pariang and Unity. When Riek returned, Garang dispatched him to the remote Melut area near Malakal. For seven months, he and Emma had no contact. "I used to ask about her at the SPLA office in Nairobi, if they had seen Emma, and if she was asking after me, but no one wanted to put us in touch," he later told her friend the journalist Madeleine Bunting. "A white woman and an SPLA commander were not supposed to have contact."

Naturally Emma, besotted, thought that she was the issue. All that year she found excuses to fly to places where the Nuer commander was rumored to be, but by the time she got there, he was always gone. She wrote Riek letters, but received no reply. She mooned to her girlfriends about him, telling Bernadette that the commander of Upper Nile "awed" her. Even Kuol Manyang knew about her crush on Riek Machar. One day Bernadette and Emma were driving back to Bor from Kapoeta. A couple of teenage SPLA soldiers armed with AK-47s stopped them on the road. The soldiers roughly demanded their travel permits and told them they were under arrest. "Your permits are invalid," they announced. The charge was ridiculous; Bernadette and Emma burst into nervous laughter. Finally they convinced the soldiers to check with a higher authority while they waited in the Land Cruiser. Bernadette remembers that "Emma was smoking herself to death. She kept saying, 'This is Kuol Manyang. He just wants to get me.'" The soldiers eventually released them, but Emma told her friend that Kuol was giving her a hard time because he knew she was soft on Riek.

At the end of May 1990, the Mossad asked Tiny Rowland to help negotiate a release of two Israeli agents captured in the Ethiopian refugee camps and marked for execution by the Sudanese government. Rowland met with President Bashir and managed to get the pair released. Rowland never said what he promised Bashir in return for the spies, but he suggested that it had something to do with Israel's cutting off its support for the SPLA. "President Bashir knew I was anxious to negotiate a peace settlement between his government and the south," he said coyly. "He is a friend, and he knew he could trust me." Many Sudanese believe that Rowland decided at this time to back a coup against Garang as a means of forcing the SPLA leader to make peace with Bashir's government.

Lam and Riek started canvassing fellow officers to see if they would support an attempt to overthrow Garang. In December 1990 Lam flew into Addis Ababa and asked Peter Adwok Nyaba, a fellow Shilluk SPLA officer, to meet him alone. "After exchanging greetings, I could notice that Lam was warm, very excited, in high spirits," Nyaba wrote later. Lam came straight to the point. "Garang has taken us all for a ride," he told Nyaba. "He has proved to be a dictator. Time has come that he must be told that enough is enough." Nyaba, a geologist who resented Garang because the rebel leader had sidelined him after he was crippled by a wound, promised to rally Shilluk support for the plot. Nyaba writes that Lam had envisioned himself as the leader of the coup, but Nyaba talked him into making Riek the leader instead in a bid for Nuer support.

A year after his meeting with Emma, Riek ran into the British writer John Ryle in Nasir. Ryle had come to write a report for Save the Children–UK. Riek said nothing to Ryle about the occasion of their last meeting, the murder of the politician Benjamin Bol. Instead he asked whether Ryle knew an aid worker called Emma McCune. As it happened, Save the Children was financing part of the schools program, and Emma and Ryle had driven down to Kenya from Kapoeta together a few weeks earlier. When Ryle admitted that he did know Emma, Riek asked him to take her a message. Ryle flew out of Nasir carrying a four-line letter from Riek on official SPLA paper. The letter invited Emma to come to Nasir to discuss "educational problems pertaining to the Zones under my command."

Emma caught a UN flight to Nasir as soon as she got Riek's message. But by the time the plane landed, Riek had disappeared again on another mysterious errand. The disappointment was crushing. After several days of waiting, she returned to Nairobi, where she furiously scanned the SPLA radio frequencies for news that he had come back to Nasir. At last Riek sent a message by radio that he had returned. She flew back up to Loki. But by this time, the government had slapped a flight ban on Nasir. Three times Emma was scheduled to fly out. Three times the flight was cancelled. Wild with frustration, she turned to Willy Knocker with an audacious plan.

She and Willy had never stopped seeing each other. Only recently he had asked her again to marry him. Now she pleaded with him to drive with her to Nasir, telling him that he must help her obey the summons of the SPLA zonal commander—the whole future of the children of Upper Nile could depend on it! The good road the aid workers used to drive up from Kenya ended at Kapoeta. Nasir was three hundred miles northwest of Kapoeta through the swamps. The dirt tracks leading to the former garrison town had been mined so extensively in the early years of the civil war that no one had attempted to drive there for years. To try it was insanity, but this is what Emma persuaded Willy to do. Perhaps he was tempted by the adventure, or perhaps he thought his show of courage might finally win her over. In any event, he agreed to take her.

They set off from Kapeota in his Land Rover, driving northwest through Bor. They passed great open savannahs where giraffes grazed with antelopes and gazelles. They camped and made love under the brilliant twinkling of the stars. Perhaps to Willy it was beginning to seem like the "best safari ever" that Emma's mother says her daughter promised him when she lured him on this journey. But soon after they crossed into Nuerland, things began going wrong. Outside the Lou Nuer town of Waat, they came to the little Nuer village of Weideang. Weideang was the site of the great mound of Ngungdeng. Back in the 1890s, the prophet had fallen into a trance in which his divinity ordered him to command the Nuer to build an enormous mound and bury all the evils of the world in it. It took hundreds of workers four years to construct the mound. When it was finished, it stood sixty feet high and was decorated with elephant tusks. To the east of it was a large fig tree that Ngungdeng named the Tree of Good Things, while he called a tree to the west the Tree of Bad Things. In 1928 the British bombed and machine-gunned that Ngungdeng's mound to punish the prophet's son, who was also possessed by divinity, for rebelling against the colonial government. They killed Ngungdeng's son and left his body hanging from the Tree of Bad Things. For fifty years, the mound lay abandoned. But since the SPLA had occupied the area, worshipers had rebuilt it and adorned it with elephant tusks to replace the ones stolen by the British. Emma and Willy left packets of salt on the mound, but their offering did not bring them luck. Past Weideang, they got lost in an acacia forest. It took them three days to hack their way out and reach the Sobat. When they waded across the river, Riek was waiting for them at Ulang. He said theirs was the first car to make it there in eight years.

Riek took one look at Willy, turned to Emma, and asked, "Why have you brought him with you?"

She sent Willy back across the river to tinker with the Land Rover.

Riek invited Emma into his *tukul*. Sitting her down on a rope bed, he told her why he had invited her to come. After their meeting at the Pan Afric, he said, he had started thinking about what she had said about the boys in Ethiopia. In April he had had a meeting with Garang. He had asked Garang if it was true that the children's camps at Panyido and elsewhere were really recruitment centers. "Why are the children being militarily trained?" he said he had asked. Garang had replied that the boys who succeeded at military training would go on to school. In the meantime, the boys in the camps were the SPLA's reserve manpower for the future.

Riek told Emma that he didn't like Garang's answer.

After his meeting with Garang, he had gone to Itang. There he had told the Nuer administrator of the camp to stop the military training of children. Riek boasted that the administrator had obeyed his orders even though he was an ardent Garang supporter. There it was. That was why he had summoned Emma: to tell her he had stopped the training that bothered her so much. He also wanted her to know that she was welcome to begin working with him and the SRRA to open schools not just in Nasir but in the whole of Upper Nile.

Emma was overjoyed. This man—this hero!—she later told friends proudly, had taken her fears, her suspicions, about the children and actually confronted the all-powerful SPLA leader with them. And when Garang admitted that the children were being trained, he dared to give orders to put a stop to it. By taking her worries to Riek, she felt, she had achieved more for the child soldiers of southern Sudan than Operation Lifeline had in months of demarches. This brave, sensitive rebel commander gave her hope for the future of this tragic country. Or so ran Emma's thoughts as she contemplated Riek's news.

For the next two days, she and Riek remained closeted in his *tukul* while Willy camped in the Land Rover. When the time came for Emma to leave, Riek sat her down again. He has a habit of looking straight into the eyes of his visitors. This time he must have regarded Emma for a few minutes before he began. He asked her if she knew about Ngungdeng's mound and the Nuer tradition of prophecy.

She said she knew a little about it.

Did she know that it had been foretold that one day an unmarked, left-handed Nuer chief would marry a white woman?

She didn't.

With his left hand, Riek reached for Emma's hand. "I am that man," he told her. "Will you be that woman?"

She later said she felt stricken, as if fate had pointed its finger at her. But she did not give in to her feelings right away. She told him she would think about it.

She was silent for much of the journey back from Nasir. Between Riek's tale of prophecy and his account of ordering the camp commander to disband the training of boy soldiers, she had a feeling that destiny was calling her to him. When she and Willy reached Kongor and started making their camp, she curtly informed him that she had something to say. She didn't love him anymore, she announced. She was in love with Riek.

RIEK DIDN'T MENTION prophecy when I asked him how he proposed to Emma. (I later heard the tale of the unmarked, left-handed chief from her awestruck girlfriends, to whom she related it.) Other educated Nuer snickered when I asked them if they had ever heard of a prediction that a Nuer chief was to marry a white woman. "Riek may have said it, but there is no such prophecy," one Nuer told me when I kept asking about it. Sally Dudmesh, whom Emma told all about Riek's proposal, thought it was love, plain and simple, that drew Emma and Riek together: "She just adored being with him." An American journalist, male, who knew them both well said it was sex: "Riek was a big sexual powerhouse." Liz Hodgkin said Emma told her she sometimes asked herself whether she would have fallen in love with Riek if he weren't an "important person." "I think she wanted to be an empress," said another British confidante of Emma's. An SPLA comrade of Riek's cited their common interests in computers and pop music. When I asked Riek why he wanted to marry Emma, he acted as if the question was too obvious to bother answering. Raising an eyebrow, he laughed out loud. "What are the reasons that a man marries a woman?" Riek cried, throwing up his hands at yet another piece of *khawaja* obtuseness.

Part Four

"They call it 'my war,'" Man Gac told me, *"that I brought it, but there was nothing that I spoiled, which I can find in my head, which I can think of. There is nothing which I spoiled that I know."*

—Eleanor Vandevort, *A Leopard Tamed,* 1968

Chapter Seventeen

MMA INFORMED the coordinator of programs at Operation Lifeline that she would be moving to Nasir. He was disappointed
and puzzled. She had been doing such good work in Kapoeta
that it seemed a shame to leave. But Emma argued passionately that by
going to Upper Nile, she might open schools that would save thousands
of boys from being forced to join the rebel army. Reluctantly the coordinator agreed to let her try. The rains had just begun when the UN plane
dropped her off near the ruins of the American Presbyterian mission, a
little ways downstream from where Gordon's lieutenant Nasir Ali had
waged his war against slavery.

The area had been open to foreigners only a short time, and it retained
a stunned, dreamlike quality, as if it had not quite awakened from the isolation and violence of the previous six years. Already strange things had
started happening to the *khawajas* there. An overweight American nurse
paddling in a dugout back to Nasir from vaccinating some villages on the
Sobat came down with grievous stomach pains. The nurse's cramps were
so agonizing that her worried colleagues steered the canoe to the riverbank to see what they could do. To their amazement—and evidently to
hers—she gave birth there in the mud to a baby boy. The distraught aid
workers managed to get nurse and baby back to Nasir, where they radioed
for an airplane. By the looks of the baby, his father must have been
Sudanese. But the nurse never told anyone the father's name, and she
insisted she had not known she was pregnant. After recuperating in
Nairobi Hospital, she took the baby to America. Later she returned to
Africa on her own.

The incident reminded some of another ill-fated romance between a white woman and a southern Sudanese man at Nasir. In the 1920s the first single white woman sent to the American Presbyterian mission had made the mistake of encouraging a young Shilluk convert to woo her with poems and songs and maybe more. In the Sudanese view, the match had much to recommend it. For a start, it offered the Americans the entrée they claimed to want into southern Sudanese society. But the colonial and missionary authorities were horrified. Declaring the woman insane, the American mission shipped her off to Switzerland. Her lover was taken to Malakal and clapped into prison. Years later I found a note from a British administrator in the Rhodes Library at Oxford making derisive reference to the incident: "Miss T.'s swain is languishing in the Malakal prison. The Americans are saying she was sent to them from a foster home—as if that were an explanation for idling with a naked savage."

I first heard of the wayward missionary girl from James Mut Kueth, Nasir's gentle young Presbyterian minister, when I visited Nasir at the end of 1990. I had made the mistake of bringing some Cadbury chocolate bars with me to Nasir. Of course the chocolate was already melting by the time the plane landed. A gaggle of children had gathered to see what the sky canoe was bringing this time. I tried to give them the candy bars, but they hung back, looking fearfully at the oil-stained purple packages. Finally Reverend Kueth came over to see what the commotion was about. The minister confessed that no one in Nasir had ever seen a chocolate bar before. The children looked at him expectantly. Obviously they felt it was his pastoral duty to test these foreign objects. Summoning his courage, Reverend Kueth unwrapped a Dairy Milk bar and took a nibble. As twenty pairs of eyes watched, he slowly let the chocolate melt in his mouth, then swallowed it.

We waited.

He licked his lips and swallowed again. Finally he gave his opinion of chocolate: "It is sweet—like the onion."

Reverand Kueth had the six parallel scars of *gaar* across his forehead, but as a Christian minister he was still a black *Turuk*. He went around buttoned up in a pair of baby-blue cotton men's pajamas with navy blue piping, and he lived with his family in the cracked and roofless concrete house that had once belonged to the American missionaries. I often sat on his veranda, waiting for the rebels to take me somewhere and watching the palette of the river and the floodplain change with the hours of the day. Early in the morning, the sky drenched the river in blue, and the long grasses of the plain turned a pale, limpid green. As the day grew hotter, the blue heavens would fade to a hard white, the river would go gray-green and the grass a stunted brown. Late in the afternoon, flickers of orange began dancing across the plain, and the reflection of the sun in the river made it look as if a fire were burning underneath the water. At last the blaze would darken to purple, and for a shimmering half hour or so, the whole landscape was bathed in the most unearthly shades of lavender and violet. I have never seen anything more gorgeous than the sunsets at Nasir.

It was just a mysteriously beautiful landscape to me, but Reverend Kueth told me local people saw more than natural splendor when they looked at the river. The Jikany Nuer, he said, believed that the mother of God lived at the bottom of the river. To them the white pelicans, crested cranes, speckled vultures, and thousands of other big birds who fed off the river symbolized Kwoth, or "Spirit," the omnipotent God whom the Nuer said was like the wind or the air—everywhere but invisible. Sitting there on Reverend Kueth's veranda, time felt as flat and still as the plain spread out before us. And I couldn't help thinking about how some of the oldest human fossils had been found just a few hundred miles south of here in Kenya. The minister told me the Nuer believed the Tree from Which Mankind Was Born still stood in another part of southern Sudan.

He added that southern Sudan was part of the Biblical Garden of Eden.

I raised my eyebrows.

Oh yes, the minister said, picking up the King James Bible in his lap and turning to Genesis 2. See, it is written here that the garden is watered by four rivers.

He put his finger on the page and read aloud. "The first is Pison: that is it which compasseth the whole land of Havilah, where there is gold...." You know that we have gold in southern Sudan, he said. Well, Pison is the White Nile. "And the name of the second river is Gihon: the same is it that compasseth the whole land of Ethiopia." Gihon is the Blue Nile, which comes out of Ethiopia.

He chuckled softly to himself. Yes, he said, closing the Bible and leaning back in his plastic chair to look out again at the Sobat, we are here in the Garden of Eden.

I was no Biblical scholar, and Nasir certainly didn't look like Paradise to me. But it was easy to imagine that mankind might have first tasted sin and death here. I quipped that Nasir certainly had enough poisonous snakes to qualify for the garden. In the space of a few days, I had seen two black mambas and our translator had warned Frank and me not to go outside at night for fear of stepping on a puff adder.

Reverend Kueth nodded seriously.

That is why we believed the missionaries when they first told us about how the serpent tempted Eve. We Nuer have always known that snakes contained divinity. That is why we don't like to kill them.

It was so still and silent in Nasir that one could almost forget the war that had brought all of us here. I sometimes felt as if I might doze off listening to the platitudes Lul and the other SPLA officers mouthed when I asked them why they were fighting. We all thought that the future oil revenues must be the movement's hidden objective, but if it was, we could never get the SPLA cadres to admit it. Yes, we are fighting for the oil, they would say. And then they would go on. We are fighting for all the riches of the south! We are fighting for education! We are fighting because the Arabs will not let us develop! We are fighting for Jesus! I felt that the northerners had a better idea what they wanted out of this war. At a village on the Sobat called Rok-Rok, I met a Nuer man who told me he knew why the army razed his village of Toryat, shot his brother, and drove his family of fourteen off their land. He said they were greedy for the oil underneath it. "The *jallaba* are wanting the oil," he said. "If the *jallaba* go away from there, we shall be rich."

There was an air of expectancy about Nasir, as if everyone was waiting for something to happen. Reverend Kueth showed me the biblical passage from Isaiah that he said the American missionaries had taught the Nuer pertained to them: "Woe to the land shadowing with wings, which lies beyond the rivers of Ethiopia...." He explained that the "swift messengers" whom Isaiah said would come to a "nation scattered and peeled" were the missionaries. He said that God had doomed the Nuer and the other southern Sudanese to war and famine because they did not convert quickly or completely enough. He said he had seen the prophecy come to pass in the years before the SPLA won Nasir. "Here Isaiah is saying there should be great hunger and birds and the animals of the forest should feed on the bodies of the people. All of this I have seen. Even the dead bodies were floating on this river, the bodies were just floating. You could see the body of a big man, and you would see that it was eaten by vultures. Even you are almost to cry. But Isaiah says it is not the end of the world. It is not doomsday.

"Jesus is our doctor from God. If all of us, we had faith in God, we couldn't get diseases, we would have the clothes. Now we have all of these problems. If we had faith in God, we would have no problems on earth."

A few days after that, I met Emma just as I was leaving Nasir. She had flown up on one of her failed attempts to find Riek, who was away at the front in Malakal. Already she seemed strangely at home in Nasir, and though I couldn't have explained why, I envied her for it.

Chapter *Eighteen*

EWER AND FEWER *khawajas* of any description were staying in
Sudan. It was as if the colonial period had been the high point of
a Western tide that was now flowing back out to sea; all of the
Western money and people that had washed into Africa earlier in the
century were now receding, exposing the shipwrecks and flotsam left
behind. In August 1990 Iraq's president, Saddam Hussein, had invaded
Kuwait. Kuwait and neighboring Saudi Arabia called on the United
States for help. The United States began assembling a huge army in
Saudi Arabia. Washington gave Saddam Hussein an ultimatum: Either
pull out of Kuwait before January 16, 1991, or face the consequences. To
the fury of the Saudis and the Americans, Sudan's Islamist government
took Iraq's side against the coalition. Hassan al-Turabi argued that it was
a sacrilege for the Saudi royal family to invite unbelievers to defend the
holy land of the prophet Muhammad. According to Quranic precept, he
said, Muslims should settle the dispute between Iraq and Kuwait among
themselves.

The United States and the European Community responded by cutting off what little nonhumanitarian assistance Sudan was still getting. At
the same time Western aid officials warned that a new famine was brew-
ing in the western part of the country. An Ethiopian who worked for
Operation Lifeline told me, "Another Christmas, another famine. I think
that in the future, the main contact between this region and the outside
world is going to be famine." The Sudanese government claimed that the
West was just trying to use a temporary "food gap" to embarrass Sudan
for its friendliness to Iraq. But since the Sudanese government would not

give me permission to travel in Darfur and Kordofan, I could not say whether they were telling the truth. For all of us *khawajas* in Khartoum, that Christmas season passed like a kind of hallucination: waiting for war to break out in the Gulf, wondering how many Sudanese were starving in the west, unable to do anything about either one.

Turabi's defiant stance in favor of secular Iraq was all the more perplexing because everyone knew that the NIF government depended on its wealthy Islamist backers in Saudi Arabia and other Gulf states. I was at the time busy writing a profile of one of Turabi's followers, an amiable young fundamentalist named Kamal el-Din. "But Saddam Hussein is a bad Muslim," I kept saying to Kamal. Usually, Kamal would brush such questions aside with a friendly smile. "Don't worry, there won't be any war." But once he said, "The Saudi royal family is worse than Saddam. At least Saddam admits to being a bad Muslim. The al-Sauds pretend to be the leaders of the whole Islamic world, when actually they are just a bunch of hypocrites."

But what will you do if the Saudis and the Kuwaitis cut off aid to Sudan—or worse yet, expel all the Sudanese working in their countries? I persisted.

"We shall have to depend on Allah," Kamal answered.

Kamal seemed to live in a world of visions and nightmares I couldn't see. "We are not yet living in an Islamic paradise, but we are moving toward one," he would say dreamily. I would think of Sudan's floggings and amputations, about the war and the famine, and shake my head. Or he would rant against the danger the West presented to Sudan with its sexual permissiveness. As if sex were Sudan's problem! But I felt sure the shrewd and practical Turabi never would have taken such a risky stand against the Saudis without something up his sleeve.

I decided to interview the finance minister, one of Turabi's closest associates and a co-founder of the Faisal Islamic Bank. Abdel Rahman Hamdi kept his office in the white Ottoman-style presidential palace with the green shutters that the British had built on the ruins of Gordon's palace. Hamdi told me his family had come to Sudan from Egypt under the Turco-Egyptian regime in the nineteenth century. He was an imposing man with a long nose, wire-rimmed glasses, and clever, heavy-lidded eyes. He greeted me in a spotless white cotton *jallabiya* and skullcap. After some desultory talk about the food gap—"they are an industry, these NGOs, and they benefit from our suffering"—and the Saudis—"we are a government of principle and in this case we will have to stand on principle"—I asked him what he thought it would take to end the war in the south. "We've told John Garang we are ready to talk," the minister said. "Everything is on the table except *sharia*."

But *sharia* is exactly what John Garang says must be on the table if the south is to remain part of Sudan, I said. The south is not Muslim and does not wish to live under *sharia*.

Hamdi waved his hands dismissively. "He can have the south if he wants the south," he said.

Really, I said. I had never before heard a Sudanese government official come out and say the north would be willing to let the south go its own way. There was a large map of Sudan on the wall behind the minister. I pointed to it. Where would you draw the line between the north and the south?

Hamdi stood up. With a quick, deliberate motion of his finger, he drew a horizontal line across the map. But the line he drew did not follow the old boundary between north and south along the Bahr el-Arab and Bahr el-Ghazal rivers. It was a couple of inches south of that boundary—just below the oil fields. His nerve was breathtaking.

But that leaves the oil fields out of the south, I protested.

Hamdi gave me an almost impish smile and sighed. "Yes," he said, and he sat down heavily in a big leather chair. "That's a problem.

"We want Chevron to resume their work, and they are very luke-warm," the minister continued. "They had some people shot, but that is not the real reason they haven't come back. They had twenty people shot in Angola, and they are still there. No, it is something else.... The Americans, the British, they are actually fighting us. But that doesn't matter. There are other companies who are interested. We are talking to them."

But surely no company will agree to drill so long as the war goes on, I persisted.

"By any sensible standard, this war should be stopped," Hamdi agreed. "Personal and political greed is all that stands between us and peace. John Garang doesn't want to settle for the south. He wants to be the supreme leader of Sudan. But the politics of this country will never allow him to be the supreme leader, for the same reason"—the minister smiled confidingly, and leaned forward, as if he were inviting me to join a club of plain-speakers—"that Jesse Jackson will never be the supreme leader of the U.S.A."

He sighed again. "But the southerners will not admit this. They have a dream which blinds them to the situation, and they just go on fighting against all the odds. Well, some of them know better. We are talking to them. John Garang does not have everyone in the south. There are the Nuer."

I assumed he was talking about the government-allied Nuer militia, Anyanya II, and changed the subject. It was only much later that I realized Hamdi had given me my first inkling of what the government had planned for the south.

THE AMERICAN EMBASSY put out a warning that if Saddam Hussein failed to respond to Washington's ultimatum and the United States was forced to bomb Iraq, Americans and Europeans might be in danger in Sudan. The U.S. ambassador pointed out that terrorist groups from all over the Middle East had found a haven in Khartoum. Abu Nidal was there. So were Carlos the Jackal, Hamas, and Hezbollah. Kamal insisted that the United States was exaggerating it all. He waved away the threats against *khawajas*, the food gap in western Sudan, the atrocities the Kuwaitis said the Iraqis had committed. "Why is your government so afraid of Islam?" he would ask me, gently shaking his head in mock disbelief. "There won't be a war with Iraq. And there won't be a famine." A government minister courteously assured me, "Americans and Europeans are perfectly safe in Sudan."

But living at the Acropole, I could not be sure. The court case of the five Palestinians who had bombed the hotel in 1988 had been inching along for two and a half years. In December it reached a climax that seemed to reveal the hostility seething underneath the sly ambiguity of the NIF government's official positions. A year earlier an Islamic judge had offered the families of Chris and Clare Rolfe and a British teacher killed in the attack the same choice they offered the Sudanese victims: either to accept blood money as compensation for the loss of their relatives or to have the bombers executed. To the Sudanese, this seemed a fair choice. To the British parents of pacifist Quakers like the Rolfes, it was intolerable. The British families begged the court to compromise and spend their blood money to keep the bombers in prison. But the Sudanese judge was adamant.

The families of the Sudanese victims chose to take the blood money. (Overnight the supposedly penniless Palestinian refugees whom prosecutors said had carried out the bombing entirely on their own came up with thousands of dollars to pay the families.) The British families, who refused to take it, got nothing. Two days after Christmas, the bombers were released. The court erupted into cheers. The judge himself congratulated the newly freed prisoners on their fortitude.

At the Acropole, we wept. Saddam Hussein refused to withdraw from Kuwait. On January 15 I was evacuated to Kenya along with the rest of the Westerners still remaining in Khartoum. To everyone's surprise, the much-feared war in the Gulf was over in a matter of weeks. Americans were filled with a new confidence; the country seemed to have recovered from the "Vietnam syndrome" that had caused it to avoid foreign entanglements. For the time being, Sudan was forgotten. But Khartoum's decision to side with Saddam Hussein was to have far-reaching consequences—first for southern Sudan, then for the rest of the world.

Sudan's pro-Iraqi stance was the last straw for the American oil company Chevron. With the promise of a tax write-off from the Bush administration, Chevron informed the Sudanese government that it would not be returning to work in Sudan. Meanwhile, in Saudi Arabia and elsewhere, Islamist militants like Osama bin Laden, humiliated and distraught over what they called *al-Azama* ("the crisis" with Iraq), moved to reward Turabi and the NIF for what they saw as their courageous stand against the West and its corrupt Gulf allies. For several years the Sudanese government had been openly calling its war on the south a jihad. At a conference held on April 25, 1991, Turabi invited Islamists from around the world to join him in attacking the wider "crusader-Zionist conspiracy." The Gulf War, the Sudanese leader told his guests, had proved beyond a doubt that conservative Arab regimes like those in Saudi Arabia and Kuwait were nothing more than puppets of the infidel West. The groups assembled for the conference agreed to form a permanent council. Its aim, Turabi said, was "to work out a global action plan in order to challenge and defy the tyrannical West, because Allah can no longer remain in our world, in the face of absolute materialistic power." Veterans of the anti-Soviet war in Afghanistan began pouring into northern Sudan by the hundreds. Bin Laden had been flying in and out of Sudan on his private Gulfstream G-8 jet since 1989. In 1991 he left Saudi Arabia for Khartoum. Turabi welcomed him with a lavish reception, announcing that "the great Islamic investor" would henceforth be a member of the NIF. Bin Laden reciprocated by announcing a $5 million donation to Turabi's party.

Chapter Nineteen

*A*T THE END of May 1991, the top brass at the United Nations' Nairobi campus began receiving a series of urgent messages from Emma in Nasir. As the representative of Street Kids International, Emma was allowed to use the UN radio in emergencies. Like other aid workers, she had been warned to be extremely cautious about what she said, since the Islamic government monitored all radio transmissions in the south. Now, in a sudden barrage of increasingly agitated messages, she reported that hundreds of thousands of hungry Sudanese refugees were fleeing Ethiopia and walking back into southern Sudan. Khartoum, she said, was bombing the refugees as they walked northwest along the Sobat River. Army planes had also bombed Nasir and its hospital on May 14 and again on May 15. Thirty-six people were dead. Dozens more were wounded. Sounding nearly hysterical, she demanded that the UN airlift food and other supplies to Nasir. She even called for the UN to dispatch peacekeeping troops to protect the refugees.

On May 30, according to written transcripts, she radioed: "All refugees have now been evacuated except [those from] Dima. Refugees from Itang have been divided into two groups. A quarter of population have headed for Pochalla. Three quarters are moving toward Nasir.... 500 Uduk arrived at Jekau yesterday they are followed by 50,000 who are coming along the highway. They are expected to arrive Jekau from today. All these people will start arriving Nasir from Saturday. Returnees are not carrying food or belongings due to suddenness of evacuation."

The following day she requested more supplies:

"By 30/5/91, 15,000 refugees reported to have arrived Jekau. Numbers expected to increase rapidly. As yet we have not received any relief supplies at all. Is it not possible to have two flights a day to Nasir so we can get some supplies in before we are swamped. There are some war-wounded reported to be moving with the returnees. Please could they be evacuated once they arrive in Nasir."

A few hours later she radioed again, this time even more urgently:

"50,000 refugees have left Jekau this evening for Nasir expected to arrive Nasir 2/6/91. This is only the first group. 200,000 will follow. Bombardment has caused panic among the refugees. The sooner a political decision is made to protect the refugees the better. Authorities requesting UN peacekeeping force to provide safe haven for refugees in the area. Food situation desperate. Please organize airdrop as there is no food, repeat no food, in Nasir for these people. Please act promptly."

Emma's messages made people at Operation Lifeline furious—furious at her, furious at the SPLA, furious at the Western donors, and furious at themselves. Mengistu had finally fallen on May 21, fleeing the country just as the Ethiopian rebels advanced on Addis Ababa. Although the details were murky, Ethiopia was in chaos, and now it seemed that southern Sudan was, too. For seven years, Mengistu's government had used the SPLA to suppress the local population in Ethiopia's Gambella province. Now the locals were ready to take their revenge against the SPLA and its supporters in the southern Sudanese refugee camps. With help from the Sudanese army, Ethiopia's Oromo Liberation Front attacked the Gambella camp on May 26. The artillery barrages could be heard twenty-five miles away at Itang. Rather than leave the refugees to flee or be massacred, the SPLA decided to evacuate Itang the next day. Other camps were soon to follow. The fall of the Ethiopian dictator ultimately would drive some 350,000 southern Sudanese out of their hiding places in Ethiopia and back into Sudan.

The refugees were marching across the border just as the rains were turning the southern grasslands into a quicksand of mud. Without food or clean drinking water, tens of thousands might die. Vincent O'Reilly, the head of Operation Lifeline's southern sector, and the others at Lifeline did not yet know why the SPLA had ordered the refugees back into Sudan, but they suspected that the rebels simply wanted to keep the civilians and the humanitarian relief they generated under their control. What the rebels did not seem to realize was that once inside southern Sudan, the United Nations could not give away a single bag of grain without Khartoum's say-so. And if the government was already bombing the refugees, it was hardly likely to agree to feed them.

It was a tense moment. Operation Lifeline officials feared that Emma, by using the UN radio to broadcast what sounded like flagrant rebel propaganda, might have doomed what little chance they had of helping the refugees. The officials knew she had to be repeating exactly what the SPLA had told her. There was no way Emma could know, on her own, how many people were gathering a hundred miles away in Jekau, a village on the border with Ethiopia, where they were going, or when they might arrive. Moreover, under international law, the refugees she described were technically no longer "refugees." They included many rebel soldiers and their families, who had had just crossed the border back into their own country. Getting permission from Khartoum to assist them was going to be a nightmare, and they feared Emma was making it worse. As the historian Douglas Johnson, one of those on the receiving end of the messages at the World Food Program, later recalled, "Emma presented the figures as if she had been able to verify them and gave no qualifications of her own (e.g., 'a reported X number,' or 'unverified report of X'). We knew all figures would be disputed (they always were) and it was important to be as careful as possible in reporting from the very start." Johnson and others became even more upset when the Sudanese government started bombing the locations Emma had named in her messages—including spots where she had mistakenly reported refugees—thereby showing that they had been listening to every word she said.

The loss of the SPLA's Ethiopian military bases and supply lines was a tremendous victory for Khartoum and one that it wasn't about to hand away on humanitarian grounds. Operation Lifeline officials feared that Emma's call for a "political solution"—ludicrous as it was, coming from a very junior relief worker with no authority over anyone—would lend credence to Khartoum's persistent suspicions that aid workers in southern Sudan were trying to mobilize the West to intervene militarily on the side of the rebels. The charge had seemed fantastic—until the United States intervened a few months earlier on behalf of the Kurds expelled from Iraq. Since then the rumors had thickened that Washington, swollen with its success in Iraq, was planning something similar for southern Sudan.

Vincent O'Reilly knew nothing about Emma's relationship with Riek, but when he started getting what he later described as "these insane messages from Nasir," he began asking questions. What was she doing in Nasir anyway? Informed that she had moved the Street Kids International office from Kapoeta to Nasir, he sent Emma a stern message that she wasn't authorized to move anywhere and should return to Kapoeta at the earliest opportunity. There had been other complaints about Emma lately—that she was absent from meetings concerning the schools program, and that even before the refugee exodus, she had been using the UN radio to relay messages for the SPLA. O'Reilly later said he did not know what was going on, but he began to suspect there was something "not neutral" about Emma.

O'Reilly and others soon learned, though, that Emma had not exaggerated the magnitude of the disaster. And they could hardly blame her or even the SPLA for the fact that Operation Lifeline was unprepared for the exodus from Ethiopia. The disintegration of the Mengistu government had been evident for months. Riek and other high-ranking SPLA officials had warned Operation Lifeline repeatedly that they intended to close the camps if Mengistu fell. In October 1990 Lifeline officials made plans to send overland convoys to stock the area across the border from Ethiopia with food, seeds, tools, and fishing equipment, but the convoys never left Kenya. Khartoum refused all UN requests to send trucks into southern Sudan during the 1991 dry season. By May the rains had made it impossible for trucks to move. Now the only way to deliver food was by costly and inefficient airlift.

Part of the reason Operation Lifeline had been slow to act was that the United States had balked at providing anything inside the Sudan for the refugees, arguing that it would be better for them to stay in Ethiopia. The United States had backed the victorious Ethiopian rebels against Mengistu. American embassy officials in Addis were busily stage-managing the dictator's departure and the rebel takeover. They insisted that the southern Sudanese would be safe in Ethiopia. Even after the Sudanese had left the camps, U.S. officials in Addis kept disputing reports of the evacuation and the number of people in flight. That spring the U.S. State Department for the first time had allowed a team of officials from Washington to visit rebel-held southern Sudan to assess the humanitarian situation. The Americans flew into Nasir on May 18, in time to be bombed by the government and only days before the deluge from Ethiopia. In Nasir, Tom Brennan, the team leader from the U.S. Agency for International Development, had a strange conversation with Riek that led Riek to conclude, evidently wrongly, that if weren't for Garang, the SPLA would be receiving military assistance from the United States. Brennan also discouraged the rebels from closing down the camps in Ethiopia. Without American support, UN officials hardly thought it worth bothering to try to press Khartoum for permission to start a relief effort inside Sudan.

VINCENT O'REILLY sent Alastair and Patta to Jekau to check out Emma's reports. On May 29, as the Scott-Villierses later wrote in an article for the journal *Disasters,* they stood and watched from the riverbank as fifteen thousand people from Itang camp crossed from Ethiopia into Sudan. The Nuer always described themselves as small black ants (*cok*) in the eyes of God. That day "they actually looked like thousands of ants coming back into Sudan," said Ian Lethbridge, an Australian who worked for UNICEF and went with the Scott-Villierses to Jekau. "It was the most incredible sight." Until three days earlier, Itang had been the biggest refugee camp in Ethiopia and one of the biggest in the world. Now it was deserted. All 150,000 of its mostly Nuer inhabitants were marching north. In the next few weeks, about 130,000 of them would arrive in Nasir.

The SPLA made a film of this exodus. In it you see women at Itang packing up. The camera pans over Itang's schools and shops. The camp looks more permanent and homelike than Nasir or the other ghost towns of southern Sudan. A handsome young SPLA officer in an olive-green uniform and his giggling wife pose in front of the rectangular grass hut that has been their home; a band of grinning boys wearing ragged gym shorts shout excitedly to one another. Chattering women pile huge bundles on their heads, and the whole procession sets off singing. When darkness falls, they make camp beside the Sobat. Small clusters of boys strike up cooking fires. A few days later thousands of people take off their clothes to cross the river. They make rafts out of water hyacinths for those too short or too weak to wade across. On the other side, they crawl up the mud banks of the Sobat. Some children fall back into the water again and again. It happens so many times that you almost think the film is stuck, but no, it was just that bad.

Between Jekau and Nasir, Sudanese planes strafed the refugee columns. Armed bandits stole their pots and clothing. Tarquin Hall, a young British journalist who flew up to Nasir, described the sight of the refugees as they converged on the town. "On the south bank of the Sobat, as far as the eye could see, huddles of dying scrawny people lay about on the cracked, sun-baked earth. Skeleton-like figures crawled across the landscape on all fours, too weak to stand. In order to protect themselves from the sun, the returnees covered their bodies from head to toe in a mixture of ash and mud. The substance turned their skin a deathly gray which made them look like corpses awaiting burial in a mass grave."

Emma's friend Bernadette Kumar was in Bor when O'Reilly radioed her with orders to go to Nasir. The Scott-Villierses, Ian Lethbridge, and Douglas Johnson were already there. The UN workers were soon joined by twenty-odd other expatriates working for a hodgepodge of charities, including some overnight hires such as Patta's younger brother Charles Villiers and Giles Thornton, a young Briton who happened to be touring Africa on a motorbike. The aid workers set up camp in mosquito domes and started organizing the refugees to dig latrines and bury the corpses they found floating in the river. Thousands of refugees squatted along the muddy banks of the river, waiting for food. The dead bodies and the raw sewage from the refugees had contaminated the Sobat. After drinking from it, people started coming down with a deadly variety of diarrhea. Torrents of rain poured over them as they lay in their own excrement. Visiting journalists dubbed the stretch between Nasir and Jekau "the swamps of hell." "The health situation was incredible," Bernadette remembered. "We were wading in mud. There was no clean water, no latrines. We were facing a real danger of cholera. It was a hellhole."

In the midst of this chaos, Emma floated about in long skirts and Wellington boots, looking mysteriously happy. At first no one paid much attention when she failed to spend the night at the UN camp. In all the confusion, O'Reilly's order for her to go back to Kapoeta was forgotten; Bernadette and the others needed every hand they could get. Operation Lifeline still had little food or medicine to give the refugees. The aid workers handed out all the high-energy protein biscuits they could fly in on the single Twin Otter airplane that Khartoum allowed them to send up to Nasir. But the Sudanese government refused permission to lay on the extra flights that would have let them establish a daily grain ration. The Nasir airstrip was too boggy to land a heavier transport plane, and the refugees were rapidly consuming the edible wild plants that grew near the abandoned town. In the wrangling over the flights, Khartoum kept insisting that certain unnamed Western aid workers in Nasir were violating Operation Lifeline's rules of neutrality. UN officials in Nairobi dismissed the allegations as typical NIF paranoia. Within a short while, however, every expatriate in Nasir knew that Khartoum was right about at least one aid worker: Emma was living openly with Riek in a thatched guesthouse that he had set up for her in his military compound ten miles up the river at Ketbek.

Emma's friends went to Ketbek to try to talk some sense into her. It was one thing to have a fling with a southern Sudanese teacher or relief official. But to shack up with the local SPLA commander in the middle of a major emergency was another matter. The essence of Khartoum's argument against increasing the food deliveries to Nasir was that Operation Lifeline was aiding the rebels. Even Alastair Scott-Villiers had been accused of being too close to Riek, on the grounds that he occasionally joined the SPLA commander for a meal at Ketbek. If another Lifeline worker was seen to be literally in bed with Riek, that hardly strengthened the United Nations' position vis-à-vis the government. Khartoum also had been complaining that unnamed aid workers were using the UN flights to deliver mail for the rebels. Emma seemed the most likely suspect. "Look, you're getting into hotter and hotter water," one friend warned her. "This isn't a brilliant idea for you or for him." Emma listened quietly. She didn't argue back, but those who confronted her felt the distance between them grow.

Ian Lethbridge had been named team leader of the Nasir relief effort. He believed Emma's romance had compromised her neutrality. Some of the other aid workers complained that Riek and his men seemed to know everything that went on in confidential UN meetings that Emma attended. Lethbridge proposed that the other expats keep their distance from her. But Bernadette Kumar refused to shun her friend. Bernadette thought it more dangerous for the UN workers to start backbiting among themselves than for Emma to be allowed in the UN camp. Emma had come to her privately to tell her about Riek's marriage proposal. Sitting cross-legged on the doctor's sleeping bag, Emma had seemed vulnerable. She said she had not decided whether she wanted to marry him, but she told Bernadette that "this time was different," and she invited the doctor to Ketbek to meet the commander.

To reach Ketbek, you took a canoe or a motorboat about ten miles down the river. Along the banks, you could see the armed silhouettes of SPLA soldiers, sometimes standing on one leg in the same odd, storklike pose that had led the ancient writer Ptolemy to call the swamps south of the Nile "the land of the one-legged men." Riek's headquarters was hidden behind a high cornstalk stockade studded with machine guns. He and the old Anyanya II chieftan Gordon Kong maintained a few *tukuls* for themselves in the front of the compound, while the bulk of the soldiers slept together at the back. Riek was surrounded at all times by a retinue of Kalashnikov-toting bodyguards. In a special *tukul* that served as his office, he kept a Good News Bible displayed on the table he used as a desk. Painted on the wall behind the table was a snake. Riek went out of his way to be gracious to Bernadette, dazzling her with his gap-toothed grin and talking with her about books and music. She felt that the commander wanted Emma's friends to like him, and that touched her. To her, he seemed "very warm, very diplomatic, very elegant," and yet there was something about him she didn't quite trust.

Sitting beside Riek, her arm tucked under his, Emma smiled proudly at the doctor; Bernadette couldn't help smiling back. Afterward Bernadette said, "I told her, 'When it is all said and done, we have to support each other. You're still the same person.' " Later she said, "My philosophy was that I accepted Emma for what she was. She was a rebel."

But perhaps the criticism bothered Emma more than she let on, for she made a decision. Less than two weeks after the expatriates arrived in Nasir, she went to the UN camp looking for Bernadette. The doctor wasn't there. That day like every other, Bernadette was out in the rain among the refugees, supervising a registration here, handing out plastic sheeting there. Each day seemed to bring new calamities. Hearing of the exodus, several dozen journalists had flown up to Nasir from Nairobi to take pictures of the dying refugees. Western embassy officials followed on their heels. The visitors all wanted a personal briefing from Bernadette on the health situation. Meanwhile newly arrived aid workers constantly interrupted her with a barrage of questions and requests about what to do.

Emma sent word from the camp that she needed the doctor urgently. Thinking Emma must be sick, Bernadette hurried back to her tent, only to find her tall friend lounging outside, listening to her Walkman. Emma jumped up when she saw the tiny dark-haired doctor walking briskly toward her. Taking off her earphones, she waved gaily. Bewildered, Bernadette waved back. Emma came outside and took the doctor's hands in hers, nearly bouncing with suppressed excitement.

"Guess what?" she whispered ecstatically.

Bernadette waited.

Emma went on. "I'm in love, and I've made up my mind. I'm going to get married—here in Nasir! And I want you to be my bridesmaid."

The doctor was thunderstruck. Of all the impetuous things Emma had done, this was the worst. Apart from the damage such an alliance would do to Emma's position as an aid worker, everyone knew Riek was already married. She sat her friend down on a wooden crate and took a deep breath. Trying to gather her thoughts, she told Emma she was being rash. Why did she have to marry Riek? For heaven's sake, it wouldn't even be legal. What about Riek's Nuer wife in England?

Emma lit a cigarette and listened, exhaling slowly as if the smoke might blow away Bernadette's objections like so many unpleasant flies. With a dreamy look on her face, she mused, "You know how when you are twelve years old, you always dream about who you are going to marry?"

Bernadette nodded.

Emma took another deep drag off her cigarette. Perhaps she was remembering those cold Yorkshire winters when she warmed herself by the story of Thumbelina, carried away from the sunless north by a swallow to marry the prince of a warm land and become his people's princess? Or was she finally putting away her girlish fantasies of a white wedding on her father's arm at Cowling Hall? She went on, "Well, this isn't what I dreamed of, but in my heart I know this is what I want."

Bernadette could tell that anything she said against the marriage would fall on deaf ears. Part of her thought Emma foolhardy and feared the danger she saw her friend getting herself into. Part of her was awed by Emma's courage in pursuing a love that both of them already knew was going to extract a high price. But she agreed to be a bridesmaid.

Emma's face suddenly turned serious. "There's something else I wanted to ask you," she said. "Do you have any clothes I could borrow for the wedding? Because I don't have anything nice with me here."

The doctor burst into whoops of laughter. Hugging her tall friend, she wiped tears from her eyes.

"Emma, you are crazy," she said. "As if anything of mine could fit you!"

TWO DAYS LATER, on June 17, the rest of the camp learned that Riek and Emma were getting married. Patta, who had been organizing a food delivery, was mustered into service as another bridesmaid. While Ian Lethbridge sputtered—"This is not acceptable. You may not travel in a

UN boat to this event"—she and Bernadette ran around Nasir's weed-covered ruins, picking wildflowers for Emma's bouquet. The wedding party set off in a Land Rover from Nasir to Ketbek, but the mud was so deep that the vehicle got stuck and they had to walk the last two miles to the church. Emma led the way through the mud, singing "Get Me to the Church on Time." She had cut her dark hair short. She was slightly sun-burned, freckled, and whippet thin. She had always loved the long snowy-white cotton shawls that Ethiopian women wrapped around their waists and over their shoulders. Somewhere she had found one with a colorfully embroidered band to wear to her wedding. Bernadette and Patta followed behind her, carrying the shawl as if it were a train. Emma "had the same languid, graceful gait as the Sudanese as she walked," Patta later recalled. One of Riek's soldiers marched alongside them in camou-flage fatigues. By the time they reached the church, all four were in mud up to their knees. A snapshot shows them grinning madly.

The service was held in a little mud chapel with a grass roof. The baby-faced young pastor James Mut Kueth performed the service. One of Riek's aides wearing a quilted pink bathrobe read aloud from the Bible. At the last minute, the group realized that Riek did not have a ring to give Emma. Quickly Patta produced a silver ring that Alastair had bought for her on a vacation in India. Patta remembers that the huge red sun was setting over the Sobat as they came out of the church. A Nuer choir was singing and playing drums. "It was just so beautiful," sighed Bernadette. She thought it was a nice touch that Emma and Riek refused to have a wedding feast. "They said, 'We'll celebrate when we have enough food for everyone here.'" Reverend Kueth remembers thinking it strange that Riek didn't seem to be paying any cows to Emma's family. Otherwise, he said, "it was just a regular marriage ceremony. Everybody was very happy."

LAM AKOL SERVED as Riek's best man, but he was not happy. The re-fugee exodus had raised the stakes of the deadly game that he and Riek were playing with Garang. They had hoped to have a Nuer among the Ethiopian security services arrest Garang on a visit to Itang. With Itang empty, that scheme was out of the question. They were engaged in furi-ous and secret efforts to recruit other SPLA commanders to their cause; Lam was also writing a manifesto called "Why Garang Must Go." Garang knew they were up to something. If he attacked now, they and the 130,000 refugees encamped with them at Nasir were doomed. More than anything, Riek and Lam needed to persuade some important Dinka officers to come over to their side. Otherwise the south's most populous people would continue to side with Garang, a fellow Dinka. From the conspirators' point of view, perhaps the most useful aspect of the UN operation was the way it allowed them to communicate with commanders in other parts of southern Sudan. Normally the rebels were cut off, not only from the rest of the world but from each other. But the young expatriates flying in and out of Nasir never minded delivering a letter or two for their friends in the SPLA. And with Western television cameras trained on the refugees at Nasir, Garang could hardly march up and crush them as he'd crushed all previous challenges to his authority. On June 17 Lam and Gordon Kong had actually been sitting in Gordon's mud *tukul* going over the latest balance of forces, when suddenly Riek and Emma appeared, holding hands and giggling. "We are getting married this afternoon," Riek told them.

Lam could hardly believe his ears. "I was shocked," he said of Riek's decision to marry right as they were hatching their plot. "From that moment I knew we had difficulty." He stared at the foolishly grinning pair. He tried to maintain his composure, but inside he was aghast. He knew Emma only slightly—"She knew me more than I knew her" was how he put it—and what he knew was not favorable. He knew of at least one other rebel officer who had slept with her. He could just imagine what Garang would say when he heard that Emma was a British spy, an agent, a whore paid to split the movement. "What will our credibility be if this is the first lady?" he thought bitterly. Lam was even more worried about what Riek's announcement revealed about his fellow conspirator. What sort of leader would be thinking about romance at a time as perilous as this? Especially romance with a woman like Emma—a *khawaja*, with a reputation! How could he be so irresponsible as to take a step like this, with such fateful consequences for his comrades, without even bothering to consult them? "Riek was the most senior among us. I knew that getting married to Emma, who is so well known in the SPLA, would put us in a bad light. It showed me that he was not so democratic after all. It showed me that Riek is a carefree fellow."

Another problem presented itself to Lam. If Riek had failed to consult his fellow conspirators, how likely was it that he had told Angelina? According to Nuer custom, a man must ask his first wife for permission before he marries again. If he marries against her will, she has the right to

ask for a divorce. Lam was distantly related to Angelina. At least one of
the other plotters, the former administrator of Itang, Taban Deng Gai,
was her first cousin. Her father was a politician with a strong following in
the key Bentiu district of the oil fields. By marrying Emma, Riek might
antagonize some powerful Nuer just at the moment they needed all the
allies they could get. "What about your wife—does your wife have information about this?" Lam wanted to know.

Both men turned to hear what Riek would say.

Riek did not lose his jaunty half smile. When he answered, his voice
was soft and full of menace. "Yes, and she has no problem," he said.

Lam could not be sure if he was lying. Emma, who had always been
hopeless at languages and spoke only a few words of Arabic and Nuer,
probably didn't understand the question. She was still smiling when Riek
took her by the hand and led her out of the *tukul*. Later Riek said, "I knew
there was a xenophobic attitude in the SPLA and every white person was
seen as a spy. Some people told me it was a silly decision to marry Emma,
but I followed the dictates of my heart."

THE WEDDING STRUCK the other aid workers as the kind of surreal
sideshow that often accompanies disasters. Everyone who was there
remembers the macabre carnival atmosphere that summer in Nasir. "It
was like all the barriers were down," one aid worker said. The UN officials were forever haggling with the rebels over the number of refugees
at Nasir. The refugees were melting away in the bush, presumably walking back to their families. But Riek's men kept insisting that Operation
Lifeline provide Nasir with the same amount of food. Young Giles
Thornton thought of a way to see how many refugees were still in the
vicinity. He rigged up a pair of wooden planks attached to Wellington
boots cut off at the ankles and used them to water-ski up and down the
crocodile-infested Sobat. Everyone rushed to the banks of the river to
watch him go past. Thornton claimed his hobby allowed the other aid
workers to get a better refugee count. More orthodox colleagues accused
him of wasting fuel on reckless showboating. Charles Villiers got hit in
the head and fell into the Sobat. Patta jumped into the river after him and
was bitten by a puff adder. For two days she lay in a near coma. Then she
suddenly came to and was back at work. And there were other romances
at Nasir that summer. More than one marriage nearly went to pieces in
the fevered atmosphere of the place.

Every few days the aid workers heard the drone of the Antonov and ran for one of the snake-ridden mud pits that served as bomb shelters. Relief arrived only intermittently, and when it did, huge food distributions had to be organized in a flash. Clan chiefs had the duty of distributing the UN sorghum among about a thousand people according to a complicated ticket system. Each head of household was supposed to receive one cupful of grain per family member, but there was always confusion, and after everybody had been waiting in line in the blazing sun, sometimes fighting broke out over how many children a man had or whose turn it was. Every so often a refugee stepped on one of the land mines planted during the fighting for the town back in the 1980s. Once the camp watched as the UN plane dropped an entire day's food into the Sobat.

When you see the starving Rwandans or Somalis or Bosnians staring out of your television screens with solemn dignity, you get the idea that such places must be like mass hospitals in the dust. You think they must be entirely populated by emaciated children lining up for food handed out by heroic aid workers. Television leaves out the manic excitement of the camps. Power is naked in such places. It comes down to who has food and who doesn't. The aid workers try to cover it up, to make the men with guns at least pretend to deny themselves in favor of the children and the women. The men play along for a while, but then the mask falls away. The strong always eat first. Then the question for the aid workers is: Are we doing more harm by feeding the men with the guns than we would by letting everyone else starve? In Nasir the question arose more quickly than usual because there was less food to go around. And very soon some of the aid workers began to wonder where Emma stood—on the side of the refugees or with Riek.

Under Operation Lifeline rules, UN food was supposed to go strictly to civilians, not to soldiers. Riek had agreed to these guidelines. In the daytime he allowed monitors from the World Food Program to watch as the chiefs carefully portioned out grain to each family. But aid workers heard that at night the rebels would go around to those who had received food and take what they needed. (Peter Adwok Nyaba confirms that such seizures did take place. "Even in cases where the expatriate relief monitors were strict and only distributed relief supplies to civilians by day, the SPLA would retrieve the food at night.") In the Sudanese view, the rebel seizures weren't necessarily unethical. Most of the civilians were related in some way to the SPLA troops, and traditionally it was the duty of women and children to share what they had with their fathers and brothers and cousins and sons. Even if the soldiers weren't related, the SPLA had taught them to use their guns to get their living from the local people. "You have the Kalashnikov—it will be your mother, your father, your food," Garang reportedly told troops graduating from SPLA training camps.

Riek's outgoing manner was part of the problem. In other parts of southern Sudan, *khawajas* seldom knew enough about local people and politics to do more than guess at what happened to food after they handed it out. But in Nasir the expatriates had gotten to knew Riek. They had whiled away the time waiting for airdrops beside the Nasir airstrip with him and Lam. They had gone to Ketbek to eat *kisra* with him. And now one of their colleagues had married him. So they recognized Riek's cook and his driver when these two lined up for rations as if they were refugees. They knew the names of his soldiers and were able to figure out which ones held back a few bags when they collected the grain from a UN airdrop. And they were not afraid to tell Riek what they'd seen. Riek's first reaction was to prevaricate. But those who kept pushing him found themselves expelled. A high-strung young veterinarian appeared at the airstrip one day and yelled at Riek for commandeering two UN motorboats to send his men on a mission to catch some fish for himself and his lieutenants. Lam Akol promptly declared the man persona non grata and ordered him to leave Nasir on the next flight.

Emma was a silent presence at these confrontations. What was she thinking? Riek said that when they were alone together, she used to try to explain what was bothering the *khawajas:* "She stood up for them a lot." He said the disputes led Emma to draw up a set of rules to govern relations between the rebels and the relief groups that Operation Lifeline later adopted for use across southern Sudan. (Operation Lifeline officials say Emma had nothing to do with the guidelines.) In the summer of 1991, Emma had just been married. It was only natural for her to give her new husband the benefit of the doubt. She probably looked at someone like Giles Thornton, a public schoolboy educated—like Britain's Prince Charles—at Gordonstoun, and knew in ways that Riek never would just how privileged Thornton really was and how many UN rules he himself was breaking when he got stoned and used the UN diesel to go water-skiing. She must have wondered where he got the nerve to criticize Riek, who, as she often said, "has given up his whole life to fight for his people!"

But to her colleagues, it seemed as if she had gone over to the other side. When Emma showed up at aid meetings, the other expatriates started to hold their tongues, fearing that she would report back to Riek whatever they said. Sensing the hostility, Emma came less often, leading UN officials to question whether she was still doing her job for Street Kids International. She was often seen escorting journalists around the camp, as if she were Riek's personal press officer. "She was no longer a colleague," said Wendy James, Douglas Johnson's wife. "She represented The Power."

JAMES, a social anthropologist at the University of Oxford, had come to Nasir in late July to produce a UN report on perhaps the most miserable group of refugees: some twenty thousand people from Blue Nile province clustered a few miles from Nasir along the banks of the Sobat. Most were Uduk, a small but distinctive people whose seven-thousand-year-old language is one of Africa's oldest. Historically the Uduk lived a little north of the Nuer, along the border with Ethiopia in Blue Nile province. James had lived with the Uduk in the 1960s and written two books about them before they were hounded out of their homeland by the civil war in the 1980s. Since she had last seen them in 1983, various armed groups had chased them all over Sudan and Ethiopia. The NIF government had been trying to Islamicize their former lands, allowing Osama bin Laden to buy a large farm near the town of Damazine in southern Blue Nile. Bin Laden grew sesame and peanuts there in addition to training Islamic fighters. The Saudi magnate also built an eighty-three-mile road from the town of Kurmuk to Damazine that the army used to defend the area against the SPLA.

The dispossessed Uduk sought shelter with the rebels at Itang, but they remained fearful of their Nilotic neighbors, whom they called "the Dhamkin." They were especially wary of the Nuer, historically terrifying enemies of the Uduk. James had tried without much success to contact her Uduk friends in the years since they fled Sudan. When she heard that they were among the twenty thousand refugees from Blue Nile squatting at Nor Deng, the site of the original *zariba* established by Gordon's lieutenant Nasir Ali, she was anxious to go see them.

James was startled when Emma—whom she had met briefly at the Fairview in Nairobi—showed up at the UN camp to welcome her to

Nasir. Emma was wearing a big hat and some ropy sandals; in her York-shire lady-of-the-manor way, she began to question James about what she intended to write in her report for the UN. James was reluctant. She felt as if Emma were probing her for information. She didn't say anything, but privately the anthropologist resented the implication that she needed the permission of another, younger *khawaja* to talk to people she'd known for more than twenty years. "I didn't like the feeling that I was her guest," she said.

When James reached Nor Deng the next day, she was horrified by the conditions she found. Nor Deng was flooded and swarming with mosquitoes. The Uduk had only plastic sheeting with which to cover themselves, and they were extremely malnourished. Many were sick. Riek's security chief at first wouldn't give James permission to stay overnight with her friends, making her wonder if the SPLA had something to hide. She soon learned they did. The Uduk said the rebels were keeping them at Nor Deng against their will. The year they had spent at Itang had been one of the worst in all their wanderings. The Nuer administrators at the camp had forced them to work for the SPLA and had not given them enough to eat. As James later wrote, they remembered Itang as "a place, and a time, of death, where four, or even five, were buried in one hole." When the rebels gave the order to abandon Itang, the Uduk had wanted to strike out on their own. Instead the rebels forced them, some at gunpoint, to go downstream to Nasir with the others. Shortly after reaching Nasir, a few Uduk tried again to start walking toward their homeland in Blue Nile province. Riek's men stopped them and ordered them back to Nor Deng. The UN had given the Uduk priority for feeding, but after more than six weeks in the camp, they were still dying. James found them eating pythons and water snails. They said they had not received their UN rations for eleven days.

Emma often took visiting journalists to Nor Deng to see the sad state of the Uduk. The journalists took pictures of the sick and dying tribesmen. Then they wrote of the need for Operation Lifeline to send more food to Nasir. James began to suspect that Riek was using the Uduk as human bait to keep relief supplies coming. At a meeting she pressed him to let the Uduk move to a place where they could grow their own food, but he was evasive. She expected Emma to back her up, but Emma said nothing. "Emma didn't want to know," she recalled. "I began to feel that Emma was a part of this."

James talked about her fears with her own husband, who believed that the SPLA was playing a similarly sinister game with about twelve hundred hungry boys at Nasir. These were some of the boys from the so-called children's camps like Panyido in Ethiopia that Operation Lifeline officials believed were actually military training camps for the SPLA. In the UN lingo, the boys were known as "unaccompanied minors." After the exodus from Ethiopia, about two thousand of them ended up in Nasir, while another ten thousand landed about 150 miles to the south, near Pochalla on the Akobo River. Reporters quickly dubbed them "The Lost Boys" after Peter Pan's band of runaway boys. They became the poster children for the relief effort to southern Sudan. But, as Emma knew better than most, Sudan was far from Neverland. The boys were *not* lost—they were more like pawns in a complicated game. The question of just who the "unaccompanied minors" were and how they came to be wandering around with the SPLA was one of the most contested issues in the whole Sudanese relief effort. It was over this issue that Emma had fallen out with Kuol Manyang in Torit. It was also the issue she had confronted Riek about in their first meeting. Soon it became the issue of a struggle between her and the other aid workers over whether Riek was really as different from Garang as she believed.

In Ethiopia UNHCR had chosen to regard the boys in the children's camps as war orphans. The organization ran special schools and feeding programs for them. But at Nasir it became clear that at least some of the boys still had families. Children are valuable in Sudan. If a child's parents are dead, his aunts, uncles, grandparents, brothers, and assorted other relatives will be eager to claim him. As soon as they arrived, about eight hundred Nuer boys melted back into nearby Jikany clans. Riek declared the remaining twelve hundred boys "orphans" and settled them in a camp of their own right across from his headquarters at Ketbek. Many of them were Dok Nuer from his own home area around Ler. No journalist could visit him without seeing them—and they were a pitiful sight. Most were between ten and thirteen years old. They had been in fairly good shape when they arrived, but their health deteriorated rapidly at Nasir. Within a few months the UN reported that malnutrition levels in the minors' camp had risen from 4 percent to 35 percent. "The children became weak, depressed, resigned," one official later wrote. Like the Uduk, the boys were supposed to receive special rations, but aid workers frequently saw them eating unripe fruit, unground wheat, and wild leaves. And like the Uduk, they kept dying.

UNICEF started off by sending the boys high-energy biscuits. But the biscuits kept disappearing into the knapsacks of the SPLA men who were sent to collect them from the site where the plane dropped its load. UNICEF switched to sending a special high-protein meal called Unimix. Unimix came in a special orange plastic feeding kit and was supposed to be especially nourishing, but it, too, kept disappearing. In spite of their label, the boys in fact were accompanied at all times by several hundred grown men. The rebels called them the boys' "caretakers." They insisted that the men distribute the boys' food. But the SPLA doctor who looked after the boys told Johnson privately that the men were taking the Unimix for themselves.

Riek and Lam called Johnson to a meeting at the landing site to complain about UNICEF's decision to stop sending high-energy biscuits to the minors' camp. Lam claimed that the switchover to Unimix was killing the boys. Emma was there, but she said nothing. Johnson was appalled and not just by Riek. After all, the boys were supposed to be Emma's cause. She claimed to be still working for Street Kids International. She was in the minors' camp all the time, handing out chalkboards and exercise books to the "caretakers." Recently she had found them a tent large enough to use as a school. And she continued to revile the SPLA boarding schools to visiting journalists. Only a few weeks before the exodus from Ethiopia, she had tipped off a Canadian reporter for *The Toronto Star* about the boys at Palataka. Speaking off the record, she told Paul Watson that the SPLA was taking boys at Palataka out of school to use as underage soldiers. Yet here was her husband holding more than a thousand boys in circumstances at least as bad as those at Palataka, and she refused to say a word against him. "She made a great crusade for children," Johnson said, "but when things began to go wrong, she took no position."

A little while later a couple of other aid workers went to the mud *tukul* Riek used as an office at Ketbek to talk to him about the boys. As usual Emma was there. While they sat talking, Riek's servant handed them some of the fried bread balls the Sudanese call *mendazis*. The bright orange plastic plate, they noticed, looked exactly like the ones in the feeding kits they had given the boys. One aid worker complimented Riek on the uncommonly tasty *mendazis*.

Riek nodded proudly. "Oh, it's made with Unimix," he said.

Few expatriates dared ask Emma why she didn't do more for the boys at Nasir. But a later incident suggests how she might have answered if they had. About a year after Riek invited the aid workers to eat the *men-dazis* made from Unimix, *The Times* of London reported that Emma and Riek were eating Unimix intended for the boys. Emma was furious. In a letter to a friend, she called the article "absurd." She sometimes spoke of the need to understand and respect Nilotic cultural traditions that led the Nuer to regard boys as warriors in training. She pointed out the hypocrisy of the West in condemning the SPLA for impressing young teenagers into its army. After all, the British army had done exactly the same thing up until the last century, she liked to say. After her marriage she grew more critical of *khawajas,* including herself, who presumed to judge the Sudanese. Without speaking any of the local languages, she relied on Riek to interpret the events she saw happening around her, and given his studied preference for avoiding arguments, it's likely he told her what he thought she wanted to hear.

Emma was not by nature introspective. By temperament she was a campaigner, a fighter, a natural partisan. And to this tendency to pick sides she added a peculiarly Western idealism that was all the more poignant for being totally out of place in the context of an African civil war. It was not a political vision that truly animated Emma as much as an ideal of romantic love. She was in love with the idea of love and with the idea of sacrificing herself to it. The lesson Emma seems to have taken from her parents' divorce and her father's suicide was not that romantic love is a flimsy shelter, but that life without it is so cold and gray that it is hardly worth living. In her book Emma's mother admits that she had never been "truly passionately in love" with Emma's father. Maggie McCune blames her own coldness toward him in part for the breakup of their marriage. "Searching for the adulation and love that was his life's oxygen and which he had not found in me, he turned elsewhere." Could it be that Emma absorbed this explanation for the family tragedy and decided to set her life in opposition to it? Maggie had married in part to escape her own reckless and dramatic mother. Perhaps in some strange way, Emma sought to reverse the pattern. If Maggie had given up love for a security that turned out to be false, Emma would give up security for a love to which she would be blindly true. If her mother had been insufficiently loyal, Emma would never yield in her commitment. If her mother had failed to believe in love at first sight, Emma would turn herself into its shining exemplar. If her mother's life seemed small and cramped, Emma's would be wide open and wildly free. However she explained it to herself, it seemed to her friends that her loyalties began to shift, so that her first allegiance was now to Riek and his cause, and no longer to the children she had once defended so courageously.

IN THE SUMMER OF 1991 there were plenty of *khawajas* at Nasir who did not judge Emma so harshly for not standing on humanitarian principle. "I could understand how she might think she could combine it all by marrying Riek," said an American missionary. "It wasn't a puzzling thing to me that Emma, a passionate person, should think, 'Maybe he's the one who will bring peace and maybe that's the avenue.' To me, those aren't mentally deranged decisions. Everybody who is there is part of that war. Some aid workers think they are not, and I think that is a terrible delusion. Emma wasn't operating on life at that level. She saw things much deeper."

They all knew that the vagaries of aid held up little better than romance under harsh scrutiny. It was so hard to pin down the facts in Sudan. Maybe the other refugees at Nasir were healthier than the Uduk and the boys because they had relatives in the area who shared food with them and the Uduk and the boys did not. Or maybe the United States and its allies were to blame for not forcing Khartoum to let the United Nations take enough food to Nasir to feed everybody without stinting. It certainly wasn't the first time the SPLA had been caught eating Operation Lifeline food. In 1989 John Garang had served a visiting U.S. congressional delegation UN high-protein biscuits, for heaven's sake. ("They're not bad," one of the congressmen told me jauntily after their return from Torit.) So the relief workers ate Riek's *mendazis* and hoped for the best. It was pointless to argue with him about the Unimix unless they were prepared to stand on principle and pull out, and they weren't.

The aid workers who had been around the longest were the first to admit that it was not easy to tell right from wrong in an emergency like the one at Nasir. By insisting that children be considered innocents more deserving of food than adults, was the UN inadvertently encouraging the SPLA to starve the "unaccompanied minors" in hopes of receiving more aid? It was not as if the aid workers themselves were going without meals. Khartoum frequently blocked airdrops for the refugees, but that didn't prevent the catering company that supplied food for the expats from making its deliveries. (The one time it did, later in the year, Lethbridge pulled out all the expatriates.) This discrepancy made some people uncomfortable, especially when grain stocks were low and the aid workers had to put the more than a hundred thousand refugees on half rations. But—face it—food tastes awfully good after a day that begins at five A.M. and continues on until nightfall with all manner of frustrations in between. Who could blame the *khawajas* if they enjoyed an extra helping of canned fish? Think what they could be eating if they were at home in Manhattan or Melbourne. True, kids were dying. But if the aid workers didn't keep up their strength, more would die. What were the moral issues involved in Emma eating a Unimix bread ball compared with those raised by the blow-dried politicians and TV reporters who flew up on planes chartered at a cost that could have fed Nasir for a week? So the discussions went at the UN camp until the old hands, who'd heard it all before in other famine camps, were ready to scream with boredom. To them, Emma's transgressions seemed a very tiny piece in a much larger and more outrageous puzzle. When she left Nasir to visit Nairobi at the end of June, they wished her well.

Emma's mother was working in a London investment bank when Emma telephoned her from Nairobi. Emma usually visited England for a few weeks in the summer, but this year she had already postponed her trip three times. "I have some news for you," she said, her voice sounding very far away on the international line. "I've got married."

"Who did you marry?" asked Maggie McCune, flabbergasted. It was the first she had heard about it. But Emma answered only that her husband was Sudanese. Probably sensing her mother's stunned disapproval, she hung up the phone suddenly. Maggie was left alone with the memory of how angry her own mother had been when she announced her plan to marry an unknown man in India. By coincidence, Willy Knocker was visiting England and happened to phone Maggie the next day. He was the one who told her that Emma had married a warlord.

In Nairobi Sally Dudmesh knew all about Riek; she had been the first to hear about the prophecy and his proposal. Emma was not the only member of their set to have upturned her life lately for a chance at great passion. Sally's fiancé, Tonio Trzebinski, had ditched her almost as dramatically as Emma had dumped Willy. Sally had been in London buying a wedding dress when a mutual friend named Anna Cunningham-Reid phoned her. Anna said that she was leaving her husband so that she and Tonio could be together. Anna later told *Vanity Fair* that she was overcome by an unstoppable attraction to Tonio after meeting him and his sister for lunch one day in Nairobi. A few weeks later, Tonio paddled by dugout canoe to a New Year's Eve party Anna and her husband were attending. Anna's husband was in a deep sleep after being bitten by a centipede. "At 4 A.M.," Anna said, "Tonio got up in front of the whole congregation and said, 'I know exactly what this woman needs.' He took me by the hand ... took me into the bushes and made love to me." Anna got her divorce, and she and Tonio were married in 1991 on a trip to California. Sally had pleaded with Emma before she went to live with Riek in Nasir, "Don't just go off to Sudan and get married to him."

Emma always stayed with Sally when she was in Nairobi. When Sally came home the night Emma arrived, she went up to the spare room where her friend slept. She took one look at Emma's grin and guessed what had happened. "Oh my God," she cried. "You've done it, haven't you? Why couldn't you wait?"

"I just couldn't," Emma said happily—and proceeded to tell Sally all about the wedding.

Sally privately was dismayed and frightened for her friend. But the rest of their friends were agog with admiration. At a dinner party that week, everyone crowded around to hear about Emma's wedding in "the swamps of hell." Emma seemed to have outdone them all with her daring. "It just seemed so fantastically romantic and dashing," said a television correspondent. "It was so unreal. I think her mother thought, 'Oh dear.' But we thought she was like a character in a movie."

When Emma returned to Nasir, Sally flew up with her to meet Riek. She found the new husband pleasant enough, but Nasir, she thought, was "pretty ghastly." She walked around Riek's camp at Ketbek in a daze of disbelief that her sophisticated, art-loving friend really planned to live there. "She was very busy with what he was doing, and it was just horrible there," she told me later. "There were mosquitoes everywhere. The only thing to do was to look at that great river, and you couldn't even swim in it because of the crocodiles. Of course, she couldn't drive most places, and it was really uncomfortable to walk in the heat. The heat was horrible to live in. The food was disgusting. The toilets—ugh! There literally was no social life."

Sally was wondering why in the world Emma wanted to stay here. Then, she said, "I got into the whole political thing with them. All they did was talk about politics all the time. It's like a drug—you want to know more. I could see the energy then. She was so excited by it and talking about it. That was probably why she loved it so much. She loved Riek, but she loved the politics, too."

Chapter *Twenty*

HEN EMMA went home to England in July, everyone could see that she was in love. She made a dramatic entrance at one party wearing a dress by the designer Ghost that must have cost several hundred pounds. "Who is that stunning woman in black?" the guests were asking. She relished answering that she was the wife of an African guerrilla chief. ("Really?" replied one elderly lady. "Which regiment?") She reveled in the attention and adulation, telling one girlfriend that she wished she could capture on videotape the reactions she got when she told people about her marriage. And yet there were already some who were not amused.

Emma knew that she wasn't Riek's only wife. In fact, she seemed to enjoy shocking British friends and relatives with the news that she had entered a polygamous marriage, chuckling over what the nuns at her old school in Richmond would think. She actually tried to call on Angelina when she got to England. Evidently she'd been told this was the proper thing for a junior Nuer wife to do. Perhaps her overture was sincere, or perhaps it was a bit of cultural cross-dressing—the domestic equivalent of the SPLA's rhetoric about democracy and human rights. But Angelina refused to see Emma. Riek's first wife wasn't about to acquiesce in what Emma insisted on describing as the admirably pragmatic Nuer system of polygamy. ("You never have to worry that your husband is having an extramarital affair," she was still enthusing two years later to an ITV correspondent. "You will know all about it.") Despite his assurances to Lam, Riek had not asked Angelina for permission to marry Emma. Instead he had written her after the wedding to announce that he had married again. Angelina was livid about the way she'd been treated.

It had been seven years now since Riek left England for Sudan— seven years of hardship and struggle for Angelina and her children. Seven years of waiting in line at government offices, of scrambling to find money to buy groceries and keep the heat on, seven years of washing dishes and clothes alone at night after the children had gone to bed. In all that time, Angelina had seen Riek for a little over one month. She was often lonely. "It's like your life is on hold," she told me later. "You might cry yourself to sleep at night, but then you've got to get up and get the children off to school, and so you go on." When I met her, she and the children had moved from Bradford to a distant suburb of London. They lived on the bottom floor of a curious house shaped like a miniature castle. (Angelina told me that a well-known architect had built a series of these castellated houses in a craze of the 1920s.) Inside, the atmosphere was striving and disciplined. Riek's children were neatly dressed. They did their homework in a room with bunk beds. Angelina checked their assignments after they'd finished them. A bookcase filled with textbooks and encyclopedias stood by the table, gleaming with polish. The walls of the living room were decorated with studio portraits of Riek with Angelina and the children in formal dress. Each photo had been taken on one of his rare visits to England.

In 1990, while Riek had been wooing Emma with his tales of prophecy, Angelina had given birth by cesarean, alone in a British hospital, to their third child, a boy named Timmy. Riek had never seen Timmy. When Angelina learned that he had broken his promise never to take a second wife, she felt "devastated." "I felt as if I had wasted all my years." She wanted to ask Riek for a divorce on the grounds that he hadn't asked her permission, but she won no sympathy from his Nuer friends and relations. "Of course Riek can marry more than one wife," scoffed Riek's cousin. "His grandfather had a hundred and fifty wives!" The same cousin told Angelina she ought to be glad her husband had found somebody to take care of him in the bush. Another man asked her why she was carrying on about what was, after all, a perfectly ordinary event in Sudan. "Wait and see how you feel if your wife were to bring home a co-husband for you," retorted Angelina. Finally Riek's first wife decided to disregard Emma. "I didn't take her seriously," she said. "I didn't consider her a true wife. What priest would marry them when Riek is already married to me?" Emma, she said, was a *lam*—a concubine whose children had no rights to their father's herd.

In public Emma was lavish in her praise for Nuer-style polygamy, irritating her mother no end. "Look how much divorce there is in the UK and how many people commit adultery," Emma told a journalist when she returned to Sudan. "Nearly everyone. There's none of that here." Her remarks embittered Angelina, who really had to live according to the Nuer traditions Emma claimed to admire. "Emma was brave to try to contact me, because the job of the first wife is to make the second wife's life hell and vice versa," she said, noting that the Nuer word for "co-wife" also means "jealousy." "Who would want to share a husband?" But in private conversations with her girlfriends in England, Emma betrayed more conventional sentiments and rationalizations about Riek's relationship with his first wife. After all, Angelina was a strikingly beautiful woman only a year older than Emma. "There's nothing between them now," she told one friend. "It's just that a Nuer man can't divorce his wife after she's borne him three children."

Angelina's coldness notwithstanding, Emma seemed to bubble with happiness in the summer of 1991. She made a point of visiting all the friends and relations she hadn't seen since she left England in 1989. She showed them photos of her wedding in Nasir and entertained them with tales of fighting off scorpions and snakes and spiders in Sudan. She described the tender love letters Riek wrote her and giggled at newlywed jokes. She slipped back into English life with characteristic ease, playing long games of tennis in the afternoons and dressing up to go out to the theater in the evenings. Her sister Erica disapproved of her marriage. Emma tried to smooth over relations by inviting Erica to come along on a trip to Spain. The sisters spent a vacation relaxing on the beach. When they returned, Emma went to Notting Hill in London to stay with John Ryle, the writer and anthropologist who had delivered Riek's message to her back in February 1990.

On the morning of August 30, Ryle's phone started to ring for Emma. The BBC had announced that Riek Machar had overthrown John Garang. "Senior commanders in the rebel Sudan People's Liberation Army have rejected their leader, Colonel John Garang, saying that peace must be the top priority, even if that means what was previously unthinkable—accepting a divided Sudan," the BBC had reported. "The man who says he's taken over the SPLA is Riek Machar." Riek was joined by fellow commanders Lam Akol and Gordon Kong, the BBC went on to say. When Emma finally managed to hear the report for herself, she listened as her husband condemned the man who had been his as well as the SPLA's leader for the last seven years.

"John Garang has run the movement alone in a very dictatorial, authoritarian manner," Riek told the BBC in an interview. "He has oppressed, humiliated, and degraded our people. He has turned this movement into warlordism and a reign of terror. He has tried to manipulate even our own children, to recruit them into the army as child soldiers."

Emma appeared stunned; she gave the impression that the coup had come as a total surprise to her. It was the weekend of the Notting Hill Carnival, and Ryle's neighborhood was jammed with people. Emma stayed in the house, calling everyone she could think of to find out more. One call came to Emma from Angelina, who had heard the BBC report, too, and was sick with anxiety, knowing that not only Riek but many of her male relatives must be involved. Stiffly she told Emma, "I am just calling you to see if you have any news about my husband." Emma said she would call her back in a few minutes. Later she phoned to say she had spoken to somebody in Nairobi who had just returned from Nasir and said everybody was fine.

Smoking cigarette after cigarette, ceaselessly dialing the telephone, Emma pieced together a picture of what had happened. At the end of August, it seemed, the plotters had learned that Garang was planning to call a meeting of the SPLA High Command at which he would arrest Lam and Riek. The two men decided it was time to act. On August 28 they sent out a message to all SPLA units calling on them to overthrow Garang. Meanwhile they asked one of the aid workers leaving for Nairobi to take an envelope to the BBC's correspondent in Nairobi. The envelope contained a thirteen-point appeal for a new SPLA based on human rights and democracy, which they called their Nasir Declaration. When the BBC correspondent flew up to Nasir, Riek told him that he, Lam, and Gordon were dropping the old goal of overthrowing Sudan's Islamic government and establishing a secular, democratic one. They argued that it was time to face the fact that the African south and the Arab north were two nations. They were no longer calling for unity. Instead they wanted independence for the south. Meanwhile Garang was alive and well. Bernard Kouchner, France's minister for humanitarian affairs and the founder of Médecins Sans Frontières, had visited Kapoeta the same day as the BBC announcement. Kouchner reported that Garang still seemed to be "very much in control." In Nairobi, Garang's deputy held a press conference saying that Garang was still the leader of the SPLA.

To Ryle and to those who called her, Emma insisted that she had not known about "the split," as Riek and Lam's announcement came to be known. Riek also told me that she had had nothing to do with it. Yet Emma seemed to thrive on the melodrama, and many detected her influence in the language Riek used to attack Garang for his conscription of child soldiers. She was plainly proud of Riek for taking a public stand against Garang. Almost certainly she knew well before the announcement that something was planned. Before she left Nasir, she had hinted to Bernadette Kumar that big events might take place while she was away. In England she had been meeting quietly with some Sudanese exiles. After the BBC report, she drove up to Ilmington to visit Liz Hodgkin with Bona Malwal, a prominent Dinka journalist and politician who had recently criticized John Garang in a newsletter. "She talked to me many times about why I ought to join Riek and Lam," Bona Malwal recalled. "She was really trying to persuade me to do it." For his part, John Garang and those loyal to him immediately assumed that Emma was behind the attempted coup.

On September 4 Emma flew back to Nairobi. She knew it would be dangerous for her, but she was determined to return to Nasir anyway. The SPLA kept a camp about eight miles away from the Operation Lifeline base camp at Lokichoggio. Garang's men controlled it. The same day she arrived in Nairobi, they kidnapped a Shilluk pharmacist from Nasir who was attending a health workshop Bernadette had organized at the Operation Lifeline camp. The United Nations and the Kenyan government protested, but the rebels refused to return the pharmacist. A few days later Garang's forces seized a woman from Nasir who was staying at the International Committee of the Red Cross hospital near Loki. The woman was returned only after the Red Cross threatened to shut down the hospital. On September 5 Riek's forces clashed with Garang's south of Nasir. After a short firefight, fighters on both sides seized the opportunity to loot civilian cattle. On September 6 an SPLA captain loyal to Garang arrested his commanding officer at Pariang, the site of an oil field in the same mixed Nuer-Dinka area that had been the home of the southerners I met at Hillat Shook back in 1988. Each day brought new reports of bloodshed along a long boggy spine of high ground shared by the Nuer and the Dinka of Upper Nile: villagers shot in the back by

Riek's forces at Pok Tap; a battle at Duk Faiwil; cattle stolen at Duk Fadiat.

Emma spotted Garang's men following her on the streets of Nairobi. On September 9 Garang put out a radio message stating that the *Turuk* had planned Riek and Lam's coup against him. "Riek's marriage to the white foreign relief worker was part of this plot.... If Riek wanted a second wife, why did he not marry from the many very beautiful young girls in Bentiu where he spent five years, just to end up marrying an old white woman he just met?" At Wilson Airport in Nairobi, Emma managed to board a UN plane to Loki. But a UN security officer there pulled her off a plane bound for Nasir. Emma knew the security officer; she'd often shared a table with him at the mess hall. Now he seemed cold, even hostile. This was no romantic adventure, the man told her roughly. Garang had accused her of engineering the split within the SPLA—a split that was about to erupt into bloody tribal warfare. The UN had to avoid any appearance of taking sides. Operation Lifeline had already pulled its personnel out of the contested area. If she insisted on going back to Nasir, she'd have to find another way of getting there.

Emma was bewildered and angry. Incredibly, she later told friends she had not realized that Riek's actions might lead Operation Lifeline to regard her as a liability. She argued with the security officer, pointing out that a dozen expatriates remained at the UN camp in Nasir. She said she still was the Street Kids International representative and had the right to join them. The man walked away to confer with his superiors by walkie-talkie. When he came back, he was more determined than ever. The only authorized SKI office was in Kapoeta, he said—and Kapoeta was closed to UN flights for the time being. His advice to her was to go back to Nairobi and stay there until further notice.

Emma stalked off. The security officer saw that she was tearful; she lit a cigarette to try to compose herself. Until now she'd regarded the UN planes almost as her own little airline. She knew all the pilots by name and often asked after their children. But the UN planes weren't the only ones that landed in southern Sudan. Some charities preferred to remain independent of Operation Lifeline. There were missionaries who flew into the south. Over the last few years, several Christian groups had begun buying back slaves that had allegedly been captured by the government's Baggara militias, despite UN warnings that such "redemptions" only encouraged the militias to capture more. The Christian "redeemers" hired their own charter flights at $10,000 per trip to fly into

Bahr el-Ghazal. Journalists and politicians also hired their own planes on occasion to get into the south. So did the SPLA and its backers, such as Tiny Rowland.

It took several days, but somehow Emma learned that one of these private charter flights was leaving for Nasir, and she talked the other passengers into letting her get on board. On September 23 she finally made it to Ketbek. Riek says she stormed straight to his *tukul* to confront him. "You can't take me for granted like that," he says she told him. "I'm facing the same risks as you, and I want to know what you are doing."

He says he took it to mean that he should have let her in on the plot. He says it was the last thing he ever tried to hide from Emma.

Chapter Twenty-one

H E *WILL* LIE TO YOU," said Lam Akol, almost admiringly, after I told him what Riek had said about his promise not to hide anything else from Emma. Lam was still angry at Riek over the blunders he claimed Riek had made in the days after they put out their fateful radio message calling for John Garang's overthrow. For a start, he said, Riek never should have come right out and admitted that they wanted to sue for peace with the Khartoum government. That alienated the government's northern opponents like Sadiq al-Mahdi, and as Lam put it, "these people have the leverage to make things difficult." In other words, northerners who wanted the south to keep on fighting stepped up their backing for Garang. It also gave Garang the chance to accuse the plotters of being in Khartoum's pocket. (Whether he and Riek were in fact already in that pocket was a question Lam did not address.)

Instead, Lam said, Riek should have stuck with the deliberately vague language asking for the "self-determination for the south" that they had agreed to in their Nasir Declaration. But as soon as the BBC man flew up to Nasir, Riek started blabbing into his tape recorder about making peace and how the SPLA shouldn't bother trying to free the whole country from Islamic fundamentalism, just the south. "There was no way of stopping it," said Lam, disgusted. Clever, devious Lam seethed with frustration; he longed to take charge of the movement, but his birth into the smallish Shilluk tribe made it impossible for him to do so. He was obliged to put Riek at the head of his plot for the same reason that Garang had been obliged to promote Riek. If a Nuer wasn't seen to be near the top of things, the Nuer wouldn't follow, and without the Nuer, the rebellion would go nowhere.

Even with the Nuer, the mutiny against Garang was in trouble. Through bad luck, bad timing, or bad judgment, Riek and Lam had failed to secure the overt support of any senior Dinka commanders. According to Nyaba, the SPLA unit in Riek's home district of Bentiu was the only one to respond to their radio message appealing for Garang's overthrow. There was widespread discontent among the rebels. But few had any reason to believe that Riek and Lam would be any better than Garang, and many Dinka suspected they'd be worse.

Garang moved swiftly to solidify his support. At an August 30 meeting of the SPLA High Command, the big bald-headed chairman told the rebels that Tiny Rowland and Sudan's National Islamic Front were behind Riek and Lam's attempted coup. This is the situation, he said in his icy way. The *jallaba* were saying they were ready to let the south secede. Really the Sudanese government wanted to take advantage of the SPLA's weakness after the fall of Mengistu and to trick the rebels into self-destructing. They had come to him with their so-called peace offer. He refused. So they turned to Riek and Lam.

The reasons he'd rejected the government's offer were these: He didn't trust the NIF, and even if he had, he did not believe they were politically strong enough to make a lasting agreement. Only a genuine constitutional convention would have the power to do that. Any peace made with this government would be a bad peace. It would leave the SPLA's allies in the north—African peoples such as the Ngok Dinka and the Nuba and the peoples of the southern Blue Nile, not to mention the traditional Muslim political parties now united with the SPLA in opposition to the NIF—stranded under a newly strengthened Islamic fundamentalist government. And it would not last. The Arabs who ran this government would never give up the south's riches willingly, rest assured of that. All they really wanted was to "use a slave to catch a slave": to divide and conquer the southern peoples so as to exploit their land.

Riek and Lam thought they could outfox the *jallaba,* but in fact the wily *jallaba* and their British allies had outsmarted them, Garang went on. He, John Garang, would try to bring them back to their senses. The commanders should not be tempted to make peace with the north just because they were running out of ammunition without Ethiopia to resupply them. The Ethiopians weren't the only *Turuk* in the world. In

June and July Garang had visited the United States and Europe. He still had a few more tricks in his bag. He controlled the gold mines outside Kapoeta. He could sell the gold from Kapoeta to buy weapons. Parts of the south still under his control contained other valuable commodities: teak forests, for example, and rare animals. In the meantime he put the choice to them: Did they want to surrender to the *jallaba,* or did they want to keep on fighting?

The commanders, I was told, said they wanted to keep fighting.

Then this mass of men flanked by their armed bodyguards silently examined one another, wondering who among them meant what he said and who did not. For as long as men could remember, the southern Sudanese had had only one way of telling whether a man was with them or not: the tribal markings scored so deeply into a boy's head that, as foreigners often noted, they remained visible on the skulls of the dead. It was the *khawajas* and their Sudanese imitators who had brought these ideas of solidarity based on Africanness, blackness, Christianity, marginality. At this catastrophic moment for the south, many southerners began to ask themselves again if the ties of blood and cattle were not the only ones that truly mattered.

WHILE JOHN GARANG was telling his commanders about Tiny Rowland, the Lonrho chairman was the subject of another sultry August meeting—this one in a Paris restaurant. Adnan Khashoggi, the Saudi Arabian wheeler-dealer who in the 1970s tried to get hold of the Sudanese oil concession by luring the Nuer into a separate agreement with the north, was sitting down to tell a prominent Libyan about some fabulous opportunities that might be opening up once again in the Sudan. The news was out that Chevron would soon be abandoning its $1 billion investment. Rumor had it the Americans would sell for a fraction of what they had put into their concession. Oil was more attractive than it had been for years. The world price had risen from $16 in 1988 to $22 a barrel in 1991. But the problem remained the same: to resume serious exploration one had to somehow neutralize the SPLA in the area of the oilfields.

Tiny Rowland was providing Riek and Lam with money, but Lonrho's share price had fallen lately. Khashoggi told the Libyan, whose name was Mohammed Obedi, that the company needed cash. Obedi had brokered some commercial deals for Qaddafi. Khashoggi proposed that he broker a joint venture between Lonrho and Latfico, the Libyan Arab Foreign Investment Company. In September, Obedi and Khashoggi met with Rowland to discuss the outlines of a possible deal. Obedi later told *The Times* of London that Lonrho's interests in Sudan were mentioned, as well as the company's 45 percent stake in Ghana's Ashanti gold mines.

Two other foreign businessmen were watching the developments in Upper Nile carefully. Lutfur Rahman Khan was a Pakistani native who had moved to Vancouver more than a decade earlier. He told Madelaine Drohan of *The Globe and Mail* that his father was a Pakistani military officer. Khan added that "friends of his father" let him know in 1991 that Chevron would soon be leaving Sudan. Later he told me that his uncle, a Pakistani diplomat, alerted him to the opportunity. He said his uncle encouraged him to meet with Sudanese officials in Washington, D.C., to talk about the possibilities for oil development. Intrigued by these talks, Khan traveled to Khartoum, where the NIF government arranged a field visit for him to the oilfields. Khan's analysts advised him that the Heglig and Unity fields alone contained three hundred million barrels of recoverable crude reserves. Khan said he told the Sudanese "we will make an attempt to raise the necessary finances to get this project onstream. If we can get the funds, we will be in action."

Evidently Turabi trusted Khan. The NIF leader had made sure party loyalists controlled every aspect of Sudan's energy industry. Other businessmen claimed that the NIF favored State Petroleum because Khan belonged to the Muslim Brotherhood. Khan scoffs at the charge. "I had no connection with any brotherhood. We were a dollar-driven business." But he agrees that his religious credentials helped win the government's trust. "It was an extra level of comfort for them that I was a Canadian Muslim." Despite Khan's lack of cash or operational expertise, NIF officials authorized Chevron to show him their seismic data from the region and he began work on a business plan. In November 1991, Khan, his brother, and two other Pakistani-born businessmen founded a Canadian oil company they named State Petroleum.

Adolf Lundin, a Swedish mine and oil promoter, was also nosing around Sudan's oilfields. Lundin had no Islamic credentials, but he prided himself on his willingness to do business with unsavory governments. "If you want to find big deposits today, you have to go to countries which are unpopular," he told a reporter. His International Petroleum Corporation (IPC) had been exploring the Horn of Africa for several years. Early in 1991, Egypt occupied the Halaib Triangle, a disputed piece of land on its border with Sudan, after Sudan authorized IPC to prospect there. Like Khan's State Petroleum, IPC was based in Vancouver. It seems to have had access to Chevron's seismic data, too. In the weeks leading up to Riek and Lam's attempted coup, the company reached an agreement with Khartoum to explore the old Chevron field at Delta Toker. Then, in November, IPC signed an agreement with Ethiopia's new government to explore another former Chevron concession, this one on the Sudanese border in Gambella province, near the refugee camps the SPLA had abandoned in May.

While Tiny Rowland sought the limelight with dramatic pronouncements about ending Sudan's civil war, the two newcomers from Vancouver remained deep in the shadows. But long after Rowland was gone, Khan and Lundin would still be profiting from their early deals with the NIF government to develop southern Sudan's oilfields.

UNLIKE THE UN staff at Loki, Emma's expatriate friends at Nasir greeted her warmly when she finally made it back. Khartoum's decision to shut down all flights to Nasir for nearly two weeks after the BBC announced the coup had fostered an unusual spirit of solidarity between the UN camp and Ketbek. Khartoum had even blocked food deliveries to the expatriates, forcing Ian Lethbridge to order a brief evacuation. On their return to Nasir, the aid workers found that death and malnutrition rates had shot up to terrifying levels among the remaining refugees. They knew it wasn't their fault, but they felt horribly about waiting out the flight ban in Loki while the refugees starved to death at Nasir. Riek's human rights rhetoric thrilled them. Perhaps Emma had been right all along, and it had been the SPLA and not Riek who was responsible for everything that had gone wrong over the summer. What Riek was saying about the SPLA—that it was a secretive dictatorial organization with unclear aims that fed like a parasite off the impoverished people of the south—was exactly what most of the aid workers thought. But until now the expatriates, like the southerners themselves, had been forced to choose between Garang and the Islamic fundamentalists who ran the northern government. Now here was Emma's husband offering liberation from both. "It was like everybody was running around saying 'We are all democrats now!' " one aid worker recalled.

At first Emma seemed to think she could carry on with her schools program as if nothing had changed. Before she left for England, she faxed

Peter Dalglish a long field report from Nairobi. "It said 'I did this and distributed this much and P.S. three weeks ago I married Riek Machar in a
short ceremony in his community,' " Dalglish remembers. Such breezy
confidence was typical Emma, and Daglish was so infatuated that his first
instinct was to go along with her. But Garang was already furious with
Operation Lifeline and the aid agencies for allegedly facilitating Riek
and Lam's mutiny. "My board said no," he told me. "They said southern
Sudan is already highly politicized. We cannot have the representative of
our agency married to the commander of the area." Emma's friends had
warned her even before the split that Street Kids International would not
keep her on if she married Riek, but she was strangely blind to the obvious conflict between her humanitarian work and her husband's war.
When she heard the rumors that Dalglish was planning to fire her, she
decided to go to Nairobi to phone him. Riek said it had never occurred to
him that Emma might lose her job because of marrying him. He encouraged her to go and talk things over with her boss. Knowing that serious
fighting had already started on the Dinka-Nuer border to the west of
Nasir, he may also have feared for her safety inside southern Sudan.

She was allowed to fly out of Nasir under a pseudonym. (Garang's
faction, like Riek's, scrutinized every UN flight manifesto and complained if any of its enemies were allowed to travel on UN planes.)
When she arrived at Loki this time, the head of UN security himself had
prepared for her arrival. After arranging for her to fly out under an
assumed name first thing in the morning, he ordered additional Kenyan
paramilitaries to stand guard around the camp that night. He gave Emma
a concrete *tukul* to herself and set an armed man right outside it. The
security chief had known Emma as the vivacious charmer of the mess
hall. To him, she now seemed "tired and withdrawn, perhaps even traumatized." Maybe she was frightened by news of the fighting or depressed
about the prospect of losing her job. Maybe she just felt resentful knowing herself to be unwelcome. He remembers how relieved he felt once
the night had passed uneventfully and Emma was on her way to Nairobi.
As soon as she had gone, he sent a message to Nairobi emphasizing that
she shouldn't be allowed to fly on UN planes or stay in UN camps in the
future.

From Nairobi Emma phoned Dalglish. Her boss admitted that he had
grave concerns about her ability to continue her work for Street Kids
International as Riek's wife. She argued that he was making up his mind
based on very little information. Before he gave up on her, he ought to

come out to Sudan and see for himself all that she was doing. Now that Riek was going to free the SPLA's child soldiers, she would be able to open more schools than ever. Dalglish was tempted, but he had to say no. He sent Emma a fax on behalf of the board saying that because Street Kids International had to preserve its impartiality, it could not renew her contract in the fall.

The board's action was utterly predictable, but it infuriated Emma. She phoned Dalglish again and said, "You're firing me because I fell in love with someone, and I resent that." Then she wrote urging him to reconsider. "I knew my marriage would not be easy, but what to do? You can't go around looking for an ideal situation and then say, 'Now I want to fall in love.'" Dalglish replied with a letter in which he quoted the Persian poet Omar Khayyám. "I had written her [a letter with] a poem about how the moving hand of time writes ['and having written, moves on']. You know that poem? Well, I was trying to say that what's done is done. I was really upset by her letter. I was really hurt. I cried. She accused me of having betrayed her and betrayed the children." Riek, too, remembered Emma's fury. "It definitely affected her because it was a good source of income," he said. "And she was angry with the behavior of Peter because he wrote her a silly poem."

Emma was beginning to feel the full weight of Operation Lifeline's disapproval, but it only made her more defiant. She no longer had an income, but she had saved enough money to keep going for a while. She'd been banned from UN flights, but she somehow made it back to Nasir—she told friends that the UN pilots sometimes let her slip on board despite orders not to—and threw herself into Riek's cause. She was twenty-seven years old. If she was afraid, she did not show it. All the energy she had poured into the schools now went into Riek's movement. The UN had donated to the education program a typewriter and a mimeograph machine. Now she sat on an old ammunition crate in the two-room hut she shared with Riek and used these machines to bang out copies of Riek's proclamations and manifestos. At his political meetings, she became the note-taker. She used her remaining school blackboards to outline strategy for his rebel faction.

Unlike Riek, she understood the power that the Western press could wield over policy toward a country like Sudan, where Europe and the United States had few tangible interests. She opened her address book and began contacting the many journalists she'd met as an aid worker and before, in the London peace group. She invited them to come to Nasir to interview her and Riek. To anyone else who would listen, she denounced Garang. "He's a monster, a tyrant, a killer," she would cry. "You have no idea how many people he's killed, how many he's holding prisoner." The danger only seemed to heighten the electricity between her and Riek. She told one friend that it was "an incredible high" to get up from love-making to draft constitutions for an independent southern Sudan.

Someone had given Emma a brown and white puppy. Riek's soldiers named the puppy Come On because she was always calling it to follow her. With Come On at her side, she rode a dugout canoe down to Nasir every morning. She would have her breakfast at the UN camp, then check the flight manifesto to see who was coming and going. If journalists or official visitors were arriving, she would be on hand to greet them and take them to Ketbek to see Riek. Hania Sholkamy, an Egyptian anthropologist whom UNICEF hired to investigate conditions in the minors' camp, was one such visitor. Sholkamy flew up to Nasir in October with a young British journalist who had known Emma in London. The young journalist was thrilled to interview Emma; the night they arrived in Nasir, she told Sholkamy in an awestruck whisper all about Emma's marriage. The next morning Emma came to the UN camp to see them, looking so glamorous that Sholkamy herself almost felt flattered to be invited back to Ketbek with her. "She was looking fantastic, as she did, wearing big Wellingtons and a beautiful sarong," Sholkamy said. They rode the UN motorboat to the SPLA compound. Thousands of tall, thin refugees came to stand by the river and watch them as they sped past. "*Khawaja! Khawaja!*" shouted the children. Emma seemed not to notice. She spoke in low, urgent tones about Garang's attacks on Riek. Sholkamy was thinking, "How exciting it must be for her to do this rather than to be an ordinary development worker."

To reach Emma's *tukul,* they had to pass through a gauntlet of armed teenage boys with the Nuer slashes across their foreheads. An old tank stood in one part of the compound. Men sat around cleaning their guns. A bare-breasted woman was pounding grain in the corner, while another woman boiled porridge over a dung fire. The young soldiers greeted Emma shyly as the visitors gaped at their surroundings. "God, Emma, it's so exciting," the journalist from London kept saying.

Inside her *tukul* Emma sat the two women down on her metal bedstead. She said she wanted to tell them all about Garang's plan to exploit the boys of southern Sudan. She talked about the boys Kuol Manyang was keeping at the abandoned Catholic mission at Palataka. She suggested the journalist visit Palataka and write an article about the recruitment camps that Garang called his FACE schools. "They are soldier factories—the children know no other culture but the gun!" she would say. She told them about how the Latuka people who lived around Torit had driven their boys into the mountains to save them from being forced to join the rebels. (Emma's pitch worked. Several months later a journalist went to Palataka and wrote an article in which she described the boys, "dressed in rags and barefooted, grim-faced and disoriented.") Emma's passion and sincerity impressed Sholkamy. She felt that Emma really cared about the children of southern Sudan.

Another journalist was even more helpful. Richard Ellis of *The Sunday Times* of London visited Emma in the fall of 1991. In a long article subtitled " 'The White Woman' Says Yes to Guerrilla Leader," Ellis called Emma's marriage to Riek a story that might have come out of a "Mills and Boon [romance] novel." He described the hole in the ground at Ketbek that she used as a toilet, the copy of *Vogue* magazine featuring "must-have tweeds" that she kept by her bedside, and the solar panel that she used to read at night and that he said attracted thousands of mosquitoes, moths, and crickets. She told him she'd awakened one night in her hut to find a rat gnawing at her forehead. She said she had been bitten by a scorpion and suffered amoebic dysentery. She showed him the muddy pit she used as a bomb shelter, confessing with self-deprecating charm that she was the first one to dive into it at the sight of an Antonov. "I'm not very brave," she commented.

The article noted that Riek and Garang were fighting for supremacy over the SPLA and that Garang's side had accused her of being a British spy. "She dismisses this as ridiculous, but is passionate in her opposition to the tactics of Garang's SPLA, which have included taking up to 50,000 boys as young as seven away from their parents and herding them into 'schools' for military training," Ellis wrote. Emma admitted that her marriage had made her enemies but brushed aside the danger with gallant assurance. "There are some people out there who would gladly put a bullet through my head, but I'm sure it won't come to that," she told Ellis. The only things she said she missed in Nasir were "the cinema and the theatre and occasionally a juicy steak." "I'm very happy," she said. "I knew exactly what I was getting myself in for. When you are in love with someone, you can go through anything."

. . .

SPLASHED ACROSS a section front, with a photo of Riek's bandoliered
soldiers next to a photo of Emma in a canoe, bare-shouldered and smiling with Come On at her side, the article caused a sensation back in
England. "Love Blooms Among the Bullets in Sudan," blared the headline. The aid workers who saw it in Nasir were less entertained. The rains
were ending. Sudan's season of coolness and peace was about to give way
to the dry fever of war. Garang's SPLA had sailed up the White Nile on
a stolen Red Cross barge to attack Riek's forces near Ler. Rumors came
trickling in that Dinka commanders were killing Nuer officers in the
areas under their control. In Nasir people began to disappear. According
to Peter Adwok Nyaba, in early September Riek's commanders began
executing officers who disapproved of the break with Garang. Around
the same time a Dinka captain who had been the aid workers' liaison with
the rebels began telling them about his fears for his life.

Michael Manyon Anyuang was one of those increasingly rare southern Sudanese men who actually seemed better equipped for life in
peacetime than in war. A former circuit court judge, Michael spoke
excellent English. He was thrilled when Douglas Johnson sent him a pair
of books on Nuer and Dinka law. As the SPLA's relief officer in Nasir, he
spent every day with the aid workers, riding up and down the Sobat in
the UN motorboat, translating, counting refugees, monitoring airdrops.
On one of these outings, Michael confided he was worried about his wife
and children. After the expulsion from Ethiopia, they had ended up at
Pochalla, an area south of Nasir that remained loyal to Garang. Michael
was afraid that Garang might take revenge against his family because
he'd remained in Nasir with Riek and Lam. He said he wished he could
join them. He asked the aid workers to try to visit them in Pochalla and
find out how they were.

Michael began to visit the UN camp in the evenings, rambling on
about how he didn't feel safe at night among the Nuer and Shilluk officers. He was often drunk, and the expatriates didn't take his fears seriously. "Oh Michael, what could happen?" they'd ask him playfully.
"You're practically living at the UN camp as it is." On the evening of
September 23, the day Emma returned to Nasir, he failed to turn up. No
one took much notice. SPLA cadres often vanished without explanation.
They got reassigned, they went home for family emergencies. One usually had to take the rebels' word for it. But Michael had been the aid

workers' conduit to the rebels; without him they had no one to tell them the position of the authorities on the refugee questions that arose each day. They started asking questions. At first they met with silence. Then Riek's security chief told them Michael had been caught trying to plant a land mine in the UN camp.

The charge was ludicrous. A coded message went out to Vincent O'Reilly in Nairobi: *Michael has been arrested. What should we do?* O'Reilly sent Alastair and another aid worker to Riek's compound at Ketbek to protest. Emma was there. She liked Michael and seemed horrified to hear that he had been arrested. But Riek was impassive. "Look, you don't really know these people," he kept telling the Westerners. "In these difficult times, your best friend can turn out to be your enemy." Riek finally agreed that Alastair could see Michael at eight the following morning, but the appointed time came and went without any sign of Michael. At ten Riek sent a message to the UN camp apologizing for the delay and telling them not to worry. Four hours later a soldier took the aid workers to one of the ruined colonial houses by the river. The soldiers wouldn't leave them alone with Michael, and they could tell he must have walked a long way to reach the house. He was dirty and sweating, and his eyes bulged with terror.

The *khawajas* were unnerved. Neither of them worked for the International Red Cross, but they tried to go through what they imagined must be a standard prisoner-of-war routine. Was Michael being fed? Would he like his law books? But Michael was too frightened to answer, and even to the aid workers, the questions seemed oddly irrelevant. Something dark and strong was happening that they felt powerless to stop. After securing a promise that they could visit the next day, the UN officials left. The next day Michael was gone. They never saw him again. When they protested to Riek, he flew into a rage and accused them of trying to abduct a criminal caught planting land mines. Amnesty International later reported that Michael was executed six months after his arrest. The Uduk told Wendy James that Michael and another Dinka officer were killed in April 1992. The Uduk heard three bursts of shots in the night; the next morning the prisoners were dead. They also told her they heard that two Dinka medical assistants and twenty-eight Nuba soldiers were executed at Nasir in July 1992.

Emma seemed as puzzled and upset as everyone else by Michael's arrest. She had wanted to go with the UN officials to see him, but they chose to go alone. Riek said that Michael's killing and the killing of one of the medical assistants were the hardest things for Emma to bear in their life together at Nasir. He said he and Emma also heard the shots that killed the men. "She knew them," he told me later. "She knew that there was no reason for them to die." Did she weep or did she rage? Riek didn't say, and he's the only person who knows. She had nagged him about the cases, he said, and he agreed with her. As he told me in his reasonable way, "When you know a woman is right, what can you do?" Riek clucked sadly at the memory of the killings.

He said a saboteur working for Garang who wanted "to project us as people who did not care about human rights" was responsible for them, adding that the man later escaped to Ethiopia and so could not be brought to justice. He said he called a meeting of his officers after he and Emma heard the shots. He said he told them, "This is disgusting. If this is what you're going to do, count me out."

I related Riek's account of Michael's death to Lam Akol. He found it hilarious. Michael was indeed executed at night, Lam said—on Riek's orders. Perhaps he and Emma did hear the shots. If they did, Lam agreed that Riek would have denied any responsibility for the murders. "Riek will say anything to stay in power," he said. Lam himself left for Nairobi in September. Deftly parrying the efforts of some church groups to organize reconciliation talks between him and Garang, Lam held what he called his "first serious meeting" with officials from the northern government in Nairobi. Tiny Rowland "facilitated" the meeting, he says. "He asked us, 'Are you ready to talk to the government?' We knew what we wanted, so we were not afraid to talk." (Riek says he had no idea Lam was meeting with the government that fall, just as Lam says he had no idea what Riek was doing in Nasir.) Their fellow conspirator, Peter Adwok Nyaba, says Rowland also began channeling funds at this time from the NIF government to "the Nasir faction," as people had started calling Riek and Lam's group.

If Emma knew of these intrigues, she gave no hint of it. As for Michael's murder, perhaps she accepted Riek's explanation and left it at that. Or perhaps, as Riek suggests, she never resolved the issue to her satisfaction but pushed it out of mind and tried to forget about it. "It was a matter of objectives," Riek said vaguely when I asked how Emma coped with the factional fighting. "We were all together in the SPLA prior to 1991. And the abuses of human rights—she saw some. But that people had to die, that she could not comprehend.... But how to stop it was the question." In public she took Riek's side no matter what he did. "You saw a whole new face of her coming out, which was to dig in and deny," said one friend. "The more you pushed her, the more she saw that this thing was going wrong, the more she denied."

AT THE END OF September 1991 Emma wrote her mother that she was "happy and relaxed" to be back with Riek in Nasir. A new prophet had arisen in Nuerland. Wut Nyang—the name means "Crocodile Man"— was a calm, soft-spoken young man whom Emma said inspired great fear and respect. He lived west of Nasir, on the Zeraf Island between the SPLA and government forces. Wut Nyang claimed to be possessed by Deng, the same divinity who had spoken through Ngungdeng. In a letter to a friend, Emma called him a "fascinating character, young in age (late twenties). A man who is illiterate, but has a very keen grasp of local politics." Wut Nyang's divinity had given him the power of cursing. Emma described how it worked. "One speech I attended he spoke about the wickedness of stealing and that all thieves present had to confess publicly or something terrible would happen to them. Sure enough people came forward, some saying they had already started to die. A few days later an old sub-chief who apparently had stolen our fishing net was bitten by a snake and died immediately."

The message from Wut Nyang's divinity in the fall of 1991 was that the Nuer should stop fighting each other. Historically the Nuer had done that by uniting against the Dinka. The prophet urged the Nasir faction to enter an all-Nuer alliance with the government-supported Anyanya II battalions still based at Bentiu. Riek's officials started reminding people of how Riek was left-handed and Ngundeng had foretold that a left-handed man would lead the Nuer to victory. On October 9 Riek's forces occupied the village of Kongor, capturing many cattle and killing many Dinka who lived in surrounding villages. The fighters came streaming back from Kongor to Ketbek, chanting war songs and dancing in formation. Emma organized a victory celebration in honor of the troops, trilling and ululating with the Nuer women as an ox was speared through the heart in sacrifice. "She was a very good wife," recalls one Nuer comrade of Riek's from this time.

Lam's secret talks with the government had begun to bear fruit. Khartoum blocked Operation Lifeline deliveries to Garang's area, while it allowed a UN barge filled with grain to sail from the government-held town of Malakal to Nasir for the first time in eight years. Riek claimed not to know why the government had given Operation Lifeline permission to send food to his area and not to Garang's, and the aid workers were so desperate to feed the refugees from Ethiopia that they didn't ask. But he insisted that they leave the off-loading of the barge a few miles outside of Nasir to Taban Deng Gai, his security chief, and his soldiers. A second relief barge arrived in early 1992. The Uduk later told Wendy James that they were ordered to send 150 men to help Riek's soldiers unload this grain onto trucks. After the trucks were loaded, the rebels wouldn't let the hungry Uduk get on them. Instead Riek's men drove off the main dirt track to Nasir and made a detour to Ketbek. "They took the lorries into the bush where they had built their houses and unloaded the grain there," a man named Dawud Hajar said. "The Dhamkin dug great holes in the ground, and the sacks of grain were stacked in the holes." The guards on the barge and the drivers of the trucks, he said, were "from Nasir—the people of Riek Machar . . . The word of Riek Machar is obeyed there. He is a powerful man."

West of Nasir, in Riek's hometown of Ler, Dutch medical workers observed unmarked planes dropping mysterious bundles to the Nasir forces. Riek's men wouldn't let the *khawajas* go outside during the air-drops, but the planes came from the north, and the aid workers guessed that the packages they delivered contained government arms and ammunition for Riek's group.

GARANG HAD MANAGED to keep a famous Nuer commander on his high command. To show that his quarrel with Riek and Lam was personal and philosophical, not tribal, Garang sent this Nuer, whose name was William Nyuon, north to quash the rebellion. In October a battalion under William Nyuon's command invaded western Upper Nile, Riek's home territory. Nyuon's men occupied the area for one week. Riek put Wut Nyang on the radio to plead with the Nuer not to attack his own people. Then Riek's forces counterattacked. With the prophet Wut Nyang at their head, a mob of Anyanya II fighters, SPLA soldiers from Nasir, and Nuer village militias began marching south. Riek used all the symbols of Nuer religion and tradition to rally his people to his side. The Nuer under the prophet's command wore white ashes on their bodies and the white sheets tied over their shoulders that were supposed to protect them from bullets. They called themselves the *Jiech Mabor*, or "White Army," after the white of their spears. They fought in the traditional age-set units composed of all the men who had recieved the *gaar* together. They made a terrifying sight as they marched, chanting war verses about their ferocity. They drove Garang's men all the way back to their leader's hometown of Bor. Then the killing really started.

Now was the Nuers' chance to avenge all the grievances that had festered over the years of war, the opportunity to act on all the "bones" that had lain under the surface of rebel unity. The Anyanya II leaders killed by the SPLA in the 1980s; the cattle seized by the SPLA from Nuer herdsmen; the belittling of Nuer chiefs by the rebel bull-boys; the local disputes between Dinka and Nuer who shared grazing areas or fishing rights—the Nuer were going to use Khartoum's weapons to pay the Bor Dinka back for it all.

It was not just that John Garang and several other top SPLA leaders, including Kuol Manyang, came from the area around Bor. The Nuer also envied the food and supplies that Operation Lifeline had been giving the Bor Dinka. As the prophet Wut Nyang remarked, "People are saying the relatives of John Garang have received a lot of food." The ordinary Nuer didn't understand that Bor received more food because it lay at the end of a road, whereas most of Nuerland could be reached only by plane. A Red Cross plan to transport grain by barge up the White Nile from Bor to Ler only exacerbated their suspicions. The Red Cross bought and transported a shiny new European barge to Bor at great expense. But once the barge arrived, Khartoum refused to give the Red Cross permission to use it. The aid workers tried to explain that it was all Khartoum's fault that the barge sat idle, but the Nuer suspected the Bor Dinka of tricking them out of their share of the foreign food and supplies. When Garang's forces seized the long-grounded barge and used it to sail up the White Nile and attack Ler after Riek and Lam proclaimed their mutiny, the Nuer were further enraged.

Some say the prophet swore that any Nuer man who stayed behind would die of sickness or be eaten by crocodiles. Others say Wut Nyang excited the White Army with promises of Dinka cattle and women. Since the attackers used guns and their victims were not Nuer, they imagined themselves safe from the moral pollution of homicide. They were mostly villagers lured by the prospect of loot and revenge. Whatever they thought they were doing, they set off an explosion of bloodletting between Nuer and Dinka that continues to this day.

·   ·   ·

DAN EIFFE WAS A FORMER Irish priest who had gone to work for a Scandinavian charity called Norwegian People's Aid. At the end of September 1991 he was driving to Bor. He was near Mongalla when he suddenly saw thousands of Dinka running toward him down the dirt road. "I couldn't believe my eyes," Eiffe recalled years later. "They said the Nuer had come south and were killing them. Bodies were everywhere. People were crawling out of the bush, naked, confused, emotional. I stopped the car and got out. I was wearing a sort of Irish jersey. I took it off and I spread it over some bodies. When I came back later, I found vultures eating around it. Some people were strangled, some men were tied and burned. There were dead cattle and bodies. The Nuer had shot the cattle they couldn't take with them. I saw a fine-looking girl naked and burnt. These beautiful women—I was told they killed them after they started fighting among themselves about who to rape. 'Let's kill them rather than fight among ourselves.' "

That night Eiffe carried calabashes of water back and forth to the dying Dinka along the road south of Bor. "They said the Nuer were still at Bor. It was like the Nuer were under the spell of witchcraft. They were coming in waves. They said the Nuer were shouting, 'We will make you Dinka drink your own blood.' It was like they were bewitched." Eiffe took pictures. He drove south to Torit, where he boarded a UN relief plane. He wanted to tell Nairobi about what was happening. But when he reached the Operation Lifeline headquarters, he found it hard to persuade UN officials of the scale of the slaughter.

Eiffe thought the expatriates who had spent the summer with Riek at Nasir were especially dismissive. Like everyone else in southern Sudan, Eiffe knew about Emma's marriage. He felt that not only she, but a number of the aid workers at Nasir, perhaps inadvertently, had encouraged Riek and Lam to stage their revolt without any idea of what they were letting loose. Now, he thought, they did not want to acknowledge the consequences of their meddling. "They were totally naïve. They were playing a game in the middle of a very dangerous situation." Until then Eiffe, who was married to a Dinka woman with whom he had twin sons, had agreed with everything Riek and Lam said about the SPLA. "I was a fairly serious critic of the SPLA, but this traumatized me." He held Riek personally responsible, because the Nuer made up most of the force that assaulted Bor.

More than a hundred thousand Dinka fled the south before the Nuer advance. Before long Operation Lifeline couldn't hold a relief meeting without the rebel factions screaming recriminations at each other over Bor. Riek's group started issuing press releases along the lines of "Bor Captured, Great Victory." The UN had evacuated its staff weeks earlier when the fighting first started. It was decided that Alastair should go inspect the scene with some private relief officials and representatives from both rebel groups. They flew up to Loki and started driving north. Once they crossed into Equatoria, they found themselves in a sea of Dinka refugees, people shrieking and wailing about what the Nuer had done. But as their Land Cruiser approached Jemeza, a village south of Bor, it went quiet outside. "The whole air stank. It was just nothing—like the only form of life was sort of buzzards and stray dogs. And just everywhere were dead cows, dead people, people hanging upside down in trees," Alastair later told me. They had to keep driving off the road to avoid all the bodies. They saw three children tied together with their heads smashed in. They saw disemboweled women. Alastair took pictures. At Bor the huts were still smoldering. They had to cover their faces to breathe inside the hospital where Bernadette Kumar had once operated. A soldier's body was rotting inside, and the floors were heaped with the cattle carcasses. They noticed Nuer government ID cards spilled on the floor. Riek's new allies among the government-allied Anyanya II had obviously been in too much of a hurry to notice their loss.

Garang's forces had just retaken the town. The *khawajas* could hear gunfire. An SPLA soldier approached Alastair menacingly. "This is what you lot have caused," he said. The relief officials turned around and drove back to Loki. Alastair was shaken. In Nairobi another Operation Lifeline official took him aside and suggested that he take a break from Sudan for his own safety. "You must not become part of it," he warned. Patta Scott-Villiers took one look at her husband's snapshots from Bor and decided she did not want to go back to Nasir. "I felt that anyone associated with it was going to be in moral danger," she said later.

Eiffe made a video of what he had seen. He thought of taking it to Emma, whom he heard was staying at Sally Dudmesh's house in Langata, waiting for news. Eiffe had been trying without any success to interest the Nairobi press corps in the slaughter at Bor. He believed part of the reason he was having so much trouble was that many reporters were friends of Emma's. "There was a journalistic group, and she was the queen bee of them," he told me. "I was going to send her the pictures, but I didn't. I just thought, poor woman, I didn't want to be the one to give her the shock." Emma had been going around saying that the war was almost over between Riek and Garang. "She kept coming to me saying, 'Hey look, you know, we're going to be in Bor and, you know, once Bor has fallen, because it's the home ground of Garang, we've won the war,' " one friend recalled. Alastair did take his photos to Emma when he came back from Bor. "Just have a look at these," he said, tossing the black-and-white prints onto a table. Taut as a cat, Emma snatched them up and started flipping through them. They showed a dead child, buzzards eating the naked body of a man, Dinka streaming down the road. Just as quickly she set them down.

"What are these?" she said impatiently. "What I want to know is—was it a victory?"

Chapter Twenty-two

I T WAS NOT A VICTORY, not for Riek and not for anyone else. It came to be known as the Bor Massacre, but it was really more like a series of raids and massacres. Amnesty International later estimated that two thousand people died in nearly two weeks of killing. The Nuer also stole thousands of Dinka cattle, which—in an ironic piece of Nilotic justice—turned out to be infected with rinderpest. The stolen cattle infected Nuer and Shilluk herds, wiping out the livelihood of more than a million people and once again leaving the south prey to famine. Looking back, however, most observers agree that the Bor Massacre was the point at which Riek and Lam's rebellion turned irrevocably tribal. Prominent Dinka who had been thinking about joining the Nasir faction turned against Riek and Lam after Bor. And every Nuer who remained in SPLA territory feared for his life. A southern Sudanese student in Egypt at the time later recalled that when Nuer and Dinka students at his school heard about Bor, they attacked each other in the dining room with steak knives. As news of the slaughter trickled in to Kakuma, a refugee camp on the Kenyan border at Narus, fights broke out everywhere. The UN had to separate the Nuer and Dinka. "Even the children were trying to kill each other," an aid worker recalled. The UN eventually had to establish two camps at Kakuma: one for the Nuer and another for the Dinka.

Why did Riek let it happen? "It got out of control" was the explanation he gave me years later—though at the time he said exactly the opposite. "Fighting at Bor did not get out of control," he told *The Daily Telegraph*'s Scott Peterson. "I was in total control of how far the troops went." Peter Adwok Nyaba offers another story. "There really were no troops," he writes in his book. "The bulk of Riek's army were officers with no soldiers to command. The only fighters were the armed civilians—*Jiech Mabor*," Wut Nyang's ashen tribesmen. Back in August Garang had taunted Riek and Lam that they had only a "lot of refugees and a few bodyguards with them" at Nasir. In truth Garang's SPLA wasn't much better trained than Wut Nyang's White Army. But Garang could exert some control by regulating the ammunition his commanders received. Those who disobeyed orders failed to get more—if they didn't get a bullet in the back. The Nuer weapons, on the other hand, came from Khartoum, and Khartoum distributed them itself to individual commanders with an eye toward causing maximum disarray among Riek's forces. Wut Nyang and Anyanya II received government weapons as well as Riek's commanders. President Bashir had worked closely with Anyanya II when he served as the army's commanding officer in Muglad. Perhaps his government urged its old friends in the Nuer militia to alienate the Dinka for good. The government was also giving Wut Nyang food and supplies. And Nuer who were determined for their own reasons to avenge themselves against the SPLA were well represented in all three groups.

Even today it is hard to find a Nuer who blames Riek or even the prophet Wut Nyang for the massacre. "Riek was not responsible, Wut Nyang was not responsible—the elders of the tribe are the only responsible party," said Samuel Tut Paul, a Nuer teacher who came from the Lou Nuer country whence much of the White Army was drawn. "The pressure came from below. The White Army are just ordinary people in their *luaks* [cattle-byres]. When the SPLA came and started putting these unmarked guys, these Dinka over the Nuer, they saw it as an invasion. The SPLA was forming a system which was unknown to the people. Even though they gave everything they had to the SPLA, their grains, their cattle, these young men were raping their girls, having forced recruitments of their boys.

"It was wrong because their anger at the SPLA was taken out on ordinary people," said Samuel Tut Paul.

Riek encouraged the White Army to go to Bor, though he himself remained in Nasir. Maybe he was spellbound by Wut Nyang's prophecies; maybe he simply wanted a victory. When Scott Peterson flew up not long after the massacre, Riek welcomed him with a big grin. As usual, he had his Good News Bible with the gold-embossed lettering prominently displayed. Peterson asked him about Ngungdeng's prophecy; the prediction that an unmarked man would come out of the west to lead the Nuer was so widespread that even journalists had heard about it. Riek laughed it off. "I'm not a messiah to anybody. If they say so, I say no. This is not a religious war we are fighting," he said, speaking, Peterson later wrote, with "a practiced humility in his voice." "The secession from the north is in their blood. [My fighters] are fighting for issues, not tribes."

In a photograph Peterson took during the interview, Riek looks cool, even cocky. He leans back, one arm draped over the back of his chair while the other rests on the desk next to some papers. To Peterson, he seemed to want to have it both ways, one moment discounting tribal loyalties as though they belonged to "a different age," the next boasting that he had yet to see a Nuer who didn't support him. He claimed to feel "embarrassment" because "so many civilians were caught in the crossfire" at Bor. But he added a naked threat: "If there is a tribal element, the Nuer would destroy all the Dinka."

For Lam, who was dealing with the fallout in Nairobi, the Bor Massacre was the beginning of the end: "Everything we had called for was shattered," he told me. "After people saw the White Army had the same status as our army, discipline broke down. You cannot motivate people with witchcraft. This is where Riek got stuck. He started as a man who wanted to make a revolution, but he became just another Nuer leader." An American missionary who knew Riek well believes he deceived himself as much as he tried to deceive others about the reality of the massacre. "He thinks he can talk his way out of anything," he said. A former Nuer commander put it this way: "Riek is weak. He lives in a world of dreams."

"Riek is two characters within one person," says Peter Adwok Nyaba in his book. "Behind the facade of a smiling and benevolent Riek, there was another Riek Machar who was ruthlessly ordering the murder of Dinka officers at Nasir. Riek pretended he was innocent of all these crimes, but nobody has been tried for the murders that took place under his nose at Nasir." The chances that Riek's patron, Tiny Rowland, could deliver a peace agreement with the whole south were smashed. As the Dinka journalist Bona Malwal later put it, "Tiny went fishing, but the fish that he caught was too small for the bait he put out." From now on the best strategy for Khartoum was to keep the south divided and obtain a separate peace with the Nuer.

Meanwhile, at Bor, the naked Christian preacher who had been warning the Dinka that they faced catastrophe if they did not heed Isaiah's prophecy walked among the smoking ruins, banging his drum and ringing his bell. "You people!" Paul Kon Ajith cried. "God spoke, and you did not listen! Now he has sent the Nuer and their sorcerer to punish you. Mark my words: Until the Dinka make a present to God of our shrines to the *jak* at the place called Zion, we will be punished again and again, and we shall remain 'a people scattered and peeled,' 'a nation meted out and trodden under foot, whose land the rivers have spoiled.'"

Part Five

Be true to your own act, and congratulate yourself if you have done some-thing strange and extravagant and broken the monotony of a decorous age.

—Ralph Waldo Emerson, "On Heroism," in *Emerson's Essays.*

Chapter Twenty-three

I WAS AT THE CARTER CENTER in Atlanta when I heard about the massacre. Jimmy Carter had been trying to mediate a settlement of Sudan's civil war since 1988. In 1989 the former U.S. president had conducted talks between Bashir's government and the SPLA that ended in a stalemate. In February 1992 Carter invited both sides to a conference on conflict resolution at the center. I was covering the conference for the *Journal-Constitution*. At one of the sessions I ran into Bona Malwal, the former editor of *The Sudan Times*. Bona asked if I would like to see what Riek's men had done at Bor.

I said I would.

Bona opened his briefcase and handed me a video. I took the tape downstairs to an empty room with a television set, popped it in, and started watching.

The camera lurched clumsily past a man's body sprawled out on the ground. I saw maggots and flies eating human flesh, and a cow stabbed through the eyes. It may have been the film Dan Eiffe took. It had a homemade quality. It made me feel dizzy.

I went to find Lam's brother, Moses Akol. A smiling man with a shiny, round face, Moses was in everyday life a public policy analyst in Alameda, California. But at the conference he was representing Riek and Lam's faction of the SPLA. He knew all about Bona's video and dismissed it with smooth assurance, insisting that Riek and Lam weren't responsible for what it showed. "It's terrible, of course," he told me. "But the video doesn't really say anything about who did it."

What he said was quite true. But after watching it, I no longer envied Emma.

Chapter Twenty-four

IT WAS A TERRIBLE TIME for Emma. Everyone was talking about the monstrous crimes the Nuer had committed at Bor. Emma had lost her job, and now she began to lose many friends. The southern Sudanese who backed Garang were the first to cut her. The Dinka teachers and others she'd gotten to know in Equatoria went out of their way to avoid her. Some hissed angrily if they happened to run into her in the Nairobi shopping district. She argued violently with Willy and several other Western friends who were appalled by the slaughter at Bor. Sam Kiley, *The Times* of London's bald, plain-spoken Nairobi correspondent, made Emma look at some pictures from Bor that his newspaper thought too gruesome to publish. "Now you see what your fucking hero has done," he told her angrily.

But she wouldn't see it. To Kiley and the others, she put forth various arguments exculpating Riek: that Garang's forces were exaggerating the number of casualties at Bor; that in fact the SPLA mainstream had done most of the killing when they retook the town; that it was a war, and in wars, innocent people lost their lives. Kiley had met Emma in Nasir about the time she married Riek; he thought she was "a beautiful and intelligent English chick who was living out a middle-class fantasy" when she went to live in Nasir. Another British friend recalls the consternation Emma caused by her stubborn refusal to acknowledge the simple human tragedy of Bor. "A lot of us were working in southern Sudan, and we were all put in a difficult position where you have someone who is a friend, who in the past you could talk about it with, then suddenly we're in the position where she tells us that the Bor Massacre didn't really happen, that it's a figment of somebody's imagination." Emma remained so ferociously loyal to Riek that some Operation Lifeline types began calling her Lady Macbeth, whispering "Out dammed spot—out I say" behind her back when she stopped by UN headquarters in Nairobi to argue for more aid to Nasir.

Kiley wouldn't stand for it. In typically blunt fashion, he pointed out to Emma that Garang's men hardly could have killed the Dinka whose dead bodies Dan Eiffe videotaped in September—weeks before the SPLA reoccupied Bor. He said the killing and looting at Bor were not ordinary occurrences but on a scale unseen in the south since the Baggara militia raids that caused the famine of 1988. The Nuer had looted a million head of cattle, and tens of thousands of Dinka refugees remained afraid to go home. As an American missionary later wrote, the assault on Bor "possessed a ferocity that indicates that the intention was to wipe out the Bor Dinka economy, the social structure of the people, and with it their will to survive." Shaking with rage, Emma denied it all. She and Kiley finally agreed never to discuss southern Sudan again; in Kiley's view, it was the only way to maintain a friendship with her.

Others arrived at the same conclusion without ever confronting her directly. If anyone ventured to question Riek's handling of Bor, Emma's face would harden. "Just what do you know about fighting a bush war?" she might say. "How do you propose to get rid of a dictator like Garang? How would you maintain control over soldiers and civilians hundreds of miles away without radios or motorized vehicles?" She would badger them until all but the most self-confident characters went away feeling wimpish and softheaded. "She always defended him," Sally recalled to me. "She believed what Riek was doing was totally right." Another woman friend told me, "Emma was terribly good at justifying herself. One was—frankly—rather intimidated by her. She had a way of making you feel as if your concerns were rather small... a way of making you feel very—well, very ordinary."

If the Bush administration had ever considered backing Riek and Lam—as Riek and others claimed they had been led to believe by the U.S. officials who visited Nasir in May—Washington changed its mind after reports of the Bor Massacre were publicized in the press. But Garang was taking no chances. After the visit of French humanitarian minister Bernard Kouchner to Torit in August, the SPLA leader made a secret visit to Paris. There he met with the son of President François Mitterand, who was in charge of African affairs, as well as officials from the Total oil company, which held the never-developed concession for oil in SPLA-held Equatoria. Garang came back confident of French support.

Meanwhile Tiny Rowland continued his secret meetings with the Libyans. In October he and Qaddafi sat down to talk business. On November 27, 1991, Lonrho and Libya signed a secret agreement to establish an offshore company that would do business in Ghana, Namibia, Kenya, Uganda, Zaire, and Sudan. In return for Qaddafi's cash, Rowland promised to put all his political influence in Africa and Britain at Libya's disposal. Libya increased its arms deliveries to Khartoum. Garang's forces were mounting revenge attacks on the Nuer. Isolated at Nasir, Riek had no one to turn to for weapons except Rowland and the Khartoum government. In January 1992 Lam signed an agreement with the government in Frankfurt, Germany, endorsing a "transitional period" of unity with the north in a federal framework. But the government gave little evidence of its stated desire to live peacefully with the south. In April 1992 it issued a fatwa setting forth the status of all who opposed it: "An insurgent who was previously a Muslim is now an apostate; and a non-Muslim is a non-believer standing as a bulwark against the spread of Islam, and Islam has granted the freedom of killing both of them."

The ruined town of Nasir remained as slow and silent as ever. Flocks of herons circled overhead; crocodiles sunned themselves on the muddy banks of the Sobat. Relations between the UN camp and the rebels had slumped back into their habitual miasma of suspicion. Bernadette had taken over from Ian Lethbridge as team leader. The Indian doctor still looked forward to Emma's daily visits. But she and Riek now argued all the time over refugee numbers, over diesel and food that went missing, over a million other things. Khartoum had blocked all flights to southern Sudan outside of territory held by Riek. Garang was furious over Operation Lifeline's decision to recognize Riek's relief officials as representatives of a new, independent aid agency, the Rehabilitation Association of Southern Sudan (RASS). The reports that Riek was receiving arms from Khartoum to use against Garang's SPLA only added to the growing distaste many aid workers felt for him, a distaste sharpened by the guilty memory of how close they had allowed themselves to get to him and Emma during the summer.

Emma resumed her publicity campaign against Garang for recruiting child soldiers. In their Nasir Declaration, Riek and Lam had drawn attention to the thousands of boys from SPLA camps who returned to

Sudan from Ethiopia after Mengistu's fall. Bernard Kouchner picked up the issue on his visit at the time of the split, making a side trip to see ten thousand boys aged eight to eighteen from the Panyido children's camp in Ethiopia who had ended up encamped at Pochalla. Afterward the French official irritated Garang by asking him if he was training the boys to join his rebel army. In a flash of candor, Garang shot back that he didn't have enough arms to turn the boys into soldiers. "Why should I be giving arms to six-year-olds when I cannot give arms to 30-year-olds who are already trained?" But Emma and the UN officials knew that even unarmed boys could be useful as porters and servants. Emma turned to the network of journalists and human rights advocates she'd known in London to keep the boys in Garang's camps in the public eye. "I have seen little children being turned into little warriors, almost being brain-washed into joining the struggle, and it is so wrong," she told Richard Ellis of *The Sunday Times.* "They are already suffering so much. I have to speak out against it—it has to be stopped."

Meanwhile Hania Sholkamy, the Egyptian anthropologist, remained in Nasir trying to sort out what to do with the twelve hundred or so boys under Riek's control. The International Committee of the Red Cross (ICRC) had taken charge of the boys at Pochalla, providing them with food, water, clothing, and schools. Emma argued that the ICRC ought to do the same for the boys at Nasir. After all, she claimed, Riek had freed the boys at Nasir from Garang's army, whereas the boys at Pochalla were just being readied to become child soldiers. She accused the UN and the Red Cross of not having the courage to stand up to Garang. The ICRC was just fattening up the boys at Pochalla for Garang to use when he got ready, she would say. "Garang advocates in his own literature for using child labor in his FACE schools! Here are a thousand boys whom Riek has rescued from Garang—and the ICRC won't give them a thing!"

She invited Sholkamy to stay with the boys at Ketbek and see for herself how they lived. Living so close to Riek's headquarters, the anthropologist saw a lot of Emma and Riek, too. The boys in the camp seemed to adore Emma. And she seemed genuinely fond of them. But the Egyptian could also see that it was terribly important to Emma that Sholkamy endorse her view of Riek as their savior. "It really mattered to the future of the splinter group if people could believe the boys were orphans," she told me. "She had a whole story about how, in Ethiopia, the bad communists had held the boys prisoner, then Garang had conscripted them, then the bad northerners had bombed them.

"None of this was completely true, but none of it was completely false, and I think this complexity was threatening to Emma," Sholkamy went on. "She had to show that Riek was different from Garang. Otherwise he would just be a traitor."

Emma knew many of the boys by name and could tell Sholkamy about their individual histories and problems. The boys called her "Emma Riek" and followed her everywhere. When the local people complained about the boys cutting down wood from a nearby forest to make charcoal for their cooking fires, Emma defended the boys. She railed to Sholkamy about the UN's refusal to set up a proper school in the boys' camp outside Ketbek. The tent Emma had given them to use for a schoolroom had collapsed in the rain; the boys had neither textbooks nor paper to write on. (Local boys and girls continued to attend the makeshift school Emma had established during her days with Street Kids International on the grounds of the old mission at Nasir. But the Nasir school could not accommodate the hundreds of boys living in the minors' camp outside Ketbek.) She never failed to ask that visiting missionaries or charity representatives donate some books or used clothing for the boys. "When it came to the minors, Emma really called the shots," Sholkamy said. And yet everyone agreed—the boys were in deplorable shape.

Relapsing fever had thinned their numbers until Bernadette managed to diagnose it and the United Nations sent tetracycline. They were hungry. Emma said Operation Lifeline failed to supply the boys with enough food; the UN workers said the boys' adult rebel "caretakers" were still stealing the food they sent. They also suffered from malaria, typhoid, and tuberculosis. Hunched beside the flimsy grass shelters they'd built for themselves in the mud, they looked fearful and sad. The mosquito nets UNICEF had sent them had vanished; the big tent that Emma had given them to use as the camp school was ripped and leaking. Sholkamy did not blame the rebels for everything that was wrong with the boys. Her work with children in other war zones had taught her that in many countries, joining an army was a rational decision for children and their parents. The sad fact of the matter was that in places like southern Sudan, child soldiers often ate better than other children.

The sentimental Western view of the boys as helpless innocents irked her. Few of the UN workers spoke Nuer or Arabic. Sholkamy felt that their view of the Sudan was in a way as skewed by their personal and political prejudices as Emma's. The Western aid workers seemed to her almost comically suspicious of the Islamic government. Because she was

Egyptian and Muslim, they seemed to think she was somehow involved with Riek and Lam's murky dealings with the government. The anthropologist thought the Westerners were blind to the reality that southern Sudan had a history of cooperation as well as conflict with the north and that southerners who reached out to the north could not just be dismissed as traitors. She found Emma, who frequently invited the anthropologist over to the *tukul* she and Riek shared, especially prone to seeing things in black and white, though not always in the same way as the other *khawajas*: "That put her in a bad position, because anyone could see that no one there was an angel or a devil."

Riek, as always, was flirtatious and winning. He told Sholkamy about his brother who lived in Alexandria. He impressed her with his "perfect Egyptian Arabic" and his knowledge of Egyptian personalities and politics. Yet she could see that this side of Riek, the side that was comfortable with Arabic culture and Islam, seemed to make Emma uneasy. Once when the three of them were together, Riek began telling Sholkamy about Angelina and his children in London. In January 1992 the Presbyterian elders at Nasir had rebuked Riek for taking a second wife. Although the Presbyterian church in Sudan allows ordinary male members to marry more than once, Riek was a church elder, and elders are supposed to set an example of monogamy. Riek dismissed the incident as the work of a few disgruntled churchmen. Sholkamy teased him that Islam wasn't so bad—under Islamic law, he would be allowed two more wives. Riek laughed roguishly, but Emma stiffened and changed the subject: "She didn't take that well," Sholkamy recalled.

Emma took her role as the leading lady of Nasir seriously. She set the barefoot teenage soldiers at Ketbek to planting seeds she saved and dried from vegetables that came in the catered meals for the UN workers. "She was determined to get the soldiers to put down their Kalashikovs and plant," said Sheila Murfitt, an aid worker at Nasir. Delegations of women had started coming from distant Nuer villages to tell her about their disputes and to ask her to use her influence with Riek in their favor. Wrapped in colorful cloths, the tall women would arrive with their hands held up to slap Emma's hands. Emma would go through all the Nuer greetings, then sit down in a plastic chair under an acacia tree. The women would squat on the ground in front of her and explain their problem. Emma would settle the matter herself if she could. Otherwise she would promise to bring their dispute to Riek for a resolution. She had long since exchanged her miniskirts for more dignified sarongs and a turban, but she still kept British fashion magazines and a bottle of duty-free vodka in her *tukul*. Sholkamy admired the way she was able to live in the wilderness with such style and panache. "She was living an enjoyable life. She was not sacrificial. I liked that."

Emma seemed fully engaged in the military and political dimensions of Riek's struggle. When she wasn't across the river at the boys' camp or meeting with the women, she was churning out paperwork for Riek's group on her ancient mimeograph machine. She no longer pretended to be bound by the humanitarian ideology of the aid workers. "They were a political team," Sholkamy said. "She was part of the struggle. She would attack Garang vehemently, saying he had slandered her and was a dictator." She was prepared for Riek to take military measures against his enemies. Sholkamy said she saw prisoners at Ketbek being held in foxholes with crude wooden covers. If she saw them, Emma saw them, too. "I cannot imagine that she was oblivious or duped by Riek. Let us say that she was not averse to winning."

Sholkamy came to feel that, despite Emma's real concern for the boys in the minors' camp, she was determined to ignore those parts of their story that cast Riek in a bad light. Emma claimed that the boys were orphans when in fact "they weren't orphans. They had been conscripted." In Itang they had been getting military training as well as going to school. "In actual fact there was a civilian and a military aspect. But it was such a political issue. Everyone had a story about them. Meanwhile these boys were being stuck." Some of the boys' families used to come at night to visit them secretly. Sholkamy would see them paddling up the river in dugout canoes by the light of the moon. The boys and their families would hold whispered reunions, and sometimes the boys would give them food. She learned that the adult "caretakers" whom the aid workers accused of stealing the boys' food were often related to the children. It was part of Nuer culture for young children to feed senior men. Like Douglas Johnson, Sholkamy noticed the bright orange UNICEF cups and plates in Riek and Emma's hut. She was not inclined to make a big deal about the violation of Operation Lifeline rules. "*Yanni*, they're all family," she told me. "Some of the aid workers took a remarkably exogenous view of the whole thing—here are civilians and here are soldiers. It wasn't like that." But she couldn't help noticing how well fed Emma and Riek were compared to the boys, whom she sometimes saw trying to weave fishing nets out of string they unraveled from UNICEF blankets and discarded grain sacks.

Sholkamy recommended that Operation Lifeline return the boys to their home areas, mostly in the Bentiu district. But Riek brought up one reason after another why the boys couldn't go. He argued that the UN had to set up schools in the Bentiu district before the boys could be resettled there. Otherwise, he said, John Garang might be able to lure them back to his army with promises of education and food at the Red Cross camp in Pochalla. To Sholkamy, he seemed to be stalling. But Operation Lifeline refused to take a firm stand. Meanwhile the boys languished, and Sholkamy and the other aid workers kept collecting their per diems.

As time went on, the anthropologist felt increasingly frustrated and disgusted with all the adults at Nasir. "There was a human tragedy, and it seemed that in trying to address it, they were overwhelmed by politics," she told me. She had worked with children in Iraq and Lebanon, but Nasir was the first place she got to know some of the people who were making the decisions. She said it was like a terrarium in which she could see exactly how the children were being at once used and ignored by everyone around them. "Sudan was a situation in which I saw a personalized aspect of these situations. Everyone was there—the people on the top and the people who were suffering—and I could see the links between them. In Iraq and the other places I had worked, I had never met Saddam Hussein. To be honest, it was disturbing that Riek and Emma were so charming and likable, and yet they were perpetrating this situation."

The supposedly neutral aid workers did not seem much better to her; she thought the ugliness of the power realities tarnished everyone. The tendency of the Westerners to see themselves as "fighting evil" offended her. "We were all there to advance our careers," she said. "I never saw anybody sacrifice anything. Everyone benefited somehow." And that was what made it so upsetting. As the Sudanese put it, they were all "eating" from the situation that kept the boys penned up in the camp across the river from Riek and Emma. "Children get caught up and they die and they lose their whole future, and someone else benefits. I found it so disturbing that I never did this work again because I really couldn't face it again," she told me later.

In February 1992 Riek finally agreed to a plan to allow 450 of the boys at Nasir to return to Ler. Sholkamy returned to Egypt. Her report was filed away, one of a truckload of official studies about the Lost Boys. Riek and the UN wrangled for a long time over what to do with the remaining 800 boys. Riek claimed that some of the boys who'd been returned to Ler had turned around and walked back to Nasir. He said they came back because the UN failed to build them a school at Ler. UN officials countered that he and Garang were fighting so much around Ler that MSF-Holland could barely run a hospital there, much less a school. In that case, Riek rejoined, UNICEF could build a school in Nasir. Two years later some 800 boys were still waiting at Nasir when UNICEF dispatched another consultant to interview them. "Life is going on the run," one of the boys told this latest consultant. "I don't feel sad, because no one can choose their life and destiny."

Chapter Twenty-five

I HAVE SOME PICTURES of Emma at Nasir. Emma's friend from London, Peter Moszynski, took them when he visited in 1992. In one black-and-white shot, Emma stands outside a rectangular mud *tukul,* squinting at the sun. She's wearing a sleeveless black lace shirt, a long skirt with a belt, and flip-flops. Her dark hair is shoulder-length and stylishly cut; her hands are clasped behind her back. Her face has lost the luscious, peachy quality it had when she still lived in England. It's sharper, with more interesting angles. The next picture is in color. It shows Emma sitting inside the hut on an iron bedstead with a thin foam mattress. A mosquito net hangs over the bed, and behind it you can see Emma's clothes strung up neatly on a line. The walls are painted with African animals, human figures, and geometric shapes in black, white, and brown. The third photo is the only one to include Riek. He and Emma are sitting in front of a big table covered with ledgers, papers, and airmail envelopes, two glasses of tea, and a shortwave radio. Riek is looking straight into the camera, dressed like a cartoon dictator in military fatigues with giant shoulder boards and a bright red beret. Emma leans on the table, looking down, half smiling at something you can't quite see.

She looks a little self-conscious, as if she were posing on the movie set for *The African Queen.* But she actually seemed to relish her position as the warlord's consort. Garang's forces had started calling the fighting with Riek "Emma's War." It was a Nilotic custom to name a feud after a woman who caused it, and many southerners blamed Riek's *khawaja* wife for the maelstrom that had descended on them so soon after his marriage. "Just because she was British, they thought she was getting support from the UN, they thought maybe it is Emma who is engineering all this," said Michael Wal Duany, a Nuer political scientist who talked to numerous Nuer and Dinka SPLA members about the split. Emma knew she was a target. When Garang's fighters began raiding Nuerland in retaliation for Bor, Riek urged her to stay in Nairobi. But she refused to leave Riek and Nasir. Instead she started traveling everywhere with a seven-foot-tall, ferociously scarred bodyguard named Forty-six, after a certain machine gun he liked to use. In a never-published article, Emma's friend Emma Marrian wrote that when Emma arrived in a Nuer village, the women would set upon her, sometimes carrying her to their houses on their shoulders. "They consider body hair freakish and would set upon her, waxing every inch of her body-hair with a carmelized mixture of lemon and sugar," Marrian wrote. "They called Emma 'Yian,' after the color of their palest, creamiest cows." She added that Emma had developed the habit in Nasir of sleeping during the hot hours from ten in the morning until four in the afternoon. In the letters Riek wrote to Emma when she left Nasir from Nairobi, he spoke of missing their extended siestas in their "love nest."

In June 1992 *The Mail on Sunday* and *YOU* sent Tarquin Hall back to Sudan to write about Emma. Hall had met her the summer before, while covering the refugee crisis at Nasir. After reaching Nasir, it took Hall four more days of traveling before he found Emma in a village near the Ethiopian border, carrying a parasol and feeding an ostrich. She was wearing one of her outlandish costumes—a floppy felt hat, blue Hush Puppy shoes with pink socks, a flowered skirt, a black sleeveless blouse, and a necklace made from sunflower seeds—and as Hall wrote, "She didn't seem the least bit amazed that I had traveled all the way from Nairobi to see her." "Do you like ostriches?" she asked him calmly. "I call this one Burty because she reminds me of one of my old teachers. Burty used to have a mate, but he was killed in a cross-border raid."

Hall spent two weeks with Emma. He noticed that she had started tying around her waist the string of beads that identifies a Nuer woman as married. The locals, he said, seemed to like her and called out greetings to her wherever she passed. At Ketbek, she served him roasted goat that her bodyguards slaughtered and prepared. He met Come On and saw the cats she had imported to catch rats but instead caught the soldiers' chickens. "The soldiers keep threatening to kill them," she said of her pets. "But Riek has forbidden them." In the year that had passed since Hall's last visit to Nasir, most of the refugees from Itang had melted back into their own communities, and a market had sprung up. Fishing spears, UN plastic sheeting, and grass building supplies were for sale, as well as dried fish, nuts, and wild potatoes. Emma told Hall she had been touring Riek's territory to encourage women to elect local representatives to a council Riek was creating. She took him to the office of the women's association she had helped found in Nasir. "It has been very important for me to help these people," she told Hall. "I feel like I'm in a unique position now because I share their lives every day and I'm not just another aid worker pretending to understand their position and telling them how to live."

Hall asked her what she found so attractive about southern Sudan. "I like the simplicity here, although it is dangerous at times and life is basic," she replied. "You realize how the life you leave behind in the West is so geared to materialism. The southern Sudanese are very romantic in a way, and people live here like they always have. Not much has changed. They are survivors, and I respect that. . . .

"I'm not going to pick up a gun myself to fight, but I married someone who is committed to a cause, so I have a certain amount of commitment to it myself."

WHAT IMPRESSED OTHER *khawajas* most about Emma's life at Nasir was the degree of danger and discomfort she was prepared to endure to be with Riek. "I really admired her for living totally the Sudanese way," said Bernadette Kumar. She had no showers, no running water, not even the concrete floors, window screens, and zinc roofs that the missionaries at Nasir had used to keep out the rain and the snakes during the British period. She and Riek dined mostly on Nile perch from the Sobat. (Nuer cooks prepared the river fish three ways: fried, boiled with maize, and stewed on top of *kisra*.) A year into her marriage, she had come to know some of the more insidious hazards plaguing the southerners who lived in the war zone: the fevers, the delirium, the petty quarrels, the fear, and above all the boredom. After Hall left, she came down with typhoid malaria. Later she would adopt the Sudanese view that malaria in an adult was the local equivalent of the common cold—uncomfortable and sometimes dangerous but rarely so bad as to stop ordinary adult life. But this first bout with the disease's bone-rattling chills, fever, and headaches left her limp with exhaustion for weeks. When Emma finally went to Nairobi, Sally was shocked to see how gaunt she'd grown. "But she didn't mind at all. She would live on rice and boiled fish for months on end without complaining. Then it was like she had two lives, because she would come out of these swamps of hell, walk into my wardrobe in Nairobi, and come out looking like something out of *Vogue*. Then she would be off to a dinner party."

EMMA WAS INEVITABLY the center of attention at such Nairobi parties. She was always laughing, always teasing some blushing young man just out from England about whether he had promised to remain faithful to his girlfriend at home. Conversation would stop when she told her stories about life in Nasir. There was the court case in which a Nuer woman claimed to have been impregnated by her female lover, and Riek had to decide whether to give paternity rights to the female lover or to a man who had slept with her, though not with the pregnant woman. (He ultimately denied the woman in favor of the man, saying, "What woman has ever produced sperm?") And there was her story about the leopard who mauled eight villagers before Riek's men finally shot him and laid his skin out to dry in front of her *tukul*. A British television correspondent remembers meeting Emma at one such party. "Emma looked absolutely stunning," she told me later. "She was wearing a red low-necked shirt, and she was very animated, telling this story about this kid she knew in southern Sudan. I thought to myself, 'What an unusual aid worker.' Because, you know, aid workers are usually quite laden, quite serious. But Emma was funny. She was a great storyteller." Her Nairobi friends called her Sudan's First Lady-in-Waiting because, as Sally said, "We were so sure that if peace finally came to the southern Sudan, she would be among the most powerful women in that area. She did so much for the people, and they all loved her and would have wanted her to be one of their leaders."

The Nuer do seem to have respected Emma's efforts to live more like they did. "The aid people had their own compound," Michael Wal Duany recalled. "They ate by themselves. We were two groups. Emma broke down that barrier, and she opened her door to the people. You can come at midnight and knock on Emma's door, and she will greet you...this was not true with other *khawajas*." Nevertheless there was always that double view. What seemed like immense hardship for an Englishwoman could be unimaginable luxury for a Sudanese. While Emma was eating boiled perch, many people at Nasir were going hungry.

While she still managed to talk her way onto planes bound for Kenya, they were condemned to stay in "the wasteland of southern Sudan," as Emma once listed her address in a friend's guestbook.

At least some of Riek's comrades were jealous of Emma's freedom and wealth and of the pull they imagined she gave Riek with the aid agencies. Peter Adwok Nyaba writes that "Riek Machar's marriage to a British relief worker was calculated to exploit her potential with the relief community." Nyaba goes on to complain about the attention Riek paid to Emma and her *khawaja* friends. "He would interrupt an important [political] meeting to receive and shake hands with even the most junior of the relief workers, especially if he happened to be European or American, and he would take his time introducing his colleagues to the relief workers." Riek's ally, the old Nuer chieftain Gordon Kong, especially disliked Emma's habit of attending their meetings. He would tell Riek roughly in Nuer, "Get that woman out of here!" When Emma—half joking, half serious—tried to talk things over with the scarred old warrior, he spat on the ground contemptuously. "She would say, 'Gordon, why don't you like me?' " Bernadette recalled. "He really didn't have time for all this." Gordon and the others knew that Riek looked to Emma for advice about how this or that action might appear to the *khawaja* world, and they disapproved of her influence. "They were resentful because he was listening to a woman," Bernadette said. "They think he's gone a bit soft, but I think he's liberated," Emma told Tarquin Hall.

Hall was present when Emma and Riek presided, as he wrote, "like royalty at Ascot" over celebrations to mark the liberation of Nasir from the government three years earlier. "Everywhere we went," he wrote, "the Sudanese seemed happy to see Emma even though she had learnt little of their language. She enjoyed the sort of star attention usually afforded to royalty and celebrities. In villages, people would run up to her car as she drove past, bringing presents and seeking advice." They looked to her, as they looked to other powerful people, not only to settle their disputes but also to dispense food and other things. But Emma, no longer employed by a relief agency, had nothing to give. It was a fact that began to bother her.

When she'd worked for Street Kids International, she'd given people lifts in her Land Cruiser, handed out books and supplies, and paid teachers' salaries with soap and salt. Now she had more ideas than ever about ways to help the women and children of southern Sudan but no way to finance them. "The problem was that it was difficult to define her role," said Bernadette. She would come to the UN camp to ask for some diesel, saying she needed it to transport women to the meetings for a women's organization she was setting up. Bernadette wanted to help, but fuel was considered a military commodity, and she was under strict orders to treat Emma as if she were one of Riek's relief officials. "She would come to me, and she would say, 'I really need two barrels of diesel,' and I had to tell her, 'Emma, I can't give you anything that belongs to the UN.' Suddenly she realized she had nothing to give any more. That began to be a bit of a problem. She would try to influence the new young people sent out by the NGOs, and then other people would say, 'Who is this woman? Who does she think she is?'"

Emma confided her frustrations to Bernadette, her feelings of fitting in nowhere. "They still see me as a white woman," she complained. "I try and I try and I eat with them and I do everything they do, but they still look at the color of my skin. In my heart I'm Sudanese, but they can't see that—"

"You have the soul of a European," Bernadette would interrupt. "You can't change that."

"No, my soul is Sudanese," Emma insisted.

She expected the Sudanese to appreciate the fact that she wanted to be one of them. Instead they thought she was mad—or a spy. Why would she want to be in the swamp of southern Sudan if she could be in London? "She was in love with being Emma Riek, with being this campaigner, with standing up for these people," Bernadette said. "I think that's where she went wrong. She went native when they wanted her to be an expat."

Loyalty was the virtue she prized above all others. But everyone doubted her loyalty. "She was always on trial with the Sudanese because she was a white woman, and with the expats because she had married Riek," said Bernadette.

"She used to ask me, 'Why don't people trust me?'

"I would say, 'Emma, think how you would feel if you were in their position.'"

To which Emma replied, "If I were them, I *wouldn't* feel that way. If I had a friend, I would believe in them no matter what other people said."

SOMETIMES EMMA PASSED on radio frequencies and news of military maneuvers to Riek's supporters abroad. Her radio call sign was Nefertiti.

From Nairobi she would often call up journalists to talk, off the record, about the war. She would tell us all sorts of titillating personal gossip about the top men in the SPLA. Most of what she said was unprintable, as well as unprovable, even if it had been on the record, but it was very amusing, and it all had the effect of burnishing Riek's image. (For example, I can remember her saying that Kenyans were supposed to be shipping Garang off to Switzerland for a drinking cure. Riek, of course, was a teetotaler.) But her closest friends believed Riek often left her in the dark about the details of his political machinations. In June 1992 Emma wrote to Emma Marrian thanking her for sending a package to Nasir that included chocolates, vodka, and a copy of *The Observer.* "Everyone is in a bit of a spin with peace talks, war and politics," she wrote. "None of which I understand but I faithfully type out constitutions, programmes and plans and policies for my beloved husband." When Tarquin Hall asked her how she felt about Riek's role as a military man who made decisions to have people killed, she replied, "I don't think Riek is in the war because he loves it, or because he loves fighting.... Riek has chosen it because of principle, as a means to an end."

Emma's former colleagues were having more trouble discerning exactly what principle Riek was fighting for, and to what end. The allegations about Lam's secret deals with the Islamic government were becoming increasingly insistent. Some of Riek's confederates defected, taking papers with them that showed the Nasir group was collaborating with the NIF. The same men accused Lam of taking money from Dr. Ali al-Haj, a close friend of Turabi's who handled foreign policy for the NIF. In February 1992 Riek allowed government forces to move unmolested through his territory all the way to Equatoria, where they attacked Garang's SPLA. To escape the government onslaught, the ten thousand Lost Boys at Pochalla were forced to march through the swamps to Narus, near the Kenyan border. The Red Cross, which had been running the camp at Pochalla, was expelled from southern Sudan. One of Riek's top lieutenants defected. In Nairobi he held a press conference in which he gave journalists a list of people whom he said Riek had had shot and another list of prisoners he was holding.

In March 1992 the Sudanese government recaptured Bor, Torit, and Kapoeta from the SPLA. The army had now retaken nearly all the ground the rebels had won in the 1980s, including much of the territory where Emma had established her bush schools. The northern troops never could have done it if Riek and Lam had not allowed them to pass through their territory. Meanwhile Khartoum blocked Operation Lifeline's land route for distributing relief and denied UN flights access to all but a few sites, mostly under the control of Riek's group. Seething, Garang's SPLA accused Operation Lifeline of conspiring with the government to favor Riek. Garang loyalists looted a UN distribution center at Balliat, near the Nuer-Dinka border, stealing five hundred tons of grain and setting the fuel stocks on fire. According to Peter Moszynski, they also massacred several hundred Nuer who had been lining up for assistance at the time of the attack. "One of the few items not looted from the UN compound was a stack of Gulf War surplus, US Army MREs—Meals Ready to Eat—donated by USAID," Moszynski wrote. "The GIs had dubbed them 'Meals Rejected by Ethiopians.'"

Nasir kept getting UN airdrops, but, Moszynski said, the Sobat was a more reliable larder for the townspeople than Operation Lifeline. "Men catch fish with traps, spears, nets, lines or even bare hands," he wrote. "They fish from river banks, pools, dugout canoes and from the newly imported UNICEF improved fishing kayaks." The Jikany Nuer, who claimed fishing rights in the area, were visibly better fed than anyone else. Moszynski observed a pecking order in which "[l]ocal Nuer are the healthiest, with the Dinka and Shilluk a good deal less fit…the most pathetic looking are the 11,000 Uduks, a small forest-dwelling people from northern Sudan." The Uduk had been asking for permission to leave their camp at Nor Deng ever since they arrived in May 1991. Six months later Riek agreed to let them move to a low-lying place across the river that some Uduk optimistically named New Chali, after Chali, the site of the main church village in their old homeland. The Uduk would have preferred to go home to the real Chali in Blue Nile province, but the town remained in government hands. They asked to move to a less frequently flooded spot upstream, but Riek refused, arguing that the UN must first provide food stocks for them there. Operation Lifeline tried to get flight access to a site near the Ethiopian foothills, but the government would not give the UN permission, and so the Uduk were stuck. "We are longing for our home," the Uduk told Wendy James when she visited. "We want our hearthstones. At this time, now, we are suffering and our livers are full of our homeland!" Riek dismissed the Uduk leaders who argued that their people wanted to move to higher ground whether the UN gave them food or not.

Emma had gone with the Uduk in January to help them get settled at New Chali. The spot was very isolated, and James feared that Riek's men had chosen it because it would be difficult for the aid workers to monitor what happened there. In April some Nuer men shot and killed a Uduk man who refused to give them some fish he'd caught. Emma told Moszynski that the locals felt the man had stealing from "their" pool; she and Riek's officials explained it as a regrettable accident brought on by the kind of backward attitudes they were working to change. Shortly afterward Riek relented and let the Uduk move upstream. Later that year all eleven thousand Uduk took off suddenly on foot, marking the beginning of a return exodus of Sudanese into Ethiopia. When Emma visited England that year, James talked to her on the phone. Emma blamed the UN agencies for the Uduk decision to leave, saying Operation Lifeline had failed to provide enough relief to feed them in Nasir and had taken too long in making arrangements for them to leave. It was a shame, she said, because the Uduk had finally started catching so many fish that they were selling them in the market. She and Riek would miss the Uduk, she said, because they had enjoyed eating their delicious fish.

A few weeks later James met up with the Uduk in Ethiopia. From them she heard an entirely different account of why they had abruptly decamped from the Nasir region. They said Riek's soldiers all along had been taking the food and the cooking pots and the clothes that Operation Lifeline gave them. They accused Nuer of stopping them from searching in the woods for firewood and from digging for wild roots and potatoes. They called Riek and his soldiers the *hakuma,* or "government," when they didn't just call them the Dhamkin—the same word they used for all the tall, Nilotic cattle-herding peoples such as the Dinka. To them, Riek was simply The Power. The Uduk said Riek's soldiers habitually followed them when they went fishing to demand a portion of their catch. "All those who used to come and gather in the place of fishing, all wore the uniform and carried Kalashnikovs in their hands. And they brought sacks, to fill with fish. Always like that." They told James that the Uduk man who was shot had refused to give Riek's men his fish, saying that his wife was hungry, and if he gave away the fish he caught, she and their children would have nothing to eat. "Because of this, they killed him."

The other Uduk found the dead man's body in a fishing pool. They carried the body to Riek to report the killing and demand that the soldier responsible be punished. They showed how the bullet had gone into his groin and come out the lower buttock. "Why should people kill us when we are fishing?" one Uduk asked Riek. "Fish are the things of God."

"What do you say about this?" another man demanded. "I want to know what you are going to do."

They said Riek just sat there. Finally he asked them, "Is it just this once that a man has been killed?"

The Uduk were outraged. "Yes, just once, but it is not right to kill even just one man," they replied. "We people do not have the power to use guns. You are the man in charge of this region, you have your soldiers, you should look into this matter. Maybe you can arrest this man and ask him 'Why did you kill this man?' "

But Riek didn't arrest anyone. Just as when the Uduk reported that his soldiers were stealing their things, nothing was done. "He used his power to release his own people," a man told James. "He just helped his own people."

Another Uduk said the death of the man at the fishing pool "was like the pointless death of some creature; just like an animal. In fact, he was killed and he died just like a dog."

James, who sat listening to this tale on a scorching Ethiopian afternoon, remembered her telephone conversation with Emma a few weeks earlier. She pictured the soldiers coming back to Ketbek with their bags of fish "from the Uduk." She remembered the time the veterinarian was expelled because he complained about Riek seizing the UN motorboat so that his men could collect some fish from an "SPLA trap" downstream. The SPLA had probably been stealing the fish from a Uduk trap. She remembered how Emma had told her about enjoying the fish the Uduk caught. "She was presumably eating fish acquired in the manner described above!" James wrote angrily in a note to herself. Could Emma really have believed Riek's soldiers had paid the Uduk for the fish? she wondered. Or had she been lying all along, watching the Uduk slowly starve to death, while she ate fish that she knew Riek's soldiers had stolen from them?

The Uduk said they gave up fishing after the murder. "They prevented us from having fish, se'd [a wild root], from searching in the forest for firewood, everything." The American anthropologist Sharon Hutchinson visited Nasir that summer and went to see the Uduk in June. "Nearly all the children below the ages of one or two appeared to be very severely malnourished, with sunken eyes, stick limbs and lightened hair and skin," she wrote in a report for Save the Children–UK. "The sight of the emaciated infants clutching the empty breasts of their mothers was profoundly disturbing. Many older children were also seriously malnourished, having protruding bellies and wizened limbs. Adults complained of frequent fainting spells while walking out long distances in search of food." Not long after Hutchinson wrote her report, the Nuer seized some maize the Uduk had grown. The Uduk decided they could stand it no longer. With or without Riek's permission, they said, they were leaving.

"We cultivated a little maize, but they stopped us from taking a few ears," they told James. "The Dhamkin came and said, 'Don't touch that maize! It's ours, not yours! Don't break off that maize! Leave it!' So we said, 'Well, this is the maize the UN gave to us. The UN gave us maize to plant and help feed the children and there is no other food.'

" 'No! No! Not at all!' they said. They chased us off and we went. We were struck by hunger, we were dying and we despaired and said, 'What shall we do?' So we agreed, 'Let's go to Ethiopia, if the Ethiopians don't seize us, we'll go there.' "

The Uduk sent a delegation to Ketbek to meet with Riek. They were afraid of him. They knew he didn't want them to leave. When one of their leaders had asked him earlier for permission to go, Riek threatened to put the man in prison. Now he said, "Don't you want to stay here and eat the things of the UN?"

The Uduk leader said, "No, your people have refused to let us eat the things of the UN. We want to go and take ourselves away from you."

Riek fixed his gaze on the Uduk men. "You have something else in your livers," he said, according to the Uduk. (The Uduk believe the liver is the center of human thought and feeling, much as Westerners might say the head or the heart is.) "You are going to say the SPLA took your share of food. You are going to say we prevented you from eating."

He warned them in his soft voice that he would not be responsible for what happened to them if they left. But the Uduk were determined; they were perishing in Nasir anyway. When they moved upstream, Riek sent only two guards to protect all eleven thousand people. Nuer tribesmen attacked them on the way, killing several Uduk and stealing everything they were carrying. "Pans, bags, clothes, all taken. Many died because there was nothing left to exchange for food," a man told James. "We were naked when we arrived," a woman said.

The Nuer themselves were beginning to break up into tribal segments. Part of Riek's problem in establishing discipline was that the lineage or even the section of any man he punished was likely to turn against him. Likewise, the sections were jealous of any perceived advantage to another section. The prophet Wut Nyang came to Nasir in the summer of 1992. Riek had told Wut Nyang and the Jikany Nuer who lived around Nasir to prepare for an attack on the government town of Malakal. But when the prophet arrived, Riek informed him and the Jikany that instead they would be assaulting Garang's forces in Equatoria. "This precipitated a crisis within the Jikany, who thought the Malakal operation was being put off because they stood to benefit from its success," Nyaba writes. Instead of attacking Garang, the prophet and his followers took off for Itang in Ethiopia. At Itang, Wut Nyang made a speech about peace. Then his followers shot a number of Ethiopians standing in the marketplace. On the way back to Nasir, they burned down several Anyuak villages. "What I have seen about this prophet," Lam observed drily, "is that he talks about peace, but he brings death."

Hutchinson attended a speech Wut Nyang made at Nasir about the tensions that the relief food was causing between the Jikany and the Lou. The Lou lived west of the Jikany, along the border with the Dinka. Because of the fighting near Bor, they could not exchange cattle and grain with the Dinka as they usually did. The shutdown of the UN flights had left them hungry. They resented the fact that Operation Lifeline was still supplying the Jikany at Nasir and not the Lou in Waat. "This relief has destroyed our relationship with the Dinka and with other groups," the prophet warned the Nuer. "Now that it is coming to you, it will divide you. The Lou Nuer are saying, 'The eastern Jikany are the ones who consume this food,' and the Jikany are saying, 'This relief operation started in our area and it is ours' and 'Why should this food be collected by other people?' This attitude is very bad."

For several weeks after the prophet's attack on Itang, the bloated and tortured bodies of dead Anyuaks could be seen floating down the Sobat. But in her June 1992 letter to Emma Marrian, Emma said nothing of the violence swirling around her. She noted that she was reading Martin Gilbert's biography of Churchill (a "fascinating read") as well as a review of Lou Cannon's biography of Ronald Reagan ("the book revealed that Hopalong was weirder than any of us ever supposed!!"). And she described Wut Nyang's return to Nasir from Ethiopia: "The day of his arrival caused a frenzy in the town with people firing into the air, others running, dancing, singing and slaughtering cows." Both Emmas planned to visit England later that summer. Emma wrote from Nasir, "I understand that there are two big exhibitions on Piero della Francesca and Rembrandt now on in London—not to be missed by us either!" She signed the letter "Your Ever Loving First Lady-In-Waiting."

TINY ROWLAND's Gulfstream jet was now making a regular shuttle between Libya, Kenya, and Sudan. In March the London newspapers reported that Libya was buying Rowland's Metropole Hotel. Lonrho admitted selling the hotel but denied discussing the sale of its African assets to Libya. (In fact the company had signed an agreement six months earlier to do just that.) Backstage, oil companies were maneuvering furiously for position in Sudan. While Emma was showing Tarquin Hall around Nasir in June 1992, Chevron quietly signed an agreement to sell its 42 million-acre concession to Concorp, a newly established Sudanese company owned by a relative of Sudan's energy minister who also happened to be a friend of Hassan al-Turabi. On the twenty-sixth of the same month, another tiny Vancouver oil company, Arakis Energy Corporation, signed a letter of intent to buy 100 percent of Lutfur Rahman Khan's State Petroleum. According to the agreement, State was completing its own purchase of the portion of the former Chevron concession containing the Heglig and Unity fields north of Bentiu. Al-Turabi and his military allies had at last achieved the goal for which a generation of northern governments had worked. With Nuerland no longer actively in rebellion against the government, the NIF had persuaded a new set of oilmen to resume exploration near Bentiu. And this time a controlling interest remained in the hands of Khan, a "good Muslim," in the words of President Bashir, whom the NIF could trust to resist pressure from the West to hold up drilling or make a separate agreement with the south that would undercut the government.

Getting wind of these developments, Garang's SPLA issued a warning that his rebels would attack any oil company that dared to restart work in Upper Nile. But without the support of the local Nuer population, Garang's threats were bluster. The government quietly moved its troops into the oil fields. With the help of Baggara militias, it began removing civilians suspected of sympathizing with the SPLA from their homes near the wells. It reassured its investors that regardless of what the SPLA said, the Nuer predominated in the area around Heglig and Unity and that, as much as Riek and Lam might deny it, they remained dependent on the government for ammunition to protect themselves from the wrath of the Bor Dinka. Tiny Rowland continued his perambulations between the government and the rebel factions. It's time to make peace, he told Garang. Garang refused. On July 28 Arakis Energy Corporation announced that Triad International, owned by Rowland's old friend Adnan Khashoggi, was ready to lend the company $25 million to develop the Sudan oil fields; Arakis later denied any connection to Triad. With help from Sudan's new ally, Iran, Concorp refined and sold oil from the Abu Jabra field in Kordofan for the first time in Sudanese history.

Despondent aid workers began to say that Riek was no better than Garang and maybe worse. Because of Riek's treachery, it was said, the SPLA had lost all the important towns and large swaths of the territory it had fought nine years to gain. Garang's forces had of course counter-attacked to take revenge for the Bor Massacre. In Upper Nile people began to say more southerners were dying in the tit-for-tat battles between the Nasir forces and the SPLA than in all the battles the rebels had fought against the army. Even the Dinka seemed to be breaking into warring segments. The Christian prophet Paul Kon Ajith was claiming that the Nuer raids and the government takeover of Bor were God's judgment against the Dinka because they'd failed to heed his warnings to destroy their traditional shrines. Against Kuol Manyang's orders, Dinka Christians in Bor district began attacking shrines and stealing their sacred objects. They took the holy spears, drums, and stools to a place just south of Bor, where they had also gathered grass, bamboo, and poles. Paul told them that peace and prosperity would not return until the Dinka destroyed all their old shrines and built a huge church on this spot. He said the location of the church and its design had been revealed to him in a dream. It was to be built in the shape of a cross. The four arms of the building were to symbolize reconciliation among the four major peoples of the region: the Dinka, the Nuer, the Murle, and the Mandari. Thousands of Dinka converged on the spot, begging for for-giveness and asking Paul to baptize them. But the peace for which they prayed failed to materialize.

NOW THAT EMMA was officially banned from boarding UN planes, she had trouble getting in and out of Nasir. Sometimes friends with Opera-tion Lifeline bent the rules to allow her on board; sometimes she hitched a ride on a missionary plane. She also chartered planes for Riek's faction out of Nairobi's Wilson Airport, sparking persistent rumors that she was smuggling weapons to Nasir. In years of asking, I have not been able to find anybody who actually caught her at it, but the gossip fed her image as the Mata Hari of southern Sudan. The rumors reached so far afield that when Emma's cousin in England wanted to raise some money for her to give to the children of southern Sudan, one of his British sponsors said he would contribute only so long as the money didn't go to buy arms for Riek. The comment made Emma very angry. She pretended not to understand why the aid agencies wanted to disassociate themselves from her. She wrote her friend Emma Marrian in 1992 complaining that "for some unknown reason" the UN refused to allow her on their planes.

In England that summer Emma went to see Amnesty International's head Sudan researcher, Andrew Mawson. Mawson had written his dissertation at Cambridge University on the Dinka religion. He knew Emma from the Sudan peace groups of the late 1980s and remembered her as an energetic advocate of human rights. When she began telling him that Amnesty had overblown the Bor Massacre, he felt embarrassed. "She spent a lot of time trying to persuade me that it didn't really happen," he told me. "I always felt she wasn't actually being very frank. She didn't seem to understand that she was acting as Riek's ambassador. She wanted to play it as a friend. I found her manipulative, and I began to feel very uncomfortable."

Three of Emma's closest English girlfriends were getting married that summer. At their weddings the talk was about getting ahead. Some of her English friends were starting to have children; her old flying companion Bill Hall asked her to be godmother to his baby daughter. Others were buying their first homes or trading in their old cars for new ones. Emma made a glamorous contrast to all this bourgeois nesting, tossing off such quips as "People are always asking me what it's like to be married to a guerrilla commander, but I haven't ever been married to a stockbroker, so I've nothing to compare it to." She helped one former classmate choose carpeting, spending hours poring over the samples. She listened to another complain about the backstabbing that went on in radio journalism, kidding that it sounded very much like the infighting among Riek's group. But inside she must have felt very far away from the concerns of England.

Repeated attacks of malaria and dysentery had left her shockingly thin. She was almost out of the money she'd saved from her job. A few months earlier she and Riek had received a small fee for an interview they did with *Hello!* magazine. Emma came up with the idea of writing her autobiography. Several people she knew had made a career out of writing. She approached two of them separately with the thought that they might want to help her work up a manuscript. Each was privately astonished that Emma saw herself as the subject of a book. "I told her, 'There isn't anything there but a black man boffing a white woman,' " one recalled. "She didn't like that." Emma showed her other friend a few pages she'd written about her childhood. The woman found them almost embarrassingly sentimental. "For God's sake, don't write about Yorkshire, no one cares about that," she told Emma.

A London literary agent who knew Africa and saw potential for a movie in Emma's story was more encouraging. She told Emma not to be intimidated. Just get something down on paper, she said. We can always bring in a ghostwriter later. She thought she might be able to get Emma an advance in the six figures. Emma's mother was excited. Maggie had been clinging to the hope that Emma's marriage to Riek and what she bitterly termed her daughter's involvement in "their politics" was a stage that would pass. Now she saw a way for Emma to turn all her reckless adventures to a useful, even lucrative purpose. Emma might even become the next Karen Blixen or Beryl Markham! Emma had always written lively letters—her letters are much more natural than the bits that have been published of her autobiography—and Maggie could easily see her as a writer.

Emma didn't pretend to be an objective observer of Sudan's civil war. If anything, she was more vociferous in her support for Riek on this visit than she'd been the summer before. Some of her friends were disturbed by what they saw as her moral obtuseness. The Bor Massacre and Riek's role in it had become fairly well known even to friends and relations in Britain who knew little about the Sudan. "Slaughter of the Innocents" had been the headline over a story about Bor that came out in *The Independent* only a week after "Love Blooms Among the Bullets" appeared in *The Sunday Times*. Emma's sister quarreled openly with her, accusing her of stupidity and selfishness, according to her mother. Emma's younger brother Johnny generally took her side in family disagreements. But once when Emma was going on about all the work she was doing for women and children in Nasir, he retorted, "If it weren't for what your husband was doing, there wouldn't be any need for what you're doing." When the summer ended and she was back in Nairobi, she told Bernadette that her family thought she was mad. "They just don't understand me," she said. In Nasir, she told Tarquin Hall, "I am so happy. Whatever happens, I'm glad that I followed my instinct, married Riek and came to live in Nasir. I have no regrets."

Chapter Twenty-six

A T THE END of September 1992, Emma was in Nasir listening to the BBC's *Focus on Africa* on a new shortwave radio she'd brought back from England when she learned that unidentified southern Sudanese rebels had killed three aid workers and a journalist in eastern Equatoria. One of the dead aid workers was Mynt Maung, the Burmese UN representative in Kapoeta, who'd been one of Emma's first friends in Kapoeta and with whom she'd been in a car accident back in 1989. "Maung, dear Mynt Maung—the last person to deserve a bullet from a southern Sudanese gun," she wrote in the journal she had started keeping. Emma always tuned her radio to *Focus on Africa* if she could. But for several days now, all of Nasir had been tuning in, too, in hopes of hearing news that Equatoria had come over to Riek's side.

Three months earlier the government and the two rebel factions had held another round of peace talks in the Nigerian city of Abuja. (These were the talks that Emma wrote Emma Marrian had everyone "in a bit of a spin" at Nasir in June.) Tiny Rowland flew Lam and the other delegates from Nasir to Abuja for the meeting and put them up in a hotel. The talks went nowhere, but Garang's Nuer chief of staff, William Nyuon, who was leading the SPLA delegation, took the surprising step of uniting the SPLA and the Nasir delegations for the purpose of the meeting. Evidently Tiny Rowland and Lam had convinced Nyuon to do it. In his book, Nyaba says Lam exploited "Commander William's weakness for money and other material incentives." Garang hastily repudiated his chief of staff's actions, telling *Focus on Africa* that Nyuon was an "illiterate person with fifteen wives who had been confused by the complexities of the outside world." But six weeks later a suntanned Rowland announced in Rome that he was on the verge of ending the civil war in Sudan. "It's going to be about six to eight weeks before an agreement is signed," he said.

Rowland was in Rome that August helping to bring about a cease-fire between the rebels and the government in Mozambique, where Lonrho owned an oil pipeline as well as some tea estates. The tycoon added that he would soon be flying with John Garang to an unspecified destination to work out the details of a Sudanese peace agreement. As usual, he brushed aside questions about whether his mediation efforts were motivated by money. "Of course not," he said, "I'm too old for that. I'm seventy-five. It's no longer business but my own personal involvement." Rowland's perfect white teeth glinted as a bevy of photographers took his picture. Around the same time he told the editor of *The Observer* that he held the fate of the Sudan "in the palm of my hand."

On September 27 Nyuon and several hundred troops stationed at Pageri in Equatoria suddenly bolted for the bush. At Nasir, Emma and the others hoped the defection of Garang's chief of staff would cause his faction of the SPLA to collapse. Instead they heard on the radio that it had led to the deaths of Emma's friend Maung and three others. It seemed that Maung, a nurse from the Philippines, a Norwegian journalist, and a UNICEF driver were driving down the road to Palataka when they interrupted a gun battle between Nyuon's forces and Garang's. Their car was found blocking the road and riddled with bullets, but it was not bloodstained. The SPLA delivered the bodies of Maung and the journalist to Operation Lifeline on September 29. Both men had been shot in the back many times, as if they had been running when they were killed. Two days after that the rebels delivered the bodies of the nurse and the Kenyan driver. The heads of both had been freshly shaved. The nurse had been shot in the neck. The Kenyan had been shot through the temple. Garang and Nyuon each blamed the murders on the other's forces. But an internal UNICEF investigation found that while Maung and the Norwegian journalist might have died in the shoot-out, soldiers answering to Kuol Manyang had captured the Filipino nurse and the Kenyan driver, cared for their wounds, and then executed them, possibly three days later.

AT OPERATION LIFELINE headquarters in Nairobi, there was grief and confusion, name-calling and second-guessing. All relief operations in eastern Equatoria were suspended pending a review of what the United Nations euphemistically called the "security situation." Garang denied all responsibility for the deaths, but many aid workers feared the SPLA had turned against Operation Lifeline. The aid workers knew that Garang believed Riek and Lam never would have dared to mount their challenge if it weren't for the relief operation at Nasir. They feared the murders might have been his revenge for what he perceived as Operation Lifeline's encouragement of Riek, a relationship symbolized by the rebellious commander's marriage to Emma.

The killings made some aid workers remorseful about the role they feared they'd inadvertently played in the summer of 1991. If Operation Lifeline hadn't been so quick to recognize Riek's relief group, the Relief Association of Southern Sudan (RASS), and to resume aid deliveries to Nasir, some said, the mutiny might have fallen apart in a few days. If we hadn't allowed ourselves to be duped into carrying mail for Lam and his buddies, some said, it might never have happened. If only we'd kept our distance... The funerals of Maung and the nurse were wrenching occasions, storms of emotion. Aid workers sobbed at the gravesides, accused each other, embraced each other, went back to their offices, locked the doors, and sobbed some more. "Everyone blamed each other," recalled Bernadette Kumar. "That whole period was an emotional blur." The Sudanese government had already declared Vincent O'Reilly persona non grata. Patta Scott-Villiers resigned from the UN, and Alastair left Operation Lifeline for UNICEF's Kenya desk. Others left the region altogether, sickened about the way the war was going and afraid to go back into southern Sudan after the killings.

Emma did not attend the funerals. Despite the sadness she recorded in her diary, she came off to her former colleagues as cool toward the deaths. She knew feelings against her were strong. To some at Operation Lifeline, she had become a symbol of how a relief operation meant to be neutral had become part of the machinery of the civil war. A senior UNICEF official who remained friendly with Emma after her marriage disagreed with those who accused her of having endangered the lives of her former colleagues through her partisanship of Riek. He called the murders of Maung and Gomez "a total fuck-up," saying the SPLA had shot up the UN car by mistake—killing Maung and the Norwegian journalist—then killed the Filipino nurse and the Kenyan driver to cover up their bungling: "It just illustrated in a way that in this type of war, you can't control all the happenings." Nevertheless he was surprised to see how removed Emma seemed to be from it all when he bumped into her in Nairobi not long after the funerals. "She just kept talking about how with Riek's faction this would never happen," he said. "There was no sign of sympathy or compassion for the dead relief workers.... It was like she tried to capitalize on it, 'See what kind of people these Garang supporters are.' I thought to myself, 'She's beginning to lose it.'"

Emma was on her own again in Nairobi. Riek and his troops had marched south from Nasir to lend support to his new ally, William Nyuon, who was still battling Garang's forces in Equatoria. Meanwhile, in the Nuba Mountains, the Sudanese government was separating thousands of Nuba families and trucking them out to desert camps in northern Kordofan to clear the oil fields that Riek had once defended. Emma knew people blamed her and Riek for what was rapidly becoming a hopeless, many-sided war. She was more of a target now than ever before. Riek gave her another bodyguard, and when he came back from Equatoria in October, they moved from Nasir to the thatched village of Waat.

Waat was the seat of the disgruntled Lou Nuer. Riek hoped to pacify the Lou by setting up his headquarters in their territory. He also hoped that his and Emma's presence would attract UN relief to Waat. Khartoum had given Operation Lifeline permission in August to land there. With relief to Garang's areas blocked, desperately hungry Dinka were flocking to the Nuer village. Riek brought thousands more refugees with him from Nasir. Waat's population swelled from three thousand to about fifteen thousand. A senior UNICEF official called it "a charnel house— one of worst things I've ever seen."

Whenever the buzz of an incoming UN plane was heard at Waat, the starving would mass at the airstrip to watch the white Buffalo aircraft unload its precious cargo of grain. At other times the crowd retreated to the edges of the village, squatting in naked little groups across the plain. For ten days in early October, the Buffalo was grounded for repairs. The delay left many dead bodies in the mud. The rains had started. Hyenas and vultures prowled the muddy plain outside the village looking for corpses. The air stank of rotting flesh. "It's considered a shame to die of hunger, and that is why we do not bury starvation victims," Thomas Tot, one of Riek's commanders, told a visiting journalist on October 25. Emma told the same reporter that at least twenty people were dying daily in Waat. "A lot of people have left the town to look for wild fruits in the surrounding areas," she said. "Many others are feeding on wild grass."

A few days later Emma and Riek set off on foot through the swamps for Ayod, a Nuer village about eighty miles to the north. The Lou elders at Ayod were to give Riek a leopard skin, a Nuer symbol of divinity. The trip took five days. Bees and mosquitoes attacked them, and they waded through stretches of chest-deep water infested with bilharzia. Riek's men offered to carry Emma, but she insisted on walking. Halfway there she was so sick that a dish of sorghum and fresh cow's milk failed to revive her. Riek tried to radio for a plane, but the government had bombed Ayod's runway to rubble, and no pilot would land there. They had to keep walking. Emma's mother writes that her daughter was near collapse by the time they reached the village. When they finally reached Ayod, they found thousands of Nuer waiting to get a glimpse of them.

Emma was allowed to attend the leopard-skin ceremony. A picture taken afterward shows Riek draped in the skin, grinning. Emma sits beside him in Ascot attire: a rather churchy, long-sleeved dress, complete with a necklace, sunglasses, and a big hat. Many bulls were sacrificed in the couple's honor. The dancing and the celebrations lasted late into the night. After it was over, Riek told Emma that any son she bore him would become a leopard-skin chief. The couple spent four more days in Ayod, then prepared for another five-day walk back to Waat. Emma's body-guards sang praise poems to the mud and the rain. Nevertheless the journey was so hard that she later told friends she wept most of the way. She wrote her mother about the beautiful *tukul* she found waiting for her at Waat. The Lou Nuer had made it and decorated it with pictures of hippos, lions, and crocodiles.

Emma and Riek had offered prayers for victory at Ayod. For a moment it seemed as if their prayers had been heard. Riek had recruited an army of Nuer to attack the government garrison town of Malakal, a hundred miles to the west of Nasir, on the White Nile. But once the Nuer were assembled, he informed them that instead they should attack Garang's forces in Equatoria. Angry and confused, the Nuer were about to start fighting among themselves when the prophet Wut Nyang intervened. Nuer should not fight Nuer, he told them, and he directed them to attack Malakal despite Riek's orders. (According to Lam, Wut Nyang had a dream that the *mor-mor* termite would come to his aid against the government's mechanized troops. Douglas Johnson heard that Wut Nyang demonstrated his control over life and death by killing a goat and then bringing it back to life, an act attributed to prophets in the past.)

When Riek learned that the Nuer had overrun a few suburbs, he claimed the attack as proof he was still fighting the government. In a delirious press release, he announced that Nasir's "gallant forces" had captured Malakal, a town of more than ten thousand people, with its own electricity and schools. But government forces swiftly drove the prophet and his followers away, reportedly slaughtering hundreds of Nuer civilians in revenge. "By then," Lam told me, "I think even Emma realized how weak Riek was."

At the end of November, Riek was off in the bush with his troops when a reporter from the BBC's French-language service visited Emma in Waat. François Visnot arrived with introductions from several of her old friends in London, and he was one of the few Western journalists willing to risk a visit to southern Sudan so soon after the killings of Maung and the other *khawajas*. He found Emma lying under a purple mosquito net in her *tukul*. She'd been eating UN sorghum cooked in the same dirty water as everyone else, and she was feverish and throwing up. She showed Visnot a U.S. military survival manual that she kept by her bed. She said she took the manual with her everywhere so that she knew what to do if Riek was away and she gotten bitten by a snake or the village came under attack and she had to fend for herself in the bush. She was in pain and probably delirious. But she dragged herself out of bed to give him a tour of the village, proudly pointing out Waat's largest building, a fifty-meter circular mud edifice that she called the Parliament. Visnot poked his head inside. He found it "dark, cool and completely empty." He later heard from a French doctor that a French aid group planning to build a hospital in Waat had had to reduce its size when Riek's authorities learned it would have been bigger than the Parliament.

Visnot remembers what a strangely haunting figure Emma cut at Waat: a tall, thin, frail Englishwoman picking her way in hat and long skirt through the crowds of half-naked, bony people shrouded in the smoke of their dung fires. Two armed bodyguards, both scarified teenagers armed with Kalashnikovs and wearing flip-flops, followed her everywhere. Visnot noticed that while the Nuer men kept their distance from Riek's wife, local women came forward frequently to clasp her hand or sing poems in her honor. Nuer women made jewelry for her, and bathed her and fed her when she was sick. Sometimes they thrust their matchstick-thin children into her arms. Emma would gently hand the babies back. People expected her to have food and money because she was white. But she had none to give them. She tried instead to give them hope.

One of her bodyguards had ambitions of becoming a pop singer. Emma excitedly commanded the youth to get his guitar and play for Visnot. "Maybe François can get you a recording contract in London!" she told the boy. His eyes shining, the boy sang a revolutionary song for Visnot that he'd composed himself. Visnot muttered awkward words of praise. He knew nothing about the music business and felt it was cruel for Emma to set up the boy for disappointment. But Emma listened happily, apparently enjoying the fantasy that this French visitor might make her young bodyguard's dreams come true.

Another famine in the Horn of Africa was much in the news in the fall of 1992. Somalia, a Muslim country bordering the Red Sea south of Sudan between Ethiopia and Kenya, had dissolved into clan fighting after its U.S.-backed president was overthrown in 1991. The fighting swiftly led to famine, and Western relief workers who were trying to distribute food to the starving were forced to pay off clan militias who controlled the roads. Alastair and Patta were now working to feed Somali nomads along the Somali border with Kenya. In another month the United States would announce its planned invasion to protect relief convoys there. Emma told Visnot she was determined not to let Somalia's tragedy push Sudan out of the limelight. She was not the only *khawaja* who felt as if the world had abandoned Sudan. An American aid worker told Visnot she frequently broke down in tears trying to persuade UN officials at Loki of the severity of the situation at Waat. Several hundred people were visibly starving to death. But Emma said wearily that she knew from bitter experience it would take more than a few hundred famine victims to put Sudan back on the world agenda. No, she said, what was needed was television images of mass starvation.

She told Visnot she had a plan. Cable News Network would soon be sending a correspondent up to Waat. Once she knew when the correspondent would arrive, she'd send word to the thousands of starving people in all the villages around Waat that an airdrop was expected. They would converge on Waat, and CNN would get the pictures she wanted them to have. Of course, there would be no food for the new arrivals; but at least, she said, she would have put Waat on the world stage. Visnot was shocked, though he tried not to let Emma know it. He could understand her reasoning. But he didn't believe anything justified getting dying people to use their last bit of energy to walk for miles in the hope of reaching food, when you knew the hope to be false. He was afraid that Emma would be hurt if he told her what he really thought of her plan to manipulate CNN. She had already told him how she felt almost everyone had betrayed her since her marriage to Riek. "I can trust you, can't I, François?" she kept asking him.

Emma introduced Visnot to some men whom she said William Nyuon had freed from Garang's jails when he joined up with Riek in September. The men told Visnot that Garang had imprisoned and tortured them. One tall, skinny former SPLA commander wearing a track suit said Garang had kept him in a tiny container for four years in punishment for a military setback his unit had suffered. The commander said that of the eighty men in his group who ran away from Garang when fighting broke out around Juba, only fifty made it to Riek's territory. It is taboo for the Nuer to eat birds or their eggs, but this man said he finally broke down and ate the vultures that had been feasting on the carcasses of his dead friends. "For the rest of my life, I should remember that I have eaten death," he told Visnot.

Emma was disappointed when Visnot said he could not devote a full-length article to the prisoners' accounts without hearing Garang's side of the story, too. But she took solace in the thought that she would be able to tell their tale, like so many others, in her own way in her book. When she was well enough, she would sit typing her book on the laptop computer she had brought back from England. She was going to call it *Wedded to the Cause,* and she informed Visnot that she intended to donate any money she made to Riek's group. In Waat she was beginning to experience more of Sudan as the Sudanese lived it, but she still had her British passport and her friendships with the UN pilots. At the end of November she left Waat to check in to Nairobi Hospital. Doctors diagnosed malaria and a rare form of hepatitis, but as soon as she was strong enough, she returned to Waat to spend Christmas of 1992 with Riek.

That holiday season was filled with evil portents. Outside Bor the Dinka followers of Paul Kon Agith had started building his giant church. Near the building site the prophet's disciples stacked hundreds of sacred Dinka objects stolen from their neighbors. The Christians intended to burn the objects in a final holocaust once the church was finished. Every few days they would interrupt their frenzied sessions of building and worshiping to rush out looking for more shrines to destroy. Other Dinka complained to Kuol Manyang that the prophet and his followers were bringing disaster down on their neighbors. In their view, the *jak*, the Dinka clan divinities, were punishing the Dinka for the faithlessness of the Christian converts to the religion of their ancestors. The SPLA commander's men were becoming divided over the raids, with some joining in and others defending the old shrines. Kuol would not tolerate such a challenge to his authority. The day after Christmas he ordered SPLA soldiers to capture the prophet. They shot Paul and hacked his body to pieces, but they left the stolen sacred objects alone. Paul's followers buried him beside the foundation of the church and kept on building.

Meanwhile CNN's Gary Strieker and several other journalists visited Waat at the end of November and broadcast a story about the starvation there. Strieker was in and out of the village in a day and doesn't remember meeting Emma. The press coverage did have the effect of increasing food deliveries to Waat. But if Emma pulled the stunt she'd told Visnot about and summoned dying people from nearby villages for a food drop she knew wasn't coming, it failed to focus Western attention on Sudan. At the end of 1992 even the worst pictures from Sudan had to compete with Somalia. And Somalia was out of this world.

Chapter Twenty-seven

I HAD BEEN WRITING more about Somalia than Sudan for some time. Somalia held none of Sudan's sleepy enchantment for me. I could see no interesting political or religious texture to its clan-based battles for loot and power. I pitied the intelligent, able Somalis who found themselves at the mercy of stoned teenage warriors driving the refitted four-wheel drive vehicles they call technicals. In Somalia as in Sudan, many people had had little experience of bureaucratic government until the twentieth century. Instead the Somali clans ran their own affairs according to their interpretation of *sharia*. During the cold war years the United States had showered aid on Somalia's president, Siad Barre. Barre used the weapons and the money he got from Washington to suppress the Somali clans he considered hostile. The United States had backed Barre as a counterweight to the Soviet-backed regime in Ethiopia. But by 1990 the Soviet threat was receding, and the United States dropped its support for Barre. The enemy clans the dictator had suppressed united to chase him from power in early 1991. Then they turned on one another, ransacking the country while they fought for control of the state apparatus they saw as the source of Barre's foreign goodies. The state collapsed, and the fighting soon led to famine.

A few months earlier the U.S. military had successfully mounted its relief operation to assist Kurds fleeing Iraq after the Gulf War. American aid groups began campaigning for a similar military intervention in Somalia's civil war. CARE had the main contract to deliver American government food to Somalia. It was then in the midst of moving its headquarters from New York to Atlanta and I spent a lot of time talking to its officials about the situation in Somalia. As early as September 1992 the group's president, Phillip Johnston, began calling for the "international community, backed by UN troops" to "move in and run Somalia, because it has no government at all." In private conversations, CARE officials complained bitterly about the payoffs required to get past militia checkpoints to the starving in Baidoa and other towns. In November Somali militias shot up a CARE convoy dispatched with instructions not to pay the militias. On November 25 CARE and two other American aid groups held a press conference in which they threatened to pull out of Somalia unless the United Nations provided military protection for their convoys. Johnston met with the secretary of state. A few days later President Bush announced that he would be sending the U.S. Marines to Somalia to guard food convoys.

For me, the echoes of the nineteenth century were resounding. Obviously the marines could get the food convoys rolling. But what would they do after that? Without any government, the Somali clans would start fighting again as soon as the foreign soldiers left. Was the U.S. "intervasion," as journalists called it, a prelude to a UN takeover of Somalia? If so, wasn't that just another name for colonialism? Had we come full circle, back to the point one hundred years earlier when Britain had justified its conquest of places like Sudan and Somalia by arguing that they were saving the inhabitants from famine and slavery? Wouldn't the return of the Western aid machine that had sustained Barre simply inspire the Somali militias to start fighting over it again, as Emma's old friend Alex de Waal and his Somali colleague at Human Rights Watch in London, Rakiya Omaar, kept saying.

"Why hasn't even one Somali been consulted?" Omar demanded to know when I called to ask her about the U.S. plan. "People like Johnston know nothing about Somalia and make no effort to find out. They look at Somalia, and they see an opportunity to be heroes! This talk about humanitarian assistance is completely misplaced if it takes place in a political vacuum.... Unless this is accompanied with a political reconciliation, you have no chance of creating the conditions to stop the cycle of hunger and greed and destructiveness."

Haunted by the faces of the starving people, I found it impossible to oppose a determined American effort to help the Somalis. But I wondered where it might lead. I wasn't the only one. In Sudan Hassan al-Turabi and his allies in the international Islamist movement fiercely condemned the U.S. invasion. They did not believe Washington's motives in Somalia were humanitarian. They called the American intervention a barely disguised form of colonialism and warned that southern Sudan might be the next target. The Islamist press speculated that Washington's real goal in Somalia was to reassert control over the oil grid that spread north from there into Sudan, Eritrea, and Yemen. (Chevron and other American oil companies had held major concessions in all four countries until the upheavals at the end of the cold war.) "One needs to realize that by intervening in Somalia, America is not only trying to put pressure on some states in the region seen to oppose its influence, but also addressing a message to some of its European allies.... It wants to tell them, 'I am standing in the oil fields and the sea lanes,' " an official Khartoum commentator wrote. In London *The Guardian* wrote that the U.S. operation was seen in the Sudan as "a U.S. effort to 'tighten the noose' around Khartoum for its support of Islamic fundamentalist groups in the Arab world and Africa." The NIF government and its new ally, Iran, began lending support to one of the leading Somali warlords, Mohammed Farah Aideed, and his Habr Gidr clan.

In his weekly lectures at the al-Qaeda guesthouse in Khartoum North, Osama bin Laden railed against U.S. designs on Somalia. Bin Laden had long argued that the United States was using its military presence in Saudi Arabia to keep the world price of oil low at the expense of Muslim producers. Now he said that the Americans were trying to weaken "the Islamic revival" in Sudan. One of bin Laden's lieutenants warned al-Qaeda, "Now they go to Somalia and if they [are] successful in Somalia, the next thing could be the south of Sudan." Bin Laden himself told them, "The snake is America and we have to stop them. We have to cut the head and stop them, what they are doing now in the Horn of Africa." Al-Qaeda's committee of religious advisers issued a fatwa making it a duty for Muslims to attack the Americans in Somalia. Three weeks after U.S. troops landed in Mogadishu on December 9, al-Qaeda associates blew up a hotel housing American troops on their way to the country, killing an Australian tourist. In early 1993 a bin Laden associate traveled from Sudan to Somalia to begin providing guns and training to a Somali Islamist militia as well as to Aideed's militia. Other al-Qaeda members began setting up a cell in Nairobi from which they could direct operations in Somalia.

Turabi and bin Laden were not entirely deluded in their paranoia. As *The Guardian* noted in 1993, the early success of the U.S. mission to Somalia caused many Western observers "to question why, with similar anarchy prevailing in Southern Sudan as in Somalia, a similar operation cannot be mounted there." Early that year the U.S. military asked other federal agencies to contribute information about the south that might help military planners in case of such an operation, according to State Department officials. The U.S. ambassador to Sudan, Donald Petterson, further alarmed Turabi and the NIF government when he violated diplomatic protocol to tour rebel areas of the south between February 27 and March 3, 1993, and meet with Riek and Garang to talk about what it would take for them to reunite against the government. Petterson visited Riek at the village of Ulang, downstream from Nasir on the Sobat. The ambassador reported in a disappointed cable back to Washington that Riek and his colleagues "would not budge from [their] insistence on total separation of the South from the North." As Petterson sat talking to Riek, "just thirty yards away, about 100 terribly emaciated women, children and old men were huddled. A group brought a man's body a few feet closer to us and laid it on the ground." Petterson remarked to "Riek's well-fed and well-clothed lieutenants" that "surely ending the factional fighting and thereby relieving the suffering of people like those we had seen was more important than continuing to fight over political or ideological differences." To the ambassador's anger, Riek's men said they disagreed. On his next stop, he found Garang equally intransigent about compromising with Riek's group.

To avoid giving Washington a pretext to intervene in the south, the Sudanese government suddenly eased permission for Operation Lifeline flights to deliver food in rebel areas. After Nigeria's president warned the Islamic government that it risked "armed intervention" if it failed to negotiate with the southern rebels, the NIF also backed down on its previous refusal to send representatives to another meeting in Abuja. Riek's group was not invited to this second round of Abuja talks. The SPLA sneered that Riek's faction was little more than a government militia anyway. Riek and Emma were too preoccupied with Nuer internal fractures to worry about the snub. Despite Riek's move to Waat, bad feelings continued to mount between the Lou and the Jikany. The fighting in Equatoria had forced the Lou to graze their cattle in Jikany lands, causing new friction. Then several Lou men went fishing in the Sobat. The Jikany considered the Sobat theirs, and they had not given the Lou permission to fish in it. When the fishermen caught a type of fish the Nuer call Lec, the Jikany seized it, much as they had done the year before with the Uduk men. In the ensuing fight, the Jikany killed three Lou fishermen.

Then they refused to give the bodies of the dead fishermen back to their clansmen.

Unlike the Uduk, however, the Lou were armed to the teeth and seething with rage about the devastation of their homeland that the fighting with the Dinka around Bor had wrought. (Although some Lou had joined the original raids on Bor, they resented the fact that they and not the Jikany had been the targets of the Dinka revenge raids.) They attacked the Jikany. A wicked cycle of Nuer raids and counterraids got under way. The Nuer interpreted this all in terms of one of Ngungdeng's prophecies, which said the Jikany and Lou would fight over the Lec fish and that the fighting would not stop until it reached a small village outside of Nasir called Kotwith. Seen this way, the fighting looked inevitable, and, inevitably, Riek's lieutenants began to enter it on the side of their relatives.

Emma believed that Riek was above such quarrels. She was trying to help him put together a record of cattle stolen in the Lou-Jikany dispute so that they could be returned at a reconciliation ceremony. But Lam says Riek began to suspect that some of his Jikany underlings were plotting against him. Emma was at Waat in January 1993 when an incident occurred that she could not ignore. One officer, Hakim Gabriel Aluong, fell afoul of the others in one of these murky disputes. In Emma's presence, he was dragged away to be shot. When she pleaded for Hakim's life, Riek's men paid no attention. "Emma came [to Nairobi] and she was very angry," recalled Lam. "She talked to everyone about it. Now it was really in front of her eyes. But she didn't blame Riek. She said it was the officers."

PERHAPS EMMA BEGAN to despair of politics around this time; perhaps, like the Dutch nurse from Wau whom I had met in Khartoum, she was beginning to think it would be better to try to save just one human being. In August 1992 twelve little Nuer boys had straggled into Riek's military compound at Waat. Emma heard that the boys had walked three months to escape Garang's forces. Emma felt that Riek had not been given enough credit for allowing the International Red Cross to reunite the first three hundred boys in Nasir with their families. (By contrast, Garang had refused to let any of the more than ten thousand boys under his control go home.) One animated eleven-year-old named Emmanuel Jai arrived carrying a gun larger than he was. Emmanuel turned out to be distantly related to Riek. He described how he had fired heavy mortars and carried ammunition for Garang's men. "You take this thing over here, you put it here and"—he would cover his ears—"bang!" Emmanuel said he had gone to Ethiopia in 1989 hoping to get an education. Instead he'd been sent to one of Garang's FACE schools. Emmanuel said the boys at the school spent all their time working or in military training. They were given books only when important visitors were expected. Then in 1992 the SPLA drafted them for its assault on Juba and for months of hard fighting afterward.

Emma was taken with Emmanuel. When she returned to Kenya, she smuggled him into the country with her. Over the next few months he was often at her side. She let him sleep in her bed, and she brought him along with her to Langata dinner parties. Emma's friends called the pair "Nancy and the Artful Dodger" after the charming pair of thieves in *Oliver Twist*. Emmanuel's eyes lit up when he saw the telescope at David and Emma Marrian's house—he assumed it was a mortar rocket launcher. Emma badgered everyone she knew in Nairobi to contribute to Emmanuel's education, and she wrote away to charities, searching for a grant that would pay for him to attend boarding school in Kenya. When her mother came to visit in February 1993, Emma infuriated her by telling Emmanuel to call her Granny and asking Maggie to baby-sit for him. "I resented his presence more than I can say," Maggie wrote, and plenty of Emma's white Nairobi friends felt the same way. Maybe the strain of her two lives had begun to wear on her; in foisting Emmanuel on her friends, she seemed to be silently forcing them to see the realities of southern Sudan that until now she had always dressed up in hilarious anecdotes.

In the eyes of her white friends, she was becoming more African in another, more troubling way: She was needy. She had always stayed with Sally or other friends in Kenya. Now when she came, she was not always the delightful dinner companion she had once been. Frequently she required nursing as well as a bed. Her illnesses were ugly, severe, and frightening. Some people feared catching them. She had no money: If she was visiting and the group wanted to go out for drinks or a meal, they knew they would have to pick up Emma's share of the bill. She had never minded asking people for things. Now she grew bold. She borrowed expensive clothes without asking. When she overheard that an expatriate she knew would be traveling to Addis Ababa, she coquettishly talked him into buying her some of the fine white Ethiopian shawls she adored. He knew she had no intention of repaying him for them. Her requests must have seemed natural and almost innocent to her, accustomed as she had grown to the constant demands of the far needier Nuer. ("The demands made on a man in the name of kinship are incessant and imperious and he resists them to the utmost," Evans-Pritchard wrote of the Nuer in the 1930s.) But to the expatriates, who spent so much time trying to insulate themselves from African begging, it was as if a bit of the squalid, angry Africa they tried so hard to avoid had managed to sneak past all their razor wire, guards, and dogs and set itself up in the guest room.

IN MARCH SHE THREW herself into preparations for a big political meeting Riek was going to hold in the Dinka settlement of Panyagor. Four high-ranking politicians, two of them Dinka, had escaped from one of Garang's prisons and joined up with Riek. Riek's group was going to change its name from SPLA-Nasir to the SPLA-United—to reflect its new all-inclusive, nontribal identity. Emma hoped that the addition of the Dinka and Equatorian leaders would induce the rest of the south to come over to Riek's side. Tiny Rowland was also taking an active part in the plans. Rowland had flown the escaped politicians from Kampala to Nairobi and paid for them to hold a press conference denouncing Garang at the 680 Hotel. The four politicians said Garang put them in holes in the ground for several days after policy disputes with him in 1987. Then for more than three months they were held with other prisoners in a container five-by-seven feet wide. A spokesman for Garang countered that they had been well taken care of in prison. "Nobody tortured them," he said. From his hotel, the Norfolk, Rowland held a surprise press conference of his own in which he announced that he had been a clandestine member of the SPLA for nine years. It was time, the Lonrho tycoon informed the BBC, for the war in Sudan to end. "The war in Sudan is unwinnable," he concluded in ringing tones.

Rory Nugent, a tall, bald, beetle-browed American writer, was in Nairobi waiting to join Riek after the big meeting at Panyagor. Nugent was writing a profile of Riek for *Men's Journal*. Emma had arranged interviews for him in Nairobi with the escaped politicians who had joined up with Riek. The plan, Emma told him, was for Riek and his new colleagues to hold a rally that would show the Dinka and the other peoples of the south that the struggle within the SPLA was not about tribes but about principles. The French had established Panyagor in 1982 as a housing complex for workers on the Jonglei Canal Commission; they had abandoned it, unfinished, a year later when John Garang brought the project to a halt with an attack on the canal's giant excavator. (Thereafter the excavator lay sinking into the mud, so enormous that it remained a landmark for pilots flying across the region.) Now Panyagor belonged to what Emma dubbed the "Hunger Triangle": a zone of starvation and fighting made up of Waat, Ayod, and Kongor. A few weeks earlier the U.S. Centers for Disease Control had reported that rates of malnutrition at Panyagor were "among the highest ever recorded"; UN officials said that the hunger was almost entirely caused by the factional fighting among the southern rebels, and they feared that Riek and Emma were inveigling them to keep delivering food to the three towns for their own strategic purposes.

A blond Frenchman named Jean-François Darcq was responsible for feeding the people in Panyagor. On March 26 Darcq listened as Riek and his comrades stood before an audience of several thousand Dinka, appealing to them to rise up against Garang. At six the next morning he was in the UN's storehouse, talking on the radio. When he heard shooting, at first he thought Riek's forces must be holding a parade. Then the UN watchman told him they were under attack by Garang's SPLA. The watchman ran. Darcq hid in the brick storehouse. When the mortars and rocket-propelled grenades died down, he peeked outside. A couple of Garang's young fighters appeared with rifles. They made Darcq open up the UN's food stores and ordered him to take off his shirt, trousers, shoes, and socks. They left him with his underpants. Darcq took this as a hopeful sign, he told me. "They were shooting guys whose underwear they had taken off, because they don't like to dirty them with blood. So then I thought that they will not kill me."

A long, terrifying day passed in which Garang's forces shot at Darcq and forced him to run through the bush before Riek's men recaptured the town and released him. Emma came limping in along with the soldiers. She later said she had hidden under an overturned cupboard until Forty-Six, her huge bodyguard, rescued her. She ran from the gun battle barefoot through the thorn scrub until her feet were bloody with cuts. One of the Nasir faction's most venerable and important supporters, an elderly Equatorian who had once served as Sudan's minister of sport, couldn't keep up. Garang's fighters shot him in the back. For a half a day Emma believed that Riek had been killed, too. They finally met up at some Toyota trucks that the group had hidden in the bushes. After Riek's forces retook the town, Darcq and Emma sat in front of one of the unfinished concrete *tukuls*—another remnant of the Jonglei project—and smoked an entire pack of Dunhill cigarettes.

Darcq told Emma that before Garang's soldiers forced him to run into the bush, they asked him where she was. They told him she was a British spy, and they accused the United Nations of supplying Riek with ammunition and food. They also caught Emma's dog, Come On. A few months later Garang recaptured Panyagor from Riek. A British journalist who visited the settlement in May found that Garang's fighters still had Come On. They had renamed the dog "Emma." They kept her alive to kick and beat. They were still beating "Emma" with sticks when he left. The fighters who did it, he said, were under the command of Kuol Manyang. This was the last recorded sighting of Emma's pet.

Emma's narrow escape at Panyagor seemed to sober her. She had spent all her savings; she and Riek owed money to everyone. The electricity and the telephones were always dead at the office that Riek's faction kept in Nairobi, even though UNICEF provided cash to pay the bills. She stayed in Nairobi and worked on her autobiography. Bit by bit crumpled sheets began to arrive at her agent's office in London. Like the Sudanese, Emma had grown to distrust the mail system. Any communication of value she sent through a circuitous route involving friends and friends of friends. The first chapter described her escape by UN plane from Panyagor:

> I climbed in and bent to kiss Riek good-bye at the door. The door closed, the engine started and we sped down the airstrip and turned sharply away from the fighting. I looked down and saw Riek and his men watch us go until they became mere dots on the earth's surface. Part of my heart remained behind with Riek. As we soared up, as if magically lifted from hell, the vastness of this great flat land overwhelmed me.... Unstoppable tears poured down my cheeks, washing away all the shock, the fear and the grief. I grieved for those who had died and those who would die in this endless struggle.

She had always wanted to have a child. "That's highly irresponsible of you," Bernadette would say whenever Emma brought up the subject. "You have to go away from here if you want to have a child. You can't raise a child in southern Sudan." Even Riek warned her that she would have to stay in Nairobi if she had a baby. "I was not going to have her in the bush with a kid!" he told me indignantly. Emma, on the other hand, always talked of raising her family on a farm in southern Sudan. She probably hoped that bearing a child would improve her standing among the Nuer. For Nuer women, barrenness is a tragedy. If Emma had been Nuer and failed to have a child after two years of marriage, she might have been divorced and left to survive through prostitution or selling beer. Other women would have shunned her for fear that she might contaminate them with her misfortune or harm their children out of spite. But Emma—who joked in the spring, on the television documentary that ITV made about her called *The Warlord's Wife*, that she had not been married for her cooking skills—had not been married for her childbearing abilities, either. And, unlike the women of southern Sudan, she was able to travel to Nairobi to visit an Indian gynecologist. The gynecologist gave her fertility pills and advised her to take better care of her health.

She made a resolution to redouble her efforts to learn Nuer. She went to visit Riek's extended family in Ler. Ululating, the women of the town carried her on their shoulders five miles from the airstrip to the *tukul* they had made for her. Sitting her down on a chair, they danced around her, waving tamarind branches. At the climax of the celebration, they slaughtered an ox at the entrance to Riek's family compound as an offering to God to end her barrenness. Riek surprised everyone by flying in unexpectedly. The village erupted into celebrations. The Nuer elders rubbed ashes on his and Emma's feet and spat on their heads. They prayed for Teny, the spirit who had entered Riek's grandfather, to grant him and Emma a son. "A son, a son, we want a son from your marriage who will help us in the future," the villagers chanted.

In the summer of 1993 she became pregnant.

RIEK AND LAM continued their secret wheeling and dealing with Khartoum, but they were also looking for an alternative source of weapons and ammunition. The international black market was flooded with small arms from the former Soviet bloc countries. Emma borrowed a friend's telephone to haggle with an arms dealer over the price of some Czech guns. But without the help of a neighboring government, it was difficult for Riek to get guns into landlocked southern Sudan. Though Kenya tolerated Riek, President Daniel Arap Moi still was betting on Garang, and

Riek's ties to Khartoum had compromised him in the eyes of Ethiopia and Uganda. Riek's officers disapproved of Emma's participation in the sensitive negotiations. "She was involved illegally in the movement," one Nuer commander later recalled to me. "It was not right. Riek listened to Emma more than the others. She [could] control Riek." They may have wanted her to behave more like their Nuer wives. Or they may simply have distrusted her discretion. In a radio message that Emma's mother quotes in her book, Emma told Riek that some of them refused to let her join a planeload of journalists going to visit him in Kongor, saying she would be interfering with his work. "They went on to say I was a political liability to you and I should get used to not seeing you, maybe for years, that it is dangerous for journalists to see me next to you and that I should go and find a job instead of sitting idle in Nairobi," Emma wrote.

Riek told Emma not to listen, and yet his fellow rebels may have had a point. Westerners always considered Emma an asset to Riek because of favorable coverage she gained for him in the Western press. It is undeniable that Emma's friendships with journalists won Riek a more sympathetic Western hearing on many occasions than he otherwise would have received. The high point in the stream of positive press came with *The Warlord's Wife* in April 1993. But the publicity was not always flattering in Sudanese eyes. A Dinka politician based in Khartoum remembers seeing a photograph in a magazine of Riek and Emma holding hands as they strolled through a jungle landscape. The picture made him laugh. "This fighter is the leader of the Nuers?" he thought. "This man became a political leader by accident. His flesh is sweet. He wants to be comfortable." Riek's Western critics felt that reporters intrigued by his marriage to an beautiful Englishwoman overlooked his ruthless side. But many southern Sudanese criticized Riek for not being ruthless enough to discipline his own men. There were arrests and kidnappings and murders in his group, but they were always carried out in a haphazard manner, and Riek never took responsibility. To many southerners, he seemed indecisive. The professed modesty that foreigners found endearing struck the Nuer as "feminine." An old man at Nasir warned him to stop speaking "with his head bowed." "My son," he said, "if this is how you plan to lead the Nuers, you are going to fail. The Nuers were led by powerful leaders when they crossed the Nile to come to the east, that is why they succeeded to have this land and to assimilate other tribes."

In the summer of 1993 Presbyterian church leaders approached Riek to try to get him to join them and settle the dispute between the Lou and the Jikany. It had already cost hundreds of lives. But Riek said he and his commanders would handle it. In October he called a conference, but his commanders sabotaged it. They were benefiting from the fighting, using the arms the Sudanese government gave them to raid cattle. Each skeleton they left rotting in the sun sowed new "bones" between clans and lineages and started another round of fighting. The Lou-Jikany elders and leopard-skin priests could not settle the conflict according to traditional law because Riek's young men would not obey them. Riek told human rights investigators that he ruled by the SPLA penal code, but the practical effect of the Nasir coup had been to abolish all systematic administration of Nuerland. "The lawlessness that reigned in Nuerland culminating in the Lou-Jikany conflict is attributable to the weak leadership of Dr. Riek Machar following the attempted coup and his inability to impose his leadership on the Nuer people," Nyaba later wrote.

Nor was Riek able to deliver as a bull-boy and a black *Turuk*. His alliance with Emma did not result in weapons or other useful Western support. Instead it turned into a propaganda bonanza for Garang. Riek relied on Khartoum for guns and ammunition, just as the illiterate southern leaders of the past had. It seemed to some southerners that the vaunted benefits of a Western-educated leadership were just another hoax perpetrated by the *Turuk*. "They should let us determine our leaders, not those two monsters—Doctor John Garang and Doctor Riek Machar," one southerner scornfully told a British reporter. "In the SPLA, the ones making all the mistakes are these so-called Ph.D.'s— poverty, hunger and disease."

EMMA ARRANGED FOR Rory Nugent to spend a month in the bush with Riek, asking only that he not mention her at all in his article. Nugent, who had already written one book about tracking a mythical dinosaur-like creature in the Congo, showed up in the thatch-mud Nuer village of Yuai carrying luggage. Riek shook his head disapprovingly. "Guerrillas walk twenty miles a day," he said. "Can you do that and still carry everything?" But the two soon developed a liking for each other. Rory was a new *khawaja* willing to listen to the political theories that irritated Riek's Nuer comrades. To the journalist, he swore that all the stories about his alliance with Khartoum were false. "My enemy is Khartoum," he told

Nugent, lowering his voice and speaking slowly. "I have a personal score to settle with Garang, but I want his troops on my side." On Sunday, Riek grabbed his Bible and hurried to join the Presbyterian choir. "I sense he privately considers himself a modern crusader battling the Muslim hordes," Nugent wrote.

Riek and Nugent were still in Yuai when Riek got word by radio that Garang had attacked Ayod, the site of a UN feeding center and an open camp that housed several thousand people. Riek counterattacked a few days later. When his forces recaptured Ayod, they found that Garang's men had razed the town and burned down the feeding center, incinerating more than one hundred people inside. The bodies of two hundred other people lay sprawled about the charred remains of the village.

Nugent was in shock. He and Riek sat in the ashes, picking flies out of a soup that Riek's cook had made from bits of dried meat boiled in swamp water. "I detest flies," Riek commented. "They are the one thing I hate about the Sudan." Nugent stared at him. *The one thing you hate about Sudan is flies?* When night fell and Nugent saw Riek looking at the stars, he asked him what he saw in the sky, away from the devastation around him. Riek responded with a rush of clichés: "Millions of green shoots that grow into tall plants that feed the world. I see what can be if we are free." The images disturbed Nugent. They suggested to him that Riek's political imagination went no deeper than a pop song or a Hallmark card.

A week later Riek's forces were back at Ayod. Despite his boast about guerrillas walking twenty miles a day, Riek told Nugent his men could not move without diesel. After five days in Ayod they heard gunshots. They were under attack by Garang. Riek and Nugent ran for one of the rebel trucks. As the truck started off toward Waat, Nugent watched out the back as a series of mortar rounds and grenades hit the UN feeding center and clinic. About sixteen hundred people, he knew, were inside the feeding center. Earlier in the day he had observed about a hundred people laid out on the floor of the clinic. "The fetor of burning flesh and hair engulfs us," he wrote later. "I stare at the aid station as war transforms it into a crematorium."

"Why the feeding center?" Nugent wanted to know. He and Riek were hanging off the back of the speeding truck. "Have your troops ever done anything like that?"

Riek admitted that they had, though he claimed that his soldiers knew he would punish them for such crimes. Nugent reminded Riek that a few days before he had said guerrilla armies make up their own rules and must be willing to do anything to win. "Our army has laws!" Riek shouted above the din of gunfire. "I believe in a heaven and a hell, and I don't want to go to hell."

"Look around you," Nugent snapped. "This *is* hell."

WHEN GARANG'S TROOPS retreated, Riek and Nugent walked along with Riek's troops back to Ayod from Waat. In every village they found the dead, mostly women split in half by machete. Often the women's killers had spread their legs and inserted sticks in their vaginas. Nugent took pictures of the dead. He pressed Riek for answers. Had he any vision of an end to this war? Riek spoke of a UN-sponsored referendum on secession, of an independent state. And then what? Nugent said. Riek's answers all seemed to involve a rescue by outsiders: a custodial government run by the UN, a peacekeeping force, national elections after three years. "The south has the potential to be rich economically," he told Nugent earnestly. "The south does have vast reserves of oil, gold and other minerals.... If the UN helps us to our feet, it won't be long before we can take care of ourselves." Nugent stared out at the empty plain. Corpses lay sprawled out around the perimeter of the village. Hyenas came trotting past with human limbs in their jaws. Riek didn't seem to notice, but Nugent couldn't keep his eyes off them.

Nugent started accompanying a Sudanese relief worker attached to Riek's faction on his trips outside Ayod to look for abandoned children. One day they found the corpse of a woman covered with vultures. The stink was enough was to ward anyone off, but the Sudanese sensed something unusual. He scattered the birds and turned over the woman's rotting body. Beneath the corpse, he uncovered a pair of infants, both alive. "A fingertip of one of the babies has been gnawed to the bone by a vulture," Nugent wrote. It was a pair of twins, the miraculous "children of God" whom the Nuer believe to be akin to birds.

At last Riek's faction hit upon a way of obtaining some diesel. They invited a party of journalists from Nairobi to visit, on the condition that they bring along some extra fuel. With their trucks refueled, they counterattacked, retaking Yuai and Ayod and killing about a thousand Garang soldiers, by Riek's calculation. At Ayod Nugent said good-bye. Riek was just about to make a speech to the survivors at Ayod. The rebel leader had told Nugent he wasn't sure what he was going to tell the people who had lost their families and their homes, but, as he approached the crowd,

Nugent later reported that the survivors began chanting, calling him "savior, liberator, champion." Several sprang to their feet yelling, "Messiah...messiah!"

With long, sure steps, Riek walked to the head of the crowd. As Nugent turned to go, he heard Riek telling them about his vision of a free southern Sudan.

On August 29, 1993, Sudan's Islamic government signed a $125 million exploration and production-sharing agreement with Arakis and State Petroleum. The agreement gave Arakis and its new president, Lutfur Rahman Khan, the right to begin pumping oil from the wells that contained the Sudan's only proven reserves: Heglig and Unity in Nuerland. Hassan el-Turabi and his National Islamic Front were jubilant. With their courtship of Riek and Lam, they had won in one stroke everything the Sudanese army had failed to gain in nine years on the battlefield. They had divided the rebel movement and obtained a separate peace that would now allow them to resume oil development. But to proceed, they knew they had to keep Riek and Lam on their side. And all of a sudden the southern mutineers had another suitor: the American government.

Also in August 1993 Turabi's old friend Sheikh Omar Abdel-Rahman had been indicted for conspiring to blow up the United Nations and other New York landmarks. The blind preacher had emigrated from Sudan to New Jersey in 1990. Six of those convicted in the plot were Sudanese, while two Sudanese diplomats at the United Nations were accused of helping the conspirators. A few days later the Clinton administration put Sudan on its list of state sponsors of terrorism, preventing many American companies from investing in the country. The International Monetary Fund also suspended Sudan's voting rights, citing the government's failure to pay interest on the country's debt. Saudi Arabia stopped sending Sudan subsidized oil. Turabi already blamed U.S. intelligence for a failed attack on his life that took place on a visit to Canada a year earlier. According to the U.S. ambassador, Donald Petterson, Khartoum responded to the sanctions with an "increasingly frenzied" series of anti-American demonstrations and press attacks. The U.S. embassy evacuated all nonessential personnel from Sudan. Petterson took a warning to President Bashir and Turabi on September 12. In his book Petterson says the U.S. government warned that if any harm came to Americans in Sudan, it would retaliate "in a way that would essentially destroy the Sudanese economy." Other accounts claim that Washington's message included a military threat. "As I knew they would, both Bashir and Turabi reacted with fury, Turabi in particular," Petterson later wrote. The Islamists feared Washington was about to intervene in southern Sudan in a way that would cast aside their carefully laid plan to establish a secure financial base for their regime.

It did seem in Washington's interest to turn up the heat on Turabi and Bashir. Not only was the NIF implicated in the New York bombing plots, but American forces in Mogadishu were also engaged in a manhunt for the Somali warlord Mohammed Farah Aideed, who had attacked UN troops in June. It had also been widely reported that the Sudanese government had been assisting Aideed. If Riek and Garang would stop fighting each other and start fighting the government again, Turabi would have less time and money to meddle in neighboring countries. The U.S. Select Committee on Hunger invited the feuding rebels to come to Washington in October and see if they couldn't find a way to patch up their quarrel. After that former President Jimmy Carter asked them to come to Atlanta for talks on October 25. President Bashir responded to Washington's overtures to Riek and Garang with a furious speech attacking the United States as an enemy of peace and Islam. More quietly the NIF government sent emissaries to Riek and Lam offering the possibility of a separate peace that would allow Arakis to proceed with petroleum exploration near Bentiu.

At the end of September Lam flew into government-held Shillukland. He said he was going to attend the installation of the Shilluk king at Tonga. Actually he was engaged in an intense round of secret talks with the government, intended to finalize the Frankfurt agreement he had signed the previous year. The government's latest proposal was for the south to hold a referendum on self-determination after an undetermined period of rule under an Islamic federal system. (The government called this plan "Peace from Within.") But the talks broke down over the division of the oil revenues between Khartoum and the provincial government that Riek and Lam envisioned for Upper Nile in an Islamic federal system. "Khartoum was claiming 100% for a period of ten years, whilst Lam Akol and his group proposed that a future autonomous government of southern Sudan would share the riches 50-50 for a period of no more than two years," reported *The Indian Ocean Newsletter* in a rare mention of the ultrasecret oil talks. To make sure the government could not ignore their wishes, Riek and Lam sent rebel units loyal to them to Bentiu to ensure control over the area. The government flew another delegation to meet personally with Riek in the village of Mankein. The plane carrying the delegation crashed, killing everyone on board.

Riek had steered clear of any personal contact with the government. In public he denied having made a deal with the Islamic fundamentalists. Emma always backed him up. Rory Nugent believes that she would not have stayed with Riek if she believed he truly had gone over to the government's side. "To her, the government was the devil," Nugent told me. But years later Riek said she knew all about his clandestine dealings. "She was facing the same risks as me," he said. "I never doubted her loyalty."

At the end of September Emma chartered a plane to pick up Riek and Lam in southern Sudan and bring them to Nairobi before going to Washington. Flying back, they ran into a storm. "We nearly crashed—she was in the plane," Riek told me later. But they made it safely back to Nairobi, where Tiny Rowland put them up at the Hotel Inter-Continental. ("Food, cars, hotels—it was all paid for by me," Rowland said when I asked him about it.) It was the first time Riek had ventured out of the south since his split with Garang. The Carter Center paid for him to fly on to the United States, while Emma stayed behind. She was four months pregnant. She told me later on the telephone that her doctor had advised her to stay at home.

LAM AKOL BELIEVES that, just before he left for Nairobi in October, Riek gave orders for the arrest of Lul, the lecherous Nasir education coordinator who first told me about Emma's fondness for Riek. Riek and Emma were staying at the Inter-Continental then. Riek had left the old Anyanya II leader Gordon Kong in charge at Nasir. Gordon had accused Lul and thirteen others of plotting against him and Riek. He put the men in one of the rebel jails at Nasir. A few weeks later Lam and John Luk, a Nuer lawyer, heard that Lul was dead.

When they asked Riek about it, he said Lul had died of typhoid. Luk was suspicious. He went to Nasir to investigate. There he heard another story. Every evening at seven P.M., he was told, the fourteen prisoners had been taken out of their huts and beaten, one by one. One night Lul was not brought back until after midnight. He was nearly unconcious and vomiting blood. That night he died.

When the lawyer returned from Nasir and confronted Riek with his report, Riek swore he hadn't known that Emma's former colleague had been tortured to death. He said he would court-martial Gordon. But nothing much happened. Gordon continued to reign in Nasir undisturbed. (Five or so years later Riek put Gordon on trial. Riek says it was for murdering Lul, among other things. Other Nuer say Riek was angry with Gordon because he tried to challenge Riek.)

I WAS GETTING READY to go to Mogadishu when I heard that Riek was staying at a hotel in Atlanta. Aideed's men had killed eighteen U.S. Rangers in Somalia. Although we did not know it at the time, at least some of the attackers had been trained by members of Osama bin Laden's al-Qaeda. ("Under cover of the United Nations, the United States tried to establish its bases in Somalia so that it could get control over Sudan and Yemen," bin Laden would later say. "My associates killed the Americans in collaboration with [Mohammed] Farah Aideed.") I was going with Phillip Johnston, the head of CARE who had lobbied the Bush administration to send troops to Somalia. I hadn't talked to Emma in more than a year, but at the suggestion of our mutual friend Gill Lusk, the editor of *Africa Confidential*, I called her at the Inter-Continental to ask about the Washington talks.

The press had been quick to see Riek's emergence from the bush for the first time in three years as a signal that the Clinton administration had somehow persuaded him to reconcile with Garang. Livid over the possible loss of its pawn, Khartoum staged a series of angry demonstrations against the talks in Washington. But the Islamists needn't have worried. In Washington Riek and Garang drove the American negotiators crazy with their bickering. Congressman Harry Johnston, a Florida Democrat who was chairman of the select committee, led the talks. Johnston's people felt Riek sabotaged their efforts. As amiable as ever, he entertained the congressional staffers with the tale of his and Emma's escape from Panyagor—"You had your *wife* with you?" one American negotiator remembered thinking incredulously—and seemed to agree to all their proposals for reunifying the SPLA. But no sooner had Johnston's staff laboriously crafted an agreement than Riek refused to sign unless they changed Garang's title to something besides "commander in chief." A shouting match ensued. Riek accused Garang of atrocities, and the meeting collapsed in mutual recriminations. Garang refused to come to Atlanta and flew back to Sudan. Riek returned alone with Jimmy Carter. Garang's group issued a press release denouncing his refusal to sign the so-called Washington agreement. "Why won't Riek sign?" the statement asked. "The reason is clear. He won't sign because his military pay-masters have threatened military action against them if he signs. He has proved himself a stooge of the Khartoum regime and we call on all our people and the world to treat them for what they are—TRAITORS!"

I read the statement aloud to Emma over the phone. She listened without saying anything, but I got the feeling she was worried and upset. After a long pause she urged me to go see Riek at the Wyndham Hotel and hear his side of the story. She insisted Riek was being unfairly blamed for the breakdown, but she wouldn't give me any details. I couldn't help asking her if she wasn't weary of it all. She said it wasn't that—it was just that being pregnant made her tired. Though it was already late in the evening, I went over to the Wyndham, more out of curiosity than anything else. With Somalia uppermost in everyone's mind, I knew my editors wouldn't want another story in the paper about complicated factional fighting in Africa. I found Riek suave and relaxed, recounting with gusto the obscure political differences and personal affronts that made it impossible for him to sign the agreement with Garang.

On his way back from Washington, Riek stopped in London. Emma phoned him there every day, making arrangements for him to meet her family for the first time. She also called the members of his faction in London, annoying them by insisting that they take down lists of people she thought it would be useful for Riek to see. Riek spent most of his time with Angelina and their children. It was the first time he'd met his three-year-old son, Timmy, and the first time he'd seen Angelina since his mar-riage to Emma.

Angelina had been waiting two years for this moment. She told him she wanted a divorce.

Riek laughed her off. Under Nuer law, he reminded her, a wife cannot be divorced after she has had three children. And by the time Riek left England two weeks later, Angelina was pregnant with a fourth. Notwith-standing Emma's apologies for polygamy, she was crushed when she found out Riek had slept with Angelina. She told Bernadette Kumar that Riek had told her when they married that his marriage to Angelina would be in name only. "She was really very upset," Bernadette recalled.

"She said, 'He betrayed me.' " Emma complained to Bernadette that African men simply did not keep their promises to be faithful. She said the tradition of polygamy was just too old and strong. (She seemed not to know that Riek had made and broken the same promise to remain monogamous when he married Angelina.) "In their hearts, they just don't see anything wrong with it. She said this happens all the time with African men." Bernadette asked Emma if she had told Riek how she felt. Emma replied that she had and that Riek had promised that he had slept with Angelina only once and that it would never happen again. Bernadette suspected Emma didn't believe him. "She found out and she was really unhappy, but she was beyond the stage where she could sit on a high horse," Bernadette said.

Emma concentrated all her energy on her pregnancy. She gave up smoking and tried to eat nutritious food. She began making plans to go to England for the birth so her child would be certain to get British citizenship. "I think she was disillusioned," Bernadette said, "but it was taken out by the fact that she was going to have a child. Southern Sudan and the peace talks were very far away in her mind. She was not concentrating on the debates. She was thinking that maybe her child would be the future of southern Sudan. She had lots of hopes and dreams about what her child might mean."

While Riek was in London, Emma had found a house, again courtesy of Tiny Rowland and the Kenyan government. It was a white stucco bungalow off Riverside Drive, a smart area where Kenyan big shots and Western diplomats live. (Emma's first choice had been the Ngong Dairy, the Karen mansion where the Hollywood movie *Out of Africa* was filmed. When Riek's lieutenants vetoed the house on the grounds that it would be too difficult to secure against assassination attempts, she talked Sally Dudmesh into renting it.) Emma had never had a house of her own. She bustled about buying things for it. Her friend the sculptor David Marrian built a big metal bed for her and Riek. For the first time in years, she started painting. "She said she didn't have enough money to buy pictures, so she might as well paint them," her brother Johnny recalled. Johnny and her sister Jennie had arrived in November for their first visit to Africa. To them, Emma had never seemed happier.

Chapter *Twenty-eight*

I THOUGHT OF GOING to see Emma in Nairobi on my way to
Mogadishu. Our telephone conversation had reawakened my curiosity about her. Did she really still believe Riek was fighting for
anything larger than his own aggrandizement? But I had no time to visit.
The Clinton administration had decided to pull the U.S. troops out of
Somalia. CARE and the American aid agencies were chagrined, certain
the country would collapse back into chaos, but apparently afraid to
challenge the widespread American belief that the lives of eighteen
American soldiers were too much to pay to avoid that. The brief
post–cold war period in which the United States and its allies had talked
of using their military power to create a "New World Order" had come
to an abrupt halt. Apparently the New World Order was desirable only if
it could be achieved without cost to American lives. There was no more
talk of intervention in southern Sudan or anywhere else in Africa. In
Haiti, a U.S. warship turned back after a few hundred Haitians rioted on
the dock at Port-au-Prince. At his headquarters in Khartoum, Bin Laden
gloated over what he claimed as al-Qaeda's victory. "One day our men
shot down an American helicopter," he later told reporters. "The pilot
got out. We caught him, tied his legs and dragged him through the streets.
After that 28,000 U.S. soldiers fled Somalia. The Americans are cowards."

Phillip Johnston had been given the task of reporting to the United
Nations on the Somali civil structures in place for a handover of power
after the U.S. departure. There were, of course, no such structures—or at
least none of the sort Washington wanted to recognize. But that didn't

[326]

stop American officials from trying to conjure up some, any more than it had stopped the British from trying to get General Gordon to cobble together some entity to cover their retreat from Sudan in 1884. Sitting through Johnston's meetings in the fantastic walled compound that Operation Restore Hope had spent $300 million to build on the grounds of the former U.S. embassy—one-third the gross national product of Somalia before the war—I doodled on my notepad. Johnston's talks were all off the record. I couldn't see how they wouldn't make any difference anyway. Somalia was already forgotten. All America cared about was when the troops were coming home. As far as Americans were concerned, the Somalis had missed their chance. No one wanted to hear about the foolish and brutal mistakes of the United States and the United Nations that allowed Aideed and his Islamist allies to build support in Mogadishu. No one wanted to consider whether it had been wise to intervene in the first place without any plan for ending the civil war. And of course no one began to imagine that events in Somalia were capable of boomeranging back on the United States once we were out of the country.

At the CARE house I lay on my bed, listening to the sinister buzz of the U.S. helicopters swooping over the city, and thought of Gordon in his shuttered palace at Khartoum. Like the British of that time, the Americans weren't interested in fighting and dying for the Somalis who had put their trust in us. We wanted our heroism on the cheap, and when the object of our benevolence turned on us, we reacted with fury. Better to smash the African mirror than to see what we had become in it. Just as the British had insisted that Gordon pretend he wasn't handing over power to Sudan's slavers, so the Americans ordered Johnston to produce councils of Somali elders, women's caucuses, youth congresses— anything to conceal the fact that they were leaving the country to the very same Somali warlords who'd caused the famine that spurred us to get involved in the first place. The mood inside the UN compound was edgy and defensive. Robert Oakley, the U.S. envoy charged with arranging the pullout, denied that outsiders like Bin Laden had played any significant role in the fatal October firefight. When I asked another American diplomat who had lost Somalia, he snapped, "CNN."

One day I borrowed a CARE truck and a couple of gunmen to visit Oxfam. Oxfam's whitewashed villa was only a block away from the CARE house, but Mogadishu was so tense that even with armed guards, few white people ventured outside the UN compound. Mobs of young

Somali men gathered daily at the UN gates chewing *qat* and muttering angrily about the luxurious, air-conditioned Quonset huts, PX shops, cafeterias, and movie theaters inside. Outside the compound, Somalia had been without running water or electricity since 1991. As I sat in the Oxfam house waiting to interview an official, I heard someone speaking with a British accent. I turned to see a white man with close-cropped, mouse-colored hair coming down the stairs. There was something familiar about him. I started—it was the journalist—the antislavery investigator who'd been taken away to jail the day I arrived in Safaha.

"It's you—" we both gasped.

I had never known his name, and I still don't know it, because suddenly we heard gunfire. Get down! the antislavery man shouted. We threw ourselves onto the floor, forgetting everything but the *pop! pop! pop!* of bullets close by. When the bullets stopped, my walkie-talkie started to squawk. CARE had placed two Bengali employees in charge of doling out Mogadishu's food ration. It was one of the Bengalis on the walkie-talkie. "You have to bring our vehicle back!" he screamed. "Our watchman is dead! The UN shot him!"

I ran outside. The gunmen I'd borrowed from CARE were just coming out from behind the truck where they had taken shelter. They grabbed their weapons, and we jumped in. Within seconds the heavy gates to the CARE compound opened and we were back inside. There was a shrieking, shouting hubbub of voices. The sun was very bright. The dead watchman lay in the dust. A couple of women wrapped in bright yellow and orange veils knelt beside him, wailing. A bunch of other Somalis had climbed onto the back of an open pickup truck. The Bengali was standing on the back of the truck, his eyes red from tears. Follow us! he shouted to the guard driving my truck. We've got a wounded man here! We're taking him to the Swedish hospital! The big gates to the street opened again, and the pickup truck lurched forward. We followed.

It was market time, but the stalls along the street were closed, and the Somalis moved aside to make room for our procession. The Malaysians had done it, my driver told me excitedly. Malaysian peacekeepers seconded to Operation Restore Hope had been on patrol in front of the CARE compound when something frightened them. They had fired into the market crowd. The watchman had been killed, and another local CARE staffer—the man in the truck—had been shot in the belly. The

Malaysians did not stop to see whom they hit, just drove straight back to the UN compound and shut the door, he said bitterly.

The Swedish hospital was inside the UN compound. An immaculate empty facility, it was open only to aid workers and military personnel affiliated with Operation Restore Hope. (The Somalis whom Operation Restore Hope was supposed to serve were relegated to a Somali hospital down the street manned by a single exhausted Somali surgeon who lacked medicine and even bedding.) The Bengali man from CARE got out and started arguing with a blond Swedish peacekeeper at the hospital gate. The CARE man was waving his Operation Restore Hope ID, but the Swede wouldn't let the truck inside the gate. He kept saying we should take the wounded man to the Somali hospital.

"You bastards!" the Bengali was shouting. "You better let him in! So what if he's Somali—he works for us! You killed our watchman!"

I pulled out my UN press card and gave it to the Swede. "Malaysian troops shot that man. He works for CARE. You'd better open the gate—"

Relief flooded the Swede's pale face. "You're American?" he asked, sweating under his blue helmet.

"Yes."

"You take responsibility?"

"Yes, but—"

I was the only person in the entire caravan not employed by Operation Restore Hope and thus without any rights to enter the Swedish hospital. But because I was white, the peacekeeper believed me and not the Bengali man from CARE. I stopped talking and nodded.

The Swede gave the signal, and the gates opened, allowing the truck to go in.

I was speechless with rage. No wonder Hassan al-Turabi found willing recruits in Somalia. This careless, vain so-called humanitarian operation had cost $2 billion, not to mention hundreds of Somali lives. If this was the best the West could do, it would be better for *khawajas* like us to stay out of Africa. What good had any of it done, anyway? Cursing, I got back into the Land Cruiser.

Back in Nairobi, I didn't feel like talking to anyone about Somalia or Sudan. I had dinner with an old friend who worked for *Newsweek*. He had just returned from covering a massacre in the central African country of Burundi. He was trembling with exhaustion and I noticed that he had taken up smoking. He told me in an expressionless voice that the

Burundi slaughter would set off an even bigger explosion of killing in neighboring Rwanda. He was trying to talk his editors into sending him there now. He asked me whether I thought Americans would be interested in the story.

If he hadn't been such a good friend, I would have laughed out loud.

You must be kidding, I said. No one in America gives a damn about Rwanda.

The next day I was on a plane home.

Chapter *Twenty-nine*

OWARD THE END of November 1993, Emma called Rory Nugent in New York. Riek had stayed at Nugent's Manhattan apartment after he left Atlanta. Maybe Emma felt that Nugent was the last of her friends with any faith in Riek. She told him she was worried, though she didn't really say why. "It was like she had a premonition," he recalled. "She made me promise that I would come back to Sudan if Riek was fucking up. I was like 'Right, Emma. Yes, Emma, of course, I'll come back. Absolutely.'" Nugent didn't expect anything to happen. A few days later, Emma phoned Bernadette. "I could really use a good chat," she said. Bernadette started to propose lunch in two weeks, but something in Emma's voice stopped her. For the first time she could remember, her friend sounded really low. She tried to probe, but Emma was evasive. "We'll have a real heart-to-heart when I see her," Bernadette thought. They made a date for November 25.

The latest fashion in Western aid was "indigenous nongovernmental organizations" (INGOs). Modeled after Western charities, these local groups were supposed to help build up "civil society" as a replacement for dissolving governments in Africa and elsewhere. On November 24, Emma sat down to write a proposal for the UN to finance an INGO that she said southern Sudanese women would run. She was going to call it Womenaid. "Womenaid," Emma typed, "wishes to help people displaced by war and famine to help themselves and their families." She was alone in the house off Riverside Drive. Her brother and sister had decided to spend an extra day on the coast at Mombasa. Riek was away at a meeting. Willy Knocker was in town. She planned to meet him and Sally Dudmesh for drinks at the Ngong Dairy in Karen.

Midway through making a list of costs for Womenaid's proposed "small income-generating projects"—restaurant, $5,000; tea shop, $3,000; vegetable gardens, $3,000—she closed the document and turned off her computer. She had given Forty-Six the day off. She borrowed a Suzuki Land Cruiser from Willy's sister, Roo, who lived nearby, promising to return it by eight o'clock. She was five months pregnant. She didn't bother with a seat belt. Hardly anyone in Africa does. For whites, it's part of the mind-set: If you were the kind of person who wore a seat belt, you wouldn't be living in Africa in the first place.

She drove out onto Gitanga Road, a busy avenue that leads to the Nairobi suburbs. At that time of day the paths beside the tarmac road were crowded with Kenyans walking home from work. The great ball of the African sun was setting. By the time she reached the intersection with James Gichuru Road, the glare would have have been in her eyes. She slowed, then started to cross the intersection. Naturally there were no traffic lights, and Emma didn't see one of Nairobi's notorious little private buses, a *matatu*, barreling down the road toward her on the left. When the *matatu* hit the Land Cruiser, she was thrown out the window. The heavy four-wheel-drive vehicle rolled on top of her.

"My baby! My baby!" she was crying when the first Kenyan passersby reached her. And she said, "SPLA." She died on the way to Nairobi Hospital. She was twenty-nine.

Chapter Thirty

I HAD JUST GOTTEN BACK from Nairobi when I heard that Emma was dead. It was Thanksgiving Day 1993. Visions of Emma being crushed by a *matatu* bus mingled with memories of Sudan and Somalia: of the queer, insectlike look that starving children get when their bodies shrink all out of proportion to their heads; of the twitchy eyes of the stoned Somali gunmen; of the prophet at Nasir with the pink flowers in his ears. *You have been coming and going, but you don't bring anything.* I could not join in the great American celebration of eating. I went to the office and read Emma's obituary in *The Times* of London. It referred to her, inevitably, as a "British aid worker."

I flung down the paper with irritation. At the time of her death it had been two years since Emma had been employed by an aid agency. But the clichés of mercy are so powerful that it was perhaps beyond the obituarist's imagination to see her as anything but a humanitarian. She was British; she was in a poor and angry part of Africa; therefore she must be helping. I thought of some of the things Emma was called in Sudan: First Lady-in-Waiting; concubine; spy; heroine. To label her an aid worker seemed another example of the West's inexcusable narcissm: the lazy refusal to see beyond our salvation fantasies and look at Africa and ourselves for what we are.

There seemed to be no escape from this hall of mirrors.

Chapter Thirty-one

EMMA HAD COURTED death in so many exotic ways that her friends at first could not believe her death had been an accident. There had to be more to it than careless driving. It seemed too neat a coincidence that her bodyguard should have been off that day. Car accidents are a time-honored method of political assassination in East Africa. Three years earlier Kenya's foreign minister had been killed in a crash that many believed President Moi's government had orchestrated. Longtime aid workers remembered the mysterious truck that had driven the SPLA's relief director Richard Mulla off the road after he threatened to expose the theft of aid funds from the SRRA's Nairobi office in 1988. Emma had mentioned receiving new death threats in the week before she died. Her family and friends had always feared that in her ever-deepening entanglement in Sudan's civil war, she was grappling with forces bigger and more dangerous than she could really comprehend. Now they speculated that one or another of Riek's enemies or perhaps even Riek himself had decided to finish her off.

Could the Sudanese government have used Riek's British wife to send him a brutal signal about the consequences of flirting with Garang and the United States? Turabi and his allies certainly wouldn't have shied from taking Emma's life if they thought it would advance their plan to split the rebel movement and move forward with the oil exploration of the south. In the weeks leading up to Emma's death, university students in several northern Sudanese towns had staged a series of antigovernment protests that the Islamists hysterically denounced as a prelude to a U.S. invasion of southern Sudan. Although Emma's friends did not know about al-Qaeda or the cell it had operating in Nairobi at the time, they knew Sudanese intelligence had operatives of it own who would not need help to pull off such a mission. (The use of cars as a weapon was not unknown to the NIF and to its Islamist friends. A few years later a Khartoum journalist would accuse the NIF of trying to run him down with a car.

Or could it have been Garang who wanted Emma dead, perhaps believing that she stood in the way of reconciliation between the two factions or maybe just wanting to punish Riek for his treachery? Garang was known to be furious about the outcome of the Washington talks. He had the support of the Kenyan government. Paid enough money, the Kenyans were capable of faking a *matatu* accident and covering it up. Between the signing of the oil agreement and the U.S. pullout from Somalia, Garang had suffered some serious setbacks that fall. One report had it that the Total Oil Company had stopped paying the SPLA to protect its concessions in Upper Nile, on the grounds that Garang's faction no longer controlled the most oil-rich land. Garang had to be yearning to lash out at Riek, and maybe at Emma, too.

Some even wondered if Riek might have set up the accident. Emma's friends knew she was angry with Riek for sleeping with Angelina. They had seen the tight-lipped way she looked at him when he came back from London. Believing that Emma would not have stayed with him if she had known about his secret dealings with the NIF government, they wondered if she might have confronted him in a way that made him want to get rid of her. The war in southern Sudan was connected to intrigues all over central Africa. In the address book found beside Emma's body at the crash site, for example, were the names and telephone numbers of some of the Tutsi guerrillas who would take over Rwanda after the 1994 Rwandan genocide that would evolve into Africa's first continental war. Emma had many enemies and it made people suspicious about the way she had died.

But against all this feverish speculation had to be set the simple fact that *matatu* accidents, even fatal ones, are an everyday reality in Kenya. Emma had never given any indication to anyone that she was planning to leave Riek. Her friends knew she was a bad driver. When the *matatu* driver accused her of pulling out in front of him, they could believe it. Several Kenyan passengers in the *matatu* were hurt in the accident, though none seriously. Far from disappearing into the woodwork, the *matatu* driver and his assistant threatened to sue Riek for the damage to their minibus. (Riek told me he turned the Kenyan driver's complaint over to his lawyer and never heard from him again.)

There was also the question of whether Emma was really so important as her friends wanted to believe. A prominent Dinka who supported Garang at the time, but has since fallen out with him, scoffed at the idea that the SPLA would have taken the trouble to kill Emma. Despite Garang's propaganda about "Emma's War," the SPLA chief was far too savvy to imagine that getting rid of her would change anything, this man said. "Emma was not the big brain to cause all this," he said. "She was really nothing. She was just an adventurer. If she were in a European setting, she would never even have been noticed." The Kenyan police ruled her death an accident.

In the end, most of Emma's friends and relations accepted the Kenyan verdict. As her mother later wrote, "It helps nobody to think that it might have been anything other than another tragic accident." Riek himself was inclined to look at Emma's death this way. Other Nuer took a more complicated view. In the old days the Nuer didn't believe in accidents—they believed in justice. They assumed that someone was to blame for every violent death, if only through the agency of *wiu*, a bleak, warlike spirit that punishes people for their sins or the sins of others close to them. Nowadays some Nuer say it was *wiu* that killed Emma; some don't. Some say Emma was a victim of sorcery, others say it was an accident. Those most inclined to suspect *wiu* or even a human hand were the least likely to talk about it. That would require them to speak ill of a dead woman, and the Nilotics prefer to leave the dead alone. In southern Sudan the dead are many, the living few.

When I e-mailed one of Riek's former friends and fellow conspirators to ask about Emma, he sent a response that to me shows how in the Sudan the steady onslaught of death in Sudan fogs the attempt to understand even one of them. "Dear Deborah," Peter Adwok Nyaba wrote. "Thanks for your query. I just came to the office to clear certain issues. I am still in a state of mourning. I lost an eleven year old son on Saturday. He drown in YMCA swimming pool in Nairobi. Our tradition does not permit one to talk much about a person who is dead, especially if the words will not be kind or for good remembrance. Late Emma was a woman of influence and that is how she found and married Riek Machar. Maybe time will come, as I said, when everything will have to be put on the table. With kind regards, Peter."

Epilogue

For four years I didn't ask about Emma. I left Africa alone. I was married by then, and I had a baby. I joined much of the rest of my generation in a cozy retreat to domesticity. A British opinion piece seemed to sum up the prevailing mood of detachment from Africa. "What can the West do for the continent?" *The Daily Telegraph* asked. "Virtually nothing.... Perhaps it is time to reverse the process begun by Stanley and his generation, to shut the door and simply steal away."

Then I happened to come across some old letters from Sudan that belonged to my husband's family. It seemed that around the turn of the century a cousin of his great-grandmother's had followed Rudyard Kipling's dictum and gone as a Presbyterian missionary to Dolieb Hill, in Shilluk country, a little more than a hundred miles up the Sobat River from Nasir. Clifford Carson and her husband, Ralph, spent five years battling fires, blackwater fever, clan warfare, and tuberculosis before they returned to the United States in 1908, their health broken and without having converted anybody. Yet they always looked back on their time in southern Sudan as the most momentous period of their lives, and they never stopped trying to persuade other Americans and Britons that God had placed the fate of southern Sudan in their hands. Back in the United States, Ralph Carson raised the money in 1911 to open the American mission at Nasir. I remembered sitting on the cracked verandas of the mission house listening to Reverend James Mut Kueth read from Isaiah. It seemed such a strange coincidence that I kept looking for more of their papers.

The more I read, the more the Carsons' earnest and continually frustrated plans to get the Shilluk to grow vegetables and to learn to sew and read and write reminded me of Emma's schemes for improvement a century later. (Long after he left Dolieb Hill, Carson was still plumping for a school. "If I were a missionary on the Sobat, I would use all my determination and persistence to get a school. If I failed, I would try, try again. You ought to have a school," he wrote another missionary in 1911.) The Carsons arrived in Sudan bursting with enthusiasm to spread Dr. Livingstone's "three C's—Commerce, Civilization and Christianity"—but in the end it was all they could do to get their own family out alive. Their daughter Catherine was the first white child born in the south. I studied a yellowed and fading photo of her and her older brother standing in the elephant grass at Dolieb Hill beside an uncomfortable-looking African nanny buttoned up to the neck in a Victorian dress. When the Carsons got ready to leave in 1908, a Shilluk nobleman approached them with an offer to pay five cows for three-year-old Catherine's hand in marriage. In an account of the incident I found among their papers, Clifford's niece concluded that "they wanted to have the little girl for a sort of queen in their village." There was no other way for Clifford's relations to conceive of the Shilluk proposal. It had been similarly impossible for Emma's obituarist to conceive of her as anything but an aid worker. For a white woman in Africa, it seemed there were only two imaginable positions: do-gooder or queen.

I thought of Emma. She had come as a missionary—not of religion but of the Western gospel of human rights—and wound up as something like a queen. But would things have turned out any differently if she hadn't gone at all? I flew to Khartoum to try to find out. It was 1997. Riek was there by then, an assistant to the president in the Islamist regime he had always professed to loathe. The first few years after Emma's death he had avoided talking about her. Emma's mother mailed him a new Church of England diary every year at Christmas, but he didn't reply. He spoke on the phone to an old friend of Emma's but failed to turn up for an appointment with her. Maybe he was busy—he had a war to fight, after all—or maybe, as he told me, it was too hurtful. But after he signed a peace agreement with the government in April of that year, many southerners branded him a traitor. "Emma's War" was revealed once and for all as a brutal piece of northern manipulation that had succeeded only in slaughtering thousands of southerners and securing the oil fields for the north. Washington threw all its support behind John Garang and his

SPLA. Isolated in the north and desperate for any positive publicity, Riek agreed to see me. I arrived in June.

The government had lent Riek one of those big half-empty stucco villas that still drowse along the avenues of British-built Khartoum. Human rights groups call some of these decaying mansions ghost houses and say the Sudanese security forces torture their opponents in them. Only a few *khawajas* remained in Khartoum. The U.S. embassy had closed down a year earlier. Hotels and shops in the old commercial quarter were even more deserted than I remembered. Even the Greek owners of the Acropole were talking about packing it up. Khartoum's new faces were Chinese: engineers come to join Arakis in drilling for oil. In Omdurman, on the other hand, men still swirled through the dusty streets in their white gowns and skullcaps as they always had, clasping each other's hands in friendly greetings and squatting over braziers to sip sweet tea. Osama bin Laden had departed the year before for Afghanistan. But lavish concrete mansions continued to sprout up out of the desert in his old Khartoum North neighborhood, nourished by petrodollars from the Gulf states. Gordon's Khartoum was half dead, but the Mahdi's former capital was thriving. And yet peeping out from abandoned lots and on the edge of the Arab town were the round *tukuls* of the refugees still pouring in from the south after all these years. Made out of discarded boxes and plastic sheeting, the Southerners tukuls remained so stubbornly African that to the Islamist rulers of the north, they must have seemed like weeds, impervious even to Allah.

Driving up to Riek's big brown villa on University Avenue, my Arab taxi driver clucked disapprovingly at the teenage Nuer boys with their scarred foreheads hanging off the fence and swaggering around the grounds in startlingly new green fatigues. At eight A.M. it was already so hot that the sand blowing in my face felt like a dirty flame. The Nuer boys grinned sweetly, hurrying me into the house and up an unlit staircase carpeted in a stained rose pattern; later I found out that some of them were Lost Boys from Nasir, now old enough to fight. "Dr. Riek is expecting you," they sang. They flung open a door, and I walked into a room dominated by a giant bed.

I could picture Emma in this place. I remembered my last conversation with her, when she was staying at the Inter-Continental in Nairobi and Riek was in Atlanta. She had joked about how Riek's fighters kept trooping in and out of her bedroom, flushing her toilet, examining her Tampax. Some of them had never seen running water, and of course there is no such thing as a private bedroom in the traditional African home. Through an open door I could see an enormous pair of men's cotton briefs drying on a clothesline; an open bottle of Brut cologne sat on a windowsill over the toilet. I had to suppress a smile. If Emma were here, I thought to myself, she would have closed that bathroom door.

Riek came forward with a dazzlingly white smile and offered me a chair at a little seating area at the foot of the bed. He wore smartly pressed blue jeans, a matching denim shirt, new loafers, and new socks. He brought me a Coke from a sweaty little refrigerator by the wall. His voice was as honeyed as I remembered from our meeting four years earlier. I thought of something one of the Washington negotiators involved in Riek's talks with Garang had said then—how he could never quite decide whether Riek was a really nice guy or a really effective murderer. All I could see was an attractive man, a little on the masterful side, but with a playful streak.

He sat down beside me, and we talked for a long while before I got up the nerve to ask him about Emma. Finally we reached the year 1989, when he met her. He started to tell me about their first encounter at the Pan Afric Hotel. "She was introduced to me by a school-days friend," he began. "We talked business."

Then he stopped. I was astonished to see his face pucker up in an expression that was almost like a pout. He cocked his head at me. His voice thickened. "Do I have to?" he said coyly.

What could I say? I said nothing. Was it this little-boy side of Riek that made Emma want to mother him?

He resumed speaking in a more normal voice. "She was very interested in education, and that attracted me." He told me about how she had come to Nasir looking for him and about her bold car journey to meet him in 1991.

"Were you flattered by that?" I asked.

"Beyond flattered," he said huskily. He leaned forward and gazed straight into my eyes.

I sat upright in my chair.

"See—there were no inhibitions on her side," he went on. "For both of us, it was just normal."

I asked him if she had been a help to him.

"Oh, yes," he said. "She saw things we did not see as somebody who was a little bit removed from Sudan. She would notice minute things to us that would have a big impact in the West. Sometimes we would have some small squabblings, and she would say, 'Don't do that.' You know, she was a politician, too. She also had her own way of dealing with issues. It took us time to harmonize."

Emma's friends in the West thought she would rather have died than see Riek here as an appendage to the Khartoum government. But he shook his head vigorously when I asked if she would have opposed the "Peace from Within," as the government called their deal. "When she died, we had actually overcome our difficulties," he said. "We were already on this course. We were clear that we would talk to the government without mediation."

His voice soared. "Now we are in a contract to enter a peace agreement which is sellable to the whole south—even to Garang. We have reached an agreement which meets the aspirations of southern Sudan, exercised through a referendum that will allow for federalism, the special status of the south, wealth sharing between the south and the north..."

Riek kept on talking, but my attention wandered. Most southerners agreed that the written terms of his agreement with the Islamic government were not bad. The problem was that they did not believe the government could be trusted to enforce them. And they knew Riek was powerless to compel it to do so. I remembered what the Belgian aid worker had said at that Khartoum roof party so many years before: *The words of the Sudanese are like birds—beautiful, but they fly away, up, up into the sky and you cannot catch them...*

"I think if Emma were alive, she would have agreed with this peace agreement," Riek said finally.

A gaggle of his advisers came into the room and sat down on the sofa next to me, at the foot of the bed. I noticed that all of the men were decked out in spanking-new blue jeans, plaid shirts, and tennis shoes. They were in Khartoum to draft the provisions that would supposedly make Riek's agreement part of Sudan's constitution. Many of them were just as fearful as other southerners that the agreement was "the jewel in the crown" of the government's plan to divide and rule the south. They had come anyway, some from as far away as England and Germany, out of loyalty to their Nuer kin. They needed Riek's approval for their latest work. (Two years later the government had still failed to implement the agreement, and Riek fled Khartoum. But by then Ler and the other areas around the oil fields were in flames, and the northern army had the better part of the south's fossil reserves firmly in its grip.) While Riek tapped away on his laptop computer, I looked out the window. Outside on the grass, two government soldiers armed with automatic rifles lolled under red carpets strung up like an Arab tent. I asked the advisers about the villa's history.

"I think it was built in the 1970s," said one man.

A sad-eyed Nuer whom Riek had introduced as his cousin corrected him. "No, it was built earlier than that, because this is where Nimeiri held the officers who tried to overthrow him in 1971," he said in flawless English. "This is where he had them executed—right here in this house."

We looked at one another. The air conditioner droned feebly. A book of Indira Gandhi's speeches from the 1960s sat on the bedside table. Like everything else in the room, the book was covered with dust. Had it belonged to one of the doomed officers? I remembered Emma's lover Khalid al-Kid, the communist who fled Sudan after trying to overthrow the government in 1966, only to die in a London traffic accident in 1995. How strange that one lover should have escaped execution in the same sort of Khartoum villa that would become a gilded prison for another. Riek said something about my going down to the basement to take some photos of him. His sad-eyed cousin turned to me with a wry expression. "Are you a Shakespearean?" he asked. Before I could reply, he began quoting from *Richard II,* " 'In the base court? Base court, where kings grow base/To come at traitors' calls and do them grace.' "

RIEK HAS A LAZY EYE. As our interview wore on and he wearied of my questions, he didn't seem so genial. The eye rolled back and clouded over. I thought I had better change the subject. I mentioned the profile I had written back in 1990 of the schoolmaster Lul. (I had no idea at this point what had become of him.) "I thought I might see him while I'm here," I said. "Do you have any idea where he is?"

"Lul Kuar Duek," said Riek, rubbing his chin as he repeated the name. "Yes, he was arrested and killed by Gordon Kong. It was a pity. It was something personal between them."

"Gordon Kong—you mean in Nasir?" I said, dimly remembering the cat-faced old warlord who had allied himself with Riek and Lam and later had been arrested.

"Yes, it was a pity," Riek said again.

I had one more question. What did Riek think about Emma's death?

An accident or *wiu?* It was late in the afternoon. Outside the bedroom a dozen or so people were waiting to see him. I could tell that Riek was eager to go. But he leaned back for a moment, still courteous, a big man in stiff new blue jeans. "I take it as an accident," he told me. "I don't want to get involved in long investigations." He told me that he had concluded that his and Emma's enemies weren't sophisticated enough to use a *matatu* bus half full of people as a murder weapon. As for the question of *wiu*, he didn't want to talk about it. "Some would say it is bad luck because of a curse or something. They will give it many interpretations. I am truthfully not going to go into it."

I apologized for bringing up painful subjects.

"It's okay," said Riek. "It's been a day of remembrance." But he stood up. I could see that his mind was already on the men waiting for him on the shabby couches out in the hall.

It was over. I went back to my room at the Acropole and lay on the bed, watching the ceiling fan go round and round.

IN LONDON I MET Emma's brother Johnny for a drink. He is a television producer. At the time he worked near Covent Garden. It was a warm summer evening. The pubs and restaurants overflowed with young people, their laughter spilling out into the pale lavender sky. We found a table in a crowded brasserie. Johnny is slight, with sandy hair and wire-rimmed glasses. He has his sister's fine features and her silvery charm.

"I still hear her voice sometimes," he said. I heard it, too, that husky, caressing voice.

He told me about her funeral and the burial at Ler. No one who witnessed either is likely to forget it. "It wasn't until I was at the funeral that I realized she had made such an impact," he said. "You know, after she died, her friends came to me in Nairobi, and they said, 'You'd better get All Saints Cathedral for the funeral.' I told them, 'You must be mad.' Because, you know, if I died, I really don't know if I could fill a village church. But we did get the cathedral, and when we went there, it was packed to the rafters." Southern Sudanese from Garang's faction as well as Riek attended; several speakers called Emma "the mother of southern Sudan."

"Then we went to Ler—Riek's from there, you know—and he and

Mum decided that Emma would have wanted to be buried there. It's quite a pretty place, but my God, the sun! When we arrived, thousands of people were waiting for us. They started rocking the plane. We were afraid to get out. Riek had to stand on a truck and use a megaphone before they would back away. Some of them had walked for days to get there. They were beating drums and crying..... There was an old man who told Mum he wanted to be buried with Emma. We were afraid we were going to end up in the grave ourselves."

He laughed shortly.

Then he said, "Emma wasn't out to better herself. When I think about her, I feel a bit guilty about my life. I'm doing something really selfish. I'm not bettering anyone."

There it was again: the noble cause, the great saving illusion. I didn't say anything. I thought of Somalia and Sudan, of all that vainglorious rhetoric about pasting nations back together with a few bags of food. No aid worker who stayed long in that part of the world imagined the kind of aid we gave could do more than keep a few people going for another day and perhaps, as one of Emma's Operation Lifeline colleagues wrote me, open some "space for the oddities of relief, tragedy, misery, sex and personal extravagance"—which is to say, some space for life itself. But it seemed impossible to transmit this small, personal knowledge back to the West; in every case it became garbled, mutated into visions of grandiosity or metastasized into furies of disappointment. It was never enough to have helped one person, to have opened some tiny window of compassion. There was no allowance for the years of warfare, no time to study the messy politics. If Africa couldn't be saved in a very short time and at very little cost, then to hell with it—anyone who went there must be a saint. Emma was a party to the delusion that she could shape Sudan's future, I thought, but at least she never pretended she was making a sacrifice to do it.

Before I went to England I called Tiny Rowland to ask him about Emma. It took him a few minutes to remember the name. Then it clicked. "Yes, of course I met her," he said. "Yes. And when she died, Riek was in a dreadful mess." But when I asked him whether her death changed anything, he seemed taken aback. He paused. "My dear," he said, "she was a white woman, a married white woman. I'm sure she helped him enormously. But in terms of Africa, she didn't play a role." I made plans to visit him the following year at his estate in Buckinghamshire and talk more about Sudan. But by then he was dead. It was skin cancer that killed him. He had always maintained a year-round suntan. I could just imagine how he must have thrown back his silver mane and roared with laughter when he got the diagnosis. *My dear, if Africa doesn't get you one way, it will get you another...*

OTHER DOORS in England were shut. When I phoned Barbara Harrell-Bond on the phone at the Refugee Studies Program in Oxford to ask about Emma, she hesitated.

"Emma was a beautiful girl, a student in photography who met me in a restaurant and asked to be a volunteer," she began. Her voice turned cold. "She was an accident waiting to happen.

"What's there to say about Emma? She's dead."

With that, she hung up on me.

IN NAIROBI, Emma's friends found it harder to put her memory aside. Sally Dudmesh missed her terribly. Every year on the anniversary of Emma's crash, she fell into gloom and depression. Still she continued to live in the Ngong Dairy, returning to Europe only in the summer, just as she had when Emma was alive. In the years since Emma's death, the mores and milieu of white Nairobi have been chronicled in books such as Francesca Marciano's *The Rules of the Game* and Kuki Gallman's *I Dreamed of Africa*—and caricatured endlessly in the British tabloid press. Now entering their forties, Emma's former safari companions find themselves regarded with almost as much curiosity as was directed a few decades ago at the relics of Happy Valley colonialism. A series of violent deaths among their number have caused some in the group to ask if the exciting lives they have carved out for themselves in "Nairobbery" are really worth the price. Dan Eldon, a Kenyan-American photographer, died at the hands of a Somali mob only a few months before Emma. Emma's old friend Giles Thornton, the British public schoolboy who water-skied up and down the Sobat counting refugees before Lam Akol declared him persona non grata, died defending Emma Marrian and a houseful of servants from Kenyan burglars in 1998. Thornton's body was cremated on the slopes of Mount Kenya—"Adventurer to Burn on African Pyre?" was the headline in *The Sunday Times*. Three years later many of the same people who had said good-bye to him reunited for the cremation of Tonio Trezbinski, the flamboyant artist who left Sally to marry Anna

Cunningham-Reid in 1991. Trezbinski was shot down in an apparent robbery early in 2002 while visiting a beautiful Scandinavian big game
hunter in Karen; *Vanity Fair* published an article about his death entitled
"The Shadow of Happy Valley."

When they thought of Emma, what pained Nairobi's diminishing
band of whites most was the loss of yet another intimate who shared their
love affair with Africa, the bittersweet black humor that colored their
relationship with the continent and gave their lives the tragic edge they
could not do without. "When the genocide happened" in Rwanda in 1994,
one longtime Nairobi television correspondent said, "I kept wishing I
could talk to Emma. She would have had so much insight into that. She
would have known all the characters and seen it in terms of a Greek
tragedy." But Emma was not there, and the West did not want to hear
about Rwanda in terms of anything. The Nairobi set were left to talk
about the genocide over their smaller and smaller dinner parties.

THOSE OF EMMA's friends who shared her special bond with the Sudan
felt her death almost like an omen. It came at a point when many of them
were beginning to lose hope for the place. "Emma's death symbolized for
me the total and complete tragedy of southern Sudan," her old boss Peter
Dalglish said later. "You could say her death had nothing to do with it, but
to me it was all the same thing." Bernadette Kumar had been on her way
to the heart-to-heart lunch she planned to have with Emma when Alastair and Patta gave her the news of Emma's death the day before. She
began weeping and didn't stop for days. "Around the time Emma died, I
started to think, 'There's never going to be light in this place.' I had to
leave. It was just too much. I was losing my friends, and it just became so
personally painful that I found it very difficult to continue. I never met
anyone who went to Sudan—I mean really went to it—whose life wasn't
changed by it. The question is, how far do you want to take it? I asked
myself, 'Do I want to be here anymore?' The answer was 'Not really.'" She
left Africa the following year. Even Alastair and Patta went away for a
while, first to Vietnam, then back to England to work as aid consultants.

IN SUDAN THINGS WENT from bad to worse. "Emma's War" did not end
with Emma's death. Not only did the fighting between Nuer and Dinka
go on its murderous way, but it split and divided and multiplied until by

the end of the millennium dozens of southern factions were battling each other across a vast region. The fighting between the Jikany and the Lou Nuer alone, which began in the dry season of 1993 and had been much on Emma's mind before she died, killed more than a thousand people before Riek finally asked the Nuer elders and church leaders to convene a major peace conference in 1994. Before the conference could take place, the Lou Nuer burned Nasir to the ground. The northern government fueled the Lou-Jikany feud as well as the south's other internal conflicts, handing out weapons to both sides. Garang managed to resist the blandishments of the Islamist regime, but he remained inflexible when it came to reconciling with the Nuer and his other southern enemies. Many of his followers abandoned him, concluding that for him, as for the south's petty warlords, the war had become a means to power and wealth that he was loath to give up. A Bor pastor composed this song to express his people's anguish:

> I am in the sinful land of Sudan.
> The birds in the sky are surprised
> By the way I have been orphaned.
> The animals of the forest
> Are startled by my skeleton.

In 1995 Rory Nugent fulfilled his promise to Emma to return to Sudan if Riek ever started "fucking up." Riek still claimed to be fighting the north, but his position had grown increasingly weak. The government had retaken Nasir. His top commanders had defected or were fighting among themselves. No outside government would give him money. On his way to meet Riek, Nugent interviewed a triumphant Hassan al-Turabi in Khartoum. Turabi warned him to prepare for "dramatic explosions." "There is a renaissance of Islam coming. We are rising with Jews all around us.... It is part of a historical cycle. Islam will be on top again. Soon the West will be forced to treat us with respect." Nugent made his way to Akobo, where he found Riek huddled with his few remaining troops. "With Russia gone from Africa, the West has abandoned us," Riek told Nugent. "The fools. Don't they realize they have left everything open to Turabi?" Two years later Riek was ensconced in the University Avenue villa, promoting his peace agreement with Turabi's government. Nugent was bitter. "I saw thousands of people die, and what did it all mean? Nothing at all."

IN ITS 1997 AGREEMENT with Riek, the Islamist government had promised to share any future oil revenues with provincial governments and a southern regional government to be established. Citing the agreement as proof of the fairness of the northern authorities, the Canadian oil giant Talisman Energy announced the following year that it was buying Arakis Energy Corporation from the Pakistani-Canadian businessman Lutfur Rahman Khan and the company's other shareholders for approximately $180 million in Talisman stock. Talisman closed its deal only days after the United States bombed Sudan in retaliation for al-Qaeda's bombing of the U.S. embassies in Nairobi and Dar es Salaam. Osama bin Laden said al-Qaeda had been emboldened by the pullout of American troops from Somalia. Nevertheless, Talisman forged ahead, lending its technology and expertise to help Chinese and Malaysian oil companies build in record time a pipeline from Upper Nile to the Red Sea. Adolf Lundin's Lundin Oil had already bought up 11 percent of Arakis at the time of its sale to Talisman. Lundin's International Petroleum Corporation went on to snap up the remaining blocks south of Heglig and Unity for sale from Chevron's former concession. On August 30, 1999, representatives from thirty Western companies as well as Chad, Saudi Arabia, and elsewhere watched as the first of 600,000 barrels of oil flowed out of the pipeline into waiting oil tankers. On the eve of the millennium, the Sudan had become an oil-exporting nation. That year oil production from Heglig and Unity added some $480 million to the government's total budget of $1.2 billion. In the year 2000, the IMF predicted, oil exports would provide the Islamist government $1.7 billion in annual revenues.

The government did not honor its agreement with Riek. The referendum it promised on self-determination for the south was never held. Riek's men were not allowed to guard the oil fields. Almost none of the oil money has reached any of the southern peoples. Instead the Sudanese government has used its new riches to buy arms that have allowed it to sharpen its war against the south. It has given his Nuer rivals weapons and money and set them to fighting against him and one another. The freshly equipped Sudanese army has gunned down southerners in the oil region from helicopters, massacred them with proxy militias, and driven them from their homes with fire. Their children have been abducted and their cattle stolen. Their water holes have been destroyed and UN relief centers bombed. Operation Lifeline, the relief consortium that began as a stopgap measure intended to feed the survivors of the 1988 famine, is now entering its fourteenth year of operation. The Operation Lifeline base camp at Lokichoggio where Emma and I once slept in tents now boasts Kenya's second-busiest airport. Cargo planes roar in and out at all hours of the day, bringing food for southern Sudan—potentially one of the richer pieces of real estate in the world, with estimated proven crude oil reserves of 262 million barrels.

Faced with complaints from human rights groups, Talisman and the other oil companies have demanded proof that the Sudanese government is mistreating civilians. But a stack of investigations by the United Nations, the Canadian government, and various independent groups showing that the government is driving Nuer and Dinka inhabitants out of the oil region to make way for development has failed to deter the companies. The oil money has created its own momentum, with more calls each year for the United States to suspend its sanctions against Sudan. In the year 2000 an eagerly awaited Canadian government report began by reviewing the evidence that the Sudanese army had conducted a military assault on the Dinka town of Pariang in 1999, intended to remove people from the Heglig field. These were the same Dinka I interviewed in the Khartoum squatter camp Hillat Shook more than ten years earlier, who told me about what they recognized even then as the *jallaba* plan to clear their land so that the north could exploit its oil. The Dinka had returned to Pariang after the government closed down Hillat Shook in 1989. Now they were being expelled again. Reading the report, I recalled the question the Dinka elder had asked me ten years earlier: "Why are you people in Britannia and Europe hearing this and not helping us?" echoed in my head. I didn't have an answer then, and I still don't.

BUT RIEK IS A CAT with nine lives. In 1997 Lundin Oil became the operational partner in a consortium to explore the oil block south of Bentiu that included Riek's hometown of Ler. The following year a government-allied Nuer militia razed Ler. The Teny-Dhurghon family compound where Emma is buried under a concrete slab was burned to the ground along with the rest of the town. In April 1999 Lundin announced its discovery of "substantial" reserves of "excellent" quality at Thar Jath outside of Ler. The government immediately moved to the area well-armed troops who began fighting against Riek's remaining remnant of a force. For Riek, the future looked grim. But then he began receiving telephone calls at his Khartoum villa from a Minnesota house-wife. Becky Hagman later told me she had first heard of Riek while help-ing Nuer refugees in Minneapolis type up press releases for his movement. Frustrated with their tortured English, she decided to phone their leader himself to ask for direction. Riek's voice was as velvet as ever. The calls grew longer. According to some of the Nuer involved, Hagman flew to Khartoum in 1999 to deliver aid from her church for southern Sudan. After her return she and her husband divorced. She returned to Africa and married Riek.

Riek's new American wife, who is still raising children from her first marriage, spends most of her time in Minnesota. Nevertheless Hagman has become a dedicated helpmeet to Riek. After Riek fled Khartoum to southern Sudan in 2000, Nuer gunmen threatened to kill him. Hagman and her parents flew to Nairobi, chartered a plane, and swooped into Sudan to pluck Riek away to safety. While in Nairobi, Hagman later told me, she had had a portrait of Emma rematted and restored to a position of honor at Riek's new headquarters. She wrote me that I was wrong to say in a magazine article that Riek was "no Thomas Jefferson." "A fierce humanitarian like Emma could not have been happily married to the man you portrayed," she wrote. "Emma was happily married to a fierce idealist who fights every day for the rights of the Sudanese to freedom, justice, democracy, and peace. You could state that he is fighting because of a deep-seated belief that 'all men are created equal' which entitles them to the right to life, liberty and the pursuit of happiness."

Angelina, who had enjoyed a brief springtime of prosperity during Riek's sojourn with the government, was outraged by this latest romantic entanglement and furious over the loss of the oil fields to the northern army. This time she promised to take action, telling me she planned to divorce Riek in British court. "It won't be recognized at home," she told me in 2000. "But he's out of my system." Two years later, Angelina's ire seemed to have faded. She called me from Washington, where she and the son she conceived just before Emma's death were traveling with Riek as part of an official delegation. She had named the boy Gordon.

WHEN I ARRIVED in the Sudan in 1988, the United Nations and others set the number of those killed in the country's civil war at about one mil-lion. Fourteen years later Sudan's war is the longest-running in Africa, and the number of dead is put above two million. Nearly all of those killed have been southerners. But whereas in 1988 a million dead Africans was a figure that could still shock, today the two million southern Sudanese corpses have been submerged by a tidal wave of death that has washed over Africa in the aftermath of the cold war and the dissolution of the postcolonial states. A million dead in Somalia; another million slaughtered in Rwanda; up to three million killed in Congo; hundreds of thousands killed in smaller wars in Sierra Leone, Liberia, Angola, Eritrea, and Ethiopia; not to mention 17 million dead of AIDS and untold millions felled even in relatively safe countries like Kenya by the everyday African scourges of crime and disease. All of this has taken in place in the last fifteen years. Even for Africans, it has become a blur. As for the West, we have shut our eyes.

For these millions upon millions, there are no days of remembrance.

ON SEPTEMBER 11, 2001, as I was finishing this book, four jets hijacked by Osama bin Laden's followers smashed the smug Western conviction that it is up to us to choose whether to tend to the world's festering sores or to turn our backs on them. In the wake of the attacks, commentators rushed to explore the roots of al-Qaeda's rage. All the footage from the Horn in the early 1990s paraded across our television screens again: Turabi's calls for jihad, wizened Somali children waiting for bowls of gruel, the first bombing of the World Trade Center, the corpses of the U.S. Rangers being dragged through the streets of Mogadishu. It seemed that these Western encounters from a decade earlier, carelessly entered and even more carelessly exited, had borne evil fruit. They had begun to have consequences not just for the continent's luckless residents but for us. There was talk of once again invading Somalia or even Sudan. Some argued in favor of a new kind of imperialism that would bring parts of the world that support terrorism under direct Western control. Calling the Mahdi "the Victorian Osama bin Laden," a British historian reminded American readers that Britain had discovered in Gordon's day that there were limits to what can be achieved by informal imperialism. Though the real bin Laden had left Sudan five years earlier, the attack's effect was immediate. Under pressure from Washington, Riek and Garang announced on January 8, 2002, that they were reuniting to resist the government. Eleven years of the most bitter fighting was over. Incredible as it seemed, we, like the Victorians fourteen years after Gordon's death, appeared to be on the verge of a new cycle of engagement with Africa. But had we learned anything from the past?

I pondered the smudged-pencil diaries of my husband's relations, the missionaries who had followed the British to Sudan after the 1898 Anglo-Egyptian reconquest, to look for clues. The Carsons were mesmerized by the snakes of southern Sudan. They killed 143 snakes inside the mission compound in their first year at Dolieb Hill. Ralph Carson wrote of putting a mirror in front of a spitting cobra he captured and watching in fascination as it spewed poison back at its own reflection. "The peculiarity of this Sudan snake is that it has the power of throwing poison from its mouth directly into the eyes of its enemy," he wrote. "The poison which it thus throws...is an active acid as to blind if not destroy the sight." The spitting cobra reminded Carson of the Tempter in the Garden of Eden. It reminded me of how the West is alternately enthralled and enraged by its own reflection in Africa.

Emma had seen spitting cobras at Nasir. What would she have made of that snake? She had been known to say that southern Sudan was like a modern-day Eden, forever sealed off from the rest of the world by the flaming sword of its war. It struck me that perhaps the saddest thing about Emma was that she never had the chance to learn from her own mistakes. She had beauty, passion, a radiant spirit. She wanted to help. Yes, she was up to her neck in horrors. But the horrors almost certainly would have happened without her. They have surely gone on without her. She never appears to have seen the damage she did to her best self when she gave in to her romantic fantasies and followed Riek into the wilderness of that war. But the lure was too powerful for her to resist. Emma had grandeur. She was not ordinary. She loved her fate.

She did not give up.

Source Notes

AUTHOR'S NOTE

ix "Emma's War": The use of the phrase "Emma's division" to describe the fighting between Riek Machar and John Garang is mentioned in an unpublished manuscript written shortly after Emma McCune's death by her friend Emma Marrian, "The Story of Emma McCune Machar," pp. 1–7. Emma's former classmate Madeleine Bunting makes reference to Garang's faction, calling the fighting "Emma's War" in her magazine article "For Love of a People," *Guardian,* May 19, 1994, as does Tarquin Hall in *Mercenaries, Missionaries, and Misfits* (London: Muncaster Press, 1997), p. 259. In her memoir, *Til the Sun Grows Cold: Searching for My Daughter, Emma* (London: Headline, 1999), Emma's mother, Maggie McCune, who has access to Emma's diary and other papers, says Garang coined the phrase as part of a campaign to show that Emma had orchestrated the split within the SPLA for British intelligence (p. 205). Eleanor Vandevort mentions another case of the Nuer naming a war after a woman whose marriage was supposed to have started it in *The Leopard Tamed: An African Pastor, His People and His Problems* (New York: Harper and Row, 1968), pp. 107–108.

ix blamed Machar's foreign wife: John Garang issued a radio message to all SPLA units on September 9, 1991, claiming that Riek's marriage to Emma was part of a plot against the movement. Copy of transcript in my files.

ix "the war of the educated": Jok Madut Jok and Sharon Hutchinson discuss this and other characterizations of the Nuer-Dinka fighting since 1991 in "Sudan's Prolonged Second Civil War and the Militarization of Nuer and Dinka Ethnic Identities," *African Studies Review* 42, no. 2 (September 1999), pp. 125–45.

Source Notes

PROLOGUE

5 An Arab slave-hunter hired: The founding of Nasir is described in Douglas H. Johnson, *Nuer Prophets: A History of Prophecy from the Upper Nile in the Nineteenth and Twentieth Centuries* (Oxford: Oxford University Press, 1994), p. 131.

PART ONE

CHAPTER ONE

17 "the politics of the belly": Jean-François Bayart, *The State in Africa: The Politics of the Belly* (New York: Longman, 1993).

17 "eating is warring": Sharon Hutchinson, *Nuer Dilemmas: Coping with Money, War and the State* (Berkeley: University of California Press, 1996), p. 165.

17 Stomach lived by itself: Vandevort, *Leopard Tamed*, pp. 89–90.

CHAPTER TWO

19 She was born: My account of Emma McCune's family background, childhood, and youth is drawn from interviews conducted with Emma's family members and friends in England and Kenya from 1997 to 1999 as well as from McCune, *Til the Sun*, pp. 21–120; Bunting's "For Love of a People"; Marrian, "Story of Emma," pp. 1–3; and Hall, *Mercenaries*, pp. 247–66. Quotations taken from my own conversations with Maggie McCune in London in the summer of 1997, like those from other personal interviews, are not noted.

20 "heavenly": McCune, *Til the Sun*, p. 37.

20 "golden and silent": Ibid.

20 "sun-downer... dancing": Ibid.

22 his indifference to work: Ibid., p. 75.

22 "bone-idle... liar": Ibid., p. 77.

23 "Her childhood ended there": Ibid., p. 89.

23 "Thumbelina": Ibid., p. 79.

23 his wife's extravagance: Ibid., p. 95.

26 "a strange dream": Ibid., pp. 102 and 194.

CHAPTER THREE

27 "the white man's burden": Rudyard Kipling, *Rudyard Kipling's Verse* (London: Hodder and Stoughton, 1958), p. 323.

29 "We will fly...ocean": Emma's remarks to the *The Oxford Times* were reprinted in Fiona Tarrant, "The Warlord's Wife," *Oxford Times,* April 23, 1999. The same article discussed Emma's photo exhibition in Oxford.

31 "so shrunken...planet": Bob Geldof's comments on the Ethiopian famine are taken from his autobiography, *Is That It?,* written with Paul Vallely (Middlesex: Penguin Books, 1986), pp. 269–71.

31 "Dawn...earth": Quoted in Paul Harrison and Robin Palmer, *News Out of Africa: Biafra to Band Aid* (London: Hilary Shipman, 1986), p. 130.

32 more than $100 million: Ibid., p. 131.

32 "Saint Bob": See Paul Vallely, "Arise Sir Bob, All Is Forgiven," *Independent,* March 12, 1999.

CHAPTER FOUR

34 Ethiopia's civil wars: See Ahmed Karadawi, *Refugee Policy in Sudan, 1967–1984* (Oxford: Berghahn Books, 1999), for his account of modern Sudanese history and the camps, as well as his views on refugee policy. See Barbara Harrell-Bond, "Planning a New Role for Refugees: Obituary Ahmed Abdel-Wardoub Karadawi," *Guardian,* December 12, 1995. Other facts are taken from the obituary of Karadawi that appeared in *The Times* of London, December 20, 1995.

35 Israel concentrated: Israel's role in Sudan's civil wars is discussed in Jacob Abadi, "Israel and Sudan: The Saga of an Enigmatic Relationship," *Middle Eastern Studies* (July 1999), pp. 1–14. See also Gerard Prunier, "Identity Crisis and the Weak State: The Making of the Sudanese Civil War," WRITENET Issue Paper, January 1996, pp. 7–8.

36 borrow more than $12 billion: The figure and the analysis of Nimeiri's financial policies is taken from Alex de Waal, *Famine Crimes: Politics and the Disaster Relief Industry in Africa* (Oxford: James Currey, 1997), pp. 88–90.

36 George Bush: Mansour Khalid describes then–UN ambassador George Bush's role in developing Sudan's oil reserves in *The Government They Deserve: The Role of the Elite in Sudan's Political Evolution* (London and New York: Kegan Paul International, 1990), p. 297, n. 59.

36 Chevron also signed: Abel Alier reports that Kafi-Kengi, an area containing uranium deposits, was secretly leased to Chevron at the end of 1979, in *Southern Sudan: Too Many Agreements Dishonored* (Exeter, U.K.: Ithaca Press, 1990), p. 219.

39 "With the government": Harrell-Bond, "Planning a New Role for Refugees."

41 *Harper's & Queen:* Marrian mentions Emma's job at *Harper's & Queen* in "Story of Emma," p. 2.

41 "I read...soon": Tayeb Zaroug, letter to Emma McCune, November 12, 1986; copy in my files.

CHAPTER FIVE

42 "Sudan...worse": Quoted in *The Warlord's Wife,* ITV News, April 1993.

43 "You are aware...matter": Quoted in Richard S. Hill, *Egypt in the Sudan, 1820–1881* (Oxford: Oxford University Press, 1959), p. 13.

43 Slavery: See P. E. Lovejoy, *Transformations in Slavery: A History of Slavery in Africa* (New York: Cambridge University Press, 1983), pp. 1–18; and Douglas Johnson, "Muslim Military Slavery," in *Encyclopedia of World Slavery,* Paul Finkelman and Joseph C. Miller, eds. (New York: Macmillan, 1998). See also Amir H. Idris, *Sudan's Civil War: Slavery, Race and Formational Identities* (Lewiston, NY: Edwin Mellen Press, 2001), pp. 29–44.

44 In classical Islamic thinking: See John Hunwick, "Islamic Law and Polemics over Race and Slavery in North and West Africa, 16th through 19th Century," in Shaun E. Marmor, ed., *Slavery in the Islamic Middle East* (Princeton, NJ: Markus Wiener Publishers, 1999), pp. 46–52.

44 "It is known...unbelief": Hunwick, "Islamic Law," p. 47.

44 "the time when the world was spoiled": Francis M. Deng, *War of Visions: Conflict of Identities in the Sudan* (Washington: Brookings Institution, 1995), p. 73.

45 a harrowing report: Quoted in Roland Werner, William Anderson, and Andrew Wheeler, *Day of Devastation, Day of Contentment: The History of the Sudanese Church Across 2000 Years* (Nairobi: Paulines Press, 2000), pp. 127–29.

46 David Livingstone: Tim Jeal, *Livingstone* (London: Pimlico, 1993), pp. 373–84.

46 the abolitionists' moral indignation: See Alice Moore-Harell and Gabriel Warburg, *Gordon and the Sudan: Prologue to the Mahdiyaa, 1877–1880* (London: Frank Cass, 2001), pp. 11–36, on Ismail's view of slavery and the pressures on him to abolish the slave trade.

46 "Ottoman slavery...place": Ehud E. Toledano, *Slavery and Its Abolition in the Ottoman Middle East* (Seattle: University of Washington Press, 1998), p. 116.

46 "derived from Islamic...society": Ibid., p. 127.

47 Sudanese slave-owners: Idris, *Sudan's Civil War,* pp. 33–44.

47 Sir Samuel Baker: The amazing story of the Bakers is told in Richard S. Hill, *Lovers on the Nile: The Incredible African Journeys of Sam and Florence Baker* (New York: Random House, 1980).

47 "It is almost...trade": Sir Samuel W. Baker, *Ismailia: A Narrative of the Expedition to Central Africa for the Suppression of the Slave Trade* (New York: Harper and Brothers, 1875), p. 4.

48 As a young British officer: My account of Gordon's youth is drawn from Charles Chenevix Trench, *The Road to Khartoum: A Life of General Charles Gordon* (New York: Dorset Press, 1978), and Anthony Nutting, *Gordon of Khartoum: Martyr and Misfit* (New York: Clarkson N. Potter, 1966).

49 "In England we are...position": Quoted in Nutting, *Gordon*, p. 76.

49 "hollow emptiness": George Birkbeck Hill, ed., *Colonel Gordon in Central Africa, 1874–1879* (London: Thomas de la Rue & Co., 1885), p. 26.

49 "gold and silver idols": Quoted in Nutting, *Gordon*, p. 97.

49 "I am like Moses...Egypt": Quoted in Trench, *Road to Khartoum*, p. 80.

50 "He was largely ignorant...characters": Douglas Johnson, "The Death of Gordon: A Victorian Myth," *Journal of Imperial and Commonwealth History* 10 (May 1982), p. 300.

50 "He is not worse...others": Hill, *Colonel Gordon*, p. 33.

51 "Up to the present...boat": Quoted in Trench, *Road to Khartoum*, p. 30.

51 Gordon himself estimated: Hill, *Colonel Gordon*, p. 351. A modern historian estimates that at the time of the Anglo-Egyptian conquest in 1898, 20 to 30 percent of the Sudanese population were slaves. Peter F. McLoughlin, "Economic Development and the Heritage of Slavery in the Sudan," *Africa* 32 (1962), pp. 355–89.

51 "would give their all...house": Trench, *Road to Khartoum*, p. 100.

51 "Has the khedive...people": Hill, *Colonel Gordon*, p. 393.

52 "When the trees hear...slaves": Ibid., p. 258.

52 "The Khedive writes me...on": Ibid., p. 393.

53 "the world's greatest living expert on the Sudan": Quoted in Johnson, "Death of Gordon," p. 300.

53 "native mind": Ibid.

53 "peace and orderly government": Ibid.

53 "Consider the effect...it.": Hill, *Colonel Gordon*, p. 225.

53 "People think you have only...slave dealers." Ibid., p. 266.

53 "When you get the ink...lands": Ibid., p. 285.

53 "I cannot shoot them all!": Ibid., p. 359.

54 "Poor creatures!...so": Ibid., p. 342.

54 "An escaped slave...Europe": Ibid., p. 225–26.

54 "Ambition was...men": Lytton Strachey, *Eminent Victorians* (San Diego: Harcourt Brace Jovanovich, 1948), p. 260.

54 "I declare that if I...it": Hill, *Colonel Gordon*, p. 347.

54 "I could not govern...death": Ibid.

54 "wished merely to help...flag": Trench, *The Road to Khartoum*, p. 163.

55 "whosoever doubts...worlds": Quoted in P. M. Holt, *The Mahdist State in the Sudan, 1881–1898: A Study of Its Origins and Overthrow* (Oxford: Clarendon Press, 1970), p. 53.

55 the godless ways: Ibid., p. 59.

56 "Nothing could...him": Rudolf C. Slatin, *Fire and Sword in the Sudan*, F. R. Wingate, trans. (New York: Edward Arnold, 1896), p. 244.

56 "Yes, those people...free": Quoted in Strachey, *Eminent Victorians,* p. 310.

57 "We cannot send...army": Quoted in Johnson, "Death of Gordon," p. 300.

57 "I feel quite happy...me": Quoted in Reid Shields's history of the American Presbyterian Mission in Sudan, *Behind the Garden of Allah* (Philadelphia: United Presbyterian Board of Foreign Missions, 1937), p. 30.

57 "In that distant...joy": Quoted in Johnson, "Death of Gordon," p. 300.

57 "The mere fact...Sudan": Slatin, *Fire and Sword,* pp. 298–99.

58 "What is...Europe": Quoted in Trench, *Road to Khartoum,* p. 237.

59 *"I will...*RISKS": C. G. Gordon, *The Journals of Major-Gen. C. G. Gordon, C.B., at Kartoum,* A. Egmont Hake, ed. (London: Kegan Paul, Trench & Co., 1885), pp. 307–308.

59 "I am ready...people": C. G. Gordon, ed. *Letters of C. G. Gordon to His Sister* (London: Kegan Paul, Trench & Co., 1888), p. 110.

59 "You send me...C.G.G.": Gordon, *Journals,* p. 395.

59 "Is not this...fallen": Slatin, *Fire and Sword,* p. 340.

60 "Mr. Gladstone...consciences": Queen Victoria, *Queen Victoria's Letters,* G. E. Buckle, ed. (London: 1926–32), 2:616.

60 "smash up the Mahdi": Thomas Pakenham, *The Scramble for Africa* (London: Abacus, 1991), p. 271.

60 "Remember Gordon!": Winston Churchill, *The River War* (New York: 1899), 1:173 and 2:205.

60 "The vindication...ever": G. W. Steevens, *With Kitchener to Khartum* (New York: Dodd, Mead, 1898), p. 325. "And there never was an Englishman who had been there but was ready and eager to go back," Steevens added.

61 Rudyard Kipling: For Kipling's view of Omdurman, see Charles Carrington, *Rudyard Kipling: His Life and Work* (London: Macmillan, 1955), pp. 273–79.

61 *"Take up...cease":* Ibid., p. 323.

CHAPTER SIX

62 anniversary of his great-grandfather's victory: The 1987 anniversary celebrations of Gordon's defeat are described in Denis Boyles, *African Lives* (New York: Ballantine Books, 1988), p. 76.

62 she wrote rapturously: McCune, *Til the Sun,* p. 140.

62 *"All Showak...*you": Tayeb Zaroug, letter to Emma McCune, November 12, 1986; copy in my files.

62 "like a queen.": Ibid., p. 141.

63 "It is...lifestyle": Ibid.

63 "In the 1970s, the Eritrean People's Liberation Front...indifference.":

The history of the Eritrean-Ethiopian conflict is described in Tekeste Negash and Kjetil Tronvoll, *Brothers at War: Making Sense of the Ethiopian-Eritrean War* (Oxford: James Currey, 2000). An account of the 1984–85 Ethiopian famine and the situation of the Ethiopian refugee camps in the late 1980s is found in Robert Kaplan, *Surrender or Starve: The Wars Behind the Famines* (Boulder, CO: Westview Press, 1988).

66 the Ethiopian Jews: Ahmed Karadawi, "The Smuggling of the Ethiopian Falashas to Israel through Sudan," *African Affairs* 70 (1991), 23–49.

67 "circumcising" girls: On female genital mutilation in Sudan, see Asma El-Dareer, *Woman, Why Do You Weep? Circumcision and Its Consequences* (London: Zed Press, 1986).

68 she no longer slept: McCune, *Til the Sun*, p. 143.

71 She spoiled a dinner party: Ibid., p. 145.

71 Dorothy Crowfoot Hodgkin: Georgina Ferry, *Dorothy Hodgkin: A Life* (London: Granta Books, 1998).

73 "I like... appeared": Emma McCune, letter to Belay Woldegabriel, undated; copy in my files.

PART TWO

CHAPTER SEVEN

79 a Nilotic myth: C. G. Seligman and Brenda Seligman, *Pagan Tribes of the Nilotic Sudan* (London: Routledge and Kegan Paul, 1932), p. 179.

79 "it becomes clear... adventure": Jamal Mahjoub, "Sudan: Dreams, Ghosts, Nightmares," *Guardian*, May 15, 1998.

86 "Chevron": Human Rights Watch/Africa, *Sudan, Oil and Human Rights Abuses*, draft report (New York: Human Rights Watch, April 11, 2000), pp. 38–41.

88 Nimeiri began supplying: The government's militia strategy is described in Alex de Waal, "Some Comments on Militias in the Contemporary Sudan," in Martin Daly and Ahmad Sikainga, eds., *Civil War in Sudan* (London: British Academic Press, 1993), pp. 142–56, as well as in David Keen's *The Benefits of Famine: A Political Economy of Famine and Relief in Southwestern Sudan, 1983–1989* (Princeton: Princeton University Press, 1994).

88 "some kind... Nile": G. Norman Anderson, *Sudan in Crisis: The Failure of Democracy* (Gainesville: University of Florida Press, 1999), p. 143.

88 a secret deal with... Kashoggi: Mansour Khalid describes Nimeiri's approach to Adnan Khashoggi to resume oil development in *Nimeiri and the Revolution of Dis-May* (London: KPI, 1985), pp. 379–86.

88 In 1984 and 1985 the Baggara Arabs: Human Rights Watch/Africa, *Famine in Sudan, 1998*, February 1999, pp. 139–43.

88 foreign aid: Anderson, *Sudan in Crisis*, p. 51, and Organization for Eco-

nomic Cooperation and Development, *Geographical Distribution of Financial Flows to Developing Countries* (Paris: OECD, various dates), quoted in African Rights, *Food and Power in Sudan* (London: African Rights, 1997), p. III.

89 Mubarak al-Mahdi: Anderson, *Sudan in Crisis,* pp. 142–43.

89 "make itself...investment": Ibid., p. 143.

CHAPTER EIGHT

93 the human rights report: Dr. Ushari Ahmad Mahmud and Suleyman Ali Baldo, *The Al Dhiein Massacre: Human Rights Violations in the Sudan* (Khartoum: University of Khartoum, 1987).

95 "The kidnapping...present": Ibid., p. 3.

96 "How much...nullified": Primo Levi's comment on slavery is taken from *The Drowned and The Saved* (London: Michael Joseph, 1988), p. 9.

97 the army commander at Wau: See Millard Burr and Robert O. Collins, *Requiem for the Sudan: War, Drought, and Disaster Relief on the Nile* (Boulder, CO: Westview Press, 1995), pp. 74–75, and Africa Watch, *Denying the Honor of Living: Sudan, a Human Rights Disaster* (New York: Human Rights Watch, March 1990), pp. 68–70.

CHAPTER NINE

106 The agribusiness schemes: The impact of the Western Savannah Development Corporation and other development projects of the 1970s in Sudan is described by David Cole in *Between a Swamp and a Hard Place: Development Challenges in Remote Rural Africa* (Cambridge: Harvard International Institute for Development, 1997).

108 a group of about five hundred Dinka: Deborah Scroggins, "Refugees Stream into Safaha Camp Fleeing War and Famine in Sudan," and "In Sudan Heat, Workers Put Children in Sweaters," *Atlanta Journal-Constitution,* April 15 and 17, 1988.

CHAPTER TEN

117 the Anti-Slavery Society: The investigator's anonymous report, "Slavery in Sudan," was published by the Anti-Slavery Society for the Protection of Human Rights, Working Report to the UN Commission on Slavery, 1988.

124 the famine of 1988: Several excellent books have been written about the famine. See Keen, *Benefits of Famine,* and Burr and Collins, *Requiem for Sudan.* African Rights, *Food and Power in Sudan,* is another.

125 "Quantifying Genocide": Millard Burr arrived at the figure of 500,000 dead in 1988 in "Quantifying Genocide in the Southern Sudan 1983–1993," a U.S. Committee for Refugees Issue Paper, October 1993, p. 28.

CHAPTER ELEVEN

126 "the Humanitarian International": De Waal, *Famine Crimes*, pp. 3–4.

128 Julia Taft: Ray Bonner, "A Reporter at Large: Famine," *New Yorker*, March 13, 1989, pp. 85–100.

128 Sadiq's government entered negotiations: The events that led up to the creation of Operation Lifeline Sudan are described in Keen, *Benefits of Famine*, pp. 165–210. See also Francis M. Deng and Larry Minear, *The Challenges of Famine Relief: Emergency Operations in the Sudan* (Washington: Brookings Institution, 1992), and de Waal, *Famine Crimes*, pp. 148–51.

129 the Sudanese army delivered the prime minister: Anderson, *Sudan in Crisis*, pp. 174–195.

130 "drop-dead handsome": quoted in James Fox, "The Shadow of Happy Valley," *Vanity Fair*, March 2002, pp. 236–50.

131 "colonial": McCune, *Til the Sun*, p. 173.

132 "There was a look…it": Quoted in Deng and Minear, *Challenges*, p. 114.

132 In their camps inside Ethiopia: Peter Adwok Nyaba's account of conditions at Itang is taken from his *The Politics of Liberation in South Sudan: An Insider's View* (Kampala: Fountain Publishers, 1997), pp. 49–56.

134 protégés of Hassan al-Turabi: Prunier, "Identity Crisis," p. 14. Also see Abd el Wahab al-Effendi, *Turabi's Revolution: Islam and Power in the Sudan* (London: Gray Seal Books, 1991).

CHAPTER TWELVE

135 Peter Dalglish: Dalglish has written about his decision to found Street Kids International in his autobiography, *The Courage of Children* (Toronto: HarperCollins, 1998), pp. 263–96.

136 "Behind is death" and "watching…responsibility": The quotes describing Dalglish's visit to Ler are taken from his article "Witness to War," *Globe and Mail*, February 18, 2000.

136 "Without education…future": Quoted in Paul Watson, "Suffer the Children of Sudan's Civil War," *Toronto Star*, May 26, 1991.

136 "on the cusp of the earth": Quoted in McCune, *Til the Sun*, p. 153.

137 secretly mining gold: *Africa Analysis* wrote about the SPLA's gold-mining in the Taposa area on August 6, 1993, suggesting that the SPLA used gold to grease relations with Kenyan and Ugandan officials.

138 The southerners' demand for education: Watson, "Suffer the Children."

138 "paper": Hutchinson discusses the Nuer concept of "paper" and their feelings of inferiority toward the north in *Nuer Dilemmas,* pp. 283–88.

139 "children of the missionaries": Marc Nikkel, "Children of Our Fathers' Divinities or Children of the Red Foreigners?" in Andrew Wheeler, ed., *Land of Promise: Church Growth in a Sudan at War* (Nairobi: Paulines Publications Africa, 1997), pp. 61–78.

139 "children of the red foreigners": Ibid., p. 61.

139 "incantory, almost ritualistic importance": Quoted in Johannes Zutt, *Children of War: Wandering Alone in Southern Sudan* (New York: UNICEF, 1994), p. 32.

139 "In Bor district... pencils": Quoted in Eric Onstad, "Children Write in Ground in Classrooms of Southern Sudan," Reuters News Service, June 7, 1990.

139 the color... testicles: Terese Svoboda, *Cleaned the Crocodile's Teeth: Nuer Song* (Greenfield Center, NY: Greenfield Review Press, 1985), p. 12.

140 "the Tall Woman from Small Britain": Marrian, "Story of Emma," p. 2.

140 the SPLA policy of putting soldiers: Nyaba, *Politics of Liberation,* p. 58.

141 three thousand young boys from the Nuba Mountains: Ibid., p. 55.

142 "There were no figures... about": Barry Sesnan, "Education: Policy and Pencils," unpublished report, June 1992; copy on file at Refugee Studies Program, University of Oxford. Sesnan discusses a December 1990 meeting at which education officers reported on how they had handled materials given by SKI, UNICEF, and the SRRA. Emma organized the meeting, and I happened to be in Lokichoggio at the time it was held. Sesnan says, "Approximately half of the two-day meeting was taken up with precise and careful reports on exactly how many pencils, erasers and exercise books had actually arrived at each school.... This concern for numbers about pencils (which are easy to count) was not matched by any concern for other, far more important, figures such as, for example, how many pupils there were and how often they attended."

142 Lual Agoth: Watson, "Suffer the Children"; Lual Agoth's quote is from the same article.

143 "I don't see any... existence": Quoted in Watson, "Suffer the Children."

143 "Emma was special... opinions": Quoted in Bunting, "For Love of a People."

143 Kuol Manyang Juk: See Scott Peterson, *Me Against My Brother: At War in Somalia, Sudan, and Rwanda* (New York: Routledge, 2000), p. 227.

144 "not very interested... war": Ibid.

144 Palataka: Zutt, *Children of War,* p. 26, and Watson, "Suffer the Children."

144 *"Oh my mother":* Quoted in Zutt, *Children of War,* p. 26.

146 the government threatened to shoot down: Africa Watch, *Denying the Honor of Living,* pp. 114–15.

146 Khartoum would not dare bomb: McCune, *Til the Sun,* pp. 159–60.

149 The Bor mutiny: Nyaba, *Politics of Liberation,* pp. 27–28.

149 Paul Kon Ajith: The story of the Christian prophet Paul Kon Ajith is taken from Werner, Anderson, and Wheeler, *Day of Devastation,* pp. 545–47.

150 "5-star dude ranch...": Ilene Prusher, "Welcome to the Town that Famine Feeds," *Scotsman,* October 24, 1998.

151 "When I saw...hundreds": The SPLA commander's comments about Loki are quoted in African Rights, *Food and Power,* p. 300.

151 Emma's mother: McCune discusses her feelings about Emma's romance with Willy in *Til the Sun,* p. 173.

152 the most extraordinary one he ever met: Dalglish, *Courage of Children,* p. 317.

PART THREE

CHAPTER THIRTEEN

158 "using their humanitarian...espionage": See Patrick Seale, *Abu Nidal: A Gun for Hire* (New York: Random House, 1992), pp. 261–65, and Anderson, *Sudan in Crisis,* pp. 219–20. Seale and Anderson are convinced that Abu Nidal's followers carried out the bombing with Libyan support. Seale suggests that the bombing was an attempt to discredit the Palestinian intifada then under way. Anderson says the attackers chose to strike the hotel and the club after finding official U.S. targets too secure. Nevertheless I detail my fears that the bombing was intended to discourage aid workers from probing into Sudan's civil war to convey the atmosphere of paranoia and suspicion hanging over Khartoum at the time.

158 its director was a known terrorist: Anderson, *Sudan in Crisis,* pp. 217–20.

161 Hassan al-Turabi: Turabi's life story and his views on the Islamic political movement are outlined in Mohamed Elhachmi Hamdi, *The Making of an Islamic Political Leader: Conversations with Hasan al-Turabi,* trans. Ashur A. Shamis (Boulder, CO: Westview Press, 1998).

163 Prince Mohammed al-Faisal: Jonathan C. Randal, "Sudan Party Puts New Face on Fundamentalism," *Washington Post,* April 7, 1988. Also, Al-Effendi, *Turabi's Revolution,* p. 116.

163 Sheikh Omar Abdel-Rahman: Mary Anne Weaver discusses Turabi's friendship with the blind sheikh and other prominent figures in the Afghan jihad in *A Portrait of Egypt: A Journey Through the World of Militant Islam* (New York: Farrar, Straus and Giroux, 2000). Peter Waldman offered one of the first accounts of the early links between Abdel-Rahman, Turabi, Abdullah Azzam, and Osama bin Laden in "Holy Terror: How Sheik Omar Rose to Lead Islamic War While Eluding the Law," *Wall Street Journal,* September 1, 1993. See also Phil Hirshkorn, Roham Gunaratna, Ed Blanche, and Stephen Leader, "Blowback," *Jane's Intelligence Review,* August 2001.

163 "It is not a major exaggeration ... the Moslem Brothers concluded ... that they were entitled to govern it": African Rights, *Food and Power in Sudan,* p. 14.

163 Turabi visited Peshwar at least six times: The Sudanese ambassador to Afghanistan told reporters about Turabi's previous visits to Peshawar when the Sudanese leader visited in 1993. See "Sudanese Peace Mediator Has Talks with Afghan President," Agence France-Press, November 20, 1993, and "Turabi Mediating in Kabul," *APS Diplomat Recorder,* Arab News Service, November 20, 1993.

163 "a springboard ... countries": Yossef Bodansky, *Bin Laden: The Man Who Declared War on America* (Rocklin, CA: Forum, 1999), p. 35.

164 Bin Laden ... began buying up land and businesses in Sudan: "Islamists Celebrated Arrival of Great Islamic Investor," *Al-Quds al-Arabi,* November 24, 2001.

164 the NIF held meetings in Peshawar with bin Laden: The founding of al-Qaeda and the meetings between the NIF and Bin Laden are detailed in Jamal al-Fadl's testimony at the 1998 embassy bombings trial, *U.S.A. vs. Usama bin Laden,* February 7 and 13, 2001.

CHAPTER FOURTEEN

165 How Emma met Riek Machar: Emma described her meeting with Riek at the Pan Afric to many people. I also interviewed Riek about it. For details of their conversations concerning education, I have drawn on the transcript of the interview that two Human Rights Watch researchers, Jemera Rone and John Prendergast, conducted with Riek in Waat on July 5, 1993, about schools and the recruitment of boy soldiers. Emma was present at the interview, and I believe the explanations Riek gave Rone and Prendergast are similar to those he gave her at their first meetings. With the kind permission of the researchers, I have used some of the language from the transcript of their interview in my recapitulation of Riek's initial discussions with Emma about southern Sudan.

169 Emma's mother writes that they slept together that night: McCune, *Til the Sun,* p. 168.

CHAPTER FIFTEEN

170 the twenty-sixth child of a headman: On Riek's childhood and youth, I have supplemented my own interviews with Riek with some material from Rory Nugent, "Sudan: Rebels of the Apocalypse," *Men's Journal*, September 1993.

171 "ordered anarchy": E. E. Evans-Pritchard, *The Nuer* (New York: Oxford University Press, 1969), p. 181.

171 "They strut about...peoples": Ibid., p. 182.

171 the Dok Nuer: My account of possession among the Dok Nuer is taken from Johnson, *Nuer Prophets*, pp. 248–52.

171 "had sex with women...penis": Ibid., p. 249.

172 "vultures who cared for no one but themselves": Vandevort, *Leopard Tamed*, p. 83.

173 "since there was no way...lay": Ibid., p. 21.

174 "bull-boys": Hutchinson describes the tensions between "bull-boys" and "bulls of the herd" among the Nuer in *Nuer Dilemmas*, pp. 288–98.

176 John Garang: See John Garang, *The Call for Democracy in Sudan* (London: Kegan Paul International, 1992).

180 the first Nuer pastor in Ler: Vandevort, *Leopard Tamed*, p. 103.

182 Tiny Rowland: Rowland has been the subject of two biographies. See Richard S. Hall, *My Life with Tiny: A Biography of Tiny Rowland* (London: Faber, 1987), and Tom Bower, *Tiny Rowland: A Rebel Tycoon* (London: Heinemann, 1993). Hall reports the Rowland was introduced to John Garang by Bob Fraser, an American diplomat then attached to the U.S. embassy in London. Nyaba discusses Rowland's role in the SPLA in *Politics of Liberation*, p. 63. On his interests in oil and Sudan, see Ivan Fallon, "A Visionary in the Rhodes Tradition," *Sunday Telegraph*, November 6, 1994. Alier discusses Rowland and Adnan Khashoggi's scheme to make Garang "Czar of the South" in *Southern Sudan*, p. 238. On his ties to Israel, see Uri Dan and Dennis Eisenberg, "A Great Friend," *Jerusalem Post*, July 30, 1998.

184 "There isn't a president...buy": "Death of a Tycoon Who Vowed He Could Buy Any African President," *East African*, August 10, 1998.

185 Mengistu lent Garang his security forces: On the struggles between Garang and Anyanya II, see Alier, *Southern Sudan*, pp. 251–57, and Nyaba, *Politics of Liberation*, pp. 45–49.

187 the gloomy Ethiopian capital: Nyaba describes the atmosphere in "Super Market" in *Politics of Liberation*, pp. 38 and 80–81. The account of Gai Tut's death is taken from p. 35.

189 "were not fully...Nuer": Quoted in Hutchinson, *Nuer Dilemmas*, p. 292.

189 "I told them that I am...word!": Ibid., pp. 296–98.

190 "embittered": I am indebted to Hutchinson, *Nuer Dilemmas*, pp. 106–109 and 122–41, for her analysis of the Nuer concept of *nueer*.

190 "the most important...concepts": E. E. Evans-Pritchard, *Nuer Religion* (Oxford: Oxford University Press, 1956), p. 183.

190 "Whereas the power...accurately": Hutchinson, *Nuer Dilemmas,* p. 140.

190 Riek's radical notions: Ibid., pp. 108, 140, and 296–98.

191 a song the prophet Ngungdeng: Johnson quotes the song by the prophet Ngungdeng that was broadcast over SPLA radio at the time of the Anyanya II–SPLA union in *Nuer Prophets,* p. 343.

192 "unmarked man...you": Johnson, *Nuer Prophets,* pp. 346–47, and Nyaba, *Politics of Liberation,* p. 83.

CHAPTER SIXTEEN

194 According to Rowland's biographer: Bower, *Tiny Rowland,* pp. 215–20.

195 peace talks under the auspices of the U.S. State Department: See Herman Cohen, *Intervening in Africa: Superpower Peacemaking in a Troubled Continent* (New York: St. Martin's Press, 2000), p. 68.

195 "I used to ask about her...contact": Bunting, "For Love of a People."

196 "President Bashir knew I was anxious...me": Rowland told Douglas Davis about his role in getting the Mossad agents released in "British Industrialist Describes Saving Mossad Agents in Sudan," *Jerusalem Post,* May 9, 1993.

196 "After exchanging greetings...enough": Nyaba described his meeting with Lam in *Politics of Liberation,* pp. 78–83.

196 a four-line letter: Bunting, "For Love of a People."

197 "best safari ever": McCune, *Til the Sun,* p. 175.

197 the great mound of Ngungdeng: Johnson details the building of the mound and its history in *Nuer Prophets,* pp. 104–108.

198 In April he had had a meeting with Garang: Riek gave Prendergast and Rone this account of how he questioned Garang about the military training of boys in his 1993 interview with them. But it is inconceivable that Riek did not know all along that the boys were being trained. What is more likely is that Riek, like the other top members of the SPLA, basically saw nothing wrong with sending boys away for an education that combined work and study with military training. Riek's children were safely in school in England. But other top SPLA leaders considered it a privilege to send their children to school in Cuba, where they worked as agricultural laborers and studied under conditions very like the ones Garang proposed for his FACE schools. See Carol Ann Berger, "From Cattle Camp to Slaughterhouse: The Politics of Identity Among Cuban-Educated Dinka Refugees in Canada," unpublished master's thesis, University of Alberta, Department of Anthropology, Fall 2001; copy in my files.

199 she curtly informed him: McCune, *Til the Sun,* p. 181.

PART FOUR

CHAPTER SEVENTEEN

206 James Mut Kueth: Deborah Scroggins, "Dour Prophecy of Isaiah Taken to Heart," *Atlanta Journal-Constitution*, March 10, 1991.
208 "Woe to the land … peeled": Isaiah 18.

CHAPTER EIGHTEEN

213 The case of the five Palestinians: The story of the Rolfe family's negotiations with the Sudanese court is told in Will Ellsworth-Jones, "An Eye for an Eye?," *Independent Magazine*, March 3, 1990, and Geraldine Brooks, "Life or Death: Fate Lies in Their Hands," *Sunday Telegraph*, February 4, 1990.
214 Turabi invited Islamists from around the world: Bodansky, *Bin Laden*, p. 36.
214 Bin Laden had been flying in and out: Osama bin Laden's biographers Yossef Bodansky and Peter Bergen agree on his move to Sudan in 1991. See Bodansky, *Bin Laden*, p. 40, and Bergen, *Holy War, Inc.: Inside the Secret World of Osama bin Laden* (New York: Free Press, 2001), p. 78. But the former head of Saudi intelligence, Prince Turki al-Faisal, has said bin Laden did not settle in Sudan until 1992. See Jamal Khashoggi, "Former Saudi Intelligence Chief Interviewed on Saudi-Afghan Ties, bin Ladin, Part 5," *Al-Quds al-Arabi*, November 8, 2001.
214 "the great Islamic investor": Turabi's reception and bin Laden's $5 million donation were reported in "The Celebrated Arrival of the Great Islamic Investor," *Al-Quds al-Arabi*, November 24, 2001.

CHAPTER NINETEEN

215 a series of urgent messages from Emma: Douglas Johnson provided me with his own transcripts of Emma's radio messages to him at the World Food Program in May 1991; copies in my files.
218 The Americans flew into Nasir on May 18: The United States Agency for International Development visit is described in Millard Burr, "Sudan 1990–1992: Food Aid, Famine and Failure," U.S. Committee for Refugees Issue Brief, 1993, p. 20. Burr says Riek asked the Americans for Stinger missiles, even though he must have known the State Department had long resisted sending military assistance to the southern rebels. "The problem was, as Riek well knew, with SPLA leader John Garang, who the department had concluded was unable to manage the dual role of military and political

leader." Riek evidently concluded that if Garang were removed, the U.S. would give the rebels weapons.

219 as the Scott-Villierses later wrote: Alastair and Patta Scott-Villiers and Cole P. Dodge wrote about the exodus from Ethiopia in "Repatriation of 150,000 Sudanese Refugees from Ethiopia: A Case Study in Manipulation of Civilians in a Situation of Civil Conflict," *Disasters* 17 (1993).

219 "On the south bank... grave": Hall, *Mercenaries,* pp. 253–55.

220 "the swamps of hell": *Observer,* June 23, 1991.

222 In a special *tukul:* Peterson, *Me Against My Brother,* p. 220.

224 arrest Garang on a visit to Itang: Nyaba, *Politics of Liberation,* p. 84. Nyaba discusses the usefulness of the UN operation to the conspirators on p. 92–93.

226 "I knew there was... heart": Riek's comment about xenophobic attitudes within the SPLA is taken from Bunting, "For Love of a People."

227 "Even in cases where... night": Nyaba describes the SPLA taking relief food in *Politics of Liberation,* p. 53.

228 "You have the Kalashnikov... food": The SPLA "graduation song" is quoted in Hutchinson, *Nuer Dilemmas,* p. 53.

228 someone like Giles Thornton: The account of Thornton water-skiing on the Sobat is from Stuart Wavell and David Orr, "Adventurer to Burn on African Pyre," *Sunday Times,* October 25, 1998.

229 James, a social anthropologist at the University of Oxford: James's report on the situation of the Uduk at Nasir is "Vulnerable Groups in the Nasir Region: Update on Nor Deng (Blue Nile Returnees)," Report for WFP/OLS Southern Sector, Nairobi, based on a field visit from 23 September to 9 October 1991. James also describes the problems of delivering food to Nasir in an unpublished report, "Managing Food Aid: Lessons from a Sudanese Returnee Center."

229 Most were Uduk: My description of the Uduk and their history is taken from Wendy James, *Kwanim Pa: The Making of the Uduk People* (Oxford: Clarendon Press, 1979), and *The Listening Ebony* (Oxford: Oxford University Press, 1999).

229 allowing Osama bin Laden to buy a large farm: Bin Laden's farm and road-building activities in Blue Nile province are described in Bergen, *Holy War, Inc.,* p. 80.

230 "a place and a time... death": James's comment on the Uduk recollections of Itang is taken from *Listening Ebony,* p. xiii.

231 twelve hundred hungry boys at Nasir: The Scott-Villierses and Cole Dodge described the manipulation of the boys' relief food in "Repatriation of Sudanese Refugees," p. 289. Zutt's *Children of War* also describes the situation of the boys at Nasir on pp. 18–19. The quote from a UN official on their mental state is taken from p. 18. Another source is Human Rights Watch/Africa, *Civilian Devastation: Abuses by All Parties in Southern Sudan* (New York: Human Rights Watch, June 1994), pp. 195–235.

232 the boys at Palataka: Watson, "Suffer the Children."

232 Riek's servant handed them some of the fried bread balls: Sam Kiley's report on Riek's officials eating Unimix appeared in *The Times* of London, June 1992. Emma denounced the article in a June letter to her friend Emma Marrian.

233 "truly passionately in love": Emma's mother discusses her feelings about Julian McCune in McCune, *Til the Sun,* p. 48.

233 "Searching for the adulation ... elsewhere": Ibid., p. 81.

236 "At 4 A.M. ... me": Fox, "Shadow of Happy Valley," p. 247.

CHAPTER TWENTY

237 "You never have to worry ... it": Emma's quote about polygamy is taken from ITV, *The Warlord's Wife.* Maggie McCune discusses her irritation in *Til the Sun,* p. 199.

239 "Look how much divorce ... here": Hall, *Mercenaries,* p. 264.

239 "Senior commanders in the rebel ... soldiers": The BBC's August 8, 1991, interview with Riek was reprinted in *Sudan Update* 3, no. 3 (September 7, 1991).

239 "Why Garang Must Go" actually mentioned the FACE Foundation by name, calling it "one of Garang's tricks to get himself some money." "Why Garang Must Go," *Southern Sudan Vision* 12 (September 1, 1992).

241 Garang still seemed to be "very much in control": Bernard Kouchner's remark was reported in *Independent,* September 3, 1991.

241 Garang's deputy held a press conference: "Sudan Rebels Say 'Ousted' Leader Garang Still in Control," Reuters News Service, August 31, 1991.

241 Garang ... immediately assumed that Emma: Emma's mother says Emma heard while she was still in England that Garang was claiming she had orchestrated the split for British intelligence and that Emma believed a Garang supporter had followed her back to Nairobi from Heathrow. See McCune, *Til the Sun,* pp. 204–5. I was unable to confirm that, but other friends remember discussing her suspicions of being followed in Nairobi.

241 Garang's men: The fighting between Garang and Riek's followers is covered in Human Rights Watch/Africa, *Civilian Devastation,* pp. 90–112. See also Amnesty International, *The Tears of Orphans: Sudan* (New York: Amnesty International, January 1995), pp. 89–95.

241 they kidnapped a Shilluk pharmacist: "A Moment of Truth," *Africa Confidential,* September 13, 1991.

242 "Riek's marriage ... met": Lam Akol gave me his handwritten transcript of the radio message mentioning Emma that Garang sent to all SPLA units on September 9, 1991; copy in my files.

245 the SPLA unit in Riek's home district: Nyaba discusses the response to Lam and Riek's radio call in *Politics of Liberation*, p. 89.

245 At an August 30 meeting of the SPLA High Command: Garang's visit to Paris was reported in *Middle East International,* November 10, 1991, and reprinted in *Sudan Update* 3, no. 6 (October 25, 1991). Deng describes the meeting of the High Command in *War of Visions,* pp. 231–32.

246 another sultry August meeting: The meeting in Paris between Khashoggi and the Libyans was revealed in Marie Colvin, Alan Ruddock, and John Cassidy, "Tiny and Gadaffi in Secret African Venture," and "Marriage of Convenience: Tiny Rowland and Colonel Gadaffi," *Times* of London, September 8, 1992. Libya's policy of supplying Sudan with free oil in 1990–1992 is described in "Sudan Doubles Fuel Prices," Agence France-Presse, August 4, 1992.

246 world price had risen: "Sudan Doubles Fuel Prices," August 4, 1992.

247 Lutfur Rahman Khan: Quotes from Khan are taken from an unpublished interview with Madelaine Drohan of *The Globe and Mail,* May 10, 1999, in Vancouver; copy in my files. In another interview held in May 1999 in Calgary, John McLeod told Drohan that Khan belonged to the Brotherhood. A Canadian securities official who asked to remain anonymous told me the same thing. See also "Negotiations Resume with Chevron Oil Company to Exploit Oil," BBC Monitoring Service, February 25, 1992, and Muriel Allen, "Oil a Political Weapon in Southern Sudanese Politics," *Middle East Times,* July 11, 1997.

247 The NIF leader had made sure party loyalists: *Middle East International* reported that Concorp's president, Muhammad Abdallah Jar al-Nabi, was related to oil minister Ab al-Wahab and was close to Turabi on January 22, 1993; reprinted in *Sudan Update* 4, no. 9 (January 31, 1993).

247 Adolf Lundin: See John Schreiner, "The Art of Darkness," *National Post,* January 18, 1997. The IPC announced reaching an agreement in principle to explore Delta Tokar and Halaib in a press release issued August 16, 1991. IPC's agreement to explore Delta Tokar was signed December 1, 1991. See also "Red Sea Oil Acquires IPC's Sudanese Assets and Firms Up Drilling Plans," statement issued by Red Sea Oil Corporation, March 9, 1996. The Halaib deal nearly brought Egypt and Sudan to war, as Egypt also claims the region. See Weaver, *Portrait of Egypt,* p. 177. IPC reported its agreement with the government of Ethiopia to explore Gambella in a press release issued November 14, 1991.

252 "dressed in rags…disoriented": On Palataka, see Emma Sharp, "Youth Learn Grim Lessons of Life in the 'New Sudan,'" *Guardian,* January 10, 1992.

252 Another journalist was even more: Richard Ellis's article, "Love

Blooms Among the Bullets in Sudan," appeared in *Sunday Times,* November 29, 1991.

252 "I'm not very brave": Quoted in ibid.

252 "She dismisses... anything": Ibid.

253 Riek's commanders began executing officers: Nyaba, *Politics of Liberation,* pp. 94–95.

253 Michael Manyon Anyuang: Amnesty International, *Tears of Orphans,* p. 95.

255 Rowland also began channeling funds: Nyaba, *Politics of Liberation,* pp. 93–94.

256 "happy and relaxed": McCune, *Til the Sun,* p. 210.

256 Wut Nyang ... young man: Hutchinson, Nuer Dilemmas, pp. 338–45, and Johnson, Nuer Prophets, pp. 348–56.

256 "fascinating character... immediately": Emma McCune, letter to Emma Marrian, June 1992; copy in my files.

257 The Uduk later told: The Uduk quotes are taken from Wendy James's unpublished notes from her interviews at Karmi and Gambella, September 1992. James also wrote a report on her visit to Gambella, "Uduk Asylum Seekers in Gambela, 1992: Community Report and Options for Resettlement," Report for UNHCR, October 31, 1992.

257 "They took the lorries... man": The Uduk quotes are taken from Wendy James's September 1992 interviews at Gambella. James says the UN officials discovered the SPLA subterfuge and sent drivers from Kenya who brought trucks from Malakal to deliver the grain themselves. Not until then did the refugees at Nasir start to receive the grain.

258 "People are saying... food.": Wut Nyang's quote about the food the Dinka were receiving is from Hutchinson, *Nuer Dilemmas,* p. 342.

258 A Red Cross plan to transport grain by barge: Neil Henry, "Life Saving Food Barge Stuck in Sudan Quagmire," *Washington Post,* June 12, 1990.

CHAPTER TWENTY-TWO

262 "Fighting at Bor... went": Peterson, *Me Against My Brother,* p. 221.

264 "I'm not a messiah... tribes": Ibid.

264 "Riek is two characters... Nasir": Nyaba, *Politics of Liberation,* p. 108.

265 "You people!... spoiled": Nikkel, "Children of Our Fathers'," p. 72.

PART FIVE

CHAPTER TWENTY-THREE

271 I was at the Carter Center: Deborah Scroggins, "Lots of Talk, But No Peace," *Atlanta Journal-Constitution,* January 18, 1992.

CHAPTER TWENTY-FOUR

273 "possessed a ferocity...survive": Quoted in Werner, Anderson, and Wheeler, *Day of Devastation*, p. 546.

274 Tiny Rowland continued his secret meetings: Colvin et al., "Tiny and Gadaffi in Secret African Venture."

274 In January 1992 Lam signed an agreement: Lam Akol's Frankfurt talks with the government are described in Deng, *War of Visions*, p. 233. The government's fatwa is quoted in Gaspar Biro, "Situation of Human Rights in the Sudan," a report to the UN Commission on Human Rights, February 1, 1994, p. 37.

275 "Why should I...trained": Garang is quoted in *Financial Times*, September 9, 1991.

275 "I have seen little children...stopped": Quoted in Ellis, "Love Blooms Among the Bullets."

276 the boys were in deplorable shape: On the conditions at the minors' camp, see Hutchinson, "Potential Development Projects," pp. 7–8.

276 "They were hungry...leaking.": Hutchinson, "Potential Development Projects for the Sobat Valley Region: A Set of Proposals Prepared for Save the Children Fund (U.K.), June 1993"; copy in my files.

277 "She was determined...plant": Quoted in Bunting, "For Love of a Country."

280 "Life is going...destiny": Quoted in Zutt, *Children of War*, p. 40.

CHAPTER TWENTY-FIVE

282 In a never-published article: Marrian, "Story of Emma," p. 5.

282 "love nest": McCune, *Til the Sun*, p. 197.

282 In June 1992 *The Mail on Sunday*: Hall's account of the two weeks he spent with Emma is taken from his *Mercenaries*, pp. 258–66.

284 the court case in which a Nuer woman: Riek also told Hutchinson about this case—see *Nuer Dilemmas*, p. 233.

284 "We were so sure...leaders": Sally's quote is from "The Tragedy of Emma McCune," *Nation*, July 12, 1999.

285 "the wasteland of southern Sudan": Peterson reports that this is how Emma once listed her address, in *Me Against My Brother*, p. 221.

285 "Riek Machar's marriage...workers": Nyaba, *Politics of Liberation*, pp. 92–93, 110.

285 "They think he's gone...liberated": Hall, *Mercenaries*, p. 261.

285 Hall was present when Emma and Riek presided: Ibid., pp. 264–65.

285 "Everywhere we went...advice": Ibid., p. 260.

286 Sometimes Emma passed on radio frequencies: Marrian, "Story of Emma," p. 6.

287 "Everyone is in a bit of a spin...husband": Emma McCune, letter to Emma Marrian, June 12, 1992.

287 "I don't think Riek...end": Hall, *Mercenaries,* p. 265.

287 Some of Riek's confederates defected: "Nasir Commanders Resign," *Sudan Democratic Gazette* (22), March 1992.

287 In February 1992 Riek allowed government forces: "'Final Push' Dry Season Offensive Begins," *Sudan Democratic Gazette* (22), March 1992, and Human Rights Watch/Africa, *Civilian Devastation,* pp. 35–37.

287 the ten thousand Lost Boys: Human Rights Watch/Africa, *Civilian Devastation,* pp. 211–14.

288 Garang loyalists looted a UN distribution center at Balliat: Peter Moszynski, "Letter from Nasir," *Middle East International,* June 12, 1992.

288 Nasir kept getting UN airdrops: Ibid.

288 "We are longing for our home...homeland": The quotes from the Uduk are taken from James's interviews with them at Gambella in Ethiopia.

289 Emma told Moszynski that the locals: Moszynski, "Letter from Nasir."

289 When Emma visited England: James kept notes of her conversation with Emma on September 13, 1992.

290 "Nearly all the children...food": Hutchinson, report for *Save the Children.*

292 Riek had told Wut Nyang and the Jikany Nuer: Nyaba, *Politics of Liberation,* 95–96.

292 "This relief has destroyed...bad": Quoted in Hutchinson, p. 342.

292 in her June 1992 letter to Emma Marrian: Emma McCune, letter to Emma Marrian, June 12, 1992.

293 Libya was buying Rowland's Metropole Hotel: Colvin et al., "Tiny and Gadaffi in Secret African Venture."

293 Chevron quietly signed an agreement: "Chevron Sells Exploration Interests in Republic of Sudan," *Worldwide Energy, Worldwide Videotext,* January 8, 1992. The price was reported in "US Chevron Prices Concession Between $23 and $26 Million," *Middle East Economic Digest,* July 3, 1992.

293 On the twenty-sixth...another tiny Vancouver oil company, Arakis: "Arakis to Acquire Oil Concession in Sudan," Reuters News Service, June 30, 1992.

293 Garang's SPLA issued a warning: "Sudan Rebels Vow to Attack Oil Workers in South," Reuters News Service, June 23, 1992.

293 Triad International: "Arakis Gets $25 Million Project Funding," Reuters News Service, July 28, 1992. Also "Sudan: Oil Production Begins Amid Much Political Controversy," *African Business,* August 1, 1992. The vice president of Arakis denied any connection to Triad in *Indian Ocean Newsletter,* December 26, 1992, reprinted in *Sudan Update* 4, no. 9 (January 31, 1993).

294 more southerners were dying in the tit-for-tat battles: Human Rights Watch/Africa, *Civilian Devastation,* pp. 91–193. Also see Scott Peterson,

"100,000 Uprooted in Sudan's Unwinnable War," *Daily Telegraph,* December 12, 1992.

294 Paul Kon Ajith: Werner, Anderson, and Wheeler, *Day of Devastation,* p. 546. Also Nikkel, "Children of Our Fathers'," p. 74–78.

294 The rumors reached so far afield: McCune, *Til the Sun,* p. 234.

295 the UN refused to allow her: McCune letter to Marrian, June 1992.

295 "People are always asking me…to": Quoted in Hall, *Mercenaries,* pp. 265–66. Emma's brother Johnny also remembered her making this comment.

296 "their politics": McCune, *Til the Sun,* p. 265.

296 "Slaughter of the Innocents": *Independent,* December 27, 1991.

296 "I am so happy…no regrets": Quoted in Hall, *Mercenaries,* p. 266.

CHAPTER TWENTY-SIX

297 "Maung, dear Mynt Maung…gun": Quoted in McCune, *Til the Sun,* pp. 224–25.

297 peace talks in the Nigerian city of Abuja: See Steven Wondu and Ann Lesch, *Battle for Peace in Sudan: An Analysis of the Abuja Conference, 1992–1993* (Lanham: University Press of America, 2000).

297 "Commander William's weakness for money…incentives": Nyaba, *Politics of Liberation,* p. 123.

297 "illiterate person with fifteen…world": Catherine Bond, *BBC Focus on Africa,* September 30, 1992; reprinted in *Sudan Update* 4, no. 3 (October 19, 1992). Garang's quotes are from this article.

298 "It's going to be about six…signed": Richard Wallis, "Peace in Sudan Next Aim, Lonrho Chief Says," Reuters News Service, August 7, 1992. Rowland's quotes are from this article.

298 the deaths of Emma's friend Maung and three others: The details of the killings and the subsequent investigations are taken from Human Rights Watch/Africa, *Civilian Devastation,* pp. 128–33. On December 11, 1992, Dr. Richard Mulla issued a press release claiming to have captured a radio transcript in which SPLA Commander Obote Momor recommended the elimination of nurse Wilma Gomez and driver Francis Ngure.

300 Waat's population swelled from three thousand: François Visnot, "The Best Little Oasis in South Sudan," *Guardian,* November 12, 1992. Riek told me he and Emma wanted to attract aid to Waat.

300 Whenever the buzz of an incoming UN plane was heard: Visnot, "Best Little Oasis."

300 "It's considered a shame…victims": Buchizya Maeteka, "Remote Sudan Town Slowly Starves to Death," Reuters News Service, October 26, 1992. Emma's quote is from the same article.

301 through the swamps for Ayod: I have supplemented my interviews

with Marrian's account in "Story of Emma," p. 6. McCune also describes it in *Til the Sun*, pp. 225–29.

301 She wrote her mother about the beautiful *tukul:* McCune, *Til the Sun,* p. 229.

302 Nasir's "gallant forces": Riek's press release entitled "Our Victory in Malakal" was published in *Southern Sudan Vision,* nos. 16 and 17, November 5 and 17, 1992, and was reprinted in *Sudan Update* 4, no. 5 (November 18, 1992).

302 François Visnot arrived with introductions: Visnot, "Best Little Oasis." Other details are taken from my conversations with him in July 2001.

303 Somalia, a Muslim country: The Somali famine and the buildup to U.S. intervention are described in de Waal, *Famine Crimes,* pp. 159–91.

304 "her friendships with the UN pilots": "South Sudan: The Territory of Death and Survival" is the title of an unpublished paper delivered by Aldo Ajou Deng to the Workshop on Current Conditions in Southern Sudan, Oxford University, February 13, 1999.

304 the Dinka followers of Paul Kon Ajith: Werner, Anderson, and Wheeler, *Day of Devastation,* p. 547. Also Nikkel, "Children of Our Fathers'," p. 72.

305 CNN's Gary Streiker: Streiker did not mention Emma in his report for CNN on October 29, 1992, and does not remember meeting her in Waat. But the press coverage did have the effect of increasing relief deliveries, according to African Rights, *Food and Power in Sudan,* p. 277.

CHAPTER TWENTY-SEVEN

307 "international community ... all": Phillip Johnston's comments were made in a letter to *The Guardian* published September 15, 1992.

307 On November 25 CARE: Deborah Scroggins, "More UN Troops Likely as Somali Warlords Grab Food," *Atlanta Journal-Constitution,* November 25, 1992.

307 Alex de Waal and ... Rakiya Omaar: Africa Watch fired Omaar and de Waal after they refused to stop speaking out against the U.S. intervention, in defiance of the group's stance. Deborah Scroggins, "Getting Out of Somalia Will Be the Hard Part," *Atlanta Journal-Constitution,* December 6, 1992.

308 "One needs to realize ... lanes'": Abd al-Rahman Ahmadun's comments on the U.S. intervention were quoted in *Sudan Update* 4, no. 6 (December 12, 1992). See also Cohen, *Intervening in Africa,* p. 82.

308 "a U.S. effort to 'tighten the noose ... Africa": *Guardian,* December 10, 1992. Turabi highlighted his fear that the United States and Britain were conspiring to prevent Sudan from exploiting the southern oil fields again in a March 1, 1997, interview with *Al-Sha'b* in Cairo: "They wanted to strike at Sudan's Islamic direction ... they knew that Sudan had woken up to its economic wealth and begun to exploit it. They view this as a very serious mat-

ter. Oil extraction has started in Sudan, which will allow the country to join the international oil club."

308 The NIF government and its new ally, Iran, began lending support: "Khartoum's Connection with Somali Warlord," *Sudan Democratic Gazette* (40), September 1993. See also Bodansky, *Bin Laden,* pp. 67–69, and David Williams, "Sudan Gave Somalia's Aideed Arms, U.S. Says: State Department Expresses Concern Over Activities Showing Anti-American Sentiment," *Washington Post,* August 19, 1993.

308 Osama bin Laden railed against the U.S. designs: The bombing of the Aden hotel is described in Bergen, *Holy War, Inc.,* p. 82. Jamal al-Fadl testified about bin Laden's statements, adding that bin Laden's lieutenant went to Somalia to assist opponents of the U.S. intervention; see *U.S.A. vs. Usama bin Ladin,* February 6, 2001. See also L'Hossaine Kherchtou's testimony, February 26, 2001, and Summation of Patrick Fitzgerald, May 8, 2001.

308 "to question why, with similar anarchy... there": "Aid Officials Call For U.S. Action on Sudan Famine," *Guardian,* February 25, 1993.

309 The U.S. ambassador to Sudan: Petterson's visits to Riek and Garang are described in Donald Petterson, *Inside Sudan* (Boulder, CO: Westview Press, 1999), pp. 52–54.

309 "armed intervention": Quoted in Wondu and Lesch, *Battle for Peace,* p. 92.

309 bad feelings continued to mount between the Lou and the Jikany: William O. Lowrey, "Passing the Peace: The Role of Religion in Peacemaking Among the Nuer," in Andrew Wheeler, ed., *Land of Promise: Church Growth in a Sudan at War* (Nairobi: Paulines Publications, 1997), pp. 129–50.

310 one of Ngungdeng's prophecies: Douglas Johnson points out to me that the Nuer seemed to have conveniently "remembered" the Ngungdeng prophecy concerning the Lec fish at the time of the feud, as it was not among the songs he collected before 1981.

310 Emmanuel Jai: The quotes from Emmanuel are taken from an article Peter Moszynski wrote about him, "Letter from Nairobi," *New Statesman and Society,* September 2, 1994.

311 "Nancy and the Artful Dodger": Marrian, "Story of Emma," p. 3.

311 "I resented his presence... say": McCune, *Til the Sun,* p. 233.

312 "The demands made on a man... utmost": Evans-Pritchard, *Nuer,* p. 184.

312 Four high-ranking politicians: Robert M. Press, "Rebel Infighting Devastates Sudan," *Christian Science Monitor,* April 14, 1993.

312 "Nobody tortured them": Ibid.

312 "The war in Sudan is unwinnable": Victoria Brittain, "Rowland 'Joined Sudan Rebels,'" *Guardian,* February 27, 1993.

313 "Hunger Triangle": Aid officials told Douglas Johnson in 1994 interviews that Emma had coined the phrase.

313 "among the highest ever recorded": Centers for Disease Control and

Prevention, "Nutrition and Mortality Assessment—Southern Sudan, March 1993," *Morbidity and Mortality Weekly Report* 24, no. 16 (Atlanta: April 1993), pp. 304–8.

314 Come On: Richard Dowden, "Why the Food Stopped," *Independent on Sunday,* June 6, 1993.

314 "I climbed in and bent...struggle": Quoted in Marrian, "Story of Emma," p. 1. I also quoted it in "Emma," *Granta* 60 (Winter 1997). McCune quotes from the same passage in *Til the Sun,* p. 248.

315 She went to visit Riek's extended family in Ler: Bunting, "For Love of a People," and McCune, *Til the Sun,* p. 251.

316 "They went on to say...Nairobi": Quoted in McCune, *Til the Sun,* p. 250.

316 "with his head bowed...tribes": The old man's warning to Riek is quoted in Nyaba, *Politics of Liberation,* p. 103.

316 Presbyterian church leaders: Lowrey, "'Passing the Peace': The Role of Religion in Peacemaking Among the Nuer in Sudan," pp. 129–50.

317 Riek told human rights investigators: Rone and Prendergrast, interview notes.

317 "The lawlessless that reigned...people": Nyaba, *Politics of Liberation,* p. 103.

317 "They should let us determine our leaders...disease": Quoted in Julie Flint, "Rebel Division Wreaks Lethal Havoc in Southern Sudan," *Guardian,* August 30, 1993.

317 Rory Nugent: Nugent's first African book was *Drums Along the Congo: On the Trail of Mokele-Mbembe, The Last Living Dinosaur* (New York: Houghton Mifflin, 1993). The tale of Nugent's travels in the bush with Riek is from his article "Sudan: Rebels of the Apocalypse," *Men's Journal,* September 1993. All quotes from this trip are taken from the article.

320 a $125 million exploration: The production-sharing agreement signed between the Sudanese government, Arakis, and State Petroleum was reported in "Little Known Firm in Canada Granted Sudan Properties," *Platt's Oilgram News,* December 8, 1992; "Sudan Financing Is Reduced," *Platt's Oilgram News,* March 30 1993; and "Arakis' Partner Gets Approval in Sudan," *Platt's Oilgram News,* July 9, 1993. In 1995 Arakis became the subject of an investigation by the British Columbia Securities Commission. The investigation found that Arakis had been shifting money through several mysterious offshore funds, including Anthem International. Terry Alexander, the company's former president, said the company was forced to raise money through "private placements." He said the U.S. State Department's opposition to the Sudan oil project scared off conventional investors. "Media Statement by Terry Alexander: Signing of Agreed Statement of Facts with the B.C. Securities Commission," *Canadian Corporate News,* February 24, 1999.

320 Sheikh Omar Abdel-Rahman was indicted for conspiring: Abdel-Rahman's involvement in the World Trade Center bombings and the con-

spiracy to bomb New York is described in Weaver, *Portrait of Egypt*, pp. 74–86 and 223–25. ABC-TV news reported that two Sudanese diplomats assigned to the UN were involved in the plot on August 16, 1993. The Saudi oil cutoff was reported in "Fuel Shortages Quadruple Petrol Prices," *Middle East Economic Digest*, October 15, 1993. Petterson describes Khartoum's response to the sanctions in *Inside Sudan*, pp. 69–74.

321 "As I knew they would...particular": Ibid., p. 82.

321 President Bashir responded to Washington's overtures: Petterson, *Inside Sudan*, p. 82. Nyaba describes the NIF offer of a separate peace in *Politics of Liberation*, pp. 149–50.

321 he was engaged in an intense round: The government's peace talks with Lam at Tonga are discussed in *Indian Ocean Newsletter*, September 11 and October 9, 1993; reprinted in *Sudan Update* 4, no. 22 (October 22, 1993). The *Sudan Democratic Gazette* (41) reported Lam's talks with the government and the plane crash in October 1993. Nyaba discusses the talks and the crash of the government plane in *Politics of Liberation*, p. 150.

323 "Under cover of the United Nations...Aideed": Bin Laden's quote regarding the U.S. withdrawal from Somalia is from *U.S.A. vs. Usama bin Laden*, Testimony of Jamal al-Fadl, February 3, 2001.

323 Khartoum staged a series of angry demonstrations: Petterson, *Inside Sudan*, pp. 82–83.

323 In Washington Riek and Garang drove: On the Washington talks, see *Middle East International*, reprinted in *Sudan Update* 4, no. 22 (October 22, 1993).

324 "Why won't Riek sign?...TRAITORS": The statement issued by Garang's faction in Nairobi on October 23, 1993, was reprinted in *Sudan Update* 4, no. 23 (November 10, 1991). Another SPLA press release, dated October 22, 1993, was reprinted in the same issue of *Sudan Update*, detailing the breakdown of the talks.

CHAPTER TWENTY-EIGHT

326 "One day our men...cowards": Quoted in Simon Reeve, *The New Jackals: Ramzi Yousef, Osama bin Laden, and the Future of Terrorism* (Boston: Northeastern University Press, 1999), p. 182.

327 the fantastic walled compound: The figure of $300 million to build the UN compound in Mogadishu is taken from de Waal, *Famine Crimes*, p. 185.

327 Robert Oakley, the U.S. envoy: Weaver, *Portrait of Egypt*, p. 195.

329 $2 billion: De Waal, *Famine Crimes*, p. 185.

CHAPTER TWENTY-NINE

331 "Womenaid...families": Emma's proposal for Womenaid was given to me by Helen Achiro; copy in my files. I quoted from it in "Emma," p. 138.

CHAPTER THIRTY

333 Emma's obituary: *Times* of London, November 27, 1993.

CHAPTER THIRTY-ONE

334 university students in several northern Sudanese towns: The November 1993 student protests and the Islamist reaction to them are described in Petterson, *Inside Sudan*, pp. 86–87.

335 a Khartoum journalist: "Sudan: Journalist Claims Hit-and-Run Accident Deliberate," Agence France-Presse, September 22, 2335.

335 Or could it have been Garang: *Africa Analysis* reported in January 1993 that Total Oil Company had stopped paying Garang "protection money" since "Garang is no longer in charge of the oil-rich areas of southern Sudan's Upper Nile State…now controlled by the rival forces of the SPLA's Nasir faction"; reprinted in *Sudan Update* 4, no. 9 (January 31, 1993).

336 In the end, most of Emma's friends and relations accepted: McCune says in *Til the Sun*, p. 277, that Emma's brother and sisters still believe she was murdered.

336 "Dear Deborah…Peter": Nyaba e-mail interview, January 27, 2000.

EPILOGUE

337 "What can the West…steal away": Kevin Myers, "The Magic Land That Turns Men Savage," *Sunday Telegraph*, March 7, 1998.

338 "If I were a missionary…school": Ralph Carson, letter to Charles R. Watson, May 15, 1915; copy in my files.

338 "they wanted to have…village": Katharine Baker Simpson, "The Reverend and Mrs. Ralph Erskine Carson: Presbyterian Missionaries to the Sudan, Africa 1903–1908," unpublished manuscript, December 3, 1963; copy in my files.

341 make Riek's agreement part of Sudan's constitution: Human Rights Watch/Africa, *Sudan, Oil and Human Rights Abuses*, pp. 93–108.

341 "the jewel in the crown": Ibid., p. 90.

343 He told me about her funeral: See also Moszynski, "Letter from Leer," *Middle East International*, January 1994, and Marrian, "Story of Emma," p. 1.

347 The fighting between the Jikany and the Lou Nuer: Lowrey, "Passing the Peace," pp. 129–50.

347 *I am in the sinful land…skeleton:* Quoted in William Finnegan, "The Invisible War," *New Yorker*, January 25, 1999.

347 Rory Nugent fulfilled his promise: Nugent wrote about his return to Sudan in "The March of the Green Flag," *Spin*, March 1996. Quotes from his

conversations with Turabi and Riek are taken from this article. Rory's comment about the war is drawn from my interviews with him.

349 estimated proven crude oil reserves of 262 million barrels: U.S. Department of Energy, http://www.eia.doe.gov/emu/cabs/sudan.html.

349 a stack of investigations: For example, John Harker, *Human Security in Sudan: The Report of a Canadian Assessment Mission* (Ottawa: Ministry of Foreign Affairs, 2000); John Ryle and Georgette Gagnon, *A Report of an Investigation into Oil Development, Conflict and Displacement in Western Upper Nile,* October 2001, online at http://www.ideationconferences.com/sudanreport2001/resourcepage.htm.; Amnesty International, *Oil in Sudan: Deteriorating Human Rights,* March 25, 2000; and Peter Verney, *Raising the Stakes: Oil and Conflict in Sudan, Sudan Update* report, 1999.

349 "substantial" reserves of "excellent" quality: On Lundin's oil find at Thar Jath, see "Lundin, OMV Claim Substantial Find in Sudan," *Platt's Oilgram News,* May 21, 1999. The fighting over the oil fields around Ler is described in Human Rights Watch/Africa, *Famine in Sudan, 1998,* pp. 143–57.

350 "no Thomas Jefferson": Scroggins, "Emma," p. 126.

350 "A fierce humanitarian like Emma...happiness": Becky Hagman e-mail to me, October 3, 2000.

351 a tidal wave of death: The International Rescue Committee's figure of three million dead in Congo, two million in Sudan, and one million in Somalia was reported by Karl Vick, "Death Toll in the Congo May Approach 3 Million," *Washington Post,* April 30, 2001.

351 17 million dead of AIDS: Joint United Nations Program on HIV/AIDS, "AIDS Becoming Africa's Top Human Security Issue, UN Warns," press release, January 10, 2000.

351 "the Victorian Osama bin Laden": Niall Ferguson compared Osama bin Laden to the Mahdi in "2011," *New York Times Magazine,* December 2, 2001.

352 "The peculiarity...sight": Ralph E. Carson, "Snakes," unpublished sermon, undated.

Select Bibliography

Abadi, Jacob. "Israel and Sudan: The Saga of an Enigmatic Relationship." *Middle Eastern Studies* (July 1991), 1–14.

Africa Watch. *Denying the Honor of Living: Sudan, a Human Rights Disaster.* New York: Human Rights Watch, March 1990.

African Rights. *Food and Power in Sudan.* London: African Rights, 1997.

Alier, Abel. *Southern Sudan: Too Many Agreements Dishonored.* Exeter, U.K.: Ithaca Press, 1990.

Amnesty International. *Sudan: The Military Government's First Year in Power: A Permanent Human Rights Crisis.* London, November 1990.

———. *Sudan: Patterns of Repression.* London, February 1993.

———. *Sudan: The Ravages of War: Political Killings and Humanitarian Disaster.* London, September 1993.

———. *The Tears of Orphans: No Future Without Human Rights.* London, January 1995.

———. *Oil in Sudan: Deteriorating Human Rights.* London, March 2000.

Anderson, G. Norman. *Sudan in Crisis: The Failure of Democracy.* Gainesville: University of Florida Press, 1999.

Select Bibliography

Baker, Sir Samuel W. *Ismailia: A Narrative of the Expedition to Central Africa for the Suppression of the Slave Trade.* New York: Harper and Brothers, 1875.

Bayart, Jean-François. *The State in Africa: The Politics of the Belly.* New York: Longman, 1993.

Bergen, Peter. *Holy War, Inc.: Inside the Secret World of Osama bin Laden.* New York: Free Press, 2001.

Bodansky, Yossef. *Bin Laden: The Man Who Declared War on America.* Rocklin, CA: Forum, 1999.

Boyles, Dennis. *African Lives.* New York: Ballantine Books, 1988.

Burr, Millard. "Sudan 1990–1992: Food Aid, Famine and Failure," U.S. Committee for Refugees Issue Brief, 1993.

Burr, Millard, and Robert O. Collins. *Requiem for the Sudan: War, Drought, and Disaster Relief on the Nile.* Boulder, CO: Westview Press, 1995.

Carrington, Charles. *Rudyard Kipling: His Life and Work.* London: Macmillan, 1955.

Churchill, Winston, Sir. *The River War: An Historical Account of the Reconquest of the Soudan,* 2 vols. F. Rhodes, ed. London, New York, and Bombay: Longmans, Green and Co., 1899.

Cohen, Herman. *Intervening in Africa: Superpower Peacemaking in a Troubled Continent.* New York: St. Martin's Press, 2000.

Cole, David. *Between a Swamp and a Hard Place: Development Challenges in Remote Rural Africa.* Cambridge: Harvard International Institute for Development, 1997.

Collins, Robert O. *Shadows in the Grass: Britain in the Southern Sudan, 1918–1956.* New Haven, CT: Yale University Press, 1962.

Dalglish, Peter. *The Courage of Children.* Toronto: HarperCollins, 1998.

Daly, Martin, and Ahmad Alawad Sikainga, eds. *Civil War in Sudan.* London: British Academic Press, 1993.

El-Dareer, Asma. *Woman, Why Do You Weep?: Circumcision and Its Consequences.* London: Zed Press, 1986.

Deng, Francis M. *War of Visions: Conflict of Identities in the Sudan.* Washington: Brookings Institution, 1995.

Deng, Francis M., and Larry Minear. *The Challenges of Famine Relief: Emergency Operations in the Sudan.* Washington: Brookings Institution, 1992.

De Waal, Alex. *Famine Crimes: Politics and the Disaster Relief Industry in Africa.* Oxford: James Currey, 1997.

Al-Effendi, Abd el-Wahab. *Turabi's Revolution: Islam and Power in the Sudan.* London: Gray Seal Books, 1991.

Evans-Pritchard, E. E. *Nuer Religion.* New York: Oxford University Press, 1956.

————. *The Nuer.* New York: Oxford University Press, 1969.

————. *Kinship and Marriage Among the Nuer.* Oxford: Clarendon Press, 1995.

Ferry, Georgina. *Dorothy Hodgkin: A Life.* London: Granta Books, 1998.

Finkelman, Paul, and Joseph C. Miller, eds. *The Encyclopedia of World Slavery.* New York: Macmillan, 1998.

Garang, John. *The Call for Democracy in Sudan.* London: Kegan Paul International, 1992.

Geldof, Bob, and Paul Vallely. *Is That It?* Middlesex: Penguin Books, 1986.

Gordon, Charles G. *The Journals of Major-Gen. C. G. Gordon, C.B., at Kartoum.* A. Egmont Hake, ed. London: Kegan Paul, Trench & Co., 1885.

Hall, Tarquin. *Mercenaries, Missionaries, and Misfits: Adventures of an Under Age Journalist.* London: Muncaster Press, 1997.

Hamdi, Mohamed Elhachmi. *The Making of an Islamic Political Leader: Conversations with Hasan al-Turabi.* Ashur A. Shamis, trans. Boulder, CO: Westview Press, 1998.

Harrison, Paul, and Robin Palmer. *News out of Africa: Biafra to Band Aid.* London: Hilary Shipman, 1986.

Hill, George Birkbeck, ed. *Colonel Gordon in Central Africa, 1874–1879.* London: Thomas de la Rue & Co., 1885.

Hill, Richard S. *Egypt in the Sudan, 1820–1881.* Oxford: Oxford University Press, 1959.

———. *Lovers on the Nile: The Incredible African Journeys of Sam and Florence Baker.* New York: Random House, 1980.

———, ed. *The Sudan Memoirs of Carl Christian Giegler Pasha, 1873–1883.* London: Oxford University Press, 1984.

Holt, P. M. *The Mahdist State in the Sudan, 1881–1898: A Study of Its Origins and Overthrow.* Oxford: Clarendon Press, 1970.

Human Rights Watch/Africa. *Civilian Devastation: Abuses by All Parties in the War in Southern Sudan.* New York: Human Rights Watch, June 1994.

———. *Famine in Sudan, 1998.* New York: Human Rights Watch, February 1999.

———. *Sudan, Oil and Human Rights Abuses.* Draft report. New York: Human Rights Watch, April 11, 2000.

Hutchinson, Sharon. *Nuer Dilemmas: Coping with Money, War and the State.* Berkeley: University of California Press, 1996.

Idris, Amir H. *Sudan's Civil War: Slavery, Race and Formational Identities.* Lewiston, NY: Edwin Mellen Press, 2001.

James, Wendy. *'Kwanim Pa: The Making of the Uduk People.* Oxford: Clarendon Press, 1979.

———. *The Listening Ebony.* Oxford: Oxford University Press, 1999.

Jeal, Tim. *Livingstone.* London: Pimlico, 1993.

Johnson, Douglas H. "The Death of Gordon: A Victorian Myth," *Journal of Imperial and Commonwealth History* 10 (May 1982), 285–310.

———. *Nuer Prophets: A History of Prophecy from the Upper Nile in the Nineteenth and Twentieth Centuries.* Oxford: Oxford University Press, 1994.

Jok, Jok Madut, and Sharon Hutchinson. "Sudan's Prolonged Second Civil War and the Militarization of Nuer and Dinka Ethnic Identities," *African Studies Review* 42, no. 2 (September 1999), 125–45.

Kaplan, Robert. *Surrender or Starve: The Wars Behind the Famines.* Boulder, CO: Westview Press, 1988.

Karadawi, Ahmed. "The Smuggling of the Ethiopian Falashas to Israel through Sudan." *African Affairs* 70 (1991), 23–49.

————. *Refugee Policy in Sudan, 1967–1984.* Oxford: Berghahn Books, 1999.

Keen, David. *The Benefits of Famine: A Political Economy of Famine and Relief in Southwestern Sudan, 1983–1989.* Princeton: Princeton University Press, 1994.

Khalid, Mansour. *Nimeiri and the Revolution of Dis-May.* London: KPI, 1985.

————. *The Government They Deserve: The Role of the Elite in Sudan's Political Evolution.* London and New York: Kegan Paul International, 1990.

Kipling, Rudyard. *Rudyard Kipling's Verse.* London: Hodder and Stoughton, 1958.

Lovejoy, P. E. *Transformations in Slavery: A History of Slavery in Africa.* New York: Cambridge University Press, 1983.

Mahmud, Ushari Ahmad, and Suleyman Ali Baldo. *The Al Dhiein Massacre: Human Rights Violations in the Sudan.* Khartoum: University of Khartoum, 1987.

Marmon, Shaun, ed. *Slavery in the Islamic Middle East.* Princeton, NJ: Markus Wiener Publishers, 1999.

McCune, Maggie. *Til the Sun Grows Cold: Searching for My Daughter, Emma.* London: Headline, 1999.

McDermott, Brian Hugh. *The Cult of the Sacred Spear: The Story of the Nuer Tribe in Ethiopia.* London: Robert Hale & Co., 1973.

McLoughlin, Peter F. "Economic Development and the Heritage of Slavery in the Sudan," *Africa* 32 (1962), 355–89.

Moore-Harell, Alice, and Gabriel Warburg. *Gordon and the Sudan: Prologue to the Mahdiyaa, 1877–1880.* London: Frank Cass, 2001.

Negash, Tekeste, and Kjetil Tronvoll. *Brothers at War: Making Sense of the Ethiopian-Eritrean War.* Oxford: James Currey, 2000.

Nikkel, Marc. "Children of Our Fathers' Divinities or Children of the Red Foreigners?" in Andrew Wheeler, ed., *Land of Promise: Church Growth in a Sudan at War.* Nairobi: Paulines Publications Africa, 1997.

Nutting, Anthony. *Gordon of Khartoum: Martyr and Misfit.* New York: Clarkson N. Potter, 1966.

Nyaba, Peter Adwok. *The Politics of Liberation in South Sudan: An Insider's View.* Kampala: Fountain Publishers, 1997.

Pakenham, Thomas. *The Scramble for Africa.* London: Abacus, 1991.

Peterson, Scott. *Me Against My Brother: At War in Somalia, Sudan, and Rwanda.* New York: Routledge, 2000.

Petterson, Donald. *Inside Sudan.* Boulder, CO: Westview Press, 1999.

Prunier, Gerard. "Identity Crisis and the Weak State: The Making of the Sudanese Civil War." WRITENET Issue Paper, January 1996.

Reeve, Simon. *The New Jackals: Ramzi Yousef, Osama Bin Laden, and the Future of Terrorism.* Boston: Northeastern University Press, 1999.

Ryle, John. *Warriors of the White Nile: The Dinka.* Amsterdam: Time-Life Books, 1982.

Sanderson, Lilian Passmore, and Neville Sanderson. *Education, Religion and Politics in Southern Sudan, 1899–1964.* London: Ithaca Press, 1981.

Seale, Patrick. *Abu Nidal: A Gun for Hire.* New York: Random House, 1992.

Seligman, C. G., and Brenda Seligman. *Pagan Tribes of the Nilotic Sudan.* London: Routledge and Kegan Paul, 1932.

Shields, Reid. *Behind the Garden of Allah.* Philadelphia: United Presbyterian Board of Foreign Missions, 1937.

Slatin, Rudolf C. *Fire and Sword in the Sudan.* F. R. Wingate, trans. London: Edward Arnold, 1896.

Steevens, G. W. *With Kitchener to Khartum.* New York: Dodd, Mead, 1898.

Strachey, Lytton. *Eminent Victorians.* San Diego: Harcourt Brace Jovanovich, 1948.

Svoboda, Terese. *Cleaned the Crocodile's Teeth: Nuer Song.* Greenfield Center, NY: Greenfield Review Press, 1985.

Toledano, Ehud E. *Slavery and Its Abolition in the Ottoman Middle East.* Seattle: University of Washington Press, 1998.

Trench, Charles Chenevix. *The Road to Khartoum: A Life of General Charles Gordon.* New York: Dorset Press, 1978.

Vandevort, Eleanor. *The Leopard Tamed: The Tale of an African Pastor, His People and His Problems.* New York: Harper and Row, 1968.

Victoria, Queen of Great Britain. *The Letters of Queen Victoria.* 6 vols. George Earle Bucke, ed. New York: Longmans, Green and Co., 1930–32.

Weaver, Mary Anne. *A Portrait of Egypt: A Journey Through the World of Militant Islam.* New York: Farrar, Straus and Giroux, 2000.

Werner, Roland, William Anderson, and Andrew Wheeler. *Day of Devastation, Day of Contentment: The History of the Sudanese Church Across 2000 Years.* Nairobi: Paulines Press, 2000.

Wheeler, Andrew, ed. *Land of Promise: Church Growth in a Sudan at War.* Nairobi: Paulines Publications Africa, 1997.

Wondu, Steven, and Ann Lesch. *Battle for Peace in Sudan: An Analysis of the Abuja Conference, 1992–1993.* Boston: University Press of America, 2000.

Zutt, Johannes. *Children of War: Wandering Alone in Southern Sudan.* New York: UNICEF, 1994.

Acknowledgments

This book owes debts to many people beyond those already mentioned in the Author's Note. At the United Nations Association–USA, the late Susan Woolfson, John Tessitore, and Edward C. Luck set me off on this journey by first assigning me to look into famine relief back in 1985. The New York Times Foundation and the Weyerhauser Foundation provided support for that first foray into the politics of humanitarian aid. I am grateful to Sonny Rawls, Bill Kovach, Hyde Post, Randal Ashley, Arnold Rosenfeld, Ron Martin, John Walter, and Plott Brice at *The Atlanta Journal-Constitution* for sending me to Sudan and for advising and supporting me while I was there and after I came back. At *Granta* magazine Ian Jack and Robert Winder encouraged me to pursue the story of Emma McCune, then helped shape the magazine article that became the genesis of this book.

Some of the many Sudanese and non-Sudanese who have shared their insights and knowledge are: Arop Madut Arop, Catherine Bond, Raymond Bonner, Victoria Butler, Timothy Carney, Catherine Carter, former President Jimmy Carter, Jeffrey Clark, Robert O. Collins, Jean-François Darcq, Madelaine Drohan, Wal and Julia Duane, Mark Duffield, Dan Eiffe, Ahmed Kamal el-Din, Clive English, Becky Hagman, Robin Hodgkin, Mark Huband, Liz Hughes, Richard Ibreck, Harry Jeene, Sam Kiley, Ian Lethbridge, John Luk, Gillian Lusk, Andrew Mawson, Lazarus Leek Mawut, Mahdi Ibrahim Mohamed, Stephen Morrison, Peter Moszynski, Richard Mulla, Rakiya Omaar, Jane Perlez, Scott Peterson, John Prendergast, Biel Torkech Rambang, Jonathan Randal, Eric Reeves, Tiny Rowland, William Shawcross, Hania Sholkamy, Dick

and Carol Steuart, Gary and Christine Strieker, David Turton, Peter
Verney, François Visnot, Gordon Wagner, Gritta Weil, Phillip Winter,
Roger Winter, and Michael Wolfers.

Godfrey Hodgson and the Reuter Foundation offered financial and
research assistance in the form of a 1998 Reuter Fellowship at the University of Oxford. The librarians at Oxford's Queen Elizabeth House,
Rhodes Hall, and the Refugee Studies Programme spent hours helping
me locate documents. My indispensable agent, Toby Eady, found me two
superb editors, Robin Desser at Pantheon Books and Michael Fishwick
at HarperCollins-UK. My friends Carol Berger, Wendy James, Douglas
Johnson, Millard Burr, and Jemera Rone shouldered the task of reading
and correcting the final draft.

Without my husband, Colin Campbell, this book would not exist. He
first fixed my sights on Sudan more than fifteen years ago, and he has
been my companion every step of the way. My parents, Frank and Gloria
Scroggins, and my late mother-in-law, Betty Campbell, were a constant
source of encouragement and inspiration. My stepson, Gray, and my two
daughters, Anna and Elizabeth, put up with many tedious hours of baby-
sitting while I was researching and writing this book. My hope is that it
will answer their persistent question: "But why do you love Sudan so
much?"

Deborah Scroggins, a former correspondent for *The Atlanta Journal-Constitution*, is currently a freelance writer and editor. She has won six national journalism awards for her reporting from Sudan and the Middle East. Her articles have been published in *Granta*, *The Independent*, *Playboy*, and elsewhere. She lives in Atlanta with her husband and two children.